Treading on Sacred Grounds

Studies in Religion, Secular Beliefs and Human Rights

VOLUME 12

The titles published in this series are listed at *brill.com/srsb*

Treading on Sacred Grounds

Places of Worship, Local Planning and Religious Freedom in Australia

By

Noel Villaroman

BRILL
NIJHOFF

LEIDEN | BOSTON

Library of Congress Cataloging-in-Publication Data

Villaroman, Noel G. author.
Treading on sacred grounds : places of worship, local planning and religious freedom in Australia / By Noel Villaroman.
pages cm. -- (Studies in religion, secular beliefs and human rights ; volume 12)
Includes bibliographical references and index.
ISBN 978-90-04-28933-8 (hardback) -- ISBN 978-90-04-28934-5 (e-book) 1. Religious minorities--Legal status, laws, etc.--Australia. 2. Religious law and legislation--Australia. 3. Freedom of religion--Australia. 4. Church and state--Australia. I. Title.

KU2168.V55 2015
342.9408'52--dc23

2014048666

ISSN 1871-7829
ISBN 978-90-04-28933-8 (hardback)
ISBN 978-90-04-28934-5 (e-book)

This book is printed on acid-free paper.

FSC www.fsc.org MIX Paper from responsible sources FSC® C109576

Printed by Printforce, the Netherlands

To Sandra and Sarah Noelle

Contents

Acknowledgements

In writing this book, I have depended upon countless acts of support, guidance and generosity from many people and institutions.

First and foremost, I thank my wife, Sandra, for her love, support and understanding. I also thank my adorable daughter, Sarah Noelle, for being my life's inspiration.

My wholehearted thanks also go to the Monash Institute of Graduate Research (MIGR) in Melbourne, Australia for the generous scholarship I received in order to finish my PhD thesis upon which this book is based. I am also hugely indebted to my thesis supervisor, Dr Paula Gerber. I have been privileged to have a scholar like Paula to oversee my PhD research. To Jintana Kurosawa, our Higher Degree by Research Coordinator at the Monash Law School, I will be forever grateful for your assistance and friendship. Many thanks also to Ms Melissa Castan, Prof Gideon Boas, Prof Jonathan Clough and Prof H.P. Lee of the Monash Law School for their helpful comments.

The analysis in this book also benefited greatly from many stimulating thoughts and questions from many distinguished academics on law and religion. I am thankful to Prof Peter Edge and Prof Lucy Vickers of Oxford Brookes University (UK), Prof Silvio Ferrari and Dr Sabrina Pastorelli of the University of Milan, and Prof Tore Lindholm of the University of Oslo.

My sincere thanks also go to Prof Carolyn Evans of the University of Melbourne and Associate Prof Jeroen Temperman of Erasmus University Rotterdam (The Netherlands), who both served as examiners of my PhD thesis. Their invaluable comments and suggestions were indeed useful in modifying and converting the thesis into this book.

I am grateful to the Law and Religion Scholars Network (LARSN) based in Cardiff University for allowing me to present the initial results of my research in a conference. I also thank the International Consortium for Law and Religion Studies (ICLARS) for the opportunity to network with other researchers and scholars working in the field of law and religion.

Finally, I am thankful to my organisation, the United Nations, for providing me with a stimulating working environment that enables me to continue my research interests on the legal protection of ethnic and religious minorities.

Noel Villaroman, PhD

Table of Cases

Afgan Community Support Association v Blacktown City Council [2008] NSWLEC 1357
Al-Kateb v Godwin (2004) 219 CLR 562
Baptist Union of Queensland v Brisbane City Council & Anor [2002] QPEC 41
Bethel New Life Christian Fellowship Inc v Greater Dandenong City Council [2009] VCAT 1778
Blackburn Community Church of Christ v Whitehorse City Council [2004] VCAT 2623
Canterbury Municipal Council v Moslem Alawy Society Ltd (1985) 1 NSWLR 525
Chabad House of Malvern Toorak Inc v Stonnington City Council [2001] VCAT 1448
Chaudhary v Minister for Immigration and Ethnic Affairs (1994) 49 FCR 84
Church of Jesus Christ v Casey City Council [2001] VCAT 322
City Gospel Trust v Nillumbik Shire Council [2010] VCAT 517
Coeriel *et al* v The Netherlands, Human Rights Committee, *Views: Communication No. 453/1991*, UN Doc CCPR/C/52/D/453/1991 (9 December 1994)
Dandenong Islamic Society v Dandenong City Council [2005] VCAT 2501
Defence of Government Schools (DOGS) Case (1981) 146 CLR 559
Derksen v The Netherlands, Human Rights Committee, *Views: Communication No. 976/2001*, UN Doc CCPR/C/80/D/976/2001 (1 April 2004)
Dietrich v The Queen, (1992) 177 CLR 292
Ferencz Baranyay Architects v Greater Dandenong City Council [2005] VCAT 934
Grace Bible Church v Reedman, 71 (1984) 36 SASR 376; 54 ALR 571
Harrison v Mornington Peninsula Shire Council [2001] VCAT 2010
Highfield Gospel Trust v Devonport City Council [2010] TASRMPAT 135
Islamic Education and Welfare Association of Dandenong v Casey City Council [2004] VCAT 1850
Jones and Harbour Pty Ltd v Trad (No 2) (EOD) [2011] NSWADTAP 62
Jones v Scully (2002) 120 FCR 243
Kioa v Minister for Immigration and Ethnic Affairs (1985) 159 CLR 550
Kotku Education and Welfare Society Inc v Brisbane City Council [2004] QPEC 68
Kruger v Commonwealth (1997) 190 CLR 1
Krygger v Williams (1912) 15 CLR 366
Lennon v Glen Eira City Council [2004] VCAT 1345
MAB, WAT and J-AYT v Canada, Human Rights Committee, *Views: Communication No. 570/1993*, UN Doc CCPR/C/50/D/570/1993 (8 April 1994)
Malakhovsky and Pikul v Belarus, Human Rights Committee, *Views: Communication No. 1207/2003*, UN Doc CCPR/C/84/D/1207/2003 (23 August 2005)
Mimar Architects Pty Ltd v Hobsons Bay City Council [2007] VCAT 1184

Minister for Aboriginal Affairs v Peko-Wallsend Ltd [1986] HCA 40; (1986) 162 CLR 24
Minister for Foreign Affairs and Trade v Magno (1992) 112 ALR 529 at 534–535
Minister for Immigration and Multicultural and Indigenous Affairs; Ex parte Lam (2003) 214 CLR 1
Minister of State for Immigration and Ethnic Affairs v Teoh (1995) 183 CLR 273
Minogue v Williams [2000] FCA 125
New Century Developments Pty Limited v Baulkham Hills Shire Council [2003] NSWLEC 154
OV and OW v Members of the Board of Wesley Mission Council (2010) 270 ALR 542
Prince v South Africa, Human Rights Committee, *Views: Communication No. 1474/2006*, UN Doc CCPR/C/91/D/1474/2006 (14 November 2007)
Rainsford v Victoria [2007] FCA 1059
Re The Macedonian Orthodox Church & Cultural Community Gold Coast Inc v Council for City Of Gold Coast [2000] QPEC 2
RE: Minister for Immigration and Ethnic Affairs and Lebanese Moslem Association (1987) 17 FCR 373
Schoenmakers v Director of Public Prosecutions (1991) 30 FCR 70
Sean Investments Pty Ltd v MacKellar (1981) 38 ALR 363
Singh Bhinder v Canada, Human Rights Committee, *Views: Communication No 208/1986*, UN Doc A/45/40 vol. 2 (9 November 1989)
Sister Immaculate Joseph et al v Sri Lanka, Human Rights Committee, Human Rights Committee, *Views: Communication No. 1249/2004*, UN Doc CCPR/C/85/D/1249/2004 (18 November 2005)
Smith v Hobsons Bay City Council [2010] VCAT 668
Steensen v Gold Coast City Council [2007] QPEC 48
Swancom Pty Ltd v Yarra City Council [2009] VCAT 923
Tabag v Minister for Immigration and Ethnic Affairs (1982) 45 ALR 705
Taraborelli v Casey City Council [2011] VCAT 2013
Telstra Corporation Ltd v Hornsby Shire Council [2006] NSWLEC 133; (2006) 146 LGERA 10
Tempora Pty Ltd v Shire of Kalamunda (1994) 10 SR (WA) 296
The Sabian Mandaean Association in Australia Ltd v Wollondilly Shire Council [2009] NSWLEC 94
Toonen v Australia, Human Rights Committee, *Views: Communication No. 488/1992*, UN Doc CCPR/C/50/D/488/1992 (31 March 1994)
Uniting Church v Happy Valley City Council [1997] SAERDC 409
Untan v Minister for Immigration and Multicultural and Indigenous Affairs (2003) FCAFC 69

Victory Worship Centre v Cardinia Shire Council [2009] VCAT 810
Walsh v Department of Social Security (1996) 67 SASR 143
Wheeler v Kingston City Council (Correction) [2012] VCAT 1094
Willrath v Greater Dandenong City Council [2000] VCAT 2124

PART 1

Laying the Foundation

CHAPTER 1

Introduction

1.1 Background

> David rose to his feet and said: "My brothers and my people! It was my desire to build a temple where the Ark of the Lord's Covenant could rest permanently. … The Lord said to me, 'Your son Solomon will build my Temple and its courtyards, for I have chosen him as my son, and I will be his father'."
>
> Then David gave Solomon the plans for the Temple and its surroundings, including the entry room, the storerooms, the upstairs rooms, the inner rooms, and the inner sanctuary – which was the place of atonement. David also gave Solomon all the plans he had in mind for the courtyards, the outside rooms, the treasuries, and the rooms for the gifts dedicated to the Lord. And he gave specifications for the items in the Temple that were to be used for worship. … David continued, 'Be strong and courageous, and do the work. The Lord will see to it that all the work related to the Temple is finished correctly'.[1]

So states the biblical account when God himself instructed David to build a magnificent temple where the people of ancient Israel could worship and offer sacrifices. David's own instructions to his son Solomon were detailed, including building plans and specifications with precise measurements. But for all its particulars as to the temple's design, layout, materials and ornamentation, David's instructions would have been seriously deficient in one crucial respect had this event taken place in 21st-century Australia where David could have possibly added, 'May the Lord be with you, Solomon, *but* whatever you build please do not forget to obtain a planning permit'.

Indeed, the requirements for building places of worship (or any structure, for that matter) are vastly different today than they were in centuries past. In Western liberal democracies, including Australia, most religious groups desiring to build a place of worship are not immune from the operation of local planning regulations. In Australia, the authorities who are primarily charged with enforcing these regulations are the local governments called 'local councils' composed of locally elected councillors. Considered the third level of government in

1 *The Holy Bible* (*New Living Translation*) 1 Chronicles 28.

 | DOI 10.1163/9789004289345_002

Australia (after the Commonwealth and the state or territory governments), 'the system of local government within each State and territory exists by virtue of State law'.[2] As discussed below, when local councils are satisfied that a proposed structure is consistent with the applicable local planning regulations, a planning permit is issued allowing the construction to proceed. However, when a proposed structure is assessed as contravening any such regulations, it is within the discretionary power of local councils to reject it.

In recent years, planning disputes involving the construction of places of worship have disrupted the once tranquil – almost sleepy – ambience of some Australian localities. In Box Hill, New South Wales, a proposed Hindu temple divided the community with many local residents complaining vociferously that the site was inappropriate for a place of worship.[3] In nearby Elermore Vale, a 'right-wing nationalist group' held a protest rally allegedly on behalf of local residents against a proposed mosque, stirring up racial tension and disturbing this once quiet suburb.[4] In Perth, Western Australia, a local council rejected an application to use the halls of an Islamic school as a prayer venue, but it continued to be used as such, resulting in an infringement notice.[5] In neighbouring Swan Valley, a proposed mosque was rejected by the local council because its design included a 21-metre high minaret, thus depriving Muslims residing in the area of an accessible place where they could pray.[6] In Sellicks Hill, South Australia, a Buddhist association waited for the outcome of its application to build a temple in what had been a '15-year approval process'.[7] In Warrnambool, Victoria, Muslim migrant workers abandoned their plans to settle there permanently because they had nowhere to pray as their application to build a mosque remained unresolved by the local council.[8]

The above examples illustrate that planning disputes involving the construction of places of worship across Australia can have wider social repercussions beyond land use and development, such as stirring up racial tension, creating community anxiety, or spoiling legitimate governmental objectives. At the

2 Gerard Carney, *The Constitutional Systems of the Australian States and Territories* (Cambridge University Press, 2006) 33–34.

3 Claire Thompson, 'Temple of Division', *Hills Shire Times*, 12 May 2009.

4 Naomi Davidson, 'Race Rally Fear Over Elermore Vale Mosque', *The Herald*, 3 December 2010.

5 'Council Rejects Use of School Hall as Mosque', *ABC News*, 27 October 2010.

6 Nicolas Perpitch, 'Bias denied as Swan Valley Mosque Rejected', *The Australian*, 18 December 2009.

7 'Buddhist Temple Close to Approval', *ABC News*, 28 September 2011.

8 Jane Metlikovec, 'Muslims Quitting Regional Victoria Due to Lack of Mosques', *The Herald Sun*, 2 June 2008.

same time, they also demonstrate the regulatory power of local councils over proposed religious structures.[9] Planning scholar William Johnson noted that:

> Planning entails choices and controls. Plans are designed to create predictable, orderly relationships and so to establish control. The power to make and carry out plans is therefore *the power to control*.[10] [emphasis added]

This book analyses the limits of that 'power to control' when it already encroaches upon or burdens the ability of religious groups in Australia to fully exercise their right to manifest their religion or belief as a result of spatial constraints – that is, their inability to appropriate sufficient physical space for their worship and other needs. In this study, the analysis is centred on the structural constraints to religious freedom occasioned by the exercise of a regulatory power by a secular authority. Here, the inquiry is focussed on how local planning regulations may impede the enabling role played by tangible space – epitomised by places of worship – in the enjoyment of intangible faith or belief.

Every type of worship necessarily requires physical space where a worshipper can pray in accordance with the rituals or ceremonies of his or her religion or belief. Even solitary worship has to be done in some physical place. Explaining the importance of places of worship, Peter Edge argues that '[t]he ability of a religious community to designate a place as sacred, particularly as a place of worship, has been seen as one of the keystones of religious liberty'.[11] As analysed in Chapter 2, the right of a religious community to establish and maintain places of worship is an integral component of the broader right to freedom of religion or belief. Anne Fornerod notes that:

> There is indeed no doubt that the effectiveness of freedom of worship depends upon the availability of sites specifically dedicated to religious celebration. The basic premise here is that access for religious groups for public space via places of worship would fully ensure this effectiveness.[12]

---

9 William Johnson, *Urban Planning and Politics* (Planners Press, 1989) 10.

10 Ibid.

11 Peter Edge, 'The Construction of Sacred Places in English Law' (2002) 14 *Journal of Environmental Law* 161.

12 Anne Fornerod, 'The Places of Worship in France and the Public/Private Divide' in Silvio Ferrari and Sabrina Pastorelli (eds), *Religion in Public Spaces: A European Perspective* (Ashgate, 2012) 323.

Writing in the American context, Douglas Laycock likewise stresses that:

> In every major religious tradition – Christian, Jewish, Muslim, Buddhist, Hindu, whatever – communities of believers assemble together, at least for shared rituals and usually for other activities as well. Churches cannot function without a physical space; creation of a church building is a core First Amendment right.[13]

Indeed, the centrality of places of worship for most religions cannot be denied.[14] Certain forms of religious manifestation can only be adequately performed inside places of worship. As shown in Chapter 2, places of worship make possible the greater exercise of religious manifestations in worship, observance, practice and even teaching. It is no surprise that many restrictions on religious freedom across the world, as illustrated in Chapter 3, are committed by state authorities by prohibiting religious groups from constructing, extending or renovating their places of worship. These restrictions, according to Paul Taylor, 'have, for the most part, historically been imposed by means of planning regulations'.[15] State authorities wishing to make organisational life harder for unpopular or disfavoured religious groups can easily turn to planning regulations and find purported planning infringements, thus justifying the curtailment of religious activities that are intimately tied to religious structures. As Silvio Ferrari and Sabrina Pastorelli aptly observe, a denial of the right of a religious group to have a place of worship 'goes to the heart of the right of religious freedom'.[16]

1.2 What is this Book About?

This book probes the engagement of religious groups with the local councils in Australia in their applications to construct, extend or renovate their places of worship. It illustrates that such applications by religious groups usually encounter opposition from local residents who are reluctant, and sometimes

---

13 Douglas Laycock, 'State RFRAs and Land-use Regulations' (1999) 32 *University of California Davies Law Review* 755, 756.

14 See generally, Annick Germain and Julie Elizabeth Gagnon, 'Minority Places of Worship and Zoning Dilemmas in Montreal' (2003) 4(3) *Planning Theory & Practice* 295, 298.

15 Paul Taylor, *Freedom of Religion: UN and European Human Rights Law and Practice* (Cambridge University Press, 2005) 242.

16 Silvio Ferrari and Sabrina Pastorelli, 'The Public Space: The Formal and Substantive Neutrality of the Public Sphere' (Working Paper No. 4, Religious Diversity and Secular Models in Europe: Innovative Approaches to Law and Policy, September 2010) 3.

even suspicious, of sharing their neighbourhood, locale or street with the newly arrived and less known religious 'other'. The local councils, being the planning authority that exercises the power to grant or refuse such applications, are caught in the middle of these disputes. Thus, an important part of the 'public space' becomes a contested terrain between those who want to preserve the *status quo* of the built environment and those who desire to affirm their collective identity through new religious structures. Using the lens of international human rights law, this book analyses the actions of local councils in resolving these disputes and their repercussions to religious freedom. In particular, the analysis focusses on the impact of planning decisions upon the constituent elements of the right to freedom of religion or belief, including the specific right to establish and maintain places of worship.

This book examines the compatibility of Australian local planning processes with the right to establish and maintain places of worship which is an important element of the right to freedom of religion or belief as guaranteed in international human rights law. It demonstrates the hypothesis that the principles and concepts that underpin the local planning processes in Australia, as they currently stand, tend to hinder the ability of religious groups to fully exercise their right to establish and maintain places of worship. Such a hindrance experienced by religious groups is inconsistent with international human rights standards on religious freedom. In this study, it is the Australian local planning system itself whose regulatory tools and underlying concepts and principles are being evaluated vis-à-vis the international human rights standards on religious freedom. Although this study analyses only a limited number of case studies, the *commonality* of the planning regulatory tools used in the local planning processes across Australia and the concepts and principles underpinning them enable conclusions to be drawn that are relevant to all planning decisions relating to religious structures across the country. The last two chapters of this book are an exercise in vertical legal analysis where certain generalisations about the Australian local planning system are made on the basis of the findings from the case studies analysed in the middle chapters.

1.3 Contextualising the Book's *Problématique*

The official recognition of cultural and religious diversity has become one of the defining attributes of modern Australian society.[17] Patrick Parkinson

17 Robert Crotty, 'Multiculturalism and Religious Pluralism' in Norman Habel (ed), *Religion and Multiculturalism in Australia: Essays in Honour of Victor Hayes* (Australian Association for the Study of Religion, 1992) 35.

observes that, although the policy has been changed since it was first introduced, the differences between the major Australian political parties 'are more on matters of detail than the principle' and that a 'commitment to multiculturalism is firmly enshrined in Government policy'.[18] It is therefore worthwhile to find out whether, in view of this official dictum, such cultural and religious diversity is adequately being taken into account by the local planning processes in Australia.

This book analyses this primary research question: Are the local planning processes in Australia consistent with the international human rights standards on religious freedom, including the right of religious groups to establish and maintain places of worship? Using the lens of international human rights law, this book elucidates this *problématique* by evaluating the functioning of the Australian local planning processes and their compatibility with international human rights standards on religious freedom. Local planning processes, owing to their profound impact upon the enjoyment of religious freedom, are not immune from such a human rights-based evaluation.

Analysing the primary research question brings to the fore the following specific research questions:

- Is there a right to establish and maintain places of worship to be found in the corpus of international human rights law? Is it part of the international human rights standards on religious freedom? If so, what are the elements that make up its conceptual core?
- In light of Australia's 'dualist' approach to international law, how do the international standards on religious freedom find their way into the Australian domestic jurisdiction? Specifically, and bearing in mind Australia's federal system of government, how are such standards given application by Australia's local councils? Can local councils, being creatures of state or territory legislation, be considered 'duty-bearers' of religious human rights?
- Are planning decisions which reject proposed places of worship on the ground that they would cause inadequate parking, excessive traffic, noise and similar inconveniences, consistent with the international standards on religious freedom, including the right to establish and maintain places of worship?

18 Patrick Parkinson, 'Enforcing Tolerance: Vilification Laws and Religious Freedom in Australia' (Paper Presented at the Eleventh Annual International Law and Religion Symposium: 'Religion in the Public Sphere: Challenges and Opportunities', Provo, Utah, 3–6 October 2004) 2.

- Are planning decisions which reject proposed places of worship on the ground that they would blemish an area's external appearance or character consistent with the international standards on religious freedom, including the right to establish and maintain places of worship? Is a regulatory tool which is based on Anglo-Celtic standards of 'beauty' or 'convenience' inherently discriminatory against non-Christian places of worship?
- Finally, when can restrictions against the right to establish and maintain places of worship be considered 'permissible limitations' and, thus, valid under international human rights law? How can the societal interests that underlie local planning be balanced vis-à-vis the significance of the right to establish and maintain places of worship? Does international human rights law provide the appropriate balancing mechanism?

The succeeding chapters of this book are arranged in such a way as to correspond to the analysis of each of the above questions.

1.4 Places of Worship, Local Planning and Religious Freedom

This book examines how respect for the right to freedom of religion or belief is being concretised in the 'religious' physical landscape of Australia – that is, its churches, temples, synagogues, mosques and other places of worship. As planning scholar Laura Beth Bugg argues, 'the right to practice religion free from discrimination [is] inseparable from the *right to the city*'[19] [emphasis added] which is the right of religious groups to appropriate physical spaces not only as a 'means to carry out the day-to-day requirements of their religion, but also the right to a symbolic public presence and open practice of their faith'.[20] States cannot sincerely proclaim that they respect the right to religious freedom whenever there exist unreasonable restrictions against the structural aspect of that freedom – that is, the establishment and maintenance of places of worship. Describing the sort of hypocrisy of some societies, W Cole Durham lamented that while some states affirm their commitment to protect religious freedom,

19 Laura Beth Bugg, 'Religious Freedom and the Right to the City: Local Government Planning and the Rejection of Islamic Schools in Sydney, Australia' (Workshop Paper, Twelfth Berlin Roundtables: Religious Pluralism, Irmgard Coninx Stiftung, 7–11 April 2010) 2.

20 Ibid.

> honoring this most fundamental commitment remains a problem in all of our countries. The practical problem is this: while virtually everyone gives lip service to freedom of worship, there is a recurrent refrain when a religious community seeks to lease, acquire, build or occupy a place of worship: "not in my back yard." Religious freedom is fine, but let religious organizations locate somewhere else.[21]

The engagement, therefore, of religious groups with the local planning authorities in their applications to build, extend or renovate places of worship provides a well-placed observatory from which to analyse a state's commitment to respecting religious freedom. As observed by Fornerod, analysing this engagement reveals an important glimpse of 'the role that governments are willing to grant to freedom of worship, of which places of worship are at first sight only the physical and visible manifestation'.[22] The success or failure of religious groups to satisfy their religious need for places of worship, which is heavily dependent on the regulatory role played by local planning authorities, provides an important indication of how much states are willing to respect the right to religious freedom beyond, as Durham suspects, giving it 'lip service'. Therefore, the aim of this book is to shed light on one important aspect of the broader question of whether the right to freedom of religion or belief is being adequately protected in Australia.

This book takes on heightened significance considering the fact that the possible *situs* of planning disputes involving places of worship are the hundreds of local councils across Australia.[23] It is ironic that, although these disputes happen in local areas, they are not 'localised' problems because they can be ubiquitous or widespread across the country. Therefore, Australia's planning law and practice concerning places of worship constitute one crucial test of how it fulfils its international legal obligation to respect the right to freedom of religion or belief. Alice Diver and John Thompson fittingly observe that the '[d]omestic regard for international human rights principle may perhaps best be gauged by an examination of local government policies on fundamental

21 W. Cole Durham, Jr, 'Places of Worship: Enhancing Implementation of a Core Right' (Introductory Remarks for Session III of the Supplementary Human Dimension Meeting on Freedom of Religion or Belief, Vienna, Austria, 9–10 July 2009) 4.

22 Fornerod, above n 12, 331.

23 There are 558 local councils throughout Australia. Victoria has 79 councils; New South Wales, 152 councils; Queensland, 73 councils; South Australia, 68 councils; Tasmania, 29 councils; Western Australia, 141 councils; and the Northern Territory, 16 councils. See especially, Nicolas Brasch, *Australia's Local Government* (Macmillan Education Australia, 2011) 10–11.

freedoms such as the right to religious worship'.[24] Following this cue, this book examines how the spatial and structural requirements of religious worship are being satisfied – or not – by the local planning system.

1.5 Local Planning and Its Interface with Religious Freedom

In Australia, when a property owner decides to build, extend or renovate a structure, a 'development application' must be submitted to a local council which evaluates it to determine its conformity with local planning regulations.[25] Such regulations are applied uniformly to all proposed structures regardless of whether they are for religious or non-religious uses. As Carolyn Evans notes, 'in the area of zoning, religious groups are obliged to go through the same planning application process as anyone else'.[26] Local planning regulations aim to protect what is referred to as the 'amenity' of local areas.[27] Thus, when a proposed place of worship is ascertained as likely to produce an unreasonable negative impact upon an area's amenity, the local council has the authority to disallow its construction, extension or renovation.

To be analysed in greater depth in Chapters 5 and 6, the concept of 'amenity' has two limbs: physical and visual. 'Physical amenity' pertains to the convenience that a place offers because of physical conditions such as a smooth flow of vehicular traffic, absence of noise, adequacy of parking spaces, cleanliness, and similar conditions.[28] On the other hand, 'visual amenity' pertains to the collective impact of the visual components which make an area pleasant to be in.[29] Having a broad and malleable nature, visual amenity pertains to elements which contribute to the visual pleasantness and character of localities or

24 Alice Diver and John Thompson, 'Prayers, Planners and Pluralism: Protecting the Rights of Minority Religious Groups' in Javaid Rehman and Susan Breau (eds), *Religion, Human Rights and International Law: A Critical Examination of Islamic State Practices* (Martinus Nijhoff Publishers, 2007) 465, 484.

25 Susan Thompson and Paul J Maginn, *Planning Australia: An Overview of Urban and Regional Planning* (Cambridge University Press, 2012) 46–49.

26 Carolyn Evans, 'Religion and the Secular State in Australia', in Javier Martinez-Torron and W. Cole Durham (General Reporters) *Religion and the Secular State/La religion et l'État laïque* (The International Center for Law and Religion Studies, 2010) 87, 94.

27 Leslie Stein, *Principles of Planning Law* (Oxford University Press, 2008) 188.

28 See, e.g., John Skennar, 'Sydney, A City Growing Within: The Establishment of Buddhist Centres in Western Sydney' (Paper presented at Centre for Cultural Research, University of Western Sydney: Post-Suburban Sydney Conference, 2005) 5.

29 Stein, above n 27, 193–195.

neighbourhoods.[30] Both types of amenity are sought to be protected by local councils when they exercise their 'power of control' over any proposed use or development of land.

One of the early definitions of 'planning' was provided by Lewis Keeble who, in 1959, defined planning as 'the art and science of ordering the use of land and the character and siting of buildings and communication routes so as to secure the maximum practicable degree of economy, convenience and beauty'.[31] The essential core of Keeble's definition is still found in how modern day planning scholars view their discipline – that is, planning is an instrument which is used to control the kind of structures to be allowed in an area and to regulate the impact of their use in a particular area (siting) and their appearance in relation to the general look of that area (character).[32] Keeble's view that planning aims to secure the 'economy, convenience and beauty' of a place essentially encapsulates the concept of amenity which, as mentioned above, has physical and visual components. In Keeble's definition, the physical component corresponds to 'economy and convenience', while the visual component corresponds to 'beauty'.

Every local council in Australia follows its own set of planning instruments that provide the policies and strategies for the use and development of land. Collectively, these planning instruments regulate the permissible land uses or activities. These instruments can be broadly categorised into two groups: first, local councils enforce 'zoning ordinances' that subdivide a locality into different zones and the allowable uses in each zone such as, for example, residential, industrial, agricultural or mixed-use zones. Zoning ordinances are called 'planning schemes' in Victoria, Queensland and Western Australia; 'development plans' in South Australia; and 'local environment plans' in New South Wales.[33] A zoning ordinance is composed of a map that shows a locality subdivided into different zones. The map is accompanied by a text that describes the purposes or objectives of each zone and usually gives examples of the uses and forms of development that are allowed in each zone.[34] Second, when a proposed structure is found to be allowable in a particular zone, local councils enforce

30 Ibid.

31 Lewis Keeble, *Principles and Practice of Town and Country Planning* (The Estates Gazette, 1959) 9.

32 For various definitions of planning offered by modern planning scholars, see especially Susan Thompson and Paul J. Maginn, *Planning Australia: An Overview of Urban and Regional Planning* (Cambridge University Press, 2012, 2nd edition) 17–28.

33 Stein, above n 27, 31.

34 Ibid.

'planning controls' that prescribe building aspects including the size, shape and height of a structure, its bulk expressed as a ratio of height to floor space, its setback from the street or adjoining houses, the open space on each lot, and the building's overall visual impost upon the area.[35] Therefore, in Australia, an application to build any structure, including places of worship, has to undergo two stages: applications are assessed according to whether the proposed buildings are allowed in a particular zone and whether they are consistent with the relevant 'planning controls'.[36]

In Australia, there is no general prohibition against the construction of places of worship in most zones such as residential, industrial and mixed-use zones, provided that they do not contravene any of the 'planning controls' applicable to the zone where they are proposed to be constructed.[37] Therefore, as shown in Chapters 5, 6 and 7, planning controversies involving proposed places of worship typically concern their alleged inconsistencies with applicable 'planning controls', rather than if they are allowed in a particular zone or not. Although they vary from one local government area to another, 'planning controls' provide guidelines pertaining to a religious structure's bulk and height, setback from the road, screening elements, parking provisions, noise control arrangement, and traffic plans.[38] Aside from these, 'planning controls' also include guidelines on a building's overall footprint, external ornamentation, as well as colour, texture and materials used. This set of guidelines affecting a structure's *qualitative* features corresponds to what Angela Carmella refers to, in the American context, as a process of 'architectural review' which is the 'governmental (usually municipal) control over the design of proposed new construction for the purpose of maintaining architectural compatibility with existing structures and preserving neighborhood character'.[39]

1.6 International Human Rights Law as a Research Paradigm

This book's analysis of the issues arising from the engagement of religious groups with the local planning processes in Australia is made by employing the

35 Ibid., 75.

36 Ibid., 31.

37 Skennar, above n 28, 4–7.

38 See, e.g., the DCPs on Places of Worship of the City of Canterbury (NSW), City of Monash (VIC) and City of Wollongong (NSW).

39 Angela Carmella, 'Houses of Worship and Religious Liberty: Constitutional Limits to Landmark Preservation and Architectural Review', (1991) 36 *Villanova Law Review* 401, 402.

paradigm of international human rights law. This research paradigm is useful for three reasons:

First, the international standards on religious freedom are the only authoritative benchmarks upon which to gauge Australia's compliance with its international law duty to respect religious freedom.[40] In the words of the Universal Declaration on Human Rights (UDHR), human rights serve as a 'common standard of achievement for all peoples and all nations'.[41] Such standards can be used as the basis for assessing Australia's performance as regards religious freedom, both from the perspective of international law and Australian law as analysed in Chapter 4. True to their description as 'common standards of achievement', the international standards on religious freedom provide a legitimate basis for evaluating Australia's compliance with its international obligation to respect the right to freedom of religion or belief. Because of such standards, it is possible to demonstrate Australia's achievements or shortcomings with regard to respecting the religious freedom of individuals and groups within its territory. More importantly, because of their legitimacy as benchmarks that are agreed upon by the international community, such standards can be used to persuade government authorities to improve their performance regarding the protection of religious freedom in Australia.

In contrast, the regional standards developed by regional human rights systems cannot be readily employed to gauge Australia's performance as regards religious freedom because they are not authoritative with respect to Australia. Because Australia is not a State Party to any regional human rights conventions like the European Convention for the Protection of Human Rights and Fundamental Freedoms (1950),[42] the American Convention on Human Rights (1969),[43] and the African Charter on Human and Peoples'

40 This 'authoritativeness' has two aspects, namely, being authoritative in the international sphere and being so in the domestic sphere. This is discussed in more detail in Sections 4.1 and 4.3.

41 *Universal Declaration of Human Rights*, GA Res 217A (III), UN GAOR, 3rd sess, 183rd plen mtg, UN Doc A/810 (10 December 1948) ('UDHR') preamble.

42 *European Convention for the Protection of Human Rights and Fundamental Freedoms*, signed 4 November 1950, 213 UNTS 221, ETS 5 (entered into force 3 September 1953) ('ECHR') art 9(1).

43 *American Convention on Human Rights* (*Pact of San José*), signed 22 November 1969, 1144 UNTS 123, OASTS 36, O.A.S. Off. Rec. OEA/Ser.L/V/11.23,doc.21,rev.6 (1979), reprinted 9 ILM 673 (1970) (entered into force 18 July 1978) art 12.

Rights (1981),[44] their provisions are not legally opposable against it. Even their use as interpretative tools in ascertaining the meaning of vague or broad provisions in international human rights instruments to which Australia is a party (like the ICCPR) must be made with reservation and caution, because they exist and operate in systems of rights protection that have their own peculiarities specifically applicable to states in the region.[45] For example, in the jurisprudence of the European Court of Human Rights, the doctrine of 'margin of appreciation' which is 'based on the notion that each society is entitled to certain latitude in resolving the inherent conflicts between individual rights and national interests or among different moral convictions'[46] has a *diluting effect* upon the protective capacity and scope of the rights recognised in the European Convention, including the right to freedom of religion or belief guaranteed in its Article 9.[47] Eyal Benvenisti similarly observes that the:

> universal aspirations are, to a large extent, compromised by the doctrine of margin of appreciation.... Margin of appreciation, with its principled recognition of moral relativism, is at odds with the concept of the universality of human rights. If applied liberally, this doctrine can undermine seriously the promise of international enforcement of human rights that overcomes national policies.[48]

---

44 *Charter on Human and Peoples' Rights*, adopted 27 June 1981, CAB/LEG/67/3 rev. 5, 21 ILM 58 (1982), (entered into force 21 October 1986) art 8.

45 See generally, Dinah Shelton and Paolo Carrozza, *Regional Protection of Human Rights* (Oxford University Press, 2013, 2nd edition) 11–13; Dinah Shelton, 'The Promise of Regional Human Rights Systems', in Burns Weston and Stephen Marks (eds), *The Future of International Human Rights* (Transnational Publishers Inc, 1999) 351, 356.

46 Eyal Benvenisti, 'Margin of Appreciation, Consensus, and Universal Standards' (1999) 31 *International Law and Politics* 843, 844.

47 Article 9 of ECHR provides that:

1. Everyone has the right to freedom of thought, conscience and religion; this right includes freedom to change his religion or belief, and freedom, either alone or in community with others and in public or private, to manifest his religion or belief, in worship, teaching, practice and observance.
2. Freedom to manifest one's religion or beliefs shall be subject only to such limitations as are prescribed by law and are necessary in a democratic society in the interests of public safety, for the protection of public order, health or morals, or the protection of the rights and freedoms of others.

48 Benvenisti, above n 46, 844.

Second, specifically with respect to the right to freedom of religion or belief, the human rights standards that have been developed at the universal level are more stringent than those developed at the regional level, and thus offer a greater degree of legal protection to individuals or groups. For example, as analysed in Chapter 8, the 'limitations clause' specifically applicable to the right to freedom of religion or belief – that is, Article 18(3) of the ICCPR – provides a set of circumstances where restrictions may be permissible which are narrower than those found in equivalent 'limitations clauses' in regional instruments.[49] This suggests that a greater degree of protection for religious freedom exists in the international standards than in the regional standards.

Last but not least, the use of international standards on religious freedom is best suited in analysing a phenomenon that occurs within the broader dynamics between a majority culture and several minority cultures which co-exist in a common social and legal order. In this context, international human rights standards provide a sort of 'quality control' of the kind of treatment the minorities receive from the majority population. Ruth Gavison cogently asserts that:

> Human rights are seen as pre-legal constraints on majorities, so that if something is defined as a human right, it may defeat not only a policy determination by a competent authority but even a statutory arrangement enacted by a majority in the legislature. This is as it should be. Human rights are seen in this way so they can function effectively as constraints on the power of states, and of majorities within states, to violate the dignity of individuals and groups. At the same time, individuals and groups often use the special strength of rights to promote their own vision of the good life.[50]

Therefore, the issue of places of worship may be viewed as one of the areas where the majority should accommodate the minorities in Australian society. How such an accommodation is accomplished should be informed and guided by values that exist *outside* the very system that sustains the majority-minority dialectic.[51] Such values are to be found precisely in international human rights

---

49 See the more detailed discussion in Section 8.2.

50 Ruth Gavison, 'Days of Worship and Days of Rest: A View from Israel' in Winfried Brugger and Michael Karayanni (eds), *Religion in the Public Sphere: A Comparative Analysis of German, Israeli, American and International Law* (Max-Planck-Institut für ausländisches öffentliches Recht und Völkerrecht, 2007) 379, 391–392.

51 To illustrate a similar point, it may be stated that 'the prohibition placed upon a government from the use of torture is not dependent at all, as a matter of law, upon its own legal

standards. In contrast, to anchor such an accommodation exclusively upon the values of the majority culture is to invite the peril of a 'tyranny of the majority'.[52]

1.7 What are Included in 'Places of Worship'?

The subject-matter of this book is limited to *built* structures which are habitually, publicly and predominantly used as 'places of worship' such as temples, mosques, synagogues, churches, chapels, *gurdwaras* and similar constructed religious edifices in Australia. Therefore, private residential dwellings, which are sometimes used by their occupants to engage in private worship activities,[53] are excluded from this analysis because they are rightfully beyond the reach of local planning regulations, provided that the nature of the religious activities performed inside such dwellings remains 'private'. The construction of 'home altars', 'home shrines' or similar sacred spaces within residential dwellings which are intended for private worship activities is excluded from this analysis.

In addition, while traditional burial grounds, sacred sites, features of the physical environment and other natural locations (where the land or the open air is regarded as sacrosanct) are sometimes used as places of worship, most notably by Indigenous Australians, such places are also excluded from this analysis. Equally deserving of legal protection, they come under the comprehensive legal regime for the protection of the rights of Indigenous Australians and the preservation of their cultural heritage, rather than the regulation of built structures specifically provided by local planning regulations.[54] Indigenous

---

system: the obligation is one of international law'. Rosalyn Higgins, *Problems and Process: International Law and How We Use It* (Oxford, Clarendon Press, 1994) 96.

52 As originally propounded by John Stuart Mill, the 'tyranny of the majority' is a description of a polity where the will of the majority of the population shapes laws or policies that are designed to advance their own interest to the detriment of the interest of the minority. See John Stuart Mill, *On Liberty* (United Kingdom, 1859) 7; See also Dale E. Miller, *The Basic Writings of John Stuart Mill: On Liberty, the Subjection of Women and Utilitarianism* (Modern Library Classics, 1980).

53 For a discussion of the types of worship activities conducted inside private dwellings, see especially, Phra Nicholas Thanissaro, 'Home Shrines in Britain and Associated Spiritual Values' (2010) 31(3) *Journal of Beliefs & Values* 353–357; Ann L. Wehener, 'When a House is not a Home but a Church: A Proposal for Protection of Home Worship from Zoning Ordinances' (1993) 22 *Capital University Law Review* 491.

54 See, e.g., Ernst Willheim, 'Australian Legal Procedures and the Protection of Secret Aboriginal Spiritual Beliefs: A Fundamental Conflict' in Peter Cane, Carolyn Evans and Zoë Robinson (eds), *Law and Religion in Theoretical and Historical Context* (Cambridge University Press, 2008) 214.

heritage protection laws in Australia may be grouped into three types, namely, 'relics legislation' which protects prehistoric Aboriginal sites or Aboriginal cultural relics; 'culture significance legislation' which protects the contemporary cultural significance of the site; and 'general heritage legislation' which are general laws designed to protect Aboriginal heritage places without necessarily specifying them.[55]

Finally, the analysis in this book excludes buildings or entire precincts which are specifically included in the 'heritage' listings administered by the Commonwealth or the state and territory governments.[56] Such districts or areas are placed in appropriate heritage listings for their *significant* historic or architectural value which the relevant government body (usually the heritage protection agencies of the Commonwealth and state and territory governments) had officially declared worthy of preservation. They are excluded in this analysis because they fall under the comprehensive legal regime on heritage protection in Australia which is administered either by the federal or state and territory governments, rather than under the regulation of built structures on the basis of local planning regulations which are enforced by the local councils.

1.8 The Structure of the Book

This book is presented in four parts. Part 1 is comprised of the present chapter which introduces the research problem and the specific research questions; justifies the research paradigm to be employed; delimits the subject-matter of the book; and provides an overview of succeeding chapters.

Part 2 is composed of three chapters that aim to establish the applicable law. Chapter 2 demonstrates that the right to establish and maintain places of worship is a constituent element of the broader right to freedom of religion or belief. It tracks the incremental development of the right to freedom of religion or belief by analysing the international human rights instruments which are regarded as the right's 'foundational instruments'. Chapter 3 analyses the substance of the right to establish and maintain places of worship by examining

---

55 See specially David Ritchie, 'Principles and Practice of Site Protection Laws in Australia', in David Carmichael, Jane Hubert, Brian Reeves and Audhild Schanche (eds), *Sacred Sites, Sacred Places* (1994) 227, 229–230.

56 For a preliminary discussion on heritage listings in Australia, see especially, Australian Heritage Council, Guidelines for the Assessment of Places for the National Heritage List (Department of the Environment, Water, Heritage and the Arts, 2009) 4–14.

the distinct elements that make up its conceptual core, as understood by the UN Human Rights Committee and the Special Rapporteur on freedom of religion or belief. It traces its evolution from its earliest appearance in human rights documents up to its current stature as a distinct human right. Finally, Chapter 4 analyses how the international standards on religious freedom (including those pertaining to places of worship) are transported and accorded applicability into the Australian domestic setting, in light of the fact that international legal obligations are not automatically incorporated into Australian domestic law.

Part 3 is comprised of three chapters that examine the compatibility of the Australian local planning processes with the applicable law – that is, the international standards on religious freedom, including the right to establish and maintain places of worship. Employing a total of 25 case studies, these chapters illustrate that the functioning of the local planning processes in Australia produces effects, or leads to outcomes, that are incompatible with such international standards. Chapter 5 analyses planning decisions involving places of worship where issues of inadequate parking, excessive traffic, noise and similar tangible 'dis-benefits' to a place played a pivotal part, and then examines their implications to the international standards on religious freedom. Meanwhile, Chapter 6 analyses planning decisions involving places of worship where alleged intrusions against an area's visual amenity – a highly subjective planning concept – were the crucial issues, and probes their implications to the international standards on religious freedom. Finally, Chapter 7 analyses the specific design controls imposed by local planning authorities on the architectural design or appearance of proposed religious structures, and demonstrates their adverse impact upon certain aspects of the right to freedom of religion or belief.

Building from previous chapters, Part 4 presents the theoretical implications of the research findings. Chapter 8 analyses the requirements of 'permissible limitations' to the right to religious manifestation under Article 18(3) of the ICCPR, and illustrates their application in the context of restrictions against the right to establish and maintain places of worship. It then unravels the primary societal interests that underpin the protection of physical and visual amenity in local planning, and measures up their importance vis-à-vis the right to establish and maintain places of worship. This 'balancing exercise' demonstrates the privileged position of the right to freedom of religion or belief under international human rights law. Finally, Chapter 9 presents the book's conclusions and highlights the contribution it makes to the existing body of knowledge and its wider significance to the understanding of the interaction between law and religion. This final chapter makes it evident that the book's analysis has wider significance *beyond* the Australian jurisdiction in assessing the compatibility of other countries' local planning processes with the right to establish and maintain places of worship. The functioning of their local planning processes – and how they are impacting the ability of religious groups to build places of worship – may similarly be evaluated using the international standards on religious freedom. The structure, methodology and arguments of this study will inform such an endeavour.

PART 2

Determining the Applicable Law

CHAPTER 2

Freedom of Religion or Belief in International Human Rights Law and the Provenance of the Right to Establish and Maintain Places of Worship

2.1 Introduction

The struggle for religious freedom precedes the discipline of international human rights law which only emerged after the Second World War. Long before the notion of systematic protection of civil and political rights was developed, religious freedom has been the battle cry of minority groups and persecuted individuals.[1] It has been aptly stated that 'the origin of the general idea of human rights lies in the long history of protecting religious minorities'.[2] However, the modern international legal protection of religious freedom began when rights associated with religion[3] were collectively incorporated as subordinate rights (or constituent elements) of what is now referred to in international human rights instruments as the 'right to freedom of religion or belief'.[4] This chapter explores the genesis of this incorporation and the ensuing incremental development of the substance of the right to freedom of religion or belief, including the express articulation of a distinct right to establish and maintain places of worship. It analyses the emergence and relative position of the right to establish and maintain places of worship within the constituent elements comprising the broader right to freedom of religion or belief.

The aim of this chapter is to demonstrate the emergence and normative strength of a distinct right to establish and maintain places of worship. As discussed below,

1 Karl Josef Partsch, 'Freedom of Conscience and Expression, and Political Freedoms' in Louis Henkin (ed), *The International Bill of Rights: The Covenant on Civil and Political Rights* (Columbia University Press, 1981) 209.

2 Martin Scheinin, 'Article 18' in Asbjørn Eide, Gudmundur Alfredsson, Göran Melander, Lars Adam Rehof and Allan Rosas (eds), *The Universal Declaration of Human Rights: A Commentary* (Scandinavian University Press, 1992) 263.

3 Some commentators refer to these rights as 'religious human rights'. See, e.g., Natan Lerner, *Religion, Secular Beliefs and Human Rights: 25 Years after the 1981 Declaration* (Martinus Nijhoff Publishers, 2006) 13–54.

4 The modern international legal protection of human rights began after the Second World War (1939–1945) when the horrors of war 'outraged the conscience of mankind'. See generally, Michael Goodhart, *Human Rights: Politics and Practice* (Oxford University Press, 2013) 15–18.

 | DOI 10.1163/9789004289345_003

this aim can be accomplished by understanding the *symbiotic* relationship between the right to establish and maintain places of worship and the other constituent elements of the right to freedom of religion or belief. An understanding of this relationship sheds light on the protective scope of the right to establish and maintain places of worship which, in later chapters, is appraised in light of local planning disputes involving proposed places of worship in Australia. Thus, this chapter prepares the groundwork for the main research task ahead – that is, to evaluate the compatibility of Australian local planning processes with the international human rights standards on religious freedom, including the right to establish and maintain places of worship.

This chapter is divided into three parts. First, it analyses the legal architecture of the right to freedom of religion or belief under international human rights law. In chronological order, it examines the key international human rights instruments that provide legal protection of the right to freedom of religion or belief. Each of these instruments has contributed to the present conception of the international legal protection of religious freedom. Second, this chapter introduces the 'permissible limitations' to the right to freedom of religion or belief which are the narrow set of circumstances under which the right may be validly restricted. Third and finally, this chapter illustrates the symbiotic relationship between the right to establish and maintain places of worship and other constituent elements of the broader right to freedom of religion or belief. Analysing this relationship is crucial in understanding the protective capacity of the right to establish and maintain places of worship.

2.2 The Incremental Development of the Substance of the Right to Freedom of Religion or Belief

Several international human rights instruments can be credited with erecting the legal architecture of the right to freedom of religion or belief under international law: the Universal Declaration of Human Rights (UDHR) adopted in 1948,[5] the International Covenant on Civil and Political Rights (ICCPR)[6]

---

5 *Universal Declaration of Human Rights*, GA Res 217A (III), UN GAOR, 3rd sess, 183rd plen mtg, UN Doc A/810 (10 December 1948) ('UDHR'); The UDHR was adopted in 1948 by 48 votes in favour, none against and eight abstentions. There were only 58 member-states of the UN at that time. Australia was among those that voted in favour of the adoption of the UDHR.

6 *International Covenant on Civil and Political Rights,* opened for signature 16 December 1966, 999 UNTS 171 (entered into force 23 March 1976) ('ICCPR'); Australia signed the ICCPR on 18 December 1972 and ratified it on 13 August 1980.

adopted in 1966, the Declaration on the Elimination of All Forms of Intolerance and of Discrimination Based on Religion or Belief (Religion Declaration) adopted in 1981,[7] and the Human Rights Committee's General Comment 22 issued in 1993.[8] This section analyses the successive and incremental contributions of each of these instruments and demonstrates that, through their interaction, the right to freedom of religion or belief has taken shape and received its substantive content, including the specific right to establish and maintain places of worship. Paul Taylor described these instruments as 'the foundational instruments' that 'constitute the basic building blocks' of the right to freedom of religion or belief.[9] Their contributions are analysed successively below.

2.2.1 *Article 18, Universal Declaration of Human Rights*

Being a resolution adopted by the United Nations' General Assembly, the UDHR is not a legally binding treaty. In its own words, it provides 'a common standard of achievement for all peoples and all nations'.[10] However, it has been argued that the UDHR, either in its entirety or some of its provisions, has crystallised into customary international law.[11] Natan Lerner opined that '[m]ost of the principles proclaimed by the [UDHR] are seen today as reflecting customary international law and some of them as constituting *jus cogens*'.[12] It has been argued that, in particular, the right to freedom of thought, conscience and religion 'exists as a binding customary norm under international law'.[13] However, as demonstrated below, the right to freedom of thought,

---

7 *Declaration on the Elimination of All Forms of Intolerance and of Discrimination Based on Religion or Belief*, GA Res 36/55, UN GAOR, 36th sess, 73rd plen mtg, Supp No 51, UN Doc A/RES/26/55 (25 November 1981) ('Religion Declaration').

8 UN Human Rights Committee, *General Comment 22: The Right to Freedom of Thought, Conscience and Religion (Art 18)*, 48th sess, UN Doc CCPR/C/21/Rev.1/Add.4 (30 July 1993) ('General Comment 22').

9 Paul Taylor, *Freedom of Religion: UN and European Human Rights Law and Practice* (Cambridge University Press, 2005) 1–2.

10 UDHR, 'Preamble'.

11 Henry Steiner, Philip Alston and Ryan Goodman, *International Human Rights in Context: Law, Politics, Morals* (Oxford University Press, 2008) 137; Rex Ahdar and Ian Leigh, *Religious Freedom in the Liberal State* (Oxford University Press, 2005) 106.

12 Natan Lerner, 'Religious Human Rights under the United Nations', in Johan van der Vyver and John Witte, Jr (eds), *Religious Human Rights in Global Perspective: Legal Perspectives* (Martinus Nijhoff, 1996) 79, 82.

13 Peter W Mason, 'Pilgrimage to Religious Shrines: An Essential Element in the Human Right to Freedom of Thought, Conscience and Religion' (1993) 25 *Case Western Reserve Journal of International Law* 619, 624.

conscience and religion is a broad concept encompassing distinct elements whose relative normativity can be described as being on a gradated scale. Thus, characterising the entire right to freedom of thought, conscience and religion as constituting a customary norm of public international law might be an over generalisation.

The right to freedom of thought, conscience and religion is embodied in Article 18 of the UDHR which provides:

> Everyone has the right to freedom of thought, conscience and religion; this right includes freedom to change his religion or belief, and freedom, either alone or in community with others and in public or private, to manifest his religion or belief in teaching, practice, worship and observance.

Four important observations can be made about this provision. First, freedom of religion is recognised alongside freedom of thought and conscience.[14] Under the all-embracing phrase 'right to freedom of thought, conscience and religion', both religious and *non*-religious belief systems are guaranteed protection. Karl Josef Partsch explained the combination of 'thought and conscience', on one hand, and 'religion', on the other, in Article 18 of the UDHR as follows:

> Although no definition of "thought" or "conscience" is provided, taken together with "religion" they include all possible attitudes of the individual toward the world, toward society, and toward that which determines his fate and the destiny of the world, be it a divinity, some superior being or just reason and rationalism, or chance. "Thought" includes political and social thought; "conscience" includes all morality.[15]

Article 18 of the UDHR expressly provides that the 'right to freedom of thought, conscience and religion' includes (1) the freedom to change 'religion or belief' and (2) the freedom to manifest 'religion or belief'. Natan Lerner noted that the term 'religion or belief' in this context carries a definite meaning. He explained that:

> in modern human rights law the word "religion," usually followed by the word "belief" refers to theistic convictions involving a transcendental view of the universe and a normative code of behaviour as well as atheistic,

14 For an analysis of the specific right to freedom of conscience, see especially Leonard M Hammer, *The International Human Right to Freedom of Conscience: Some Suggestions for its Development and Application* (Ashgate, 2001).

15 Partsch, above n 1, 213–214.

> agnostic, rationalistic, and other views in which such elements are absent. "Beliefs," in this context, *always relate to religion* and *exclude beliefs of a different character in the political or social fields.*[16] [emphasis added]

Therefore, the protection of the 'right to freedom of religion or belief' under Article 18 of the UDHR extends to religious belief systems and belief systems which are *related to* religion. Its protective scope is broad to encompass traditional and non-traditional, established and new, dominant and minority, as well as organised and diffused religions. In addition, and equally significant, the 'right to freedom of religion or belief' protects belief systems which 'relate to religion' such as atheism, agnosticism, humanism, rationalism and similar beliefs, but *excludes* those beliefs of a political or social character such as political ideologies, economic philosophies and scientific theories. Lerner further explained that "[t]he term 'belief' has a particular meaning in the [UDHR]. Its inclusion in Article 18, and in similar articles in other instruments, should be interpreted strictly in connection with the term 'religion'."[17] Hence, for example, a Catholic's belief in the Holy Trinity or a Muslim's conviction that Muhammad is the final prophet and messenger of Allah comes within the protective scope of the 'right to freedom of religion or belief'. In contrast, however, a communist's belief in establishing the utopia of a classless society by armed struggle or a scientist's belief in the theory of evolution by natural selection, while both deserving and worthy of legal protection, do not fall under the protective scope of the 'right to freedom of religion or belief' but is encompassed by the broader 'right to freedom of thought, conscience and religion' which is also guaranteed by Article 18 of the UDHR.

Second, Article 18 of the UDHR expressly states that an individual has the freedom to 'change his religion or belief'. This express inclusion of the right to change one's religion or belief is significant because later international instruments omitted such unequivocal affirmation by replacing it with a milder formulation to appease certain Islamic countries during the drafting process.[18] Carolyn Evans states that the right to change religion or belief in Article 18 entitles 'every individual to decide at any point in his or her life to maintain,

---

16 Natan Lerner, 'The Nature and Minimum Standards of Freedom of Religion or Belief' in Tore Lindholm, W. Cole Durham, Jr and Bahia G. Tahzib-Lie (eds) and Elizabeth A. Sewell and Lena Larsen (associate eds), *Facilitating Freedom of Religion or Belief: A Deskbook* (Martinus Nijhoff Publishers, 2004) 63, 81–82.

17 Lerner, *Religion, Secular Beliefs and Human Rights,* above n 3, 14.

18 See discussion on Article 18(1) of the ICCPR below.

change or abandon his or her current religion or belief'.[19] Bahiyyih Tahzib identifies the right to change one's religion or belief as the 'first prong' of the right to freedom of religion or belief. It 'concern[s] the internal sphere of the right to freedom of thought, conscience and religion – the *forum internum*' which is absolute and cannot be restricted.[20] Thus, under Tahzib's view, the protection of the *forum internum* can be accomplished when the right to change religion or belief is guaranteed. However, as analysed below, later human rights documents have expounded on the meaning and import of the *forum internum* beyond the right to change religion or belief. In other words, there are other *forum internum* rights beyond the right to change religion or belief.

Third, if an individual manifests (that is, externalises into action) his or her religion or belief, then he or she crosses the realm of the *forum externum* which is also protected by Article 18 of the UDHR. Article 18 enumerates the four areas where the manifestation of one's religion or belief can take place, namely, in worship, observance, practice and teaching. It does not, however, elaborate on the possible forms of manifestations that fall under these four broad areas. Acts of manifestation of religion or belief may take on different forms but they are all outward demonstrations of one's religious or other beliefs which may affect other individuals, and thus may be validly restricted pursuant to Article 29 of the UDHR which provides the 'permissible limitations'[21] applicable to all the rights recognised in the Declaration.[22]

Finally, Article 18 of the UDHR guarantees the freedom to manifest one's religion or belief 'either alone or in community with others' which is an acknowledgement of both the individual and collective dimensions of the right to manifest one's religion or belief. Tahzib referred to both aspects as '[t]he second prong pertain[ing] to the external sphere of that right – the *forum externum*'.[23]

---

19 Carolyn Maree Evans, *Legal Protection of Religious Freedom in Australia* (The Federation Press, 2012) 25.

20 Bahiyyih Tahzib, *Freedom of Religion or Belief: Ensuring Effective International Legal Protection* (Martinus Nijhoff Publishers, 1996) 73.

21 Article 29(2) of the UDHR provides a 'generic' limitation clause, as follows: 'In the exercise of his rights and freedoms, everyone shall be subject only to such limitations as are determined by law solely for the purpose of securing due recognition and respect for the rights and freedoms of others and of meeting the just requirements of morality, public order and the general welfare in a democratic society'.

22 The analysis of the permissible limitations to the right to freedom of religion or belief is made separately in Section 2.3 below in order to preserve the continuity of the present discussion about the chronological development of the substance (as opposed to the limitations) of the right to freedom of religion or belief.

23 Tahzib, above n 20, 73.

In particular, the recognition of the collective dimension of the right implies that religious organisations in their own capacity possess certain rights exercisable by them as a group. Stressing the significance of the collective dimension of the right to manifest religion or belief, Lerner stated that a "right to be exercised 'in community with others' must therefore refer to something more than a purely arithmetic addition of individuals."[24] The UDHR does not, however, give examples of such 'organisational' rights but later human rights instruments do, notably the Religion Declaration and the Human Rights Committee's General Comment 22, as discussed in Sections 2.2.3 and 2.2.4 below.

In summary, the most important contribution of Article 18 of the UDHR in the normative development of the right to freedom of religion or belief is its erection of the right's basic skeletal framework as having two broad pillars, namely the *forum internum* and *forum externum,* and its identification of the four general areas where religion or belief can be externalised, namely in teaching, practice, worship and observance. This basic skeletal framework has endured since 1948 and has become the foundation of the present international legal architecture of the right to freedom of religion or belief. As analysed below, the ICCPR and the Religion Declaration subsequently adopted this basic skeletal framework and incrementally built from there the substantive constituent elements of the right to freedom of religion or belief, including the specific right to establish and maintain places of worship.

The UDHR has had an impact on the drafting of subsequent human rights treaties. Peter Cumper observed that 'the [UDHR] has been very influential in the formulation of the principles of national and international law'.[25] He observed that Article 18 of the UDHR provided the common and usual 'template used as the basis for drafting provisions that guarantee freedom of religion in a wide range of international human rights documents'.[26] The basic legal structure of Article 18 of the UDHR has been replicated in international human rights instruments like the ICCPR; in regional instruments like the European Convention for the Protection of Human Rights and Fundamental Freedoms (1950),[27] the

24 Lerner, 'Religious Human Rights under the United Nations', above n 12, 88.

25 Peter Cumper, 'Religion, Belief and International Human Rights in the Twenty-First Century' in Sarah Joseph and Adam McBeth (eds), *Research Handbook on International Human Rights Law* (Edward Elgar Publishing, 2010) 467, 470.

26 Ibid.

27 *European Convention for the Protection of Human Rights and Fundamental Freedoms,* signed 4 November 1950, 213 UNTS 221, ETS 5 (entered into force 3 September 1953)('ECHR') art 9(1).

American Convention on Human Rights (1969),[28] and the African Charter on Human and Peoples' Rights (1981)[29]; and even in national human rights statutes like the *New Zealand Bill of Rights Act 1990*.[30] With the skeletal framework of the right to freedom of religion or belief firmly established, the particulars of its substance as a human right have been developed in later instruments, including the ICCPR which is discussed in the next section.

2.2.2 *Articles 18 and 27, International Covenant on Civil and Political Rights*

Unlike the UDHR, the ICCPR legally binds all states that have ratified it. State Parties have agreed 'to ensure to all within their jurisdiction the rights guaranteed [and], if necessary, taking legislative or other action to do so'.[31] Of direct relevance to the right to freedom of religion or belief is Article 18 of the ICCPR which provides that:

1. Everyone shall have the right to freedom of thought, conscience and religion. This right shall include freedom to have or to adopt a religion or belief of his choice, and freedom, either individually or in community with others and in public or private, to manifest his religion or belief in worship, observance, practice and teaching.
2. No one shall be subject to coercion which would impair his freedom to have or to adopt a religion or belief of his choice.
3. Freedom to manifest one's religion or beliefs may be subject only to such limitations as are prescribed by law and are necessary to protect public safety, order, health, or morals or the fundamental rights and freedoms of others.
4. The States Parties to the present Covenant undertake to have respect for the liberty of parents and, when applicable, legal guardians to ensure the religious and moral education of their children in conformity with their own convictions.

Taken together, the above four sub-sections of Article 18 of the ICCPR 'contain the core international law commitments on the protection of freedom of

---

28 *American Convention on Human Rights (Pact of San José)*, signed 22 November 1969, 1144 UNTS 123, OASTS 36, O.A.S. Off. Rec. OEA/Ser.L/V/11.23,doc.21,rev.6 (1979), reprinted 9 ILM 673 (1970) (entered into force 18 July 1978) art 12.

29 *Charter on Human and Peoples' Rights*, adopted 27 June 1981, CAB/LEG/67/3 rev. 5, 21 ILM 58 (1982), (entered into force 21 October 1986) art 8.

30 *New Zealand Bill of Rights Act 1990*, s 15.

31 ICCPR, art 2.

religion'[32] made by those states that have ratified the ICCPR. Five important observations can be made about this provision:

First, Article 18(1) of the ICCPR echoes closely the phraseology of Article 18 of the UDHR. It reaffirms the protection given not only to 'religion' but also to the broader concepts of 'thought' and 'conscience' to encompass beliefs or belief systems that are non-religious in nature. Like Article 18 of the UDHR, Article 18(1) of the ICCPR reaffirms that the right to freedom of religion or belief has two broad components: the *forum internum* and the *forum externum*. Like Article 18 of the UDHR, Article 18(1) of the ICCPR also guarantees an individual's freedom to manifest his or her religion or belief in four distinct areas: worship, observance, practice and teaching. Human rights academics Sarah Joseph and Melissa Castan observed that:

> Manifestation of a religion may be termed the 'active' component of one's religious freedom, as opposed to the 'passive' component, which consists of mere adherence to certain beliefs. 'Manifestation' of religion or belief includes worship, teaching of the particular beliefs, and observance of specified canons of conduct or rituals. As such activities can interfere with the rights of others, or even pose a danger to society, the freedom to manifest religion or belief is not absolute.[33]

One notable difference between the UDHR and ICCPR provisions is that Article 18(1) of the ICCPR has omitted the *express* statement in Article 18 of the UDHR that an individual has the 'freedom to change his religion or belief' and replaced it with the rather mild formulation 'freedom to have or to adopt a religion or belief of his choice'. The latter is a compromised phraseology which was proposed by the Philippines and Brazil during the negotiations[34] because of the dominant stance of some Islamic states at the time of drafting that opposed the inclusion of a right to change one's religion.[35] Malcolm Evans opined that this change in phraseology can be read as retaining an individual's right to change religion, but it is also 'open to the interpretation that it allows

32 Kevin Boyle, 'Freedom of Religion in International Law' in Javaid Rehman and Susan Breau (eds), *Religion, Human Rights and International Law* (Martinus Nijhoff Publishers, 2007) 23, 39.

33 Sarah Joseph and Melissa Castan, *The International Covenant and Civil and Political Rights: Cases, Materials, and Commentary* (Oxford University Press, 2013, 3rd edition) 567.

34 Nihal Jayawickrama, *The Judicial Application of Human Rights Law: National, Regional and International Jurisprudence* (Cambridge University Press, 2002) 647–648.

35 Javaid Rehman, *Islamic State Practices: International Law and the Threat from Terrorism, A Critique of the 'Clash of Civilizations' in the New World Order* (Hart Publications, 2005) 68.

an individual to continue in a faith, to adopt a faith but not abandon a faith already held'.[36] Malcolm Evans added that the *travaux préparatoires* of Article 18 of the ICCPR did not show any consensus on this question and added that 'Muslim countries continued to express their dissent'[37] that there is such a right to change one's religion or belief. This conflict in interpretation has ultimately been resolved by the Human Rights Committee's General Comment 22, issued in 1993, which is the most authoritative elaboration of Article 18 of the ICCPR (discussed in Section 2.2.4 below).

Second, it will be recalled that, in Article 18 of the UDHR, the *forum internum* was equated with (i) the freedom of thought and conscience and (ii) the freedom of religious choice – that is, the right to change one's religion or belief, both of which are protected absolutely. Article 18(1) of the ICCPR reiterates both such freedoms. Significantly, however, Article 18(2) of the ICCPR represents a normative progression of the *forum internum* guarantee. By providing that no one 'shall be subject to coercion which would impair his freedom to have or to adopt a religion or belief of his choice', Article 18(2) contemplates *all* types and degrees of compulsion aimed at undermining an individual's freedom to choose a religion or belief, or not to choose at all. Hence, serious forms of coercion such as brainwashing, indoctrination, and the use or threat of force to compel an individual to convert to or recant a religion or belief are inconsistent with the freedom of religious choice. In addition, offering or withholding material or pecuniary benefits aimed at gaining new religious members,[38] as well as exerting improper pressure on individuals in dire need or distress with the aim of converting them into a religion or belief (or making them renounce a religion or belief) are also a violation of Article 18(2) of the ICCPR. Such covert forms of influence are referred to as 'improper proselytism'[39] which is

---

36 Malcom Evans, *Religious Liberty and International Law in Europe* (Cambridge University Press, 1997) 202.

37 Ibid., 221.

38 However, it must be recognised that this is not always easy to determine. For example, the act of a Christian religious group offering 'free rides' to and from its place of worship to assist in convincing a non-member to join the group may, depending on the circumstances, only be a gesture of kindness.

39 For a comparison between 'improper proselytism' and 'true evangelism', see especially Paul Taylor, 'Religion and Freedom of Choice' in John Witte Jr and M. Christian Green (eds), *Religion & Human Rights: An Introduction* (Oxford University Press, 2012) 170, 175–180; See also, Tad Stahnke, 'The Right to Engage in Religious Persuasion' in Tore Lindholm, W. Cole Durham, Jr and Bahia G. Tahzib-Lie (eds), and Elizabeth A. Sewell and Lena Larsen (associate eds) *Facilitating Freedom of Religion or Belief: A Deskbook* (Martinus Nijhoff Publishers, 2004) 619–649.

elaborated further by General Comment 22 to be discussed below. Therefore, Article 18(2) of the ICCPR casts the net wider, so to speak, and captures all types of coercion that would impair the freedom to choose or not to choose a religion or belief. Sylvie Langlaude opines that Article 18(2) of the ICCPR is in fact 'a measure that prohibits coercion and pressure on the individual's *forum internum*'.[40]

More significantly, however, the protection of the *forum internum* encompasses all kinds of compulsion on religious matters which do *not* necessarily impair an individual's freedom to choose or not to choose a religion or belief. Taylor suggested the existence of 'the numerous facets of religious choice'[41] which are distinct from the right to change one's religion or belief. Explaining the expanded scope of the *forum internum*, Taylor stated that:

> The *forum internum* is taken to denote the internal and private realm of the individual against which no State interference is justified in any circumstances. It comprises not only the individual's absolute freedom of choice of religion or belief... but also a range of additional freedoms (which shall be referred to as the residual scope of the *forum internum*).[42]

On the 'residual' *forum internum*, W Cole Durham, Jr similarly noted that:

> the precise outer boundaries of the non-regulable *forum internum* have never been precisely demarcated. Accordingly, one can at least argue that matters of doctrine, beliefs about internal ecclesiastical structure, membership and discipline, a variety of other organizational matters, and possibly even beliefs about how donations should be made and administered, are all themselves matters of religious belief linked to the internal forum.[43]

This means that the legal protection of the *forum internum* extends beyond its traditional conception of safeguarding the right to maintain or change one's religion or belief, but it also encompasses the right not to be compelled, in any

40 Sylvie Langlaude, *The Right of the Child to Religious Freedom in International Law* (Martinus Nijhoff Publishers, 2007) 70.

41 Taylor, 'Religion and Freedom of Choice', above n 39, 170.

42 Taylor, *Freedom of Religion: UN and European Human Rights Law and Practice,* above n 9, 115.

43 W. Cole Durham, Jr, 'Facilitating Freedom of Religion or Belief through Religious Association Laws' in Tore Lindholm, W. Cole Durham, Jr and Bahia G. Tahzib-Lie (eds) and Elizabeth A. Sewell and Lena Larsen (associate eds), *Facilitating Freedom of Religion or Belief: A Deskbook* (Martinus Nijhoff Publishers, 2004) 321, 360.

manner, to act or behave in contradiction with one's religion or belief. Thus, for example, an individual cannot be compelled to salute a flag if it contravenes his or her inner beliefs, nor a religious group be forced to perform worship activities different from those prescribed in its religious tenets. As observed by Taylor, even the Human Rights Committee exhibits a 'greater willingness to admit that coercion to act contrary to belief falls within the *forum internum*'.[44] Chapters 6 and 7 illustrate that architectural design choices in building places of worship are part and parcel of a religious group's *forum internum*. As analysed in those chapters, while the act of building places of worship is a form of religious manifestation (and hence, classified as *forum externum*), how the act is done is *inextricably tied* with religious beliefs which dictate the design or appearance of religious edifices. In building places of worship, the belief-action dichotomy is therefore less pronounced. Instead, 'belief' and 'action' exist in a sort of continuum where religious beliefs take on physical forms and become almost indistinguishable from the other. The analysis in Section 7.2 further bolsters this point.

Third, Article 18(3) of the ICCPR provides the permissible limitations which are specific or applicable only to the right to freedom of religion or belief, unlike the general limitations clause in Article 29 of the UDHR which applies to all the rights recognised therein. An introductory analysis of the permissible limitations under Article 18(3) of the ICCPR is made separately in Section 2.3 below.

Fourth, Article 18(4) of the ICCPR mandates that States Parties respect the liberty of parents or legal guardians to guide the religious education of their children 'in conformity with their own convictions'. Such liberty can be regarded as a specific form of manifestation which is already protected in Article 18(1) which guarantees the freedom to manifest one's religion or belief in teaching.[45] With respect to educating children in matters of religion or belief, the right of parents or legal guardians always prevails over the religious education provided by either the state or religious organisations.

Finally, the right to freedom of religion or belief guaranteed in Article 18 of the ICCPR is non-derogable. It is one of the few human rights where States Parties are not allowed to take measures which derogate from their international obligations under the ICCPR during an officially proclaimed public emergency which threatens the life of the nation. Article 4 of the ICCPR provides that:

---

44 Taylor, *Freedom of Religion: UN and European Human Rights Law and Practice*, above n 9, 200.

45 Malcolm Evans, above n 36, 219.

1. In time of public emergency which threatens the life of the nation and the existence of which is officially proclaimed, the States Parties to the present Covenant may take measures derogating from their obligations under the present Covenant to the extent strictly required by the exigencies of the situation, provided that such measures are not inconsistent with their other obligations under international law and do not involve discrimination solely on the ground of race, colour, sex, language, religion or social origin.
2. No derogation from articles 6, 7, 8 (paragraphs 1 and 2), 11, 15, 16 and 18 may be made under this provision.

The non-derogable nature of the right to freedom of religion or belief suggests its relatively privileged position in the hierarchy of human rights. It may be stated that international human rights law accords it with a greater degree of protection as compared with those human rights that can be derogated during times of grave public emergencies. Alexandre Kiss supports this view when he stated that:

> certain rights recognized by the Covenant *have a special character and are therefore entitled to greater protection than the others.* According to Article 4, no derogation may be made in time of public emergency from Articles 6, right to life; 7, prohibition of torture; 8(1) and (2), prohibition of slavery; 11, prohibition of imprisonment for contractual debt; 15, non-retroactivity of criminal legislation; 16, recognition as a person before the law; and 18, right to freedom of conscience, religion and thought. These … rights and freedoms form the hard core of the rights recognized by the Covenant and *it is normal that they should be given special consideration should a conflict arise with other rights and freedoms.*[46] [emphasis added]

Based on the foregoing, other human rights which do not share the 'special character' of non-derogable rights cannot prevail over the right to freedom of religion or belief (which is non-derogable). Taylor observed that '[w]hat is particularly interesting about the treatment of Article 18 among the non-derogable rights is that the whole of Article 18 is non-derogable, not just those parts that, according to the terms of Article 18, may not be restricted'.[47] Because the *whole*

---

46 Alexandre Kiss, 'Commentary by the Rapporteur on the Limitation Provisions' (1985) 7(1) *Human Rights Quarterly* 15, 22.

47 Taylor, 'Religion and Freedom of Choice', above n 39, 171.

of Article 18 is non-derogable,[48] it follows that all of the constituent elements of the right to freedom of religion or belief (including the right to establish and maintain places of worship) enjoy a greater degree of protection as compared to other human rights which may be derogated.

Another provision of the ICCPR which is directly relevant to the right to freedom of religion or belief is Article 27 on the rights of minorities. The complementary relationship between Articles 18 and 27 of the ICCPR was recognised by the Human Rights Committee when it stated that the 'respect for the rights of religious minorities under article 27 is necessary for the Committee to assess the extent to which the right to freedom of thought, conscience, religion and belief has been implemented by States parties'.[49] Article 27 of the ICCPR provides that:

> In those States in which ethnic, *religious* or linguistic *minorities* exist, persons belonging to such minorities shall not be denied the right, in community with the other members of their group, to enjoy their own culture, *to profess and practise their own religion,* or to use their own language.[50] [emphasis added]

Two observations can be made about Article 27. First, it applies only to certain types of minorities existing in a state, namely, the ethnic, religious and linguistic minorities.[51] A 'minority' has been defined as:

> [a] group numerically inferior to the rest of the population of a state, in a non-dominant position, whose members – being nationals of the state – possess ethnic, religious or linguistic characteristics differing from those of the rest of the population and show, if only implicitly, a sense of solidarity, directed towards preserving their culture, traditions, religion or language.[52]

---

48 Partsch, above n 1, 212.

49 General Comment 22, para 9.

50 ICCPR, art 27.

51 For an introductory discussion of the regime of international legal protection of minorities, see especially Asbjorn Eide, 'Minority Protection and World Order: Towards a Framework for Law and Policy' in Alan Philips and Allan Rosas (eds), *Universal Minority Rights* (Institute for Human Rights, Abo Akademi University, 1995) 87–112.

52 Francesco Capotorti, UN Special Rapporteur of the Sub-Commission on Prevention of Discrimination and Protection of Minorities, *Study on the Rights of Persons Belonging to Ethnic, Religious and Linguistic Minorities,* E/CN.4/Sub.2/384/Rev.1 (1979), para 242.

The protection given to minorities by Article 27 is *additional* to the protection given by the principle of non-discrimination 'in order to ensure them real equality of status with the majority population'.[53] Since a State Party is required by the principle of non-discrimination to ensure that the rights protected under the ICCPR are available to all individuals within its territory and subject to its jurisdiction,[54] a State Party may not restrict the rights under Article 27 to its citizens alone,[55] contrary to the definition of 'minority' quoted above which confines the protective scope of Article 27 to the 'nationals of the state'.

Second, the substantive rights which are recognised in Article 27 have a collective dimension because such rights are to be exercised in community with the other members of their group. The Human Rights Committee commented that the protection of the rights recognised in Article 27 is 'directed towards ensuring the survival and continued development of the cultural, religious and social identity of the minorities concerned'.[56] Hence, the right 'to profess and practise their own religion' in Article 27 is conferred to a religious minority as a group. Yoram Dinstein commented that one of the purposes of Article 27 of the ICCPR is to confer 'collective human rights to members of a religious minority *qua* a group'.[57] It recognises certain rights as belonging to minorities 'which [are] distinct from, and additional to, all the other rights which, as individuals in common with everyone else, they are already entitled to enjoy'.[58] Therefore, the significance of Article 27 of the ICCPR to the international legal protection of religious freedom is its reinforcement, as applied to religious minorities, of the collective dimension of the right to manifest religion or belief.

In addition, Articles 2(1) and 26 of the ICCPR,[59] also significantly contributed to the protective scope of the right to freedom of religion or belief by enunciating

---

53 Jayawickrama, above n 34, 843.

54 Exceptions to this rule include those rights which are expressly made to apply to citizens such as the political rights guaranteed in Article 25, ICCPR.

55 Human Rights Committee, General Comment 23 (1994): *The Rights of Minorities (Art 27)*: CCPR/C/21?Rev.1/Add.5 ('General Comment 23'), para 5.

56 Ibid., para 9.

57 Yoram Dinstein, 'Freedom of Religion and the Protection of Religious Minorities', in Yoram Dinstein and Mala Tabory (eds), *The Protection of Minorities and Human Rights* (Martinus Nijhoff Publishers, 1992) 157.

58 General Comment 23, para 1.

59 Article 2(1) of the ICCPR provides 'Each State Party to the present Covenant undertakes to respect and to ensure to all individuals within its territory and subject to its jurisdiction the rights recognized in the present Covenant, without distinction of any kind, such as race, colour, sex, language, religion, political or other opinion, national or social origin, property, birth or other status'.

the right not to be discriminated against on the basis of one's religion or belief. Owing to its singular importance, an analysis of the legal fusion between the right to freedom of religion or belief and the principle of non-discrimination in the enjoyment of human rights is made separately in Section 2.2.5 below.

The foregoing analysis shows how the basic skeletal framework of the right to freedom of religion or belief (which was first erected by Article 18 of the UDHR) was expounded by Article 18 of the ICCPR and further bolstered by Article 27 of the ICCPR with respect to religious minorities. This process of building up the substantive content of the right to freedom of religion or belief continued with the adoption of the Religion Declaration, another foundational instrument of the right to freedom of religion or belief, whose contribution to the norm standard-setting on religious freedom is discussed in the next section.

2.2.3 *Declaration on the Elimination of All Forms of Intolerance and of Discrimination Based on Religion or Belief*

Like the UDHR, the Religion Declaration is not a legally binding treaty. By consensus, it has been adopted by the members of the UN General Assembly in the form of a resolution.[60] While UN General Assembly resolutions are not *per se* sources of international law, their utility lies in being authoritative elaborations of existing legal norms as understood by states. International law expert Oscar Schachter argued that these resolutions may be authoritative evidence of binding international law on one or more of the following grounds: "(a) as 'authentic' interpretations of the UN Charter [or one of its principles] as agreed by all the parties; (b) as affirmations of recognized customary law; and (c) as expressions of general principles of law accepted by states."[61]

Article 26 of the ICCPR provides: 'All persons are equal before the law and are entitled without any discrimination to the equal protection of the law. In this respect, the law shall prohibit any discrimination and guarantee to all persons equal and effective protection against discrimination on any ground such as race, colour, sex, language, religion, political or other opinion, national or social origin, property, birth or other status'.

60 Donna Sullivan, 'Advancing the Freedom of Religion or Belief Through the UN Declaration on the Elimination of Discrimination and Intolerance' (1988) 82 *American Journal of International Law* 487.

61 Oscar Schachter, 'The UN Legal Order: An Overview' in Christopher Joyner (ed), *The United Nations and International Law* (Cambridge University Press, 1997) 3, 5; Donna Sullivan argued that, because the Religion Declaration was 'enunciated in *normative terms*, elevating the rights and freedoms in question to normative status, *the Declaration has a certain legal effect*'. [emphasis added] Sullivan seems to suggest that the Religion Declaration does not merely evidence nor interpret the law, but it is in fact responsible for the creation of the law. See Sullivan, above n 60, 488.

Notwithstanding its non-legally binding character, the Religion Declaration contributed significantly to the development of the right to freedom of religion or belief by providing specific substantive content to the otherwise broadly formulated right to freedom of religion or belief, more particularly its *forum externum*. Lerner observed that 'Articles 1 and 6 of the [Religion] Declaration contain a catalogue of rights that seem to be the universally agreed *minimum standard* in the area of religious human rights'.[62] [emphasis added] For this reason, Donna Sullivan observed that 'the [Religion] Declaration stands as a milestone in the progressive development of human rights norms'.[63] In the same vein, Lerner characterised the Religion Declaration as 'the most important international instrument regarding religious rights'.[64] The Religion Declaration is concerned with two broad themes: addressing religious discrimination and intolerance, and fleshing out the substance of the right to freedom of religion or belief.[65] The former is discussed in Section 2.2.5 below, while the latter is dealt with here.

Echoing the language of Article 18 of the UDHR and Article 18 of the ICCPR, Article 1 of the Religion Declaration provides that:

1. Everyone shall have the right to freedom of thought, conscience and religion. This right shall include freedom to have a religion or whatever belief of his choice, and freedom, either individually or in community with others and in public or private, to manifest his religion or belief in worship, observance, practice and teaching.
2. No one shall be subject to coercion which would impair his freedom to have a religion or belief of his choice.
3. Freedom to manifest one's religion or belief may be subject only to such limitations as are prescribed by law and are necessary to protect public safety, order, health or morals or the fundamental rights and freedoms of others.

Article 1(1) of the Religion Declaration is almost identical with the language of Article 18 of the UDHR and Article 18(1) of the ICCPR analysed above. It

62 Lerner, 'Religious Human Rights under the United Nations', above n 12, 117–118.

63 Sullivan, above n 60, 488; See also, Jeroen Temperman, '25th Anniversary Commemoration of the adoption of the 1981 UN Declaration on the elimination of intolerance and discrimination based on religion or belief – A Report' (2007) 2(1) *Religion and Human Rights* 19, 20–21.

64 Lerner, 'Religious Human Rights under the United Nations', above n 12, 114.

65 Carolyn Evans, 'Time for a Treaty?: The Legal Sufficiency of the Declaration on the Elimination of All Forms of Discrimination and Intolerance' [2007] *Brigham Young University Law Review* 617, 625.

reaffirmed the basic skeletal framework of the right to freedom of religion or belief – that is, it consists of an absolute and non-regulable *forum internum* and a *forum externum* which may be manifested in four areas and may be validly restricted. It is apparent that Article 1 of the Religion Declaration made no significant addition to what Article 18(1) of the ICCPR already provides for in terms of the substance of the right to freedom of religion or belief. The use of the word 'whatever' to describe 'belief' in Article 1 merely emphasises what has already been settled: that a broad range of belief systems such as atheism, agnosticism, humanism and other belief systems related to religion fall under the general rubric of 'belief', and hence should also be protected in the same manner as religious beliefs. Notwithstanding the fact that its Article 1 is a mere reaffirmation of Article 18 of the UDHR and Article 18(1) of the ICCPR, the Religion Declaration has made two principal contributions towards the normative development of the right to freedom of religion or belief.

First, Articles 2, 3 and 4 of the Religion Declaration deal with the prohibition against discrimination on the ground of religion or belief. By virtue of these provisions, the Religion Declaration has in fact fused together the principle of non-discrimination and the right to freedom of religion or belief into one legal formulation. This fusion may be considered an incremental development of the substance of the right to freedom of religion or belief. Owing to the utmost significance of this fusion in the international legal protection of religious freedom, it merits a separate analysis which is made in Section 2.2.5 below.

Second, the Religion Declaration further advanced the development of the substantive content of the right to freedom of religion or belief through, most crucially, Article 6 which enumerates in a non-exhaustive fashion the different forms of manifestation of religion or belief, one of which is the establishment and maintenance of places of worship. Article 6 of the Religion Declaration states that:

> In accordance with article 1 of the present Declaration, and subject to the provisions of article 1, paragraph 3, the right to freedom of thought, conscience, religion or belief shall include, *inter alia,* the following freedoms:
>
> (a) To worship or assemble in connection with a religion or belief, and *to establish and maintain places for these purposes;*
> (b) To establish and maintain appropriate charitable or humanitarian institutions;
> (c) To make, acquire and use to an adequate extent the necessary articles and materials related to the rites or customs of a religion or belief;
> (d) To write, issue and disseminate relevant publications in these areas;

(e) To teach a religion or belief in places suitable for these purposes;
(f) To solicit and receive voluntary financial and other contributions from individuals and institutions;
(g) To train, appoint, elect or designate by succession appropriate leaders called for by the requirements and standards of any religion or belief;
(h) To observe days of rest and to celebrate holidays and ceremonies in accordance with the precepts of one's religion or belief;
(i) To establish and maintain communications with individuals and communities in matters of religion and belief at the national and international levels.[66] [emphasis added]

Article 6 has improved the "condensed formula of 'teaching, practice, worship and observance'" found in the UDHR and the ICCPR by providing a 'detailed list of various forms of manifestation'.[67] There seems to be a general agreement among various law and religion scholars that Article 6 represents an important milestone in the development of religious freedom norms. For example, Boyle described these forms of manifestation as 'the major concrete components of religious freedom that are to be recognised and guaranteed by the state'.[68] Lerner regarded them as 'a detailed enunciation of rights belonging to the accepted minimum standard'[69] of the right to religious freedom. While Rex Ahdar and Ian Leigh described these forms of manifestation as 'the incidents of freedom of religion',[70] the Religion Declaration itself referred to them as separate 'freedoms'. This detailed enumeration of concrete forms of manifestation represents a progression from earlier efforts to conceive the international legal protection of the right to freedom of religion or belief. As Carolyn Evans observed, '[t]his new development in the effort to protect the freedom of religion does not have a clear counterpart in the earlier treaties and instruments'.[71]

For this analysis, Article 6 of the Religion Declaration is most significant because it is the first *explicit* articulation in an international human rights instrument that a religious group has the right to establish and maintain places of worship. While such a right may be implied from the right to manifest religion or belief 'in community with others', because communal worship necessarily

66 Religion Declaration, art 6.
67 Taylor, *Freedom of Religion: UN and European Human Rights Law and Practice*, above n 9, 22.
68 Boyle, above n 32, 49.
69 Lerner, 'Religious Human Rights under the United Nations', above n 12, 118.
70 Rex Ahdar and Ian Leigh, *Religious Freedom in the Liberal State* (Oxford University Press, 2005) 107.
71 Evans, 'Time for a Treaty?: The Legal Sufficiency of the Declaration on the Elimination of All Forms of Discrimination and Intolerance', above n 65, 626.

presupposes having an appropriate physical space for worship activities, its express inclusion in the list of the accepted minimum standards of the right to freedom of religion or belief leaves no doubt as to its existence as a distinct international human rights norm. However, it should be stressed that while Article 6 of the Religion Declaration expressly recognised its existence, it is the later efforts towards international human rights standard-setting on freedom of religion or belief which substantially gave the right to establish and maintain places of worship its own substantive metes and bounds, as discussed in Chapter 3.

Under Article 6 of the Religion Declaration, the right to establish and maintain places of worship was recognised as emerging from the nucleus of – and thus its legal foundation anchored on – the freedom to manifest one's religion or belief. Yoram Dinstein aptly observed that 'freedom of religion, as an individual right, may be nullified unless complemented by a collective human right of the religious group to construct the infrastructure making possible the full enjoyment of that freedom by the individuals'.[72] Silvio Ferrari and Sabrina Pastorelli also emphasised the importance of this organisational right:

> Having a place of worship was regarded as a manifestation of religious freedom, which is a right that had to be recognized to every human being. In this new perspective any religious group, independently from its relations with the State, is entitled to have its own place of worship and this right cannot be made dependent on an authorization by or an agreement with the public administration and cannot be limited to the religious communities that have been registered or recognized at national or local level.[73]

By virtue of its express articulation in Article 6 of the Religion Declaration, the right to establish and maintain places of worship has been entrenched as a constituent element of the right to freedom of religion or belief and, therefore, as an important part of the broader corpus of international human rights law.

It is clear that Article 6 of the Religion Declaration is not concerned much with religious manifestations by an individual, but rather it involves the freedoms of the religious group, community, or organisation as such. Carolyn Evans referred to this as the 'institutional elements of religious freedom'.[74] For the

---

72 Dinstein, above n 57, 158.

73 Silvio Ferrari and Sabrina Pastorelli, 'The Public Space: The Formal and Substantive Neutrality of the Public Sphere' (Working Paper No. 4, Religious Diversity and Secular Models in Europe, September 2010) 5.

74 Evans, 'Time for a Treaty?: The Legal Sufficiency of the Declaration on the Elimination of All Forms of Discrimination and Intolerance', above n 65, 626.

first time, the following *organisational* rights pertinent to religious freedom were expressly and collectively recognised in an international human rights instrument:

1. The right to establish and maintain places of worship,
2. The right to make, acquire and use religious articles and materials,
3. The right to establish and maintain charitable or humanitarian institutions,
4. The right to write, issue and disseminate religious publications,
5. The right to teach religion or belief,
6. The right to solicit and receive voluntary financial and other contributions,
7. The right to train and choose religious leaders in accordance with the requirements of one's religion or belief,
8. The right to observe days of rest and to celebrate holidays and ceremonies in accordance with the precepts of one's religion or belief, and
9. The right to establish and maintain communications with individuals and communities in matters of religion and belief at the national and international levels.

All of the foregoing 'concrete components of religious freedom'[75] are exercisable only by religious groups or associations in their own capacity. Even the right to observe days of rest in accordance with the precept of one's religion or belief, while ostensibly a right exercised by an individual, only becomes meaningful if exercised with co-religionists.[76] Lerner observed that Article 6 made a unique contribution to the normative development of the right to freedom of religion or belief. He observed that Article 6:

> involves progress as compared to previous instruments. Only groups can establish and maintain places of worship and institutions, or appoint religious leaders, or establish federations. The [Religion] Declaration thus contemplates the needs of religious communities or congregations – needs that are not satisfied by the instruments that follow the orientation of the early years of the UN, based exclusively on individual rights.[77]

75 Boyle, above n 32, 49.

76 See especially, Ruth Gavison and Nahshon Perez, 'Days of rest in multicultural societies: private, public, separate?' in Peter Cane, Carolyn Evans and Zoö Robinson (eds), *Law and Religion in Theoretical and Historical Context* (Cambridge University Press, 2008) 195.

77 Lerner, 'Religious Human Rights under the United Nations', above n 12, 120.

In sum, the thrust of Article 6 is the entrenchment of the collective dimension of the right to manifest religion or belief. The Religion Declaration 'is of unique significance in the development of the freedom of religion since it was the first, and remains the only, United Nations instrument dedicated solely to that freedom'.[78] Its practical value comes from the fact that it has been utilised by the human rights bodies that have a direct influence on international standard setting as regards the right to freedom of religion or belief (namely, the Human Rights Committee and the Special Rapporteur on the freedom of religion or belief) whose pronouncements are analysed in Chapter 3 for their standard setting value.

The final key document which contributed to the incremental development of the substance of the right to freedom of religion or belief is the Human Rights Committee's General Comment 22 which is discussed in the next section.

2.2.4 *Human Rights Committee's General Comment 22*

The Human Rights Committee, the treaty body mandated to monitor states' compliance with their obligations under the ICCPR, performs crucial functions of international human rights standard-setting with respect to the freedom of religion or belief.[79] The Committee performs such function in three ways. First, States Parties to the ICCPR are required to submit periodic reports about the 'measures they have adopted which give effect to the rights recognized [in the ICCPR] and on the progress made in the enjoyment of those rights'.[80] The Committee, in turn, issues its 'Concluding Observations' on these state reports. Second, an individual who alleges a violation of his or her civil or political rights as guaranteed in the ICCPR can lodge a communication with the Human Rights Committee, provided that his or her state has ratified the First Optional Protocol to the ICCPR.[81] The Committee then issues its 'Views' on such communications which also contribute in the understanding of the rights enshrined in the ICCPR. Third and finally, the Human Rights Committee issues 'General Comments' which are authoritative interpretations of the provisions of the ICCPR. Strictly speaking, these interpretations are not legally

---

78 Taylor, *Freedom of Religion: UN and European Human Rights Law and Practice,* above n 9, xii.

79 Peter Cumper, 'Religion, Belief and International Human Rights in the Twenty-First Century' in Sarah Joseph and Adam McBeth (eds), *Research Handbook on International Human Rights Law* (Edward Elgar Publishing, 2010) 467, 472.

80 ICCPR, art 40(1).

81 *Optional Protocol to the ICCPR,* opened for signature 16 December 1966, 999 UNTS 302 (entered into force 23 March 1976) art 41.

binding upon states but they are 'generally respected as an authoritative and expert source for interpreting the ICCPR'.[82] While noting that different commentators assign varying degrees of 'authoritativeness' to General Comments, Paula Gerber *et al* stated that:

> it is clear that the legal status of general comments has grown beyond a mere technical recommendation into an *authoritative* source of interpretation. That status seems to fall short of positive law, but general comments nonetheless play a substantive legal role in the elaboration of standards and possible future custom within the complex matrix of international law.[83] [emphasis added]

Recognising the treaty bodies' contributions to international human rights standard-setting in general, human rights academic Makau Mutua similarly observed that:

> [t]hrough their interpretive powers, treaty bodies have made significant contributions to human rights. Many treaties tend to be either broad or vague, so it has fallen on treaty bodies to elaborate, clarify, and elucidate standards by more clearly defining their meaning and the scope of states' obligations. Without a doubt, treaty bodies serve not merely an interpretive function, but rather, in effect, engage in standard-setting.[84]

Pursuant to such international standard-setting function, the Human Rights Committee issued General Comment 22 in July 1993, which constitutes the Committee's authoritative statement of the meaning and application of Article 18 of the ICCPR. Carolyn Evans described General Comment 22 as 'the best distillation of the international law obligation to protect freedom of religion or belief'.[85] She further commented that:

> General Comment 22 is the most comprehensive and detailed international law instrument giving substance to the protection of freedom of

---

82 Evans, *Legal Protection of Religious Freedom in Australia*, above n 19, 32.

83 Paula Gerber, Joanna Kyriakakis and Katie O'Byrne, '*General Comment 16* on State Obligations Regarding the Impact of the Business Sector on Children's Rights: What is its Standing, Meaning and Effect?' (2013) 14 *Melbourne Journal of International Law* 1, 9.

84 Makau Mutua, 'Standard Setting in Human Rights: Critique and Prognosis' (2007) 29 *Human Rights Quarterly* 547, 615.

85 Evans, *Legal Protection of Religious Freedom in Australia*, above n 19, 32.

> religion or belief under art 18 of the ICCPR. It should be understood as an authoritative and expert overview of the obligations under the ICCPR.[86]

General Comment 22 makes five key contributions to the substantive content of the right to freedom of religion or belief. First, General Comment 22 provides that:

> Article 18 protects theistic, non-theistic and atheistic beliefs, as well as the right not to profess any religion or belief. The terms "belief" and "religion" are to be broadly construed. Article 18 is not limited in its application to traditional religions or to religions and beliefs with institutional characteristics or practices analogous to those of traditional religions.[87]

Through this elaboration, the Human Rights Committee made clear that the term 'religion or belief' should be accorded a wide and inclusive meaning in order to bring new and not so well-established religions or beliefs under the protective mantle of Article 18 of the ICCPR. Thus, traditional and non-traditional, majority and minority, and registered and non-registered religions or beliefs are encompassed by its protective scope.

Second, General Comment 22 resolved any lingering doubt or ambiguity as to whether there exists a right to change one's religion or belief under international human rights law by providing unequivocally that:

> the freedom to "have or to adopt" a religion or belief necessarily entails the freedom to choose a religion or belief, including the *right to replace* one's current religion or belief with another or to adopt atheistic views, as well as the right to retain one's religion or belief.[88] [emphasis added]

Whether or not there is a right to replace one's religion or belief is an issue that had been left unresolved by the use of the muted provision 'right to have or to adopt a religion or belief' in Article 18(1) of the ICCPR, in lieu of the unequivocal 'freedom to change his religion or belief' in the earlier Article 18 of the UDHR. In General Comment 22, the Human Rights Committee settled the issue once and for all. Religious freedom includes the right to maintain or replace one's religion or belief, or not to have any religion or belief at all.

---

86 Ibid., 33.

87 General Comment 22, para 2.

88 General Comment 22, para 5.

Third, General Comment 22 also elaborated on the non-coercion guarantee found in Article 18(2) of the ICCPR by stating that:

> Article 18.2 bars coercion that would impair the right to have or adopt a religion or belief, including the use of threat of physical force or penal sanctions to compel believers or non-believers to adhere to their religious beliefs and congregations, to recant their religion or belief or to convert. Policies or practices having the same intention or effect, such as, for example, those restricting access to education, medical care, employment or the rights guaranteed by article 25 and other provisions of the Covenant, are similarly inconsistent with article 18.2.[89]

Thus, the Human Rights Committee provides concrete examples of the non-coercion guarantee found in Article 18(2) of the ICCPR. 'Coercion' on religious matters does not only cover grave forms of compulsion to undermine an individual's right to choose or not to choose a religion or belief such as brainwashing, indoctrination and the use or threat of force to compel an individual to convert to or recant a religion or belief, but also includes other means of compulsion such as restricting access to education, medical care, employment, suffrage or other rights to force an individual to convert into a religion or belief or to renounce an existing religion or belief. Lerner states that it is 'reasonable to interpret [coercion] as meaning not only the use of force or threats but also *more subtle forms* of illegitimate influence'.[90] [emphasis added] In the above paragraph, the Human Rights Committee made it clear that the non-coercion guarantee in Article 18(2) of the ICCPR is an expansion of the protective scope of the *forum internum* guarantee.

Fourth, General Comment 22 recognises an individual's right to a 'conscientious objection' by stating that:

> [t]he Covenant does not explicitly refer to a right to conscientious objection, but the Committee believes that such a right can be derived from article 18, inasmuch as the obligation to use lethal force may seriously conflict with the freedom of conscience and the right to manifest one's religion or belief.[91]

---

89 Ibid.

90 Lerner, 'Religious Human Rights under the United Nations', above n 12, 91.

91 General Comment 22, para 11.

The right to a conscientious objection springs from the legal protection of the *forum internum*. It protects individuals who hold a genuine belief that using lethal force while performing military service is contrary to their religious or other convictions. The right to conscientious objection may exempt them from rendering military service. In addition, General Comment 22 provides that, when the right to conscientious objection is recognised, 'there shall be no differentiation among conscientious objectors on the basis of the nature of their particular beliefs; likewise, there shall be no discrimination against conscientious objectors because they have failed to perform military service'.[92] The right to conscientious objection is one of the easily discernible *forum internum* rights whose essence is the prohibition against compelling an individual to act contrary to one's inner beliefs. As previously discussed, the expanded conception of the *forum internum* encompasses other guarantees against any type of compulsion in matters of religion or belief, whose relevance to building places of worship will be analysed in Chapters 6 and 7 when religious groups are required to vary their faith-dictated architectural designs on their religious edifices in order to comply with local planning regulations.

Fifth, General Comment 22 elaborated on the 'broad range of activities' encompassed by the freedom to manifest one's religion or belief. The Human Rights Committee defined religious manifestation by giving concrete examples of the four general types of manifestation (that is, worship, observance, practice and teaching).[93] It must be emphasised that the four types of manifestation are exhaustive,[94] but the concrete examples given by the Committee are not. The examples cover a broad range of activities that connote an outward expression of one's religion or belief. In General Comment 22, the Human Rights Committee "sought to give specific content to the 'broad range of activities' encompassed by the right to manifest religion in worship, observance, practice and teaching."[95] The Committee explained in detail that:

> The freedom to manifest religion or belief in worship, observance, practice and teaching encompasses a broad range of acts. *The concept of worship extends to ritual and ceremonial acts* giving direct expression to belief, *as*

92 Ibid.

93 Malcolm Evans, above n 36, 216.

94 Bahiyyih Tahzib argued that 'there are only four explicitly defined means by which religion or belief may be manifested, i.e., teaching, practice, worship, and observance'. See Tahzib, above n 20, 170–171.

95 Boyle, above n 32, 42.

> *well as various practices integral to such acts, including the building of places of worship,* the use of ritual formulae and objects, the display of symbols, and the observance of holidays and days of rest. The observance and practice of religion or belief may include not only ceremonial acts but also such customs as the observance of dietary regulations, the wearing of distinctive clothing or head coverings, participation in rituals associated with certain stages of life, and the use of a particular language customarily spoken by a group. In addition, the practice and teaching of religion or belief includes acts integral to the conduct by religious groups of their basic affairs, such as the freedom to choose their religious leaders, priests and teachers, the freedom to establish seminaries or religious schools and the freedom to prepare and distribute religious texts or publications.[96] [emphasis added]

What is immediately apparent in the Human Rights Committee's elaboration of the right to manifest religion or belief is the fact that the four areas of worship, observance, practice and teaching are not rigidly compartmentalised into separate and distinct types of activities. On the contrary, there is significant overlap in their scope in such a manner that one particular religious manifestation can be both performed in worship and in observance, or in observance and in practice, and other possible combinations. As Cornelis de Jong notes:

> the distinctions between the right to manifest in worship, in observance or in practice are not rigid: the separate examination of these various elements can be of help in singling out the specific aspects of the freedom to manifest one's religion or belief, but it should never be forgotten that the elements are interlinked and sometimes overlap.[97]

Thus, a Sikh religious congregation which prepares food inside their *gurdwara* and shares it with everyone present is doing so *both* as part of their faith-prescribed manner of worshipping as well as the observance of a religious tenet to share one's blessings. Similarly, a Catholic baptism ceremony involves acts of worship as well as the observance of a ritual associated with a certain stage of a Catholic's life.

Von Keetch and Matthew Richards observed that '[t]he right to erect buildings where communities of faith may gather or to make use of existing buildings to fulfil a religiously mandated mode of worship is ... a fundamental and

96 General Comment 22, para 4.

97 Cornelis de Jong, *The Freedom of Thought, Conscience and Religion or Belief in the United Nations (1946–1992)* (Hart-Intersentia, 2000) 105.

indispensable aspect of the right to worship'.[98] It may appear therefore that the construction of temples, mosques, *gurdwaras,* churches, synagogues or other similar edifices is relevant exclusively to the right to religious manifestation in worship. But this is not the case because the building places of worship may also be 'in observance' of fundamental religious beliefs, as analysed in Chapter 7. In addition, the building of places of worship may also be relevant to religious manifestation 'in teaching' in so far as they have educative and expressive functions meant to inform religious members and the general public, as discussed in Chapter 6. In General Comment 22, the Human Rights Committee characterised the 'concept of worship' as extending to 'ritual and ceremonial acts' and that the construction of places of worship as 'integral' to such acts. Thus, while places of worship have a direct and obvious relevance to religious manifestation in worship, they may also be indispensable to religious manifestations in observance, practice and teaching.

In summary, the utility of General Comment 22 in clarifying the metes and bounds of the right to freedom of religion or belief may be attributed to the internal consistency and coherence of its elaborations. General Comment 22 is able to explain the grey areas of Article 18 of the ICCPR while successfully avoiding the temptation of going beyond its confines, thereby preventing the dilution of its normative strength.

Another substantive element of the right to freedom of religion or belief requires a separate analysis due to its singular importance as an augmentation to the right's protective capacity. That substantive element is the principle of non-discrimination based on religion or belief discussed in the next section.

2.2.5 *The Principle of Non-Discrimination Based on Religion or Belief*

The principle of non-discrimination cuts across all human rights, including the right to freedom of religion or belief. Together with the principle of equal protection of the laws, the principle of non-discrimination underpins 'all human rights instruments' and both are 'the pre-eminent norms of the human rights movement'.[99] Strictly speaking, therefore, the right to freedom of religion or belief and the principle of non-discrimination are distinct and separate concepts.

However, violations of the right to freedom of religion or belief are often committed with a discriminatory intent.[100] The curtailment of religious exercise

98 Von Keetch and Mathew Richards, 'The Need for Legislation to Enshrine Free Exercise in the Land Use Context' (1999) 32 *University of California Davis Law Review* 725, 726.

99 Mutua, above n 84, 623.

100 See especially the reports of the mandate-holders of the office of the UN Special Rapporteur on freedom of religion or belief discussed in Chapter 3.

is often the result of policies or practices that single out individuals or groups unfairly on the basis of their religion or belief. In many cases, it appears that violations of religious freedom are precipitated by acts of discrimination on the basis of religion or belief. Kris Hanna has similarly observed this sort of cause-and-effect relationship when he stated that '[a]llowing people to be discriminated against on the basis of their religious beliefs or practices *limits* their right to freedom of religion'.[101] [emphasis added] To prevent these limitations, the principle of non-discrimination is given a central, almost indispensable, role to play in safeguarding the right to freedom of religion or belief. It was accomplished, not by the earlier 'generic' anti-discrimination provisions in the UDHR[102] and the ICCPR,[103] but by Articles 2 and 3 of the Religion Declaration which provide that:

> Article 2
> 1. No one shall be subject to discrimination by any State, institution, group of persons, or person on the grounds of religion or other belief.
> 2. For the purposes of the present Declaration, the expression "intolerance and discrimination based on religion or belief" means any distinction, exclusion, restriction or preference based on religion or belief and having as its purpose or as its effect nullification or impairment of the recognition, enjoyment or exercise of human rights and fundamental freedoms on an equal basis.
>
> Article 3
> Discrimination between human beings on the grounds of religion or belief constitutes an affront to human dignity and a disavowal of the principles of the Charter of the United Nations, and shall be condemned as a violation of the human rights and fundamental freedoms proclaimed in the Universal Declaration of Human Rights and enunciated in detail in the International Covenants on Human Rights, and as an obstacle to friendly and peaceful relations between nations.

The above provisions of the Religion Declaration have fused the non-discrimination principle and the right to freedom of religion or belief into one legal formulation. Zdenka Machnyikova observed that this combination or

101 Kris Hanna, 'Freedom of Discrimination on the Basis of Religion' in Paul Babie and Neville Rochow (eds), *Freedom of Religion under Bills of Rights* (University of Adelaide Press, 2012) 365.

102 UDHR, art 2.

103 ICCPR, arts 2(1) and 26.

tandem between religious freedom and non-discrimination norms is clearly stated and unique in the above-quoted provisions. She stated that:

> a specific connection between protection of the rights to freedom of religion and non-discrimination has been made in the [Religion Declaration], which distils many of the principles articulated in Article 18 of the CCPR, and in Articles 2, 3 and 4 [of the Religion Declaration], *and directly connects the anti-discrimination norms to the protection of religion and belief.*[104] [emphasis added]

This legal fusion may be considered another incremental development of the substantive content of the right to freedom of religion or belief. Machnyikova explained the effects of this combination when she commented that "[t]he substantive protection guaranteed by the freedom of religion is reinforced in these instruments by non-discrimination clauses and by provisions guaranteeing equality before the law and equal protection of the law, which prohibit any discrimination on the grounds of 'religion'."[105] Thus, the non-discrimination principle is strongly welded with the right to freedom of religion or belief to such an extent that the former has effectively been incorporated into the conceptual core of the latter.

Referring to Articles 1 and 2 of the Religion Declaration, David Little commented that:

> The distinction between what we shall call "the right of free exercise" (Article 1) and "the right of non-discrimination" (Article 2) is a commendable way of classifying "religious human rights." ... it reliably sorts out two of the most fundamental interests religious people have: being able to affirm, express, and manifest their convictions, and being able to avoid unfair discrimination or bias on account of religion.[106]

Little underscored the importance of including the non-discrimination principle in the provisions of the Religion Declaration and how it augments the legal

104 Zdenka Machnyikova, 'Religious Rights' in Marc Weller (ed), *Universal Minority Rights: A Commentary on the Jurisprudence of International Courts and Treaty Bodies* (Oxford University Press, 2007) 179, 181.

105 Ibid.

106 David Little, 'Studying Religious Human Rights: Methodological Foundations' in Johan van der Vyver and John Witte, Jr (eds), *Religious Human Rights in Global Perspective: Legal Perspectives* (Martinus Nijhoff Publishers, 1996) 45, 48.

protection of freedom of religion or belief. Combining the principle of non-discrimination and the right to freedom of religion or belief into one legal formulation in a key human rights instrument devoted solely to religious freedom has therefore bolstered the latter's protective capacity.

The Religion Declaration also sought to create a 'positive' obligation on the part of states to address the problem of discrimination based on religion or belief. Article 4 of the Religion Declaration provides:

> Article 4
> 1. All States shall take effective measures to prevent and eliminate discrimination on the grounds of religion or belief in the recognition, exercise and enjoyment of human rights and fundamental freedoms in all fields of civil, economic, political, social and cultural life.
> 2. All States shall make all efforts to enact or rescind legislation where necessary to prohibit any such discrimination, and to take all appropriate measures to combat intolerance on the grounds of religion or other beliefs in this matter.

As provided above, states have a positive duty to actively address the problem of religious discrimination and intolerance by taking 'effective measures', including but not limited to legislative, judicial and administrative measures. This represents another incremental development of the substance of the right to freedom of religion or belief because, traditionally, it was protected when states merely *refrain from acts* that impede religious freedom. The obligation to undertake positive actions 'to prevent and eliminate discrimination on the grounds of religion or belief' is an additional duty. It should be noted that the non-discrimination guarantees in Articles 2(1) and 26 of the ICCPR do not provide a similar 'positive' obligation.

Thus far, what has been analysed is the substance of the right to freedom of religion or belief. The next section briefly introduces the 'limitations clauses' which identify the narrow set of circumstances under which a state may validly restrict the exercise of the right to freedom of religion or belief.[107] The operation of these limitations clauses (particularly in the context of exercising

107 A 'limitations clause' which may be implicit or explicit, spells out the circumstances where a human right can be legitimately restricted by a state; while a 'granting clause' is that part of a legal provision which recognises a human right and enunciates its substance. See especially, T. Jeremy Gunn, 'Permissible Limitations on Freedom of Religion or Belief' in John Witte, Jr and M. Christian Green (eds), *Religion and Human Rights: An Introduction* (Oxford University Press, 2012) 254, 254–257.

the right to establish and maintain places of worship) is analysed extensively in Chapter 8.

2.3 The Limitations Clauses: When Manifestation of Religion or Belief may be Validly Restricted

The right to manifest one's religion or belief is not absolute and may be validly restricted by the state. R S Clark explained the rationale behind these valid restrictions when he commented that the '[m]anifestation of belief... impacts directly on society at large, so that limiting such manifestations may be a legitimate goal of overall social policy'.[108] To be valid, however, a restriction against religious manifestation must satisfy the requisites laid down by the relevant limitations clauses, namely, Article 29(2) of the UDHR, Article 18(3) of the ICCPR and Article 1(3) of the Religion Declaration whose texts are reproduced below.

The UDHR provides a *generic* limitations clause that applies to all the rights recognised in its provisions. Article 29(2) provides that:

> [i]n the exercise of his rights and freedoms, everyone shall be subject only to such limitations as are determined by law solely for the purpose of securing due recognition and respect for the rights and freedoms of others and of meeting the just requirements of morality, public order and the general welfare in a democratic society.

In contrast, Article 18(3) of the ICCPR provides a tailored and specific limitations clause which is applicable only to the right to freedom of religion or belief. It is replicated *en toto* in Article 1(3) of the Religion Declaration.[109] Chapter 8 analyses how Article 18(3) of the ICCPR states *the* law on the permissible limitations on the right to freedom of religion or belief. Article 18(3) of the ICCPR states that:

> Freedom to manifest one's religion or beliefs may be subject only to such limitations as are prescribed by law and are necessary to protect public

108 R S Clark, 'The United Nations and Religious Freedom' (1978) 11 *New York University Journal of International Law and Politics* 197, 215.

109 Article 1(3) of the Religion Declaration provides that: 'Freedom to manifest one's religion or beliefs may be subject only to such limitations as are prescribed by law and are necessary to protect public safety, order, health, or morals or the fundamental rights and freedoms of others'.

> safety, order, health, or morals or the fundamental rights and freedoms of others.

By enumerating the permissible limitations on the freedom to manifest religion or belief, Article 18(3) of the ICCPR made a significant contribution in delineating the general contours of the right to freedom of religion or belief. As Manfred Nowak aptly observed, 'the interplay between the principle of freedom of religion and its restrictions is what truly determines the actual scope of the individual's right'.[110] Article 18(3) allows limitations against the right to manifest religion or belief only if certain requirements are satisfied, namely, the limitations are: (i) prescribed by law, (ii) necessary to protect public safety, order, health, or morals or the fundamental rights and freedoms of others, and (iii) directly related and proportionate to the specific need on which they are predicated. In General Comment 22, the Human Rights Committee offered some guidance on how to apply Article 18(3) of the ICCPR when it stated that the:

> [l]imitations imposed must be established by law and must not be applied in a manner that would vitiate the rights guaranteed in article 18. The Committee observes that paragraph 3 of article 18 is to be strictly interpreted: restrictions are not allowed on grounds not specified there, even if they would be allowed as restrictions to other rights protected in the Covenant, such as national security. Limitations may be applied only for those purposes for which they were prescribed and must be directly related and proportionate to the specific need on which they are predicated. Restrictions may not be imposed for discriminatory purposes or applied in a discriminatory manner.[111]

This elaboration from the Human Rights Committee yields five key guidelines in evaluating the permissibility of limitations against the right to manifest religion or belief – that is, whether the restrictions are legally valid:

First, the burden of proof is upon the state authorities whose actions restricted the manifestation of religion or belief to prove that their actions satisfy the requisites of permissible limitations under Article 18(3) of the ICCPR. Tahzib agreed with this reasoning and argued that '[s]tates have, therefore, the

---

110 Manfred Nowak, *U.N. Covenant on Civil and Political Rights: CCPR Commentary* (N.P. Engel, 2005, 2nd revised edition) 311.

111 General Comment 22, para 8.

burden of demonstrating that a limitation imposed complies with the requirements of paragraph 3'.[112]

Second, the grounds for permissible limitations on the freedom to manifest one's religion or belief are an exhaustive list. The *only* possible grounds are public safety, order, health, morals or the fundamental rights and freedoms of others, all of which must be strictly interpreted. If any kind of restriction is based on grounds other than those mentioned in Article 18(3) of the ICCPR, then the restriction is invalid 'even if they would be allowed as restrictions to other rights protected in the Covenant, such as national security'.[113]

Third, Article 18(3) of the ICCPR is unique for its inclusion of 'the fundamental rights and freedoms of others' as a ground for permissible limitation on religious manifestation. The Special Rapporteur on freedom of religion or belief, whose mandate and contribution to international human rights standard-setting is discussed in the next chapter, observed that:

> this article allows for restrictions only in very exceptional cases. In particular the fact that it mentions the protection of "*fundamental* rights and freedoms" of others as a ground for restriction indicates a stronger protection than for some other rights whose limitation clauses refer simply to the "rights and freedoms of others" (e.g. article 12, 21 and 22).[114] [emphasis original]

The placement of the adjective 'fundamental' which describes the 'rights and freedoms of others' is deliberate. Taylor opined that '[i]f the "rights and freedoms of others" are to be the legitimate basis of State restrictions on the manifestation of religion, they must be "fundamental." '[115] Therefore, forms of manifestation in worship, observance, practice and teaching should not be restricted by the state based on the need to protect the human rights of others that are not considered 'fundamental'. The meaning of 'the fundamental rights and freedoms of others' and its susceptibility to be invoked as a ground for restricting the right to establish and maintain places of worship are analysed in depth in Sections 8.2.2.5 and 8.3, respectively.

Fourth, even in situations where the restrictions to the freedom to manifest one's religion or belief are allowed (that is, they are based on public safety,

---

112 Tahzib, above n 20, 170.

113 General Comment 22, para 8.

114 *Report of the UN Special Rapporteur on Freedom of Religion or Belief*, UN Doc A/60/399 (30 September 2005), para 62.

115 Taylor, 'Religion and Freedom of Choice', above n 39, 171.

order, health, morals or the fundamental rights and freedoms of others), they 'may not be imposed for discriminatory purposes or applied in a discriminatory manner'.[116]

Finally, even in situations where the restrictions against the freedom to manifest one's religion or belief are allowed (that is, they are based on public safety, order, health, morals or the fundamental rights and freedoms of others), they must still be 'directly related and proportionate to the specific need on which they are predicated'.[117] This test of relevance and proportionality calls for a delicate balancing between religious freedom and other societal values. For example, if a local authority decides to temporarily close down a local temple because of a bomb threat, the restriction seems to be justifiable on the ground of protecting public safety. However, if the temple remains closed for an unreasonably long period of time, such a restriction is no longer 'proportionate to the specific need' on which it is predicated.

In Chapter 8, the restrictions against the right to establish and maintain places of worship as a consequence of the enforcement of local planning regulations are analysed in light of the above key guidelines.

2.4 The Key Principles Underlying the International Legal Protection of Religious Freedom and How they Relate to the Right to Establish and Maintain Places of Worship

Based on the foregoing discussion of the legal architecture of the right to freedom of religion or belief, it is now possible to summarise four key principles underlying the international legal protection of religious freedom. These principles have a direct positive bearing on the right to establish and maintain places of worship as a distinct human rights norm by augmenting the latter's protective capacity.

First, the internal realm of thought, conscience and belief is absolutely protected. As analysed in Section 2.2.2 above, this protection of the *forum internum* goes beyond the right to replace one's religion or belief and extends to all kinds of coercion on matters of religion or belief – that is, according to Taylor, the 'residual' *forum internum*. This expanded conception of the *forum internum* guarantee is especially relevant in protecting the right to establish and maintain places of worship in two important ways. First, the choice of the fundamental

116 General Comment 22, para 8.

117 Ibid.

religious or other beliefs worthy of being spatially expressed in the design of places of worship belongs exclusively to religious organisations which, in this context, act on behalf of their individual members. For instance, if a Christian church wants to structurally depict the concept of the Holy Trinity, the state authorities cannot substitute their own judgment and insist on depicting Jesus Christ's resurrection instead. That choice is protected by the *forum internum* guarantee. However, as analysed in Chapters 6 and 7, there is an ever present danger that that choice may be interfered with by local planning authorities in discharging their mandate. Second, when pressure or compulsion is exerted by state authorities in the architectural design of places of worship, religious organisations may be forced to accept variations in designs which are contrary to, or at least different from, what their religious or other beliefs prescribe. Thus, for example, if a domed roof is religiously significant in a group's belief system, the state cannot alter that choice and force any other shape of roof. The protection of the *forum internum* requires that state authorities refrain from making an assessment of the validity, importance, or hierarchy of religious beliefs. The protection of the *forum internum* – which is guaranteed to all individual members but, in this context, is exercised on their behalf by the religious organisation – entails that such an assessment be made by the religious organisation itself and without the interference of the state.

Second, the right to establish and maintain places of worship has important repercussions for the exercise of other religious freedom rights encompassed by the overarching right to manifest one's religion or belief (*forum externum*). This is because places of worship perform an indispensable function in manifesting religion or belief in the areas of worship, observance, practice or teaching. In fact, certain forms of religious manifestation cannot be performed except inside a place of worship. Therefore, religious communities cannot function completely and effectively without a physical space to perform the ceremonies or rituals required by their faith.[118] The importance of establishing places of worship becomes even more pronounced when acts of worship are performed 'in community with others' for, indeed, in some religions, worshipping as a group is obligatory.[119] The significance of places of worship permeates all areas of the *forum externum*. Therefore, the legal protection of the right to establish and maintain places of worship has a *multiplier effect* on religious

118 See generally, Douglas Laycock, 'State RFRAs and Land-use Regulations' (1999) 32 *University of California Davies Law Review* 755, 756.

119 For example, the Quakers are religiously mandated to engage in silent communal worship. See especially, Daniel Steinbock, *Making Silence Together: Collaboration in the Silent Gatherings of Quakers* (PhD Thesis, Stanford University, August 2012) 1–146.

manifestation because places of worship make possible the performance of more forms of religious manifestation in worship, observance, practice and teaching – that is, a net result of greater exercise of religious manifestation.

Third, the principle of non-discrimination based on religion or belief offers a crucial protection for religious organisations desiring to build their own places of worship. It assumes greater importance in societies where there are religious minorities who may be vulnerable to being singled out and treated unfairly in planning applications simply on the basis of their religion or belief. Carolyn Evans has stressed that anti-discrimination laws 'may play an important role in protecting members of minority or unpopular religious groups from discrimination'.[120] Chapters 5 and 6 further illustrate the relevance of the prohibition against discrimination, both its direct and indirect forms, in the protection of the right to establish and maintain places of worship.

Finally, because the right to establish and maintain places of worship is an inherent part of the broader right to freedom of religion or belief, it logically follows that the former is covered by the international legal guarantees that protect the latter. As pointed out by de Jong, '[t]he right to establish places of worship and assembly is subject to the same limitations as the general freedom to manifest one's religion or belief'.[121] Therefore, planning decisions that restrict the right to establish and maintain places of worship should be dissected and scrutinised in light of the provisions in Article 18(3) of the ICCPR. This is analysed further in Chapter 8.

In sum, the above four key principles underlying the international legal protection of religious freedom operate simultaneously, with the effect of enhancing the protective capacity of the right to establish and maintain places of worship in the scheme of related rights. Thus, there exists a *symbiotic* relationship between such principles and the right to establish and maintain places of worship. Owing to this mutually beneficial relationship, the right to establish and maintain places of worship becomes a more robust religious freedom norm.

2.5 Conclusion

The 'foundational instruments' of religious freedom (namely, the UDHR, ICCPR, Religion Declaration and General Comment 22) have incrementally built up

120 Carolyn Evans, 'Balancing Religious Freedom Rights and Other Human Rights', in Paula Gerber and Melissa Castan (ed), *Contemporary Perspectives on Human Rights Law in Australia* (Thomson Reuters, 2013) 475, 481.

121 De Jong, above n 97, 360.

the substance of the right to freedom of religion or belief. Carolyn Evans described this development as 'a long, slow, and ongoing process of generating consensus around the fundamental need to protect religious freedom'.[122] Since the inception of the right to freedom of religion or belief in the UDHR in 1948, its substantive build-up has been a gradual process that eventually led to the express articulation of its subordinate rights, including the specific right to establish and maintain places of worship whose own substantive elements are analysed in the next chapter. It has been observed that:

> [i]t is their inherent compatibility that binds related norms together. The net effect is to bring about a group of related norms operating concertedly, while maintaining their separate and distinct existence, like different parts of a clock.... As part of a cohesive group, a constituent norm is regarded as being more authoritative or legally binding than when it is standing alone.[123]

In many respects, the different elements of the right to freedom of religion or belief exhibit the same behaviour by operating 'like different parts of a clock' working in unison towards the same objective – that is, to produce the greatest possible exercise of religious freedom. The right to establish and maintain places of worship plays an important part in maximising that freedom. Indeed, the right to freedom of religion or belief may be rendered nugatory unless the state guarantees the right of religious communities to build and keep the physical infrastructure that enables the full exercise and enjoyment of that freedom.

The four key principles underlying the international legal protection of religious freedom interrelate with the right to establish and maintain places of worship, with the effect of bolstering the latter's protective capacity. First, the freedom of religious choice which flows from the protection given to the *forum internum* allows religious groups to decide the significance and hierarchy of their religious beliefs, and which of them should be conveyed or expressed through the architectural designs or features of their places of worship. Second, the utility of places of worship to the exercise of various forms of religious manifestation *rationalises* the international legal protection given to the right

---

122 Evans, 'Time for a Treaty?: The Legal Sufficiency of the Declaration on the Elimination of All Forms of Discrimination and Intolerance', above n 65, 632.

123 Noel Villaroman, 'Rescuing a Troubled Concept: An Alternative View of the Right to Development' (2011) 29(1) *Netherlands Quarterly of Human Rights* 13, 27.

to establish and maintain places of worship. As discussed in this chapter, the existence of places of worship makes possible the greater exercise of the right to manifest one's religion or belief in worship, observance, practice and teaching. Third, the principle of non-discrimination based on religion or belief assumes greater relevance in the process of securing planning permits to construct places of worship where local decision-makers are highly susceptible to pressure or influence exerted by local residents who may be opposed to the building of such places. Finally, the narrow set of circumstances comprising the permissible limitations to the right to freedom of religion or belief under Article 18(3) of the ICCPR is the same set of circumstances where restrictions to the building of places of worship are to be adjudged as valid or not. If the rejection of a proposed place of worship cannot be justified on any of the grounds in Article 18(3), then such rejection is an impermissible limitation, and thus a breach of Article 18 of the ICCPR.

Building on this chapter's analysis, the next chapter traces the normative development of the right to establish and maintain places of worship by analysing and synthesising the various outputs of the human rights authorities which have a direct influence on international human rights standard-setting pertaining to the right to religious freedom, namely, the UN Human Rights Committee and the Special Rapporteur on freedom of religion or belief.

CHAPTER 3

The Right to Establish and Maintain Places of Worship

Unpacking the Substance of a Human Right

3.1 Introduction

As analysed in the previous chapter, the 'foundational instruments' of the right to freedom of religion or belief have only established the broad contours of this right because the process of elaborating its substantive contents is ongoing and far from complete. Kevin Boyle notes that '[t]he effort to enhance religious freedom through the adoption of new standards is a continuing process.'[1] While the foundational instruments have delineated the general shape and form of the right to freedom of religion or belief, on closer analysis it becomes apparent that some of its constituent elements remain imprecise and blurred, including the right to establish and maintain places of worship. Through the process of international standard-setting in human rights, the substance of the right to freedom of religion or belief is continually being refined and given precision. This chapter illustrates this important process by discussing how, through the work of relevant human rights standard-setting authorities, the substance of the right to establish and maintain places of worship is further elaborated.

This chapter draws primarily from the work of UN bodies directly responsible for international human rights standard-setting in the area of religious freedom, namely, the Human Rights Committee and the Special Rapporteur on freedom of religion or belief. It dissects the substance of the right to establish and maintain places of worship in order to reveal the elements that make up its conceptual core. This chapter consists of two parts. First, the process of international standard-setting in human rights is explained. In particular, the unique contribution of the Special Rapporteur on freedom of religion or belief to standard-setting in the area of religious freedom is highlighted. Second, and this is the crux of this chapter, it synthesises the outcomes of the standard-setting activities of the Human Rights Committee and the Special Rapporteur

1 Kevin Boyle, 'Freedom of Religion in International Law' in Javaid Rechman and Susan Breau (eds), *Religion, Human Rights and International Law* (Martinus Nijhoff Publishers, 2007) 23, 32.

 | DOI 10.1163/9789004289345_004

relevant to the right to establish and maintain places of worship. What emerges from this analysis is a distinct right which is made up of its own constituent elements. This analysis is important in order to further understand the protective scope of the right to establish and maintain places of worship which, in subsequent chapters, is appraised in light of planning disputes involving places of worship in Australia.

3.2 International Human Rights Standard-Setting on the Right to Freedom of Religion or Belief

The entry of the right to establish and maintain places of worship into the ranks of recognised human rights, while being a notable milestone, does not guarantee its implementation by states. Across the world, violations of the right to establish and maintain places of worship have been observed. For example, the Special Rapporteur on freedom of religion or belief has reported a litany of such violations:

> In Brunei Darussalam and Kuwait, the authorities are said to have refused permission to build, enlarge or renovate non-Muslim places of worship.... [I]n Myanmar, construction of a church was stopped by the authorities despite the fact that a construction permit had been obtained. In Greece, a Muslim religious leader was purportedly taken to court and then released after being accused of illegally building a mosque. In Azerbaijan, Christians were reportedly driven from the establishments where they were carrying out religious activities. In Georgia and Azerbaijan, Armenian Orthodox churches are said to have been closed. In Azerbaijan and the Russian Federation, religious minorities are reportedly having difficulty renting rooms to be used as places of worship. In Bulgaria, in one city, Jehovah's Witnesses are apparently banned from renting buildings. In Bosnia and Herzegovina and in Nepal, places of worship are said to have been attacked and even destroyed. In Pakistan, in Karachi, peaceful demonstrations by Christians protesting against the destruction of Christian properties including churches were allegedly suppressed by the police. In Romania and Georgia, the problem of restitution of goods and properties confiscated under the former regime has been raised.[2]

---

2 *Interim Report of the Special Rapporteur on the Elimination of all Forms of Religious Intolerance*, UN Doc A/52/477 (16 October 1997), para 34(a).

In almost every region of the world, religious communities 'face insurmountable obstacles when trying to construct or renovate visible places of worship, such as churches, mosques, pagodas, synagogues or temples.'[3] The bare and austere language of Article 6(a) of the Religion Declaration, where the right to establish and maintain places of worship was first expressly recognised, is of limited use in promoting compliance. The simple formulation 'to establish and maintain' masks several difficulties that may arise when the right is claimed or invoked. In other words, the explicit manner in which the right was articulated did not completely fill up the 'normative gap'[4] and left much to be implied from the text of the Religion Declaration. Hence, there arises a need to flesh out the particulars of the substance of the right to establish and maintain places of worship.

International human rights instruments are usually phrased in general and broad language. Before they can be effectively implemented, the meaning and practical consequences of their provisions must be elaborated. Such elaboration is an important aspect of the process of international standard-setting in human rights.[5] The end-product of this process assumes different forms, including general comments, views and concluding observations of treaty-based human rights bodies as well as studies, reports and even 'soft law' instruments prepared through the Special Procedures of the UN human rights machinery. Whatever form it takes, the end-product of human rights standard-setting serves the same purpose – that is, the elaboration of broadly articulated human rights norms. The UN General Assembly has recognised the importance of standard-setting and called on UN bodies charged with elaborating human rights norms to '[b]e sufficiently precise to give rise to identifiable and practicable rights and obligations.'[6]

Emphasising the importance of formulating sufficiently clear standards, human rights academic Makau Mutua stated that 'human rights norms cannot be effective unless they are unpacked into clear components, spelling out

3 Heiner Bielefeldt, 'Statement of the Special Rapporteur on Freedom of Religion or Belief,' 65th session of the General Assembly, Third Committee, Item 68 (b) (21 October 2010) 4 <http://www2.ohchr.org/english/issues/religion/> at 15 September 2014.

4 A 'normative gap' exists when acts or omissions that violate human rights are not adequately covered by existing human rights instruments. See especially, International Council on Human Rights Policy, *Human Rights Standards: Learning from Experience* (ICHRP, 2006) 7.

5 See, e.g., UN General Assembly Resolution, 97th plen mtg, *Setting International Standards in the Field of Human Rights,* UN Doc A/RES/41/120 (4 December 1986).

6 Ibid., art 4(c).

obligations and rights, and identifying the path to their implementation at the national level.'[7] Mutua noted that:

> Broad norms and standards must be unpacked, broken down, elucidated, revised, and may even need to be rejected and replaced by new and different standards. The scope, reach, and content of norms must be comprehensible to their beneficiaries, as well as to those who bear the responsibility for their implementation. Vacuous, rhetorical, and vague standards accomplish little.[8]

Thus, all human rights must be 'operationalised' into identifiable duties or obligations on the part of states which can guide their actions, and into clear entitlements on the part of rights-holders. Because they serve as guideposts in implementing broadly articulated norms, human rights standards 'have transformed the nature of the relationship between governments and individuals, and made public authorities far more accountable.'[9]

Given the non-detailed manner in which the right to establish and maintain places of worship was articulated in the Religion Declaration, it is therefore necessary to resort to the relevant authorities on human rights standard-setting and to synthesise their work into a coherent whole. In this chapter, the relevant pronouncements of the two human rights authorities whose mandates are directly relevant to the right to freedom of religion or belief are examined, namely, the Human Rights Committee and the Special Rapporteur on freedom of religion or belief. Their pronouncements – that is, the Committee's 'Concluding Observations' and 'Views' as well as the various reports of the Special Rapporteur on freedom of religion or belief – are distilled for their standard-setting value with respect to the right to establish and maintain places of worship.

The Human Rights Committee established under the ICCPR is a quintessential example of a human rights standard-setter. Because the Committee's mandate and functions were discussed in the previous chapter,[10] it is only necessary here to explain those of the Special Rapporteur on freedom of religion or belief.

---

7 Makau Mutua, 'Standard Setting in Human Rights: Critique and Prognosis' (2007) 29 *Human Rights Quarterly* 547, 618.

8 Ibid., 620.

9 International Council on Human Rights Policy, above n 4, 2.

10 See the discussion on Section 2.2.4.

The UN has established a mechanism for promoting and protecting human rights known as the 'Special Procedures.'[11] It consists of country mandates where human rights experts prepare reports on the human rights situation of particular states, and thematic mandates where experts prepare reports on particular human rights, or issues relevant to human rights.[12] There are different official titles used to refer to thematic mandate-holders, namely, Special Rapporteur, Independent Expert, Representative or Special Representative of the Secretary-General, Working Group or High-Level Panel. While the designations differ, their function is essentially the same. Special Procedures have been described as being:

> at the core of the UN human rights machinery. As independent and objective experts who are able to monitor and rapidly respond to situations and allegations of violations against individuals or groups occurring anywhere in the world, they play a critical and often unique role in promoting and protecting human rights.[13]

Mandate-holders in the Special Procedures 'have played a vital role in standard-setting. They regularly identify protection gaps and initiate new standards.'[14] Henry Steiner *et al* have observed that most mandate-holders use their annual reports in order to 'provide an overview of current and pressing issues ... and to develop particular interpretations of the norms in question.'[15] As of 1 October 2014, there were 39 thematic mandates in the Special Procedures system,[16] including the Special Rapporteur on freedom of religion or belief.[17]

---

11 For a comprehensive discussion on the functions of the Special Procedures, see especially Philip Alston and Ryan Goodman, *International Human Rights: Text and Materials, The Successor to International Human Rights in Context* (Oxford University Press, 2013) 699–741.

12 Ibid., 699.

13 Amnesty International, *United Nations Special Procedures: Building on a Cornerstone of Human Rights Protection* (2005) 5.

14 International Council on Human Rights Policy, above n 4, 27.

15 Henry Steiner, Philip Alston and Ryan Goodman, *International Human Rights in Context: Law, Politics, Morals* (Oxford University Press, 2008, 3rd edition) 769.

16 Office of the High Commissioner for Human Rights, *Thematic Mandates* <http://www.ohchr.org/EN/HRBodies/SP/Pages/Themes.aspx> at 7 October 2014.

17 The former Commission on Human Rights appointed a 'Special Rapporteur on religious intolerance' in 1986, but the Commission changed the mandate's title to 'Special Rapporteur on freedom of religion or belief' in 2000. The Commission on Human Rights was replaced by the Human Rights Council in March 2006 by virtue of UN General Assembly Resolution 60/251.

The Special Rapporteur on freedom of religion or belief is an independent expert appointed by the UN Human Rights Council[18] who 'identif[ies] existing and emerging obstacles to the enjoyment of the right to freedom of religion or belief and present[s] recommendations on ways and means to overcome such obstacles.'[19] The Special Rapporteur on freedom of religion or belief undertakes fact-finding country visits, conducts in-depth studies, transmits urgent appeals and letters of allegation to governments, and submits annual reports to the UN Human Rights Council.[20] Unlike the Human Rights Committee which monitors the full range of civil and political rights in the ICCPR, the Special Rapporteur on freedom of religion or belief is given the particular mandate of 'examin[ing] incidents and governmental actions in all parts of the world inconsistent with the provisions of the [Religion Declaration], and to recommend remedial measures for such situations.'[21] In the 28 years of the mandate's existence, which is one of the longest among the thematic mandates in the Special Procedures of the UN human rights machinery, the Special Rapporteurs on freedom of religion or belief have contributed to the elaboration of the right to freedom of religion or belief through the undertaking of technical studies and the preparation of reports.[22] Referring to a former mandate-holder, Carolyn Evans has commented that the Special Rapporteur's work has brought 'a greater awareness of some of [the religious freedom issues] and it may be that her time in office leads to a greater clarity in relation to obligations.'[23] The next section analyses the standard-setting contributions of the Special Rapporteur on freedom of religion or belief, along with those of the Human Rights Committee.

---

18 Thus far, four individuals have held this position, as follows: Angelo d'Almeida Ribeiro (Portugal), from March 1986 to March 1993; Abdelfattah Amor (Tunisia), from April 1993 to July 2004; Asma Jahangir (Pakistan), from August 2004 to July 2010; and Heiner Bielefeldt (Germany), from August 2010 up to present.

19 Rapporteur's Digest on Freedom of Religion or Belief: Excerpts of the Reports from 1986 to 2011 by the Special Rapporteur on Freedom of Religion or Belief Arranged by Topics of the Framework for Communications (2011) 2.

20 Ibid.

21 UN Commission on Human Rights Resolution 1986/20, 42 UN ESCOR Supp. (No. 2) at 66, UN Doc E/CN.4/1986/65 (1986).

22 For a discussion of the contribution of the Special Rapporteur on freedom of religion or belief in the subsequent elaboration of the right to freedom of religion or belief, see generally Malcolm Evans, *Religious Liberty and International Law in Europe* (Cambridge University Press, 1997) 245–250.

23 Carolyn Evans, 'Strengthening the Role of the Special Rapporteur on Freedom of Religion or Belief' (2006) 1 *Religion & Human Rights: An International Journal* 75, 96.

3.3 The Substance of the Right to Establish and Maintain Places of Worship

This section analyses the pronouncements of the Human Rights Committee and the Special Rapporteur on freedom of religion or belief, and distils their standard-setting value relevant to the right to establish and maintain places of worship. What emerges from this analysis is a composite of individual entitlements that benefit religious groups, as well as corresponding duties on the part of the state. In the discussion of these entitlements and duties, there is an underlying recognition that 'places of worship are an essential element of the manifestation of the right to freedom of religion or belief to the extent that the great majority of religious communities ... need the existence of a place of worship where their members can manifest their faith.'[24] As analysed below, the substance of the right to establish and maintain places of worship can be unpacked or broken down into the following nine substantive elements:

1. The right to a legal entity status,
2. The right to acquire or possess real property for religious use,
3. The right to be free from 'bureaucratic' or 'administrative obstacles' in obtaining permit to build places of worship,
4. The right to 'make, acquire and use to an adequate extent the necessary articles and materials related to the rites or customs of a religion or belief,'[25]
5. The right to express religious or other beliefs in physical structures,
6. The right to access, use and peaceful enjoyment of places of worship,
7. The right to 'solicit and receive voluntary financial and other contributions from individuals and institutions,'[26]
8. The right to physical protection of places of worship, and
9. The right to be free from discrimination based on religion or belief in the local planning process.

Each of these substantive elements is analysed below.

---

24 *Report of the Special Rapporteur on Freedom of Religion or Belief*, 'Summary of cases transmitted to Governments and replies received,' UN Doc A/HRC/13/40/Add.1 (16 February 2010), para 146.

25 Religion Declaration, art 6(c).

26 Ibid., art 6(f).

3.3.1 *The Right to a Legal Entity Status*

The ability of a religious group to fully exercise its right to establish and maintain places of worship is directly affected by its status as a recognised legal entity within a domestic jurisdiction. In turn, its legal entity status depends on whether or not it has satisfied the registration requirements prescribed by state authorities. A legal entity status is indispensable for any religious group to 'carry out the full range of a group's legitimate religious activities.'[27] A legal entity status is therefore a condition *sine qua non* for the greater exercise of religious freedom, including the ability of a religious group to establish and maintain places of worship. As Tymen van der Ploeg aptly observed:

> There is a clear connection between places of worship and a religious community being recognized as a legal entity. Without legal personality, a religious community cannot own or rent a permanent place where it can worship. As a general rule, the right to legal personality follows from the freedom of religion.[28]

Similarly, Paul Taylor examined the direct relationship between a religious group's registration status and its ability to construct a place of worship. He observed that '[r]estrictions on the use of buildings have, for the most part, historically been imposed by means of planning regulations, although in recent years registration procedures have taken centre stage in the means by which States constrain the structural aspects of religious practice.'[29] The lack of legal entity status prevents a religious group from accomplishing the first crucial step in building a place of worship – that is, formally engaging with state authorities responsible for the issuance of development permits for new structures.

In *Malakhovsky and Pikul v Belarus*,[30] the Human Rights Committee found a violation of Article 18 of the ICCPR, following the refusal by the Belarus authorities to register the Minsk Vaishnava community as a religious association

---

27 W. Cole Durham, Jr, 'Facilitating Freedom of Religion or Belief through Religious Association Laws' in Tore Lindholm, W. Cole Durham, Jr and Bahia G. Tahzib-Lie (eds) and Elizabeth A. Sewell and Lena Larsen (associate eds), *Facilitating Freedom of Religion or Belief: A Deskbook* (Martinus Nijhoff Publishers, 2004) 321, 324.

28 Tymen van der Ploeg, 'Places of Worship: Between Public and Private: A Comparison between Bulgaria, Italy and the Netherlands' in Silvio Ferrari and Sabrina Pastorelli (eds), *Religion in Public Spaces: A European Perspective* (Ashgate, 2012) 353, 355.

29 Paul Taylor, *Freedom of Religion: UN and European Human Rights Law and Practice* (Cambridge University Press, 2005) 242.

30 Human Rights Committee, *Views: Communication No. 1207/2003*, UN Doc CCPR/C/84/D/1207/2003 (23 August 2005) ('*Malakhovsky and Pikul v Belarus*').

which deprived it of a legal entity status. The authorities required the community to have both an office address and a place of worship before it could be registered as a religious association. The Committee found this requirement as unreasonable and stated that:

> the State party has not advanced any argument as to why it is necessary for the purposes of article 18, paragraph 3, for a religious association, in order to be registered, to have an approved legal address which not only meets the standards required for the administrative seat of the association but also those necessary for premises used for purposes of religious ceremonies, rituals, and other group undertakings. Appropriate premises for such use could be obtained subsequent to registration.… Also taking into account the consequences of refusal of registration, namely the impossibility of carrying out such activities as establishing educational institutions and inviting foreign religious dignitaries to visit the country, the Committee concludes that the refusal to register amounts to a limitation of the authors' right to manifest their religion under article 18, paragraph 1 that is disproportionate and so does not meet the requirements of article 18, paragraph 3. The authors' rights under article 18, paragraph 1 have therefore been violated.[31]

Similarly, in *Sister Immaculate Joseph et al v Sri Lanka,*[32] a group of Catholic nuns engaged in teaching and other charity works was denied legal entity status when the Sri Lankan authorities had refused its incorporation as a juridical entity. The authorities claimed that the activities of the Catholic nuns, especially its teaching and spreading of Catholicism, would impair the very existence of Buddhism or the *Buddha Sasana* which is the predominant religion or belief in Sri Lanka. The Human Rights Committee found that refusing the incorporation of the group has violated the Catholic nuns' right to manifest their religious beliefs in worship, observance, practice and teaching. The Human Rights Committee stated that:

> The [Catholic nuns] have advanced, and the State party has not refuted, that incorporation of the Order would better enable them to realize the objects of their Order, religious as well as secular, *including for example the construction of places of worship.*[33] [emphasis added]

31 Ibid., para 7.6.

32 Human Rights Committee, *Views: Communication No. 1249/2004,* UN Doc CCPR/C/85/D/1249/2004 (18 November 2005) (*'Sister Immaculate Joseph et al v Sri Lanka'*).

33 Ibid., para 7.2.

As the above two cases illustrate, the right to a legal entity status is an enabling right because, without it, religious groups or associations cannot engage in activities which require them to have the legal capacity to act, including purchasing or renting property for religious use. The Human Rights Committee emphasised that states 'should guarantee the right of all persons to manifest their religion or belief in community with others through the recognition of their right to organize themselves in the form of associations or foundations.'[34] To deny a legal entity status to a religious group can have a tremendous impact on its exercise of religious freedom. In one reported case, for example, the action of the Azerbaijani authorities in stripping a Muslim association of its legal entity status has deprived a town's 40,000 Muslim residents of a place of worship where they can manifest their faith.[35]

The Special Rapporteur on freedom of religion or belief observed how the right to a legal entity status is being restricted, indirectly yet effectively, in many states through the misuse of the registration process for religious groups. As observed by Sylvie Langlaude, a 'legal entity status may be the only way for a religious association to be able to carry out a number of essential functions, such as entering into contracts, renting a place of worship, owning property, publishing religious literature or having a bank account.'[36] Enumerating the benefits of obtaining official registration, and thus a legal entity status, the Special Rapporteur on freedom of religion or belief stated that:

> Legal status enables religious groups to act as juridical persons in the court system; *it entitles religious communities to build places of worship,* exempts religious communities from customs duties, entitles the community to open bank accounts, secures their standing as officially registered denominations and means that such communities can be fully fledged partners with the Government.[37] [emphasis added]

In several reports, the Special Rapporteur on freedom of religion or belief illustrated the adverse implications to a religious group when the registration

34 Human Rights Committee, *Concluding Observation on the Report of Turkey,* adopted by the Committee at its 106th session, Geneva (15 October–2 November 2012), para 21.

35 Felix Corley, Azerbaijan: No legal place of worship for 40,000-strong town, Forum 18 News Service, 17 January 2013, at <http://wwrn.org/articles/38908/> last accessed 7 September 2014.

36 Sylvie Langlaude, 'The Rights of Religious Associations to External Relations' (2010) 32(3) *Human Rights Quarterly* 502, 507.

37 *Report of the Special Rapporteur on Freedom of Religion or Belief on Angola,* UN Doc A/HRC/7/10/Add.4 (6 March 2008), para 18.

requirements imposed by state authorities included a stringent or unreasonable criterion. In the Slovak Republic, religious minorities have complained about a piece of legislation that prohibits religious communities with fewer than 20,000 members from obtaining legal status, which they needed *inter alia* to construct a place of worship.[38] In relation to Angola, the Special Rapporteur criticised the government for implementing a law that, for registration purposes, prescribes a membership of at least 100,000 persons who are domiciled in Angola and, at the same time, who are from at least two-thirds of Angola's provinces. In both these examples, the required number of members presented a real obstacle to religious groups obtaining registration, especially new religious groups. Explaining the potential repercussions of this requirement, particularly to the right to establish and maintain places of worship, the Special Rapporteur stated that:

> the law contains stringent requirements for registration ... It has potential practical implications for religious communities, such as a denial of permission to build places of worship, the closure of places of worship or the prohibition of religious organizations. The Special Rapporteur recommends that the law is reformed ... [39]

The requirement to have a minimum number of members impacts most acutely on new or startup religious groups. It presents a serious hurdle for them because, pending satisfaction of the recruitment of enough members, their activities are restricted. It impedes their operational capacity to do acts as basic as, for example, opening a bank account, recruiting members of the clergy or claiming tax exemptions.

In situations similar to the above, the Special Rapporteur on freedom of religion or belief noted that 'registration appeared often to be used as a means to limit the right of freedom of religion or belief of members of certain religious communities.'[40] In another report, the Special Rapporteur expressed alarm over reports that local government authorities in Tajikistan had misused the registration process in order to hinder the activities of a religious group, including the construction of new places of worship. In the Tajik city of Tursundale, the religious group Jehovah's Witnesses 'has repeatedly been denied local

---

38 *Report of the Special Rapporteur on Freedom of Religion or Belief*, UN Doc E/CN.4/2004/63 (16 January 2004), para 90.

39 *Report of the Special Rapporteur on Freedom of Religion or Belief on Angola*, UN Doc A/HRC/7/10/Add.4 (6 March 2008), para 47.

40 *Report of the Special Rapporteur on Freedom of Religion or Belief*, UN Doc E/CN.4/2005/61 (20 December 2004), para 56.

registration as a legal entity. Obtaining all necessary official documents for registration is cumbersome and in some cases authorities reportedly obstruct this process.'[41]

The Special Rapporteur commented that registration *per se* for the acquisition of a legal entity status does not contravene the right to freedom of religion or belief but, when it is required, 'registration should not be a mandatory precondition for practicing one's religion.'[42] In addition, the registration process 'should be easy and quick and should not depend on extensive formal requirements in terms of the number of members or the length of existence of a particular religious group.'[43] The Special Rapporteur added that registration cannot be made contingent on a review of the substantive content of the applicant's religion or belief, the structure of its faith group or its methods of appointing clergy. Finally, vague registration requirements and those which authorise excessive governmental discretion should not be allowed.[44]

From the above pronouncements of the Human Rights Committee and the Special Rapporteur on freedom of religion or belief, it may be concluded that the crucial starting point for guaranteeing the right to establish and maintain places of worship is when state authorities grant religious groups the legal entity status which, in turn, endows them with the legal capacity to acquire ownership or lawful possession of property for religious uses.

3.3.2 *The Right to Own or Possess Real Property for Religious Use*

One of the first considerations by a religious group desiring to build a place of worship is whether to purchase a piece of land. But land ownership is not always indispensable as a religious group can instead construct a place of worship on a rented piece of land, provided that the lease agreement does not prohibit such construction. However, for some religious communities, their ownership of the land where their place of worship stands is significant because 'the right of ownership may enhance the feeling of security or sanctity.'[45]

Article 6(a) of the Religion Declaration recognising the right 'to worship or assemble in connection with a religion or belief, and to establish and maintain places for these purposes' traces its legislative history from the draft Declaration

---

41 *Report of the Special Rapporteur on Freedom of Religion or Belief on Tajikistan*, UN Doc A/HRC/7/10/Add.2 (27 November 2007), para 32.

42 Ibid., para 58.

43 Ibid.

44 Ibid.

45 Cornelis de Jong, *The Freedom of Thought, Conscience and Religion or Belief in the United Nations (1946–1992)* (Hart-Intersentia, 2000) 384.

on the Elimination of All Forms of Religious Intolerance which was developed by the Sub-Commission on Prevention of Discrimination and Protection of Minorities in 1964.[46] During its drafting, Nicaragua proposed the inclusion of 'the right to own and acquire property' and 'the right to administer such property in accordance with the law'[47] but the proposal was not approved. However, this non-inclusion does not mean that 'the right to own and acquire property' may not be logically inferred from the broader formulation of 'the right to establish and maintain places of worship' under Article 6(a) of the Religion Declaration. As de Jong observed:

> [t]he fact that early proposals of a more detailed nature were not taken on board, should not be interpreted as restricting the right in any way... the codification process of the [Religion] Declaration shows that consensus could only be obtained by avoiding such detailed references. Those in favour of short texts usually argued that these detailed elements would be covered by the broader formulations.[48]

Thus, by necessary implication, the right to own or possess a piece of land on which to construct a place of worship is encompassed within the meaning and intent of Article 6(a) of the Religion Declaration.

The Special Rapporteur on freedom of religion or belief has stated that '[i]f people join together in religious or belief communities – old ones or new ones – such communities should be able to undertake important functions, such as owning property.'[49] However, in many states, there are either absolute prohibitions or restrictions against religious groups acquiring or leasing real property for religious purposes. The prohibition or restriction against the acquisition or lease of real property for religious use is a complete negation of the right to establish and maintain places of worship.

One of the actions that state authorities may take in order to seriously undermine religious freedom is the outright prohibition against religious groups owning or possessing land for the purpose of building places of worship. On many situations, the Special Rapporteur on freedom of religion or belief has observed

---

46 Ibid., 360.

47 *Comments by Governments on the Draft Declaration on the Elimination of All Forms of Religious Intolerance,* UN Doc E/CN.4/Sub.2/235, p. 6, also cited in the *United Nations Juridical Yearbook* (United Nations, 1964) 288.

48 De Jong, above n 45, 360.

49 Heiner Bielefeldt, 'Freedom of Religion or Belief – A Human Right Under Pressure' (2012) 1(1) *Oxford Journal of Law and Religion* 1, 8.

this type of grave violation of religious freedom. For example, in the Kingdom of Saudi Arabia, it was reported that no religious group, other than Muslims, can purchase or lease real property to be used as places of worship.[50] Because of this prohibition against non-Muslim religious groups, their members are forced to hold worship activities in private dwellings and in strict secrecy. Because there were no officially recognised non-Muslim places of worship in Saudi Arabia, this led to incidents where 'individuals have been arrested and detained for non-Muslim worship, even though the worship was non-public.'[51] In March 2009, it was reported that three Christians were arrested after organising a private religious gathering which was raided by members of the Saudi government's Commission to Promote Virtue and Prevent Vice.[52] Similarly, in Iran, one particular religious group (the Baha'is) has 'allegedly continued to be denied any right to have places of worship.'[53]

While the acquisition or lease of real property for religious purposes is not prohibited in other states, both are severely restricted by state authorities. For example, in relation to Turkmenistan, the Special Rapporteur on freedom of religion or belief has observed that in practice 'there are still numerous tight restrictions imposed by the authorities on the building, opening, renting and use of such facilities for a number of registered and unregistered religious communities.'[54] Some private property owners who had previously allowed their properties to be rented and used as places of worship 'have however been pressured by the authorities to refrain from doing so again. As a result, it has become very difficult for religious groups to find public meeting places.'[55] These examples of restrictions are a direct infringement of the right to establish and maintain places of worship.

3.3.3 *The Right to be Free from 'Bureaucratic' or 'Administrative Obstacles' in Obtaining Permit to Build Places of Worship*

A more prevalent type of violation of the right to establish and maintain places of worship is the imposition of certain 'bureaucratic' or 'administrative obstacles' that, in their severity, sometimes amount to a *de facto* obstruction to the full

50 *Report of the Special Rapporteur on Contemporary Forms of Racism, Racial Discrimination, Xenophobia and Related Intolerance*, UN Doc A/HRC/15/53 (12 July 2010), para 23.

51 Ibid.

52 Ibid.

53 De Jong, above n 45, 381.

54 *Report of the Special Rapporteur on freedom of religion or belief on Turkmenistan*, UN Doc A/HRC/10/8/Add.4 (12 January 2009), para 38.

55 Ibid.

exercise of the right to have a place of worship. W. Cole Durham observed that, in many states, it is the 'bureaucratic roadblocks which cumulatively have the effect of significantly impairing religious liberty.'[56] Thus, the construction of places of worship is not prohibited *per se* but religious groups encounter different types of obstacles along the administrative processes that must be satisfied in order to obtain a planning permit to build, extend or renovate places of worship. Such obstacles may include inordinate delays before planning applications are acted upon; the requirement to show enough funds for the construction of a place of worship and the source of those funds; the need to justify such construction when zoning ordinances do not envisage places of worship; and the condition that the dominant religious group in a particular community 'attests' to the existence of the applicant group and that its need for a place of worship is genuine. Below are some examples of these obstacles.

As regards delay in resolving applications to build, extend or renovate places of worship, what are inconsistent with the right to establish and maintain places of worship are situations involving inordinate delays (for example, several years of waiting) and malicious delays, as illustrated by the situations pointed out by the Special Rapporteur below. However, depending on the particular circumstances of each case, ordinary delays which are occasioned by the need to comply with reasonable administrative requirements may be consistent with respecting the right to establish and maintain places of worship.

The Special Rapporteur on freedom of religion or belief has repeatedly advised states that they 'should ensure that religious communities do not encounter obstructions with regard to the building, opening, renting or use of places of worship.'[57] For example, in relation to Belarus, the Special Rapporteur expressed concern over reports that religious communities experience many difficulties in building places of worship when she reported that:

> [a] building permission for a social centre in which services could have been held was withdrawn at the last minute from the leader of the Full Gospel Church in Minsk, whose community is desperately short of places of worship. Lutherans and Calvinists are also said to have great difficulty

56 W. Cole Durham, Jr, 'Perspectives on Religious Liberty: A Comparative Framework' in Johan van der Vyver and John Witte, Jr (eds), *Religious Human Rights in Global Perspective: Legal Perspectives* (Martinus Nijhoff Publishers, 1996) 1, 12.

57 *Report of the Special Rapporteur on freedom of religion or belief on Turkmenistan,* UN Doc A/HRC/10/8/Add.4 (12 January 2009) Summary.

> in obtaining the return of churches handed over to the Orthodox Church.[58]

During his visit to Turkey, a secular country but where Islam is the dominant religion, the Special Rapporteur on freedom of religion or belief took notice of the administrative hurdles that long prevented Christian, Greek Orthodox and Armenian minorities from erecting their respective places of worship.[59] In another report, the Special Rapporteur characterised planning regulations in Macedonia as '*de facto* obstruction' that religious groups faced in applying for official permission to build places of worship.[60] The Special Rapporteur was concerned that:

> When applying for such building permits, they allegedly underwent numerous bureaucratic procedures, which resulted in long waiting periods for the necessary documentation, and intervention from the local community which is against such projects. The relevant authorities often reject applications for building permits by religious minorities arguing that the development plan does not foresee a religious building on this piece of land. However, the small religious communities claim that the development plans often do not provide any such designated areas at all, which obviously adversely affects their possibility to manifest their religion or belief in worship, observance, practice and teaching.[61]

When administrative obstacles in the application process result in unreasonable delays, religious groups may have to choose less accessible places of worship, or set up prayer venues in locations less suitable for performing acts of worship such as garages, private homes, meeting rooms in shopping centres or community centres. Concerned with these inordinate delays, the Special Rapporteur on freedom of religion or belief strongly criticised the Government of Egypt after the minority Coptic Church suffered 'building and renovating restrictions which resulted in delays of up to thirty years in the grant of permission

58 *Report of the Special Rapporteur on freedom of religion or belief*, UN Doc E/CN.4/2004/63 (16 January 2004), para 32.

59 *Report of the Special Rapporteur on freedom of religion or belief on Turkey*, UN Doc A/55/280/Add.1 (10 September 2000), para 160.

60 *Report of the Special Rapporteur on freedom of religion or belief on Macedonia*, UN Doc A/HRC/13/40/Add.2 (28 December 2009), para 43.

61 Ibid.

for building or renovation work, and the closure of buildings in the interim.'[62] Similarly, the Special Rapporteur criticised the practice of intentionally delaying the grant of planning permits for the building of Christian places of worship in Malaysia.[63]

In sum, bureaucratic hurdles against the building of places of worship are anathema to the right to freedom of religion or belief. Aware of such obstructions, the UN Human Rights Council expressed its serious concern over 'the obstacles placed in the way of construction of places of worship [which are] inconsistent with the exercise of the right to freedom of religion or belief.'[64] Arising from their duty to respect the right to religious freedom, states have an obligation to remove these administrative obstructions in order to facilitate the construction of places of worship.

3.3.4 *The Right to 'Make, Acquire and Use the Necessary Articles and Materials Related to the Rites or Customs of a Religion or Belief'*

Article 6(c) of the Religion Declaration recognises the indispensability of certain articles, materials, or other objects in the conduct of religious ceremonies or rituals. It states that religious organisations have the right '[t]o make, acquire and use to an adequate extent the necessary articles and materials related to the rites or customs of a religion or belief.'[65] This provision broadly contemplates all kinds of items used during religious rites or rituals performed inside or outside a place of worship. It encompasses movable religious liturgical items such as crucifixes, statues, menorah (a Jewish candle holder), sacred books and other religious literature, incense holders and religious relics. It also includes larger and more permanent religious liturgical objects that are attached to the place of worship itself and structurally forming an integral part of it, such as, but not limited to, Christian altars, baptismal basins or fonts, confessional booths, concrete blocks depicting 'The Ten Commandments,' and similar religious objects which are physically attached to a place of worship.

---

62 *Report of the Special Rapporteur on freedom of religion or belief*, UN Doc E/CN.4/1990/46 (12 January 1990), para 40.

63 *Report of the Special Rapporteur on freedom of religion or belief*, UN Doc E/CN.4/1995/91 (22 December 1994) 59 (Malaysia).

64 UN Human Rights Council, Resolution 6/37: *Elimination of all Forms of Intolerance and of Discrimination based on Religion or Belief* (14 December 2007) 2.

65 Religion Declaration, art 6(c).

In General Comment 22, the Human Rights Committee recognised the indispensability of these religious items and objects when it stated that the freedom to manifest one's religion or belief in worship:

> extends to ritual and ceremonial acts giving direct expression to belief, as well as various practices integral to such acts, including the building of places of worship, *the use of ritual formulae and objects, the display of symbols,* and the observance of holidays and days of rest.[66] [emphasis added]

According to Taylor, the above paragraph "is not directed at a detailed description of worship but is aimed instead at extending the term 'worship' to cover the essential prerequisites or means of worship, such as buildings and liturgical objects."[67] However, not all liturgical objects used in religious rites or customs may be protected under Article 6(c) of the Religion Declaration. For example, in *MAB, WAT and J-AYT v Canada,*[68] the Human Rights Committee dismissed as inadmissible the claim by a religious group (the Assembly of the Church of the Universe) that marijuana is a liturgical object which is religiously mandated by their faith. The group considered marijuana as a 'sacrament' or 'God's tree of life.' The Human Rights Committee stated that:

> a belief consisting primarily or exclusively in the worship and distribution of a narcotic drug cannot conceivably be brought within the scope of article 18 of the Covenant (freedom of religion and conscience), nor can arrest for possession and distribution of a narcotic drug conceivably come within the scope of article 9, paragraph 1, of the Covenant (freedom from arbitrary arrest and detention).[69]

Similarly, in *Prince v South Africa,*[70] the Human Rights Committee found that the possession and use of marijuana by members of the Rastafarian religion as a liturgical object during religious ceremonies may be validly

---

66 General Comment 22, para 4.

67 Taylor, above n 29, 238.

68 Human Rights Committee, *Views: Communication No. 570/1993,* UN Doc CCPR/C/50/D/570/1993 (8 April 1994) (*'mab, wat and j-ayt v Canada'*).

69 Ibid., para 4.2.

70 Human Rights Committee, *Views: Communication No. 1474/2006,* UN Doc CCPR/C/91/D/1474/2006 (14 November 2007) (*'Prince v South Africa'*).

prohibited by the state without violating Article 18 of the ICCPR. The Committee stated that:

> the prohibition of the possession and use of cannabis, which constitutes the limitation on the author's freedom to manifest his religion, is prescribed by the law ... It further notes the State party's conclusion that the law in question was designed to protect public safety, order, health, morals or the fundamental rights and freedoms of others, based on the harmful effects of cannabis, and that an exemption allowing a system of importation, transportation and distribution to Rastafarians may constitute a threat to the public at large, were any of the cannabis enter into general circulation.... The Committee finds that the failure of the State party to grant Rastafarians an exemption to its general prohibition of possession and use of cannabis is ... justified under article 18, paragraph 3.[71]

Like the Human Rights Committee, the Special Rapporteur on freedom of religion or belief underscored the significance of the articles and materials related to the rites or customs of a religion or belief. The Special Rapporteur stated that:

> In order to ensure the freedom of the individual to profess and practice religion or belief, the participating State will, *inter alia*, ... respect the right of individual believers and communities of believers to acquire, possess, and use sacred books, religious publications in the language of their choice and other articles and materials related to the practice of religion or belief.[72]

Recognising the significance of religious items or objects, the Special Rapporteur on freedom of religion or belief criticised some states for confiscating religious objects or materials used by religious groups. For example, in June 2005, a community of Jehovah's Witnesses in Azerbaijan was the object of a raid conducted by police officers. Some of the community's religious objects 'were broken and religious literature was confiscated.'[73] The Special Rapporteur criticised the Government for the conduct of the raid even though 'the

---

71 Ibid., para 7.3.

72 *Report of the Special Rapporteur on freedom of religion or belief*, UN Doc E/CN.4/2006/5 (9 January 2006), para 40.

73 *Report of the Special Rapporteur on freedom of religion or belief on Azerbaijan*, UN Doc A/HRC/4/21/Add.2 (18 October 2006), paras 41–43.

[religious] literature confiscated was returned after a few months.'[74] In relation to Belarus, the Special Rapporteur reported on the difficulties experienced by religious communities in recovering places of worship and religious items or objects that were seized by state authorities during the Soviet period.[75]

Both the Human Rights Committee and the Special Rapporteur on freedom of religion or belief, in the above pronouncements, directly correlated the right to religious manifestation with the acquisition, possession and use of religious items or objects, many of which are either found inside places of worship or are physically attached to them. Article 6(c) of the Religion Declaration, in so far as it contemplates religious liturgical items or objects which are indispensably used in places of worship, should be understood as being subsumed under Article 6(a) which recognises the right to establish and maintain places of worship. This is because such items or objects effectively form an integral part of places of worship, many of which are structurally attached to them. The conduct of many forms of religious manifestation inside places of worship is impossible without such items or objects. Thus, in reality, sub-paragraphs (a) and (c) of Article 6 of the Religion Declaration do overlap and provide a greater degree of legal protection to places of worship.

3.3.5 *The Right to Express Religious or other Beliefs in Physical Structures*

All human rights are characterised as 'universal, indivisible and interdependent and interrelated.'[76] They are exercised in a context where they coexist with each other. This is particularly true with respect to the right to freedom of religion or belief which 'should therefore not be seen in isolation but rather as forming an integral part of the entire system of human rights.'[77] Specifically, there exists an especially close connection between freedom of religion or belief and freedom of expression. This connection is recognised by the Human Rights Committee when it stated that states should 'fully respect the rights of persons within its jurisdiction to full and free expression of their religious beliefs, as required by article 18.'[78] Similarly, the Special Rapporteur on freedom of religion or belief 'emphasized that freedom of religion or belief and

74 Ibid.

75 *Report of the Special Rapporteur on freedom of religion or belief*, UN Doc E/CN.4/2004/63 (16 January 2004), para 32.

76 *Vienna Declaration and Programme of Action*, adopted by the World Conference on Human Rights, UN Doc A/CONF.157/24 (Part I), Ch III, s I (25 June 1993), para 5.

77 Bielefeldt, above n 49, 9.

78 Human Rights Committee, *Concluding observation on the report of the Republic of Moldova*, UN Doc CCPR/CO/75/MDA (5 August 2002), para 13.

freedom of expression are interdependent and interrelated.'[79] The Special Rapporteur explained further that:

> the coexistence of rights ... implies the fundamental notion of interdependency of human rights. The right to freedom of religion or belief needs other human rights to be fully exercised, including ... the right to freedom of expression. *The right to freedom of expression* as it is protected by international standards, including article 19 of the Covenant, *constitutes an essential aspect of the right to freedom of religion or belief.*[80] [emphasis added]

Most forms of religious manifestation are in fact expressions of religious beliefs. As Carolyn Evans noted, 'much that is currently protected as religion could equally be covered as a manifestation of freedom of expression.'[81] For instance, the freedom to 'write, issue and disseminate relevant [religious] publications' guaranteed in Article 6(d) of the Religion Declaration is both an exercise of religious manifestation and an exercise of freedom of speech (that is, religious speech). Such an act is protected both by the right to religious freedom and the freedom of expression. The same characterisation may be said about the construction of places of worship because, aside from being prayer facilities or venues, they are also *intended* to express or communicate certain religious claims through their architectural designs, features and ornamentations. Places of worship are not only relevant for the exercise of the right to manifest one's religion or belief, but they are also an important exercise of the right to freedom of expression guaranteed by Article 19(2) of the ICCPR which provides that:

> Everyone shall have the right to freedom of expression; this right shall include freedom to seek, receive and impart information and ideas of all kinds, regardless of frontiers, either orally, in writing or in print, *in the form of art, or through any other media of his choice.*[82] [emphasis added]

---

79 *Interim report of the Special Rapporteur on freedom of religion or belief*, UN Doc A/65/207 (29 July 2010), para 42.

80 *Report of the Special Rapporteur on freedom of religion or belief*, UN Doc A/HRC/2/3 (20 September 2006), para 41.

81 Carolyn Evans, 'Religion and Freedom of Expression' in John Witte, Jr and M. Christian Green (eds), *Religion and Human Rights: An Introduction* (Oxford University Press, 2012) 188.

82 ICCPR, art 19(2).

Therefore, when constructing a place of worship, a religious group enjoys the freedom to communicate its fundamental religious beliefs through the building itself. A place of worship, more than just being a physical venue for praying, is also a vehicle for the expression of ideas, two of which are very important. First, places of worship serve as a religious community's proud proclamation of their arrival or existence to the general public.[83] As observed by Malcolm Evans:

> One of the clearest manifestations of religion within a community is the presence of religious structures. Religious buildings are a symbolic presence in and of themselves and their distinctive architecture and adornment, as well as the activities which take place in and around them, again take on a symbolic meaning which is both 'conceptual' and 'tangible': the presence of a minaret or church tower dominating the skyline in a town or village is more than the mere physical display of a symbol *but is a statement of a physical presence within the community,* with the size and location of such buildings being similarly significant.[84] [emphasis added]

Therefore, by building a place of worship, a religious group affirms its unique identity and announces its symbolic public presence in the larger community. This symbolic public presence amounts to a religious group's share of the contested public sphere, as discussed in Chapter 6.

Second, a place of worship is also a medium for expressing certain religious beliefs chosen by a religious group for their centrality in its belief system. In its architecture, a place of worship may be replete with designs or features that express fundamental theological beliefs. The religious edifice therefore becomes the spatial expression of core religious tenets. '[T]hrough its shapes, symbols, decorations, ornamentations and monumentality,' religious architecture is anchored on 'a strong intention to communicate a particularized message about a group's religious beliefs.'[85] Through them, individually and collectively, a religious community conveys, affirms and propagates its

---

83 Leonie Sandercock, 'Planning in the Ethno-culturally Diverse City: A Comment' (2001) 4(3) *Planning Theory and Practice* 319–323; Michael Burayidi, 'The Multicultural City as Planners' Enigma' (2001) 4(3) *Planning Theory and Practice* 259–273.

84 Malcolm Evans, 'Religious Symbols: An Introduction' in Silvio Ferrari and Rinaldo Cristofori (eds), *Law and Religion in the 21st Century: Relations between States and Religious Communities* (Ashgate, 2010) 291, 292.

85 Thomas Pak, 'Free Exercise, Free Expression, and Landmarks Preservation' (1991) 91(7) *Columbia Law Review* 1813, 1840.

fundamental theological doctrines concerning the divine existence and humanity's relationship with it. Section 7.2 further analyses this direct association between a religious group's belief system and the physical features of its place of worship.

Being an exercise of both freedom of religion and freedom of expression, the physical symbols forming part of places of worship (for example, a mosque's star and crescent moon or a Buddhist temple's pagoda) should be protected even more by the state. Any governmental action that restricts such exercise, including the disallowance, removal, hiding or altering of these religious symbols, should be scrutinised under the strict requirements of Article 18(3) of the ICCPR. Chapter 7 discusses the means of suppressing religious expression which is inherent in the architectural design or features of places of worship.

3.3.6 *The Right to Access, Use and Peaceful Enjoyment of Places of Worship*

After a place of worship has been constructed, there is a need to guarantee that it can be accessed, used and enjoyed peacefully by members of a religious community. The access, use and enjoyment of places of worship should be free from threats of closure, confiscation or seizure, interruptions, harassments and other similar restrictions by state or non-state actors. The freedom of worship will be rendered nugatory if there is a danger that its exercise may be hindered at any time as a result of any of these restrictions.

The Human Rights Committee has stressed the need to guarantee a religious minority's access to its places of worship. In a concluding observation, the Committee disapproved of Israel's unequal and discriminatory manner of granting religious minorities access to their holy places and voiced its concern over the:

> restrictions on access to places of worship for non-Jews. It further notes with concern that the regulations containing a list of holy sites only include Jewish holy places... The State party should increase its efforts to protect the rights of religious minorities and ensure equal and non-discriminatory access to places of worship. Furthermore, the State party should pursue its plan also to include holy sites of religious minorities in its list.[86]

The right to access places of worship takes on heightened significance when places of worship belonging to religious minorities are located inside the territory of another state with an official or dominant religion or belief, like in the case of Israel.

---

86 Human Rights Committee, *Concluding Observation on the Report of Israel*, UN Doc CCPR/C/ISR/CO/3 (3 September 2010), para 20.

Furthermore, the Special Rapporteur on freedom of religion or belief reported on the various ways in which the right to the use and peaceful enjoyment of places of worship has been infringed. For example, such use and enjoyment may be interrupted by government action such as, in Azerbaijan, where members of the Muslim community in Juma were temporarily deprived of the use and enjoyment of their mosque after local authorities closed it down allegedly for renovation works. The Special Rapporteur on freedom of religion or belief stated that:

> [t]he Government should ensure that religious communities are not unduly deprived of their places of worship. In cases where such deprivation is justified by lawful reasons and after judicial review, it should provide the community concerned with a suitable alternative place of worship.[87]

When a state action interrupts the use and enjoyment of a place of worship, such an interruption constitutes a restriction to the right to manifest religion or belief whose validity should be determined on the basis of the requirements of Article 18(3) of the ICCPR, as analysed in Chapter 8. When there is a legitimate ground to interrupt the use and enjoyment of a place of worship, the state has the obligation to reduce such interruption to the minimum in accordance with the 'proportionality' requirement also discussed in Chapter 8. In the Juma mosque incident above, the state had the duty to provide the affected religious community with 'a suitable alternative place of worship' in the interregnum to mitigate the adverse impact of the mosque's temporary closure.

The right to the use and peaceful enjoyment of places of worship may also be infringed when non-state actors unlawfully confiscate or seize them, thus depriving religious communities with the space needed for worship activities. For example, in Romania, a place of worship was seized by a rival religious group but the Government did not immediately address the incident by ensuring the return of the place of worship to its rightful owner. The Special Rapporteur on freedom of religion or belief criticised the Romanian Government for such inaction and stated that 'in cases where members of the community are prevented from using a place of worship that belongs to them, this thereby constituting a violation of their right to freedom of religion or belief.'[88]

---

87 *Report of the Special Rapporteur on freedom of religion or belief on Azerbaijan*, UN Doc A/HRC/4/21/Add.2 (18 October 2006), para 99.

88 *Report of the Special Rapporteur on freedom of religion or belief on Romania*, UN Doc E/CN.4/2004/63/Add.2 (16 December 2003), para 104.

Therefore, the state's failure to remedy the confiscation or seizure of places of worship constitutes another type of violation. For example, in Georgia, the 'problems related to the restitution of places of worship and related properties of religious minorities [which were] confiscated during the Communist era have not been solved'[89] by the succeeding governments. Similarly, in Belarus, religious groups experienced difficulties in recovering places of worship seized during the Soviet period.[90] In both examples, the state responsible for the confiscation or seizure (that is, the former Soviet Union) was no longer in existence, but the duty to return the confiscated places of worship to their rightful owners have devolved to the successor states, namely, Georgia and Belarus.

3.3.7 *The Right to 'Solicit and Receive Voluntary Financial and other Contributions'*

Article 6(f) of the Religion Declaration provides that the right to freedom of religion or belief includes the right '[t]o solicit and receive voluntary financial and other contributions from individuals and institutions.' An earlier version of this provision stated that '[r]eligious communities shall have the right to receive the funds necessary for the carrying out of their functions'[91] which did not emphasise the voluntary nature of the contributions. The aim of Article 6(f) is to ensure the continuous financing of a religious group's various activities including charity or humanitarian work. That is why Article 6(f) is oftentimes invoked in conjunction with Article 6(b) of the Religion Declaration which guarantees the right '[t]o establish and maintain appropriate charitable or humanitarian institutions.'

Aside from running charitable or humanitarian institutions, the right to solicit and receive voluntary financial and other contributions is, in practice, closely associated with the right to establish and maintain places of worship, because the construction, extension or renovation of religious edifices usually require a huge amount of resources. Especially for startup and small religious groups, owning or renting real property for religious use present a real financial challenge. Article 6(f) enables a religious group to appeal from members and non-members, on a voluntary basis, for financial and other contributions.

---

89 Human Rights Committee, *Concluding Observation on the Report of Georgia*, UN Doc CCPR/C/GEO/CO/3/CRP.1 (19 October 2007), para 15.

90 *Report of the Special Rapporteur on freedom of religion or belief*, UN Doc E/CN.4/2004/63 (16 January 2004), para 32.

91 Sub-Commission on Prevention of Discrimination and Protection of Minorities, *Draft Declaration on the Elimination of All Forms of Religious Intolerance*, UN Doc E/CN.4/873 (28 January 1964) 68, article X.

By guaranteeing the right to solicit and receive voluntary financial and other contributions from individuals and institutions, Article 6(f) of the Religion Declaration aims to ensure that religious groups have the necessary means to raise enough funds and other resources to establish and maintain places of worship. Therefore, the right to solicit or receive contributions, because of its enabling and complementary nature, may be subsumed as an element of the right to establish and maintain places of worship in this analysis.

However, Article 6(f) of the Religion Declaration cannot be made the basis for religious groups to demand financial assistance from the state in order to support their activities, including the building of places of worship. As noted by De Jong, the practice of states does 'not provide enough indications to change the conclusion drawn from the codification process that governments are not obliged to contribute financially or otherwise to the establishment or preservation of places of worship or assembly.'[92] But in those states where religious groups are receiving state support in the form of tax deductions, direct grants, credits or similar benefits, such support should be provided in a non-discriminatory manner. In relation to Luxembourg, the Human Rights Committee expressed concern that the Government is providing financial assistance only to the Christian and Jewish communities. The Committee stated that '[t]he State party should guarantee non-discriminatory treatment of communities of religion and belief in respect of financial assistance and, to this end, ensure that all criteria in this regard are revised to guarantee that they are in keeping with the Covenant.'[93]

In a couple of reports, the Special Rapporteur on freedom of religion or belief expressed concern over violations of the right to solicit and receive voluntary financial and other contributions from individuals and institutions. For example, in relation to Tibet, the Special Rapporteur criticised the situation where certain funds donated to Buddhist monasteries had to be deposited in a particular bank account and could only be withdrawn after obtaining government approval.[94] In relation to the Lao People's Democratic Republic, the Special Rapporteur voiced concern over the arrest of Christians for allegedly undermining the government and for receiving financial donations from overseas sources.[95] These illustrations of how the right to solicit and receive voluntary

92 De Jong, above n 45, 419.

93 Human Rights Committee, *Concluding Observation on the Report of Luxembourg*, UN Doc CCPR/CO/77/LUX (15 April 2003), para 7.

94 *Report of the Special Rapporteur on freedom of religion or belief*, UN Doc E/CN.4/1988/45 (6 January 1988), para 45.

95 *Report of the Special Rapporteur on freedom of religion or belief*, UN Doc E/CN.4/1999/58 (11 January 1999), para 86.

financial and other contributions have been infringed demonstrate the existence of the right and how it has been interpreted by the Special Rapporteur.

Commenting on a report that the Chinese government had announced that 'no donations for monasteries may be requested or given,'[96] De Jong stated that:

> I consider this a restriction of the right to maintain places of worship that cannot be justified on the basis of the limitation grounds mentioned in Article 18, paragraph 3 of the [ICCPR]. In this regard, it should be taken into account that donations tend to be a regular source of income for religious communities to enable them to take care of regular maintenance of their places of worship.[97]

Regarding the permissible limitations on the right to solicit and receive voluntary financial and other contributions, the Special Rapporteur on freedom of religion or belief stated that:

> While the right to ... receive funding is not unlimited, any restrictions imposed must be prescribed by law and must be necessary to protect public safety, order, health or morals, or the fundamental rights and freedoms of others, for example in order to prevent such institutions being misused to advance their cause through violence.[98]

Contributions, particularly those coming from overseas donors, to religious associations purportedly for the purpose of building places of worship but actually intended to further acts of terrorism are therefore within a state's power to prohibit without infringing on the right to establish and maintain places of worship. However, when the purpose of a religious group's solicitation or receipt of financial contributions is the building of a place of worship, any restriction imposed against such solicitation or receipt ought to be subjected to a close scrutiny in order to assess its compatibility with Article 18(3) of the ICCPR. Because the right to solicit and receive financial and other contributions is an enabling complementary right, any restriction against it adversely affects *other* forms of religious manifestation that crucially depend on such contributions, like the construction of places of worship.

---

96 *Report of the Special Rapporteur on freedom of religion or belief*, UN Doc E/CN.4/1990/46 (22 January 1990), para 37.

97 De Jong, above n 45, 386–387.

98 *Interim Report of the Special Rapporteur on freedom of religion or belief*, UN Doc A/65/207 (29 July 2010), para 36.

3.3.8 *The Right to Physical Protection of Places of Worship*

Thus far, the above-discussed elements of the right to establish and maintain places of worship provide the necessary legal guarantees to build and use such places. However, 'the full enjoyment of these rights also requires some kind of State involvement in offering adequate forms of protection against outside interference.'[99] In other words, in order to guarantee the continued use and enjoyment of places of worship, they require physical protection from the state.

Places of worship have more than a material significance for a religious community[100]; they 'have an emotional and spiritual significance for the believers.'[101] Because of this significance, they need to be protected from violence, attacks, desecration, destruction or other forms of physical damage inflicted by state and non-state actors. For example, the Human Rights Committee expressed concern over the 'manifestations of intolerance towards religious minorities and non-traditional religious groups in Bulgaria [including] 110 cases of reported vandalism against mosques in the last two decades.'[102] The Committee also expressed worry over 'the sharp rise in apparent anti-Semitic incidents occurring in the State party [including] the arson fire that destroyed the largest synagogue in Geneva in 2007.'[103] The Committee was also concerned at the reported failure of the police in Geneva to fully investigate the pattern of these incidents.[104]

The Special Rapporteur on freedom of religion or belief affirmed the right to physical protection of places of worship when, after his mission to Tajikistan, he denounced the Government's plan to demolish the country's only synagogue which has been used for decades by the Jewish community but which was scheduled to be demolished in order to give way to the construction of a national park and a government palace. The Special Rapporteur called the attention of the Tajikistan Government to Article 6(a) of the Religion Declaration, and stated that:

> mosques, churches and other places of worship need to be fully respected and protected by the authorities. The Special Rapporteur would like to

---

99 De Jong, above n 45, 363.

100 *Report of the Special Rapporteur on freedom of religion or belief*, UN Doc E/CN.4/2005/61 (20 December 2004), paras 49–50.

101 *Report of the Special Rapporteur on freedom of religion or belief on Macedonia*, UN Doc A/HRC/13/40/Add.2 (28 December 2009), para 45.

102 Human Rights Committee, *Concluding Observation on the report of Bulgaria*, UN Doc CCPR/C/BGR/CO/3 (19 August 2011), para 9.

103 Human Rights Committee, *Concluding Observation on the report of Switzerland*, UN Doc CCPR/C/CHE/CO/3 (3 November 2009), para 9.

104 Ibid.

> remind the Government of article 6(a) of the [Religion Declaration] which states that the right to freedom of thought, conscience, religion or belief includes the freedom "to worship or assemble in connection with a religion or belief, and to establish and maintain places for these purposes." [States must exert efforts], in accordance with their national legislation and in conformity with international human rights law, to ensure that religious places, sites, shrines and religious expressions are fully respected and protected and to take additional measures in cases where they are vulnerable to desecration or destruction.[105]

Attacks, desecration, destruction or other forms of physical damage against places of worship may also be committed by non-state actors. For example, in relation to Indonesia, the Special Rapporteur on freedom of religion or belief condemned the destruction of places of worship belonging to Christian denominations by extremist groups, the violence having been triggered by the long-running tension between Muslim and Christian communities in a locality.[106] In relation to an incident in Chiapas, Mexico, the Special Rapporteur reported the destruction of Protestant churches in the area allegedly committed by traditional rural leaders.[107] In India, violations of the right to freedom of religion or belief have been committed by rival Hindu and Muslim communities against each other in relation to a dispute over the ownership of a place of worship.[108]

Non-state actors are not 'duty-bearers' in regards to the right to freedom of religion or belief. However, it is the obligation of the state to ensure that non-state actors do not violate the right to freedom of religion or belief. As regards violations by non-state actors, the Special Rapporteur stated that:

> a large number of the violations of the right to freedom of religion or belief are committed by non-State actors, whether members of religious groups themselves or others. The Special Rapporteur notes ... that there is still a tendency even today to forget about the *positive human rights obligations* of States. States have an obligation to ensure freedom of religion

105 *Report of the Special Rapporteur on freedom of religion or belief on Tajikistan*, UN Doc A/HRC/7/10/Add.2 (27 November 2007), para 55.

106 *Report of the Special Rapporteur on freedom of religion or belief*, UN Doc E/CN.4/2000/65 (15 February 2000), para 49.

107 Ibid., para 66.

108 *Report of the Special Rapporteur on freedom of religion or belief on India*, UN Doc E/CN.4/1997/91/Add.1 (14 February 1997), para 93.

> or belief to the persons finding themselves within their jurisdiction. Where acts of violence or other acts of religious intolerance are committed against individuals, States have both an obligation to protect and an obligation to remedy the situation.[109] [emphasis added]

The positive human rights obligation of states obliges them to take all necessary actions to prevent attacks, desecration, destruction or other forms of physical damage against places of worship committed by non-state actors. Equally important, such an obligation includes the states' duty to exact accountability against the perpetrators through civil or criminal actions in order to deter future violations. The Special Rapporteur on freedom of religion or belief stated that:

> unlike other forms of violations of the right to freedom of religion or belief, attacks or other forms of restriction on places of worship or other religious sites and shrines in many cases violate the right not only of a single individual, *but the rights of a group of individuals forming the community that is attached to the place in question.*[110] [emphasis added]

Thus, because the entire membership of a religious community benefits from places of worship, any deliberate physical damage against such places results in the victimisation of the entire membership. The 'rights-holder' that stands to be harmed in the event of any impairment or restriction against the right to establish places of worship is not just the individual members of a religious group but the group itself as a collective rights-holder.

The right to physical protection of places of worship assumes greater urgency during an international armed conflict.[111] For this reason, David Llewellyn and H Victor Conde commented that '[p]laces of worship are specially protected under [international] humanitarian law from military use and military attack.... Religious and cultural sites are granted presumptions in

---

109 *Report of the Special Rapporteur on freedom of religion or belief*, UN Doc E/CN.4/2005/61 (20 December 2004), para 75.

110 *Report of the Special Rapporteur on freedom of religion or belief*, Summary of cases transmitted to Governments and replies received, UN Doc A/HRC/13/40/Add.1 (16 February 2010), para 146.

111 See especially, Marina Lostal, 'The Meaning and Protection of Cultural and Places of Worship under the 1977 Additional Protocols' (2012) 59(3) *Netherlands International Law Review* 455–472.

favor of their protection.'[112] The legal protection of such places is codified in Article 53 of the First Additional Protocol to the Geneva Convention which provides that:

> Without prejudice to the provisions of the Hague Convention for the Protection of Cultural Property in the Event of Armed Conflict of 14 May 1954, and of other relevant international instruments, it is prohibited:
>
> (a) To commit any acts of hostility directed against the historic monuments, works of art or *places of worship* which constitute the cultural or spiritual heritage of peoples;
> (b) To use such objects in support of the military effort;
> (c) To make such objects the object of reprisals.[113] [emphasis added]

The legal protection of the above provision has been extended in situations of non-international armed conflict such as civil wars or rebellions by Article 16 of the Second Additional Protocol to the Geneva Convention which provides for a similar provision.[114]

3.3.9 *The Right to be Free from Discrimination Based on Religion or Belief in the Local Planning Process*

Religious groups may be discriminated against in the enforcement of local planning regulations. It has been observed that the enforcement of such regulations may appear 'to be neutral (such as regulating the flow of traffic, harmony with other buildings or activities, or noise restrictions), but are selectively enforced for discriminatory purposes against disfavoured religious groups.'[115] Aside from

---

112 David Llewellyn and H. Victor Conde, 'Freedom of Religion or Belief under International Humanitarian Law and International Criminal Law' in Tore Lindholm, W. Cole Durham, Jr and Bahia G. Tahzib-Lie (eds) and Elizabeth A. Sewell and Lena Larsen (associate eds), *Facilitating Freedom of Religion or Belief: A Deskbook* (Martinus Nijhoff Publishers, 2004) 125, 140.

113 *Protocol Additional to the Geneva Conventions of 12 August 1949, and Relating to the Protection of Victims of International Armed Conflicts (Protocol I)*, 8 June 1977 (entered into force 7 December 1978), 1125 UNTS 3, art 53.

114 *Protocol Additional to the Geneva Conventions of 12 August 1949, and Relating to the Protection of Victims of Non-International Armed Conflicts (Protocol II)*, 8 June 1977 (entered into force 7 December 1978), 1125 UNTS 609, art 16.

115 OSCE/ODIHR Advisory Panel of Experts on Freedom of Religion or Belief, 'Guidelines for Review of Legislation Pertaining to Religion or Belief,' adopted by the Council of Europe's Commission for Democracy Through Law, 59th plen sess (18–19 June 2004) 25.

direct forms of discrimination, a religious group may also be subjected to indirect forms of discrimination in the local planning process. These forms of discrimination in the context of planning applications to construct, extend or renovate places of worship are analysed in greater detail in Chapters 5 and 6.

As noted in Chapter 2, the prohibition against discrimination on the basis of religion or belief bolsters the legal protection of religious freedom. This is especially true in the context of local planning where state authorities, in the exercise of discretion, determine the grant or refusal of planning permits. The danger that a religious group is singled out and treated unfairly on the basis of its religion or belief is ever present. Thus, for example, in relation to Kuwait, the Human Rights Committee expressed its concern over the 'discrimination by the State party on grounds of religion, including… the restrictions imposed for the construction and access to places of worship, especially for Hindus, Sikhs and Buddhists.'[116] The Committee stated that '[t]he State party should guarantee the right of all persons to practice their religion or belief in an appropriate place of worship… without discrimination on the basis of religion.'[117]

In relation to Georgia, the Special Rapporteur on freedom of religion or belief observed that local government authorities made it difficult for Protestant and Armenian Orthodox religious communities to obtain planning permits to build places of worship because of the pressure and influence exerted on such authorities by the dominant religion, the Georgian Orthodox Church.[118] As regards an incident in Turkey involving the rejection of applications to build places of worship lodged by Christian, Greek Orthodox and Armenian minorities, the Special Rapporteur stated that:

> The Government should guarantee minorities the right to establish and maintain their own places of worship, and should allow them to build such facilities in places where new communities have taken root. Any limitations in this respect… should be consistent with international jurisprudence (see General Comment of the Human Rights Committee), and this means that any non-conforming regulations should be repealed or revised.[119]

116 Human Rights Committee, *Concluding Observation on the Report of Kuwait*, UN Doc CCPR/C/KWT/CO/2 (18 November 2011), para 23.

117 Ibid.

118 *Report of the Special Rapporteur on freedom of religion or belief*, UN Doc. E/CN.4/2000/65 (15 February 2000), para 40.

119 *Interim Report of the Special Rapporteur on freedom of religion or belief*, UN Doc A/55/280/Add.1 (country visit to Turkey) (11 August 2000), para 160(d).

Furthermore, the Special Rapporteur on freedom of religion or belief stated that migrants are especially 'vulnerable to discrimination based on their religion or belief and [they] face related prejudices on a societal level.'[120] Their vulnerability is explained by the difficulties associated with being transplanted to a foreign environment, the linguistic and cultural barrier and the economic displacement they experience as new-comers. The Special Rapporteur stated that:

> all persons within a particular country, and not just the citizens of that country, have the right to freedom of religion or belief, including the manifestation of their religion or belief in worship, observance, practice and teaching. In her reports, the Special Rapporteur has pointed to practical limitations imposed on the freedom of migrants to manifest their religion or belief publicly, for example with regard to building places of worship, carrying out religious rituals openly or conducting missionary activities.[121]

In summary, states have the primary obligation to protect individuals and groups from acts of discrimination on the basis of religion or belief. In the context of applications to build places of worship, this duty assumes greater relevance because of the influence and pressure being exerted upon the state (specifically, upon its local planning authorities) by local residents or neighbourhood associations that usually oppose such applications. A state should remain impartial in exercising its regulatory power over the temporal activities of religious groups including, most especially, the usually contested terrain of establishing and maintaining places of worship.

3.4 Conclusion

The right to establish and maintain places of worship is an integral component of the right to freedom of religion or belief. A denial of the former always results in the curtailment of the latter. States therefore cannot sincerely proclaim that they respect and protect religious freedom when there are pervasive violations of the right to establish and maintain places of worship.

The Human Rights Committee has repeatedly stressed the centrality of places of worship in the life of religious communities. In relation to Iran, the Committee

120 *Interim Report of the Special Rapporteur on freedom of religion or belief,* UN Doc A/64/159 (17 July 2009), para 32.

121 Ibid., para 33.

emphasised that '[t]he State party should guarantee the freedom to manifest a religion or belief and that it can be exercised either individually or in community with others and in public or private. The Committee reminds the State party that this right also entails the building of places of worship.'[122] In relation to the Maldives, the Human Rights Committee expressed its concern that 'non-Muslims can only practise their religion in private and do not have public places of worship.... The State party should revise its legislation to authorize non-Muslims to practice and manifest their religion, including in places of public worship.'[123] Furthermore, in relation to Belgium, the Human Rights Committee expressed concern that no 'mosque has been granted official recognition in Belgium.'[124] In addition, concerned about the reports that 'religious practice is repressed or strongly discouraged' in North Korea, the Human Rights Committee asked the Pyongyang Government:

> to provide the Committee with up-to-date information about the number of citizens of the Democratic People's Republic of Korea belonging to religious communities and the number of places of worship, as well as the practical measures taken by the authorities to guarantee the freedom of exercise of religious practice by the communities mentioned in [the report].[125]

This pronouncement suggests that the Human Rights Committee equates the existence of places of worship as a necessary precondition for the exercise of religious freedom. Regarding the non-recognition of mosques in Belgium mentioned above, Joseph and Castan observed that while the Human Rights Committee did not comment about 'any discrimination entailed in that circumstance: clearly it spoke of itself in raising article 18 issues.'[126] Thus, in the Committee's pronouncements, there is an underlying premise that places of worship are a condition *sine qua non* for the full and meaningful exercise of the right to manifest one's religion or belief.

---

122 Human Rights Committee, *Concluding Observation on the report of Iran*, UN Doc CCPR/C/IRN/CO/3 (29 November 2011), para 25.

123 Human Rights Committee, *Concluding Observation on the report of Maldives*, UN Doc CCPR/C/MDV/CO/1 (31 August 2012), para 24.

124 Human Rights Committee, *Concluding Observation on the report of Belgium*, UN Doc CCPR/CO/81/BEL (2004), para 26.

125 Human Rights Committee, *Concluding Observation on the report of the Democratic People's Republic of Korea*, UN Doc CCPR/CO/72/PRK (27 August 2001), para 22.

126 Sarah Joseph and Melissa Castan, *The International Covenant on Civil and Political Rights: Cases, Materials, and Commentary* (Oxford University Press, 2013, 3rd edition) 565.

This chapter demonstrated how the right to establish and maintain places of worship has received its own substantive contents through the process of international human rights standard-setting. It illustrated how the bare and austere manner in which it was articulated in Article 6(a) of the Religion Declaration was compensated by resorting to and synthesising the pronouncements of the Human Rights Committee and the Special Rapporteur on freedom of religion or belief, both of which have a direct influence on international standard-setting pertaining to the right to freedom of religion or belief.

The right to establish and maintain places of worship has a composite character, in that it is comprised of distinct but related elements that make up its conceptual core. These elements coalesce under the general rubric of the right to establish and maintain places of worship, and operate concertedly to achieve one goal – that is, to ensure that the structural requirements of religious manifestation are adequately met. Reinforcing one another, they contribute to the right's legal validity and strength. Thus, it is only when these elements are taken together that the substance of the right to establish and maintain places of worship is adequately captured.

The foregoing analysis of the substance of the right to establish and maintain places of worship under international human rights law makes it imperative to explore several issues that logically ensue from the discussion: How can such an international human rights norm be transported and given applicability into the Australian domestic setting, especially in light of the 'dualist' barrier that maintains a strict wall of separation between Australian domestic law and international law? Can the right to establish and maintain places of worship be invoked against the lowest tier of government in Australia – the local councils? Are local councils 'duty-bearers' of religious freedom norms? The next chapter analyses these issues.

CHAPTER 4

International Standards on Religious Freedom

An Analysis of Their Existence and Applicability in Australia

4.1 Introduction

The preceding two chapters demonstrated the place of the right to freedom of religion or belief in the corpus of international human rights law. In particular, Chapter 2 discussed the right's legal architecture and located within its constituent sub-rights the relative position of the human rights norm examined in this book, that is, the right to establish and maintain places of worship. Building on this foundation, Chapter 3 analysed the substance of the right to establish and maintain places of worship by synthesising the relevant pronouncements of the UN Human Rights Committee and the Special Rapporteur on freedom of religion or belief.

Notwithstanding their firm status as international law norms, the significance of human rights, including the right to freedom of religion or belief, must be measured against their capacity to benefit rights-holders in concrete, real-life situations. At the international level, states may agree to recognise an entitlement as a human right and enshrine it in a document which they consider as binding *inter se*. But this may mean little in a country like Australia which does not automatically give legal effect to international human rights instruments in its domestic jurisdiction. Thus, they remain as promissory documents which, although legally binding in the international sphere, are largely ineffectual in the domestic sphere.

Australia has an international legal obligation to give effect domestically to the rights guaranteed in the ICCPR.[1] That is the essence of Australia's obligation under the Covenant which, although consented to in the international sphere, is intended to be complied with primarily in the domestic sphere.[2] From the perspective of international law, Australia's six states and two territories comprise an indivisible juridical entity. Australia's international human

1 ICCPR, art 2(2); See especially, Oscar Schachter, 'The Obligation to Implement the Covenant in Domestic Law' in Louis Henkin (ed), *The International Bill of Rights: The Covenant on Civil and Political Rights* (Columbia University Press, 1981), 311–331.

2 Elizabeth Evatt, 'National Implementation: The Cutting Edge of International Human Rights Law', Centre for International and Public Law, Law and Policy Paper 12 (Federation Press, 1999), 2–6.

 | DOI 10.1163/9789004289345_005

rights obligations under the ICCPR (including those pertaining to religious freedom) are demandable against it, notwithstanding that, under its municipal constitutional set-up, it is the individual states and territories which have the greater capacity to guarantee those rights.[3] This is an application of the customary rule of international law (also codified in Article 27 of the Vienna Convention on the Law of Treaties)[4] that a state cannot invoke the provisions of its internal law as justification for its failure to perform treaty obligations.

This chapter analyses the ways in which the international standards pertaining to the right to freedom of religion or belief are 'transported'[5] into Australian domestic jurisdiction and, thereafter, how such standards are accorded domestic application. This chapter distinguishes between, on the one hand, the existence of international human rights standards in the Australian domestic setting and, on the other hand, their application by the legislative, judicial and administrative authorities in Australia. As analysed below, their existence and application in the domestic setting are two separate concepts. Correspondingly, the analysis in this chapter has two levels. First, this chapter analyses whether or not the international standards on religious freedom[6] *exist* in Australian domestic law. The strict 'dualist approach' in Australia as regards the effect of international law in its domestic law implies that international human rights standards, even though they exist as norms in the international sphere, may be completely absent from Australian law.[7] As analysed below, there are different vehicles through which international law norms are transported into the domestic arena, including, *but not limited to*, the process

3 Specifically directed towards States Parties that have a federal form of government, Article 50 of the ICCPR provides that '[t]he provisions of the present Covenant shall extend to all parts of federal States without any limitations or exceptions'.

4 *Vienna Convention on the Law of Treaties*, opened for signature 23 May 1969, 1155 UNTS 331, art 27 (entered into force 27 January 1980); For international case-law on this customary rule, see especially Antonio Cassese, *International Law* (Oxford University Press, 2nd edition, 2005), 217–220.

5 The generic term 'transported' is used here to encompass not just incorporation by legislation but also other ways by which international law norms intersect with the domestic legal order, including the reception of international human rights norms into the administrative decision-making processes as discussed in Section 4.3 below.

6 Such standards are the constituent elements of the right to freedom of religion or belief, including the right to establish and maintain places of worship, which are encapsulated in Article 18 of the ICCPR and its subsequent elaboration, as discussed in Chapters 2 and 3.

7 For an analysis of the strict operation of the 'dualist' approach in Australia, see especially, Alice de Jonge, 'Australia' in Dinah Shelton (ed), *International Law and Domestic Legal Systems: Incorporation, Transformation and Persuasion* (Oxford University Press, 2011), 23–54.

of incorporation whereby international law is transformed into domestic law via the enactment of statutes. Another important vehicle is the reception of international human rights standards in the administrative decision-making processes in Australia.

Second, after the existence of the international standards on religious freedom in Australian law is demonstrated, this chapter analyses how such standards are given domestic application through different means including, *but not limited to*, judicial enforceability, that is, the capacity that they can be directly invoked in courts of law which adjudicate legal claims. As analysed below, the capacity of international human rights standards to be directly invoked before courts is just one of the means by which international human rights standards find domestic application. The legislative, judicial and administrative authorities may employ such standards in their respective domains for different but equally important purposes or objectives. That an international human rights standard is weakly enforced (or not enforced at all) through judicial remedies does not diminish its existence in domestic law and does not preclude *other* means of giving it domestic application.

This chapter is in three parts. First, it analyses the inadequacy of the legal protection of religious freedom under the Australian Constitution, the *Australian Human Rights Commission Act 1986* (Cth) (AHRC Act), and the common law.[8] This inadequacy, coupled with Australia's lack of a comprehensive and legally entrenched Bill of Rights,[9] is the impetus for resorting to international human rights standards on religious freedom. Second, this chapter analyses the vehicles through which international human rights standards are transported into Australian domestic law and given application. Two such vehicles are particularly relevant, namely, the incorporation of religious freedom standards via the enactment of statutes and the reception of such standards in administrative decision-making processes in Australia. Finally, this chapter concludes that the existence and application of the international standards on religious freedom in the Australian states and territories are incomplete and uneven, but they nevertheless demonstrate, along with other human rights norms, the increasing influence of international human rights law in Australian domestic law.

---

8 The AHRC Act is formerly called the *Human Rights and Equal Opportunity Commission Act 1986 (Cth)*.

9 George Williams, *A Charter of Rights for Australia* (University of New South Wales Press, 2007).

4.2 The Inadequate Legal Protection of Religious Freedom in Australia

The legal protection of human rights in Australia, as a whole, has been described as a 'patchwork [which] is fragmented and incomplete, and its inadequacies are felt most keenly by the marginalised and the vulnerable'.[10] This description is also specifically applicable to the legal protection of religious freedom in Australia, as illustrated by the following discussion.

4.2.1 *Limited Protection of Religious Freedom under Section 116 of the Australian Constitution*

The Australian Constitution is, by and large, a document that establishes the general structure of the Australian state, rather than one that defines the relationship between the state and its people by enumerating a list of individual rights.[11] Unlike the Constitution of the United States, the Australian Constitution does not contain a Bill of Rights that enshrines the fundamental rights and freedoms guaranteed to every individual within its territory. Upon federation of the erstwhile British colonial governments in 1901, most of the framers of the Australian Constitution had utmost confidence that the rights of individuals were sufficiently protected by the common law, the courts and parliament,[12] and they regarded an instrument that enumerates fundamental rights and freedoms of individuals as 'unnecessary'.[13] Sir Anthony Mason described the Australian Constitution as a document:

> that confines itself mainly to prescribing a framework for federal government, setting out the various powers of government and limiting them as between federal and state governments and the three branches of

10 *National Human Rights Consultation Report* (Commonwealth of Australia, 2009), 127.

11 Ryszard Piotrowicz and Stuart Kaye, *Human Rights in International and Australian Law* (Butterworths, 2000), 260.

12 One of the delegates, for example, stated that 'it seems to me to be utterly impossible to conceive that such a Parliament will proceed to infringe any of the liberties of the citizens'. *Official Record of the Debates of the Australasian Federal Convention, 1891–1898* ('*Convention Debates*) vol 5, Melbourne, 1898, 1761 (Mr Trenwith); Another delegate dismissively stated that "People would say that – 'Pretty things these States of Australia; they have to be prevented by a provision in the Constitution from doing the grossest injustice'." *Convention Debates*, vol 5, Melbourne, 1898, 688 (Dr Cockburn).

13 Julie Debeljak, 'Does Australia Need a Bill of Rights?' in Paula Gerber and Melissa Castan (eds), *Contemporary Perspectives on Human Rights Law in Australia* (Thomson Reuters, 2013), 37.

> government without attempting to define the rights of citizens except in minor respects.[14]

The presence, therefore, of some express rights and freedoms in the Australian Constitution is 'rather peculiar'.[15] One such right is the freedom of religion found in Section 116 of the Australian Constitution which provides:

> The Commonwealth shall not make any law for establishing any religion, or for imposing any religious observance, or for prohibiting the free exercise of any religion, and no religious test shall be required as a qualification for any office or public trust under the Commonwealth.[16]

Section 116 has four distinct elements that only offer limited protection to religious freedom in Australia, namely[17]: the prohibition against establishing an official state religion, the prohibition against imposing any religious observance, the prohibition against hindering the free exercise of religion, and the prohibition against prescribing religious qualification for holding public office.[18] Despite the inclusion of the right to religious freedom in the Australian Constitution, its contribution towards the legal protection of religious freedom is limited in three ways.

First, as explicitly stated in the constitutional text, these proscriptions are addressed to the Commonwealth Parliament and *not* to the individual states and territories. Hence, if any of the state parliaments chose to enact a law that curtailed religious exercise or created an official religion, Section 116 could not be invoked to nullify such a law on the ground that it contravenes the Constitution. In a similar vein, if a state planning statute or its administration has the effect of restricting important aspects of religious freedom, Section 116 cannot be relied upon to alleviate the restriction. Such a legislative or administrative action by state authorities is not covered by Section 116. As Reid

---

14 Sir Anthony Mason, 'Human Rights and Courts' in Paul Babie and Neville Rochow (eds), *Freedom of Religion under Bills of Rights* (University of Adelaide Press, 2012), xi.

15 Carolyn Maree Evans, *Legal Protection of Religious Freedom in Australia* (Federation Press, 2012), 69.

16 Australian Constitution, s 116.

17 S. McLeish, 'Making Sense of Religion and the Constitution: A Fresh Start to 116' (1992) 18(2) *Monash University Law Review* 207–236.

18 Mirko Bagaric, Peter Faris and Theo Alexander, *Australian Human Rights Law* (CCH Australia Limited, 2011), 198–199.

Mortensen observed, '[t]he Australian Constitution has no provision equivalent to the U.S. Constitution's Fourteenth Amendment, by which restrictions placed on the federal government are incorporated as equivalent restrictions applicable to states'.[19]

Second, Section 116 operates as a mere restriction to the law-making power of the Commonwealth Parliament. Its scope is limited to the action of the Commonwealth at the legislative level and it 'does not apply to the executive or the community generally'.[20] In *RE: Minister for Immigration and Ethnic Affairs and Lebanese Moslem Association*,[21] the Full Federal Court overruled a decision which had invalidated the Minister's deportation order of an imam of a Sydney mosque as violating Section 116 of the Constitution. The Full Federal Court ruled that Section 116 has no application to executive action under the *Migration Act 1958* (Cth) because its application is confined to legislative actions that impair religious freedom.

Finally, Section 116 has not received an expanded elaboration through judicial interpretation which could have contributed to a greater legal protection of religious freedom in Australia. In *Krygger v Williams*,[22] the appellant was convicted for failing to render military service as required by the *Defence Act 1903* (Cth). He argued that the law prohibited him from freely exercising his religious beliefs. The High Court rejected assertions regarding the appellant's firm belief against taking part in war which, in turn, arises from his deeply held religious conviction against using lethal force. Chief Justice Griffith stated that '[t]o require a man to do a thing *which has nothing at all to do with religion* is not prohibiting him from a free exercise of religion'.[23] [emphasis added] The ruling in this case set '[t]he tone for later cases',[24] some of which are analysed below, where Section 116 of the Constitution was given a restricted interpretation which, in turn, weakened its capacity to protect the exercise of religious freedom in Australia.

The *Defence of Government Schools* (DOGS) *Case*[25] involved a challenge against the federal funding of church schools as contrary to Section 116 of the

19 Reid Mortensen, 'The Unfinished Experiment: A Report on Religious Freedom in Australia' (2007) 21 *Emory International Law Review* 167, 170.

20 Peter Bailey, *The Human Rights Enterprise in Australia and Internationally* (LexisNexis, 2009), 300.

21 (1987) 17 FCR 373, 378–379 (Jackson J.).

22 (1912) 15 CLR 366.

23 Ibid., 369.

24 Evans, above n 15, 74.

25 (1981) 146 CLR 559.

Constitution, particularly its non-establishment limb which states that '[t]he Commonwealth shall not make any law for establishing any religion'. The applicants argued that such funding amounted to an establishment of religion which is proscribed by Section 116. The High Court rejected this argument. The majority of the justices took a narrow view of Section 116 and held that it only proscribes a law which was specifically enacted for the purpose of creating a single, national religion for Australia. Chief Justice Barwick stated that the word 'for' in the non-establishment limb of Section 116 meant that the creation of an official state religion in Australia must be the law's 'express and... single purpose'.[26] The High Court held that the funding of church schools did not amount to creating an official state religion.

The case of *Kruger v Commonwealth*[27] also illustrates the narrow judicial interpretation that has been given to Section 116 of the Constitution, particularly on its free exercise component. In that case, an Aboriginal group commenced an action for compensation alleging they were victims of government policies in the Northern Territory between 1925 and 1960 meant to place Aboriginal children in foster care in church and state-run homes. The action was based on, among others, the protection of religious exercise under Section 116 of the Constitution. They alleged that the policies impeded them from freely exercising their religious freedom. The majority of the Court chose to accord a narrow interpretation of the word 'for' in Section 116, and ruled that the *Aboriginals Protection Ordinance 1918* (NT) was not meant 'for' impeding the exercise of religious freedom but, on the contrary, it was actually enacted in order to protect Aboriginal children. Justice Gaudron stated that:

> s 116 must be construed as no more than a limitation on Commonwealth legislative power. More precisely, it cannot be construed as impliedly conferring an independent or free-standing right which, if breached, sounds in damages at the suit of the individual whose interests are thereby affected.[28]

The case-law on Section 116 of the Constitution shows its inadequacy in protecting the right to religious freedom of individuals or groups when an infringement results from either a legislative or executive action of states or territories. The above cases represent a missed opportunity to constitutionally entrench the protection of religious freedom in Australia. They reveal that attempts to rely on Section 116 have all been in vain. Carolyn Evans observed that Section 116:

26 Ibid., 579.

27 (1997) 190 CLR 1.

28 *Kruger v The Commonwealth* (1997) 190 CLR 1, 175.

> is not, in itself a free-standing right of an individual, but a limitation on the legislative power of the Commonwealth Parliament. One consequence of this is that the right to religious freedom cannot be asserted to protect an individual against actions by private individuals or organisations. Nor does s 116 create a positive obligation on the Commonwealth Parliament to take action to protect religious freedom.[29]

Therefore, the protection of the right to freedom of religion or belief in Australia, including the right to establish and maintain places of worship, cannot be anchored on Section 116 of the Constitution which has a limited protective scope. Such limited protection to religious freedom (as a result of the narrow judicial interpretation given to it) means that individuals and religious organisations cannot effectively invoke it before the courts in response to a state's legislative or executive action which violates the exercise of religious freedom. Thus, there is a need to look for another source of legal protection.[30]

4.2.2 *Limited Protection of Religious Freedom under the* **Australian Human Rights Commission Act 1986** (*Cth*) (*AHRC Act*)

The Australian Constitution was patterned after the United States Constitution in terms of the division of powers between the federal and state governments.[31] The Commonwealth Parliament can legislate only within the parameters of a specific list of powers (also referred to as 'heads of power'), while everything else was left to the states (that is, their residual legislative powers).[32] Although the protection of human rights, including the right to freedom of religion or belief, is not one of the 'heads of power',[33] the Commonwealth Parliament can enact legislation that may touch upon the protection of a particular human right.[34]

---

29 Evans, above n 15, 72–73.

30 There is another constitutional recognition of freedom of religion in an Australian jurisdiction – that is, Section 46 of the Tasmanian Constitution or the *Constitution Act 1934* (Tas). However, despite the fact that it has been part of the statute books since 1934, there has been no litigation brought under Section 46. See Peter Bailey, *Human Rights Law* (Thompson Reuters, 2012), 74; Evans, above n 15, 96–97.

31 Piotrowicz and Kaye, above n 11, 259.

32 Ibid., 259–261.

33 Anthony Mason, 'The Role of the Judiciary in Developing Human Rights in Australian Law' in David Kinley (ed), *Human Rights in Australian Law* (Federation Press, 1998), 26, 28.

34 For example, Section 51(xxix) of the Australian Constitution (also called the 'external affairs power') may be the basis for the Commonwealth Parliament to enact laws which implement Australia's international human rights obligations under international human rights treaties. In a similar vein, Section 51(xxxi) of the Australian Constitution provides

One such piece of Commonwealth legislation that touches upon human rights is the AHRC Act[35] which provides for the creation of the Australian Human Rights Commission (Commission).[36] The Commission is empowered to handle complaints involving alleged violations of federal anti-discrimination legislation, including the *Age Discrimination Act 2004* (Cth), *Racial Discrimination Act 1975* (Cth), *Sex Discrimination Act 1984* (Cth), and *Disability Discrimination Act 1992* (Cth). The statutory responsibilities of the Commission include education and public awareness, discrimination and human rights complaints, and policy and legislative development.[37]

The term 'human rights' is defined in the AHRC Act as including *inter alia* the human rights recognised in the ICCPR, including the right to freedom of religion or belief, and the international standards on religious freedom elaborated in the Religion Declaration.[38] Both the ICCPR and the Religion Declaration have been included in the schedule of the AHRC Act. However, despite such inclusion, the AHRC Act did not transport *en masse* the international human rights standards (including those on religious freedom) into Australian domestic law. The High Court held in *Dietrich v The Queen*[39] that such inclusion does not legally constitute an 'incorporation' of an international treaty (or an international obligation) into Australian domestic law. Notwithstanding that they are appended to a federal Act, the ICCPR and the Religion Declaration are not part of Australian law, except that the ACT and Victoria have incorporated most of the rights recognised in the ICCPR through the enactment of statutory bills of rights, as discussed in Section 4.3.1 below.

---

that the Commonwealth Parliament has the power to enact laws with respect to 'the acquisition of property on just terms from any State or person for any purpose in respect of which the Parliament has power to make laws' (also called the 'acquisition of property power'). This constitutional provision operates both as a granting clause that gives the Commonwealth the power to acquire property, and as a guarantee that such acquisition can only be made 'on just terms'. Thus, the right to property is protected by the Australian Constitution to the extent that acquisition of property for public purposes by the Commonwealth should be on 'just terms'. For an illustration of acquired property in consideration of 'just terms', see especially *Wurridjal v Commonwealth* (2009) 237 CLR 309, and where a claim to be paid in 'just terms' was unsuccessful, see *Tobacco Plain Packaging Case JT International SA v Commonwealth* (2012) 86 ALJR 1297; (2012) 291 ALR 669.

35 *Australian Human Rights Commission Act 1986* (Cth) ('AHRC Act'); The AHRC Act is formerly known as the *Human Rights and Equal Opportunity Commission Act 1986* (Cth).

36 The AHRC is formerly named the Human Rights and Equal Opportunity Commission.

37 AHRC Act s 11.

38 AHRC Act s 3.

39 *Dietrich v The Queen* (1992) 177 CLR 292 at [17]; See also, *Minogue v Williams* [2000] FCA 125.

The AHRC Act does not create independent or free-standing substantive human rights, and the Commission provides inadequate protection of those human rights that are recognised in Australian law because it only has 'indirect methods of enforcement'.[40] When a complaint is made in writing to the Commission alleging that an act or practice is inconsistent with or contrary to a human right recognised in Australia, including the right to freedom of religion or belief, the Commission is required to conduct an inquiry and, if it considers appropriate, to effect a settlement of the dispute by conciliation.[41] The Commission has no power to impose binding decisions regarding any alleged violations of human rights. Therefore, the legal protection of human rights, including the right to freedom of religion or belief, cannot be sufficiently anchored on the limited protective capacity of the AHRC Act.

4.2.3 *Lack of Protection of Religious Freedom under the Common Law*

Over the years, the courts have developed case by case a body of law called the 'common law'.[42] In rendering decisions over time, they have come to identify the existence of certain human rights. These include, for example, the right of the accused to have a fair trial,[43] the right against self-incrimination,[44] the right against a warrantless search,[45] and the requirement of proof beyond reasonable doubt to secure a conviction in a criminal proceeding.[46] However, there is no similar unequivocal recognition of the right to freedom of religion or belief in the common law. As noted by Carolyn Evans, 'the common law quite possibly does not protect religious freedom'.[47] The case of *Grace Bible Church v Reedman*[48] supports this conclusion. In that case, the appellant was convicted of violating the *Education Act* (SA) for operating an unregistered Christian school. In support of his appeal, the appellant contended that he had 'an inalienable right to religious freedom and that that freedom cannot be

40 Debeljak, above n 13, 43.

41 AHRC Act s 20(1)(b).

42 Bailey, *Human Rights Law*, above n 30, 63; Nick O'Neill, Simon Rice and Roger Douglas, *Retreat from Injustice: Human Rights in Australian Law* (Federation Press, 2004, 2nd edition), 108–112.

43 See, e.g., *Dietrich v The Queen* (1992) 177 CLR 292.

44 See, e.g., *Sorby v Commonwealth* (1983) 152 CLR 281.

45 See, e.g., *George v Rockett* (1990) 170 CLR 104.

46 See, e.g., *Woolmington v DPP* (1935) AC 462.

47 Evans, above n 15, 88; See also, O'Neill *et al.*, above n 42, 110.

48 71 (1984) 36 SASR 376; 54 ALR 571.

abridged by any statute of the South Australian Parliament'.[49] On this point, Justice Zelling dismissively stated that, in order for the invoked 'inalienable right to religious freedom' to be a valid claim, it needed nothing less than 'a complete rewriting of history'.[50] The appeal was unanimously dismissed by the Full Court of the Supreme Court of South Australia (Zelling, White and Millhouse JJ). Justice White held that:

> There is nothing in that common law which inhibits or is capable of inhibiting the power of the Parliament of the State to make laws for the peace, welfare and good government of this State, including laws which affect the freedom of religious worship and religious expression.[51]

Regarding a possible common law protection of religious freedom, Justice White stated that 'the common law has never contained a fundamental guarantee of the inalienable right of religious freedom and expression'.[52] This decision illustrates the state's exercise of plenary legislative power – seemingly unfettered and unconstrained – which in turn springs from the concept of 'parliamentary sovereignty'.[53]

To summarise, while religious freedom is expressly protected in Section 116 of the Australian Constitution, its protective scope is constrained by judicial interpretation. At the federal level, the AHRC Act recognises religious freedom but the law itself only provides indirect and weak protection. Worse still, religious freedom is not recognised as a right which is protected by the common law. Given this serious deficiency in the legal protection of religious freedom in Australia, individuals or groups whose right to freedom of religion or belief has been infringed must look for other sources of legal protection. One such alternative is the international human rights standards applicable to the right to freedom of religion or belief. Such standards offer a viable alternative source of legal protection of religious freedom in Australia if, and only if, they are first transported into Australian domestic law and then given application in the domestic setting.

---

49 Ibid., 377.

50 Ibid., 379.

51 Ibid., at SASR 385; ALR 580.

52 Ibid., 388.

53 Debeljak explains that the concept of 'parliamentary sovereignty' means that the 'parliament is the supreme authority within government'. She continues: 'In the positive sense, this means that parliament can legally pass any law whatsoever; in a negative sense, this means that there is no person or body whose legislative power competes with parliament, or is superior to it'. See Debeljak, above n 13, 45.

4.3 How International Human Rights Standards on Religious Freedom are Transported into Australian Law and Given Domestic Application

Australia follows the 'dualist' perspective of international law under which the treaty commitments assumed by Australia in the international sphere do not automatically form part of the domestic law.[54] Thus, when Australia became a State Party to the ICCPR, the fundamental rights and freedoms guaranteed therein, including the right to freedom of religion or belief, did not automatically become part of Australian domestic law. The Australian 'dualist' approach to the relationship between domestic and international law may be attributed to its firm adherence to the supremacy of Parliament from which all substantive rights exclusively emanate.[55]

Julian Burnside asserted that a human right that is recognised in international law, but not incorporated into Australian domestic law, 'is nothing but a pious hope'.[56] However, as discussed below, this assertion is not entirely accurate and does not adequately capture the way in which international human rights law intersects with the Australian domestic legal order. Burnside mistakenly assumed that human rights lose their validity and significance as binding norms simply because they cannot be judicially enforced.

International law, including international human rights law, has several points of contact with the Australian legal structure.[57] It is quite simplistic to assume that international law exclusively intersects with the legislature (for example, when it decides to transform an international law norm into domestic law). Nor is it correct to state that international law only intersects with the judicial arm of

---

54 The dualist view may be contrasted with the 'monist' view that regards international law and domestic law as parts of one universal legal order. See generally, Gerald McGinley and Harry Reicher, 'The Relationship of International Law to Australian Law' in Harry Reicher (ed), *Australian International Law: Cases and Materials* (LBC Casebooks, 1995), 67–115; For a comprehensive discussion on the transformation of international law into Australian law, see especially J. Crawford and W. Edison, 'International Law and Australian Law' in K. Ryan (ed), *International Law in Australian Law* (Law Book Company, 1984), 71; Bailey, *The Human Rights Enterprise in Australia and Internationally*, above n 20, 260–268.

55 For a discussion of the concept of parliamentary sovereignty and its impact on human rights protection in Australia, see Debeljak, above n 13, 44–48.

56 Julian Burnside, 'It's Time. A Bill of Rights for Australia' (Speech delivered at the 2008 International Human Rights Day Address, Bob Hawke Prime Ministerial Centre, University of South Australia).

57 Chief Justice Robert French, 'Oil and Water? – International Law and Domestic Law in Australia' Bond University Brennan Lecture, 2009, para 4.

government when courts, in the exercise of judicial power, directly apply international standards to resolve legal disputes. Equally important, international law norms also inform executive or administrative decision-making in Australia. The Chief Justice of the High Court of Australia, Robert French, has noted that:

> It is important at the outset that we recognise that the story about the role of international law and our domestic law is not told simply by describing its consideration in the courts. *Much of the interaction takes place at the level of legislative, administrative and commercial practice which will never see the inside of a courtroom.*[58] [emphasis added]

From the above statement, it can be explicated that the judicial enforceability of international law norms (such as the international human rights standards on religious freedom), while very important, is not the only way that such norms influence the Australian domestic legal order. To equate the validity of an international law norm with judicial enforceability leaves out the other significant influences of international law on the domestic law. Commenting on the extent to which international legal principles affect Australia's legal order, Hilary Charlesworth *et al.* observed that:

> the literature's focus on the judicial role has led to a lopsided emphasis on the judiciary compared to that of the executive and legislature. Activity by the executive, in contrast to the judiciary, usually occurs out of the public eye and legislative action, while often giving rise to strong debate, is far less frequent. Nevertheless, activity by these limbs of government is certainly no less significant.[59]

Indeed, examining how international law norms influence the legislative, judicial and executive or administrative branches of government 'allows a more comprehensive understanding of the context in which international law intersects with the Australian legal order'.[60] The international human rights standards on religious freedom do exhibit the same behaviour – that is, they intersect with the legislative, judicial and executive or administrative branches of the Australian government. Therefore, the significance of international human rights standards on religious freedom goes beyond judicial enforceability.

---

58 Ibid.

59 Hilary Charlesworth, Madelaine Chiam, Devika Hovell and George Williams, 'Deep Anxieties: Australia and the International Legal Order' (2003) 25 *Sydney Law Review* 423, 428.

60 Ibid., 425.

The next three sections analyse how the international human rights standards on religious freedom are transported into Australian law. They also analyse how, in addition to judicial enforceability, such standards are given domestic applicability. The international standards on religious freedom are transported into Australian domestic law and given domestic applicability by virtue of three processes, namely: (i) the incorporation of the international standards on religious freedom in Victoria and the Australian Capital Territory (ACT), (ii) the incorporation of the norm of non-discrimination based on religion or belief in most Australian jurisdictions, and (iii) the use of international human rights standards, including those pertaining to the right to freedom of religion or belief, to inform administrative decision-making processes in Australia. Each of these processes is analysed below.

4.3.1 *Incorporation of International Human Rights Standards on Religious Freedom in Victoria and ACT*

In what many commentators believe is a positive development,[61] two Australian jurisdictions – the Australian Capital Territory (ACT) and the state of Victoria – have enacted legislation incorporating human rights which are based on the ICCPR, including the right to freedom of religion or belief.[62] The ACT enacted the *Human Rights Act 2004* (ACT) (ACT HRA) and Victoria the *Charter of Human Rights and Responsibilities Act 2006* (Vic) (Victorian Charter).[63] Peter Bailey described both human rights Acts as 'look[ing] beyond the domestic common law to international human rights law, and particularly to the ICCPR, for the rights they promote'[64] and noted that 'they are *explicitly*

---

61 See, e.g., Diane Sisely, 'Inspired by the Human Rights Act: The Victorian Charter of Human Rights and Responsibilities' in Nicolas Kang-Riou, Jo Milner and Suryia Nayak (eds), *Confronting the Human Rights Act: Contemporary Themes and Perspectives* (Routledge, 2012), 85; Williams, above n 9, 15.

62 In recent years, other Australian jurisdictions have also considered enacting human rights Acts. For example, Tasmania and Western Australia constituted independent committees which recommended the adoption of human rights Acts in their respective jurisdictions, but no such Acts has been enacted so far. In Queensland and New South Wales, parliamentary committees have rejected the idea of enacting human rights Acts but recommended other measures. See especially, *National Human Rights Consultation Report*, above n 10, 237–240.

63 The *Human Rights Act 2004* (ACT) ('ACT HRA') took effect on 1 July 2004; while the *Charter of Human Rights and Responsibilities Act 2006* (Vic) ('Victorian Charter') took effect on 1 January 2008.

64 Bailey, *The Human Rights Enterprise in Australia and Internationally*, above n 20, 174.

based on the internationally accepted legal standards of human rights'.[65] [emphasis added] With respect to the ACT HRA, Dinah Shelton similarly observed that 'the primary source for the Act was the ICCPR'.[66] Section 5 of ACT HRA defines 'human rights' to mean the human rights enumerated in Part 3 of the Act,[67] while Section 3 of the Victorian Charter defines the term 'human rights' to mean the human rights enumerated in Part 2 of the Act.[68]

4.3.1.1 *The Existence of the International Human Rights Standards on Religious Freedom in the Victorian and ACT Jurisdictions*

The incorporation of the above human rights in the ACT and Victoria means that the international standards pertaining to those rights, including the right to freedom of religion or belief, have been transported from the international

---

65 Ibid., 175; For a general discussion of the influence of international human rights law in Australian law, see especially, Jim Kennan, 'The Role of International Human Rights Law in Australian Law' (2009–10) 44 *Valparaiso University Law Review* 895.

66 Dinah Shelton, 'Introduction' in Dinah Shelton (ed), *International Law and Domestic Legal Systems: Incorporation, Transformation and Persuasion* (Oxford University Press, 2011), 22–23.

67 ACT HRA ss 8–28; These human rights are the following:
a. right to recognition and equality before the law,
b. right to life,
c. right against torture and cruel, inhuman or degrading treatment,
d. protection of the family and children,
e. right to privacy and reputation,
f. freedom of movement,
g. freedom of thought, conscience, religion and belief,
h. right to peaceful assembly and freedom of association,
i. freedom of expression,
j. right to take part in public life,
k. right to liberty and security of person,
l. right to humane treatment when deprived of liberty,
m. rights of children in the criminal process,
n. right to a fair trial,
o. rights in criminal proceeding,
p. right to compensation for wrongful conviction,
q. right not to be tried or punished more than once,
r. right against retrospective criminal laws,
s. freedom from forced work, and
t. rights of minorities.

68 Victorian Charter ss 7–27; These human rights include the rights enumerated in the above footnote and the following rights:
a. cultural rights
b. property rights

arena into these two domestic jurisdictions. Formerly existing only in international law, such standards now exist also as part of the law of the ACT and Victorian jurisdictions. Substantially repeating the substance of Article 18 of the ICCPR,[69] both human rights Acts guarantee the right to freedom of thought, conscience, religion and belief. Section 14 of ACT HRA provides that:

(1) Everyone has the right to freedom of thought, conscience and religion. This right includes –
   (a) the freedom to have or to adopt a religion or belief of his or her choice; and
   (b) the *freedom to demonstrate* his or her religion or belief in worship, observance, practice and teaching, either individually or as part of a community and whether in public or private.
(2) No-one may be *coerced* in a way that would limit his or her freedom to have or adopt a religion or belief in worship, observance, practice or teaching. [emphasis added]

Section 14 of the Victorian Charter similarly provides that:

(1) Every person has the right to freedom of thought, conscience, religion and belief, including –
   (a) the freedom to have or to adopt a religion or belief of his or her choice; and
   (b) the *freedom to demonstrate* his or her religion or belief in worship, observance, practice and teaching, either individually or as part of a community, in public or in private.
(2) A person must not be *coerced or restrained* in a way that limits his or her freedom to have or adopt a religion or belief in worship, observance, practice or teaching. [emphasis added]

Both the ACT HRA and the Victorian Charter preserve the legal architecture of the right to freedom of religion or belief as erected in the international sphere by the 'foundational instruments'[70] and extend their applicability into the ACT and Victorian jurisdictions. Both Acts preserve the dichotomy of the *forum internum* and *forum externum* limbs of the right. A textual examination of

---

69 Bagaric *et al.*, above n 18, 199–200.

70 As discussed in Chapter 2, these are the UDHR, the ICCPR, the Religion Declaration and General Comment 22.

Section 14 of ACT HRA and Section 14 of the Victorian Charter shows minor differences with their counterpart phrases in the foundational instruments.

First, the term 'freedom to demonstrate' religion or belief is used in both Acts instead of the term freedom to 'manifest' religion or belief which is used in the foundational instruments. Such difference in phraseology does not dilute the potency of the *forum externum* limb of the right to freedom of religion or belief as guaranteed in the foundational instruments. The framers of the Acts intended to employ a simpler or more familiar language, rather than to deviate from the settled meaning and import of the freedom to 'manifest' one's religion or belief. This conclusion may be gleaned from the overall object or purpose of the Acts which is to 'bring the rights home'[71] to Victoria and the ACT. The intention not to deviate from the meaning of the freedom to 'manifest' religion or belief may also be inferred from the purpose of the interpretative rules found in Section 31(1) of ACT HRA and Section 32(2) of the Victorian Charter which is to resolve legal ambiguities in a manner consistent with *inter alia* the foundational instruments. With respect to Section 31(1) of ACT HRA, Reid Mortensen commented that it ensured '[t]he comprehensive implementation of the language of international law in the ACT'.[72]

Second, Section 14 of the Victorian Charter states that a person must not be 'coerced or restrained' in a way that limits the freedom to have or adopt a religion or belief, while the counterpart phrase in the foundational instruments state that no one shall be subjected to 'coercion' which would impair the freedom to have or to adopt a religion or belief. Again, this difference in phraseology does not veer away from the meaning of the freedom to choose (or not to choose) a religion or belief as guaranteed in the foundational instruments. Not to be 'coerced' and not to be 'restrained' are two sides of the same coin – that is, the freedom of religious choice. The difference in phraseology is thus the result of the legislative intent to prohibit, in an unequivocal manner, all types of impairment of the freedom of religious choice. Thus, for example, a woman who was forced to adopt the religion of her husband upon marriage (coercion) and a man who was prevented by his family from converting to his preferred religion because the family could be ostracised by the community (restraint) are equally repugnant as violations of the freedom of religious choice.

Thus, despite minor differences with their counterpart formulation in the foundational instruments, Section 14 of ACT HRA and Section 14 of the Victorian

71 Julie Debeljak, 'Balancing Rights in a Democracy: The Problems with Limitations and Overrides of Rights under the Victorian Charter of Human Rights and Responsibilities Act 2006' (2008) 32 *Melbourne University Law Review* 422, 433.

72 Mortensen, above n 19, 181; Cf Evans, above n 15, 100.

Charter *substantially* brought home, so to speak, the international standards on the right to freedom of religion or belief into the ACT and Victorian jurisdictions.

4.3.1.2 *The Application of the International Human Rights Standards on Religious Freedom in the Victorian and ACT Jurisdictions*

The ACT HRA and the Victorian Charter contemplate different means by which international human rights standards (including those pertaining to religious freedom) may find application in their respective jurisdictions, including but not limited to judicial enforcement. As noted by Carolyn Evans and Simon Evans:

> Courts and tribunals are not intended to be the sole focus, or even the primary focus, of the Australian human rights Acts. Instead, creating a culture of rights within parliament and the executive is intended to be the primary method for enhancing rights protection. Both the Australian Capital Territory and Victorian governments were determined to avoid overreliance on courts and tribunals. They were particularly anxious to avoid the impression that the human rights Acts would be a 'lawyers' picnic'.[73]

The ACT HRA and the Victorian Charter provide the following three primary methods for enhancing the protection of human rights:

First, the ACT HRA and the Victorian Charter provide for interpretative rules which allow the courts and tribunals to consider international human rights standards in resolving a legal ambiguity. Section 31(1) of ACT HRA provides that when interpreting statutory provisions, the following instruments may be considered: the ICCPR, other human rights treaties ratified by Australia, the General Comments and views of the human rights treaty bodies, declarations adopted by the UN General Assembly pertinent to human rights, and decisions of international courts and tribunals.[74] Similarly, Section 32(2) of the Victorian Charter provides that international law and the judgments of domestic, foreign and international courts and tribunals relevant to a human right may be considered in interpreting a statutory provision.[75] On this point, Julie Debeljak commented that:

> First, by adopting the essence of the ICCPR rights, the Victorian Charter implicitly 'brings rights home' for Victorians. Secondly, 'international law

73 Carolyn Evans and Simon Evans, *Australian Bills of Rights: The Law of the Victorian Charter and the ACT Human Rights Act* (LexisNexis Butterworth, 2008), 113.

74 ACT HRA s 31(1).

75 Victorian Charter s 32(2).

> and the judgments of domestic, foreign and international courts and tribunals relevant to a human right may be considered in interpreting a statutory provision' under s 32(2) of the Victorian Charter, thereby making international human rights norms relevant.[76]

Based on the above, these interpretative rules open the 'dualist' door, so to speak, in order to allow the entry and use of international human rights standards, including those pertaining to the right to freedom of religion or belief, into the ACT and Victorian jurisdictions in the event that there is ambiguity in the law.

However, it must be stressed that the interpretative rules' contribution towards human rights protection is possible only where there is an ambiguity in the statute under consideration. If the law is understandable in its plain terms, there is no occasion for interpretative rules to apply. In *Al-Kateb v Godwin*,[77] it was held that the *Migration Act 1958* (Cth) as it applied to Mr Al-Kateb's case was unambiguous and, therefore, there was no need to consider the international human rights norm prohibiting arbitrary detention. Thus, the main source of weakness in the use of interpretative principles to protect human rights is that, as a mere rule of statutory construction, it only applies when there is legal ambiguity and that 'any express or implied parliamentary indication circumscribing rights *prevents* judicial rights-based interpretation'.[78] [emphasis original]

Second, the ACT HRA and the Victorian Charter provide for the so-called 'dialogue model' that enables the courts and the legislature to engage in a joint enterprise in order to protect human rights without compromising each other's prerogative.[79] If a court finds that a law is not consistent with a particular human right, it may make a 'declaration of incompatibility'[80] or a 'declaration of inconsistent interpretation'[81] which does not affect the validity or enforcement of the law. The declaration is presented to the legislature which may or may

76 Debeljak, 'Balancing Rights in a Democracy', above n 71, 433.

77 (2004) 219 CLR 562.

78 Debeljak, 'Does Australia Need a Bill of Rights?', above n 13, 49.

79 See especially, George Williams, 'The Victorian Charter of Human Rights and Responsibilities: Origins and Scope' (2006) 30 *Melbourne University Law Review* 887; Julie Debeljak, 'Parliamentary Sovereignty and Dialogue under the Victorian Charter of Human Rights and Responsibilities: Drawing the Line Between Judicial Interpretation and Judicial Law-Making' (2007) 33 *Monash University Law Review* 9, 9–10.

80 ACT HRA s 32(2).

81 Victorian Charter s 36(2).

not amend the law which a court has found to be human rights-incompatible.[82] However, it must be emphasised that the opportunity for a court to make a declaration of incompatibility (ACT HRA) or a declaration of inconsistent interpretation (Victorian Charter) arises only if there is a legal ambiguity requiring interpretation. Without such ambiguity, there is no occasion for a court to make a declaration of incompatibility or inconsistent interpretation. In both Acts, an individual does not have a free-standing right to request a court to issue such a declaration.

Third, and most significantly, the ACT HRA and the Victorian Charter impose (i) an obligation upon 'public authorities' to perform their powers and functions compatibly with human rights, including the right to freedom of religion or belief, and (ii) an obligation to take human rights into account when discharging their powers and functions.[83] The failure to comply with either of these mandatory obligations may be a ground to challenge the decision of a public authority. Section 40(c) of the ACT HRA 'create[s] a new cause of action for breach of human rights'[84] which allows a person to bring an action against a public authority who has acted in breach of the obligations in Section 40B(1) of the ACT HRA. In contrast, Section 39 of the Victorian Charter has 'no express provision establishing a direct cause of action for breach of human rights'[85] but it may 'provid[e] the element of unlawfulness to other causes of action that require proof of this element'.[86] As analysed below, local councils are 'public authorities' under the Acts and thus they carry these dual obligations, namely, to act consistently with human rights and to give proper consideration to them in arriving at a decision. Underscoring the importance of these two mandatory obligations imposed upon public authorities in the context of the Victorian Charter, Diane Sisely stated that:

> The cornerstone of the [Victorian] Charter is the provision (s 38) that makes it unlawful for a public authority *to act* in a way that is incompatible

82 ACT HRA s 33(2)(3); Victorian Charter s 37; In *R v Momcilovic* [2010] VSCA 50 (17 March 2010), the Victorian Court of Appeal ruled that a legal presumption relating to the finding of illegal drugs that transferred the burden of proof to the accused violated the right to be presumed innocent. The court then signified its intention to issue a declaration of incompatibility which would be transmitted to the Victorian Parliament.

83 ACT HRA s 40B(1); Victorian Charter ss 38 and 39.

84 Evans and Evans, above n 73, 120.

85 Ibid., 123.

86 Ibid., 124; See also, Melissa Castan and Julie Debeljak, 'Indigenous peoples' human rights and the Victorian Charter: a framework for reorienting recordkeeping and archival practice' (2012) 12(2) *Archival Science* 213, 229.

> with a human right or, in making a decision, *to fail to give proper consideration* to a relevant human right. This is similar to s 6(1) of the [United Kingdom's Human Rights Act]. As Lord Bingham observed, 'Thus Parliament was requiring compliance with the scheduled Convention rights across the whole spectrum of government.[87] [emphasis added]

Similarly, describing the dual obligations of public authorities under the Victorian Charter, Melissa Castan and Julie Debeljak stated that:

> Section 38 of the Charter imposes two obligations on public authorities. Under s 38(1), it is unlawful for a public authority *to act* in a way that is incompatible with protected rights. This imposes an obligation to act compatibly with the substance of the rights. It is also unlawful for a public authority, *when making a decision*, to fail to give proper consideration to a human right. This is a procedural right which ensures that rights are a relevant part of the decision-making process.[88] [emphasis original]

Therefore, the legal obligation bestowed upon public authorities in the ACT and Victoria consists of two separate duties. First, there is a negative duty not to infringe human rights, including freedom of religion or belief. This duty addresses the *effect* of governmental actions, such that, if they resulted in a breach of human rights, they can be declared unlawful. Second, there is a positive duty on the part of all public authorities to take human rights into consideration in making a decision, especially the particular human right which is most prone to be infringed by that decision. This second duty seeks to improve the decision-making process itself in order to saturate, or at least infuse, it with relevant human rights considerations. It is a critical task to be followed by all public authorities in balancing the importance of human rights vis-à-vis the societal interests they are mandated to look after (for example, environmental protection, public health, peace and order, the protection of amenity, and other societal interests). This duty does not necessarily result in the 'trumping' of such societal interests in favour of the relevant human rights in every situation that requires a balancing; but it ensures that the decision-makers have adequately pondered over the relevant human rights that will be affected by their decisions.

87 Sisely, above n 61, 93.

88 Castan and Debeljak, above n 86, 229.

As enforcers of local planning regulations, local councils fall within the purview of 'public authorities' under the ACT HRA[89] and the Victorian Charter,[90] because they are entrusted with governmental powers and functions. Peter Bailey argues that both human rights Acts 'expressly bind administration in the broad sense, in that they apply to bodies discharging a public function as well as to traditional government agencies such as departments'.[91] Local councils, 'as public authorities under the Charter … are legally obligated to take human rights into consideration when drafting local laws, policies and programs'.[92] Being public authorities within the meaning of the ACT HRA and the Victorian Charter, local councils have a duty not to breach human rights, including freedom of religion, and are obliged to inform their planning decision-making process with human rights considerations, including the freedom of religion or belief.

In *Swancom Pty Ltd v Yarra City Council*,[93] the Victorian Civil and Administrative Tribunal held that local councils have a legal duty to factor in human rights considerations 'when making decisions, developing local laws and policies, and in providing services'.[94] In this case, a decision by the local council to refuse planning consent to a pub seeking to extend its trading hours in its beer garden located in a mixed-use zone was held to be lawful. The Tribunal recognised that the same legal duty applies to itself, when it stated that: 'We agree with the Council that the Tribunal is also bound by the [Victorian] Charter in a case of this nature – i.e. exercising its review jurisdiction on a planning application'.[95]

Similarly, in *Smith v Hobsons Bay City Council*,[96] the Victorian Civil and Administrative Tribunal emphasised that an administrative decision-maker should comply with the legal duty under the Victorian Charter to give proper consideration to any relevant human right as part of his or her decision-making process. In this case, the Tribunal held that a local council's decision to remove the condition in a planning permit requiring a balcony screen to prevent overlooking to a neighbour's property did not infringe the human right to privacy protected under Section 13 of the Victorian Charter.

89 ACT HRA s 40.
90 Victorian Charter s 4.
91 Bailey, *The Human Rights Enterprise in Australia and Internationally*, above n 20, 176.
92 Victorian Local Government Association, 'Human Rights Matter Locally: Preparing your local government to understand and implement the Charter' Manual 1 (2011), 1–2.
93 [2009] VCAT 923 (10 June 2009).
94 Ibid., para 22.
95 Ibid.
96 [2010] VCAT 668 (12 May 2010) paras 37, 40.

While the incorporation of international human rights standards on religious freedom into the ACT and Victorian jurisdictions is a significant contribution towards the legal protection of the right to freedom of religion or belief, their positive impact is confined only to those two jurisdictions. In contrast, there is one legal principle that exists in most Australian jurisdictions which is central to the legal protection of the right to freedom of religion or belief. As discussed in the next section, it is derived from international human rights law and is enforceable in Australia by virtue of incorporation.

4.3.2 *Incorporation of the Norm of Non-Discrimination Based on Religion or Belief in the Australian Domestic Jurisdiction*

Carolyn Evans has noted that 'the principle of non-discrimination on the basis of religion is one of the clearest principles of international human rights law'.[97] Such a principle has been incorporated into the Australian domestic jurisdiction, albeit in a rather unsystematic manner. At the federal level, there are two relevant laws that prohibit discrimination based on religion or belief in specific contexts, namely, the *Racial Discrimination Act 1975* (Cth) and the *Fair Work Act 2009* (Cth). While at the state level, the prohibition against discrimination based on religion or belief is provided in *most* state and territory jurisdictions.[98] These are discussed consecutively below.

First, Section 9(1) of the *Racial Discrimination Act 1975* (Cth) provides that:

> It is unlawful for a person to do any act involving a distinction, exclusion, restriction or preference based on *race, colour, descent or national or ethnic origin* which has the purpose or effect of nullifying or impairing the recognition, enjoyment or exercise, on an equal footing, of any human right or fundamental freedom in the political, economic, social, cultural or any other field of public life.[99] [emphasis added]

---

97 Evans, above n 15, 138; Evans also stated that anti-discrimination laws in Australia 'may play an important role in protecting members of minority or unpopular religious groups from discrimination in areas such as employment or housing'. Carolyn Evans, 'Balancing Religious Freedom Rights and Other Human Rights' in Paula Gerber and Melissa Castan (eds), *Contemporary Perspectives on Human Rights Law in Australia* (Thomson Reuters, 2013), 475, 481.

98 *Equal Opportunity Act 2010* (Vic) ss 16–21, 30–31; *Discrimination Act 1991* (ACT) ss 7–8; *Equal Opportunity Act 1984* (WA) ss 11–17; *Anti-Discrimination Act 2004* (NT) s 19(m); *Anti-Discrimination Act 1991* (Qld) s 7(i); *Anti-Discrimination Act 1998* (Tas) s 16(o).

99 *Racial Discrimination Act 1975* (Cth) s 9(1).

While the *Racial Discrimination Act 1975* (Cth) does not expressly prohibit discrimination based on religion or belief, it "may in effect be prohibited given the above references in s10 to 'ethnic origin'."[100] In *Jones v Scully*,[101] it was held that the Jewish people can be considered an ethnic group for purposes of applying the *Racial Discrimination Act 1975* (Cth). The court took note of the fact that the Jews regard themselves as a distinct community bound by common customs, beliefs, language and other characteristics. However, the Jones ruling may only be applicable to the unique situation of the Jewish people. The same ratiocination may not apply to other religious groups who do not share the same degree of commonality in many significant respects as do Jewish people. On this point, Anthony Gray commented that '[i]t remains an open question in Australia whether followers of the Islamic faith [or other religious groups] constitute an 'ethnic group' within the meaning of the *Racial Discrimination Act 1975* (Cth)'.[102]

Second, unlike the *Racial Discrimination Act 1975* (Cth), the *Fair Work Act 2009* (Cth) provides a '[m]ore specific legal protection'[103] to non-discrimination on the basis or religion or belief, albeit only in the workplace context. Section 351(1) of the *Fair Work Act 2009* (Cth) provides that:

> An employer must not take adverse action against a person who is an employee, or prospective employee, of the employer because of the person's race, colour, sex, sexual preference, age, physical or mental disability, marital status, family or carer's responsibilities, pregnancy, *religion*, political opinion, national extraction or social origin. [emphasis added]

This provision has broadened the legal protection to include non-discrimination guarantees in the workplace in the contexts of hiring prospective employees and dismissing existing employees, unlike the former *Workplace Relations Act 1996* (Cth) which merely covered anti-discrimination guarantees in the context of terminating employment.[104] However, the non-religious discrimination guarantee in the *Fair Work Act 2009* (Cth) operates only in the context of employment. As Carolyn Evans observed, 'outside the area of employment, there is no general protection under Commonwealth law to protect people from being discriminated against on the basis of their religion or

---

100 Anthony Gray, 'Section 116 of the Australian Constitution and Dress Restrictions' (2011) 16(2) *Deakin Law Review* 293, 321.

101 (2002) 120 FCR 243, 271–273.

102 Gray, above n 100, 322.

103 Evans, above n 15, 141.

104 *Workplace Relations Act 1996* (Cth) s 659(2)(f).

belief'.[105] The state or territory legislation substantially, but not completely, fills up this gap in the law as discussed below.

Finally, all Australian jurisdictions, except New South Wales[106] and South Australia,[107] have a corresponding state or territory legislation which prohibits discrimination based on religion or belief.[108] The prohibition can be judicially enforced in those state or territory jurisdictions. It may be invoked in the courts to address unfavourable treatment in different areas including employment, education and accommodation. Another important area where the prohibition against discrimination based on religion or belief may be invoked is the 'provision of government services'.[109] It is defined by some anti-discrimination laws as 'the services of the kind provided by a government, a government authority or a local government body'.[110] As analysed below, acting on and resolving development applications for planning permits to build, extend or renovate structures constitute a 'government service', and are therefore covered by anti-discrimination legislation in most Australian jurisdictions.

The important criterion before an act can be considered a government service, as explained in *Rainsford v Victoria*,[111] is whether it is 'helpful or beneficial' to a class of individuals. As observed by Chris Ronalds and Elizabeth Raper, "a wide variety of government services have been the subject of discrimination complaints. Authorities demonstrate that the word 'services' is *of a general application* to a range of 'things' delivered by government."[112] [emphasis added]

---

105 Evans, above n 15, 141.

106 In New South Wales, it was held that, although the addition of the words 'ethno-religious' to the definition of the word 'race' did not extend the coverage of the *Anti-Discrimination Act 1977* (NSW) to include discrimination based on religion or belief, it can nevertheless cover particular groups such as Muslims. See *Jones and Harbour Pty Ltd v Trad (No 2) (eod)* [2011] NSWADTAP 62.

107 In South Australia, the *Equal Opportunity Act 1984* (SA) was amended to prohibit discrimination based on religious appearance or dress in the context of education or employment.

108 Chris Ronalds and Elizabeth Raper, *Discrimination Law and Practice* (The Federation Press, 2012), 28; Evans, above n 15, 142.

109 See, for example, the following state legislation prohibiting discrimination based on religion or belief in the provision of government services: *Equal Opportunity Act 2010* (Vic) s 73; *Anti-Discrimination Act 1998* (Tas) s 22(1)(f); *Anti-Discrimination Act 1991* (Qld) ss 101–102.

110 See, e.g., *Disability Discrimination Act 1992* (Cth) s 4(1); *Sex Discrimination Act 1984* (Cth) s 4(1).

111 [2007] FCA 1059, at [77] (Sundberg J.).

112 Ronalds and Raper, above n 108, 112.

Hence, for example, it was held that receiving and assessing applications by the relevant state government department from foster carers in relation to adoption and foster services constituted a 'government service' for purposes of applying the relevant anti-discrimination legislation.[113]

By analogous reasoning, receiving and assessing a development application for a planning permit to construct, extend or renovate a structure also constitutes a 'government service' because the applicants are being 'helped or benefited', generally construed, in the local planning process. For example, at the initial stage of a development application, applicants are apprised by the local council's planning department of the deficiencies in their proposals and given the opportunity to amend them. As noted by Nicolas Brasch, a '[l]ocal government provides important *services* in areas such as: *building and planning*, the environment, health, parking and transport, parks and gardens, and waste management'.[114] [emphasis added]

Discrimination on the basis of religion or belief may either be direct or indirect.[115] Direct forms of religious discrimination may be committed when an individual or an organisation is treated unfavourably compared with similarly situated individuals or organisations and the differential treatment is based not upon any relevant criteria other than religion or belief.[116] In the context of applications to build places of worship, a religious group may be directly discriminated against when, for example, its application is rejected simply because the local council is biased against its religion or belief.

On the other hand, indirect forms of religious discrimination may be committed when a condition or a requirement is uniformly imposed on all individuals or groups, but a particular individual or group cannot comply with such condition or requirement because of religion or belief. Ronalds and Raper explained that:

> Indirect discrimination requires a detailed examination of the facts of a situation to ascertain whether the operation of the requirement or condition appears on the face of it to be neutral and applies equally to all persons, but in fact disadvantages a particular group ...[117]

---

113 *OV and OW v Members of the Board of Wesley Mission Council* (2010) 270 ALR 542.

114 Nicolas Brasch, *Australia's Local Government* (Macmillan Education Australia, 2011), 12–13.

115 Neil Rees, Katherine Lindsay and Simon Rice, *Australian Anti-Discrimination Law: Text, Cases and Materials* (Federation Press, 2008), 74–146; Ronalds and Raper, above n 108, 31–52; Evans, above n 15, 143.

116 Bagaric *et al.*, above n 18, 165.

117 Ronalds and Raper, above n 108, 41.

In the planning context, indirect religious discrimination is perhaps more prevalent than direct religious discrimination. Chapter 6 demonstrates that facially neutral planning regulations that aim to preserve the Anglo-Celtic standards of convenience and beauty in the built environment are *inherently* discriminatory. This is because minority religious groups who have their own standards on the design and appearance of their places of worship – which are usually faith-dictated – are more likely unable to comply with such planning regulations. Although meant to have a uniform application, these regulations tend to cause more rejections of proposed places of worship with non-Anglo-Celtic architectural designs, compared to those with a 'familiar' or 'accustomed' appearance.

In summary, the principle of non-discrimination on the basis of religion or belief finds its domestic application in most Australian state or territory jurisdictions (except New South Wales and South Australia) by virtue of state legislation. Queensland, Tasmania, Victoria, Western Australia, the ACT and Northern Territory have enacted legislation which prohibits discrimination on the basis of 'religion', 'religious belief', 'religious activity', or 'religious conviction'.[118] Being part of Australian law, the principle of non-discrimination on the basis of religion or belief binds all public authorities exercising governmental functions, including local councils.

4.3.3 *Using International Human Rights Standards to Inform Administrative Decision-Making in Australia*

The two preceding sections discussed how the international standards on religious freedom are transported and accorded application into the Australian domestic jurisdiction. The ACT HRA, the Victorian Charter, and the state or territory laws prohibiting discrimination based on religion or belief are examples of incorporating such standards into the domestic legal system via the enactment of ordinary statutes. They illustrate the process whereby 'human rights norms are directly incorporated into the domestic legislation'.[119] However, the protective scope of the ACT HRA and Victorian Charter is confined only to their respective jurisdictions. And while the prohibition against discrimination based on religion

---

118 *Anti-Discrimination Act 1991* (Qld) s 7(i), Pt 4 (ss 12–102); *Anti-Discrimination Act 1998* (Tas) ss 16(o), (p), 40–42; *Equal Opportunity Act 1995* (Vic) ss 6(j), 7, Pt 3 (ss 13–68); *Equal Opportunity Act 1994* (WA) Pt IV (ss 53–66); *Discrimination Act 1994* (ACT) ss 7(h), 8, Pt 3 (ss 10–23) ss 42–43; *Anti-Discrimination Act 1992* (NT) ss 19(1)(m), 20, Pt 4 (ss 28–49).

119 Robin Creyke, 'The Performance of Administrative Law in Protecting Rights' in Tom Campbell, Jeffrey Goldsworthy and Adrienne Stone (eds), *Protecting Rights Without a Bill of Rights: Institutional Performance and Reform in Australia* (Ashgate, 2006) 101, 126.

or belief is present in most Australian state and territory jurisdictions, the other equally important elements of the right to freedom of religion or belief are not protected in those jurisdictions (except Victoria and ACT). There is, therefore, a lacuna in the statutory protection of religious freedom in Australia.

4.3.3.1 Reception of International Human Rights Standards in Administrative Decision-Making

This section discusses that such a lacuna may be filled by the reception of international human rights standards (including those pertaining to religious freedom) into the administrative decision-making processes. Like in judicial decision-making or in legislative actions, international human rights standards can permeate administrative decision-making so that those who administer or enforce the law do so in a rights-compatible manner. This section analyses the manner in which such standards are infused into administrative decision-making, including local planning processes.

In discharging their functions, administrative decision-makers exercise the power of the state. They are, for all intents and purposes, state agents. As John McMillan and Neil Williams observed:

> The capacity of the administrative arm of government to affect the human rights of individuals is great. The coercive powers exercised by government law enforcers and investigators can result in the involuntary detention of people, the confiscation of private property and papers, and intrusion into the privacy of residential and business premises.... In the distribution of grants, licenses, benefits and other concessions, government policies can exhibit discriminatory tendencies that favour one social group over another. Routine decisions by government – to provide income support, grant a visa to enter or remain in Australia, issue a business license, or approve enrolment in an educational course – will often shape the fortunes of those to whom they apply.[120]

Thus, administrative decisions can affect many aspects of a person's life that involve his or her human rights. Administrative decision-makers can respect human rights not only through their decisions but also through the manner in which they exercise the power vested in them.[121] This is particularly true with

---

120 John McMillan and Neil Williams, 'Administrative Law and Human Rights' in David Kinley (ed), *Human Rights in Australian Law* (Federation Press, 1998), 63.

121 The Hon Catherine Branson Q.C., former President of the Australian Human Rights Commission, 'Using Human Rights to Inform Administrative Decision-Making', Speech to the Council of Australasian Tribunals, 25 August 2009.

respect to local planning decisions. Kevin Sproats and Roslyn Crichton noted that '[t]he regulation of land and building development is a significant part of a broader portfolio of regulation administered by local councils across Australia'.[122] In regulating the allowable and non-allowable uses of land, local councils are acting as administrative decision-makers whose decisions potentially impact human rights. One such impact of this regulation is the restriction against the right to establish and maintain places of worship.

Given that administrative decision-making can potentially infringe on the rights of individuals or groups, administrative law was developed as 'one of the chief methods adopted in a liberal democratic society to check the exercise of governmental powers'.[123] Ryszard Piotrowicz and Stuart Kaye argued that, because administrative law is essentially at the interface between individuals and government and has the potential to impinge upon human rights, 'it occupies an important and relevant position in the recognition and protection of human rights in Australian society'.[124] On the relationship between administrative decision-making and human rights, Catherine Branson commented that:

> Administrative decision-making plays an important role in the protection of human rights. Administrative law and human rights are closely connected in their objectives. They are both concerned with the relationship between the state and the individual. Administrative law is premised upon the protection of individuals against the unlawful or arbitrary exercise of state power; and human rights impose obligations on the state to respect and protect the rights and freedoms of individuals.[125]

Therefore, the protection of human rights, including the right to freedom of religion or belief, may be accomplished not only through the enactment of legislation (that incorporates them into domestic law) but also through the adoption of 'other measures' including administrative measures. Article 2(2) of the ICCPR recognises this important alternative when it provides that 'each State Party to the present Covenant undertakes to take the necessary steps ... to adopt such legislative *or other measures* as may be necessary to give effect to the rights recognized in the present Covenant'.[126] [emphasis added] Bolstering

122 Kevin Sproats and Roslyn Crichton, 'Regulatory Reforms: Balancing Interests' in Brian Dollery and Neil Marshall (eds), *Australian Local Government: Reform and Renewal* (MacMillan Education, 1997), 247.

123 McMillan and Williams, above n 120, 63.

124 Pietrowicz and Kaye, above n 11, 281.

125 Branson, above n 121.

126 ICCPR art 2(2).

the protection provided by legislative measures or judicial remedies, administrative measures are equally important means of providing redress to individuals or groups whose human rights are violated by government action. Peter Bailey similarly argued that, in a common law system like Australia, the protection of human rights 'should be inherent in all legislative and administrative processes, with court-enforced consequences being only one part of the process. Protection and promotion of rights should not be seen as the exclusive preserve of the courts'.[127]

4.3.3.2 International Human Rights Standards as Relevant Considerations in Administrative Decision-Making

The opportunity for international human rights standards to permeate the administrative decision-making processes in Australia takes place in two contexts. They do so either because (i) there is a legal duty on the part of administrative decision-makers to consider such standards in their decision-making processes, or (ii) they *may* do so because well-settled administrative law doctrines provide them with sufficient latitude to consider such standards in arriving at just or reasonable decisions.

a *When the Use of Human Rights to Inform Administrative Decision-Making Is Mandatory*

As discussed in Section 4.3.1, the ACT HRA and the Victorian Charter impose upon public authorities the mandatory obligations: (i) to perform their powers and functions compatibly with human rights, and (ii) to take human rights into account when discharging their powers and functions.[128] These mandatory obligations consist of two parts. First, there is a negative duty not to infringe human rights, including the right to freedom of religion or belief. This duty addresses the effect of governmental actions, such that, if they resulted in a human rights breach, they can be declared unlawful. Second, there is a positive duty on the part of all public authorities to take human rights into consideration in making a decision, especially the particular human right which is most prone to be infringed by that decision.[129] This duty seeks to improve the decision-making process itself in order to infuse it with human rights considerations. Both obligations can be demanded – or in human rights parlance, 'opposable' – vis-à-vis all public authorities in Australia, including the local councils.

---

127 Bailey, *The Human Rights Enterprise in Australia and Internationally*, above n 20, 177.

128 ACT HRA s 40B(1); Victorian Charter ss 38 and 39.

129 See, e.g., *Swancom Pty Ltd v Yarra City Council* [2009] VCAT 923 (10 June 2009) and *Smith v Hobsons Bay City Council* [2010] VCAT 668 (12 May 2010), paras 37, 40.

The legal duty to take human rights into consideration in the context of planning decisions has been explained by the Victorian Equal Opportunity and Human Rights Commission (VEOHRC) when it made a submission to the Casey City Council in Victoria regarding a development application to build a mosque in January 2013. The VEOHRC emphasised the local council's legal duty as a 'public authority' to consider human rights in its deliberations. The VEOHRC stated that:

> In the context of planning decisions, human rights are vital considerations. Council must consider relevant human rights that are relevant to the mosque application, including evaluating potentially competing human rights. Through the planning process, the Council has an opportunity both to demonstrate how it protects and promotes the human rights of its residents, and that any limitations on human rights are reasonable.[130]

Independent of any statutory command like that of the ACT HRA or the Victorian Charter, the use of human rights considerations when discharging administrative powers and functions has a life of its own which is derived from the application of administrative law in Australia. As argued by John McMillan and Neil Williams, '[a]bsent a Bill of Rights, it is nevertheless the case that human rights considerations have been of growing importance in Australian administrative law'.[131] Absent any express statutory command, the use of human rights considerations in administrative decision-making in Australia is discretionary, as discussed in the next section.

b *When the Use of Human Rights to Inform Administrative Decision-Making Is Discretionary*

When there is no express statutory command to use human rights considerations, administrative decision-makers (including local councils) may nevertheless consider them in their decision-making, while at all times being guided by Australia's international human rights obligations even if they remain unincorporated into its domestic law.[132] Catherine Branson explains the rationale of this approach in administrative decision-making by stating that:

130 Victorian Equal Opportunity and Human Rights Commission, 'Submission to the Casey City Council regarding an application to build a mosque', January 2013, para 2.

131 McMillan and Wiliams, above n 120, 69.

132 Employing an analogous reasoning, Justin Glyn argues that peremptory norms of international law (*ius cogens*) may provide an objective source of human rights that can be

> even without a Human Rights Act, I believe that *there is considerable scope for Australian decision-makers to take human rights principles into account.* Decisions which are informed by human rights principles are likely ... to be better decisions leading to better outcomes for individuals while nonetheless being based on sound legal principle.[133] [emphasis added]

In *Minister for Foreign Affairs and Trade v Magno*,[134] it was stated that an international law obligation which has not been incorporated into domestic law may nevertheless be considered by a decision-maker in making a decision. Justice Gummow stated that:

> whilst the international obligation or agreement in question is not in terms imported into municipal law and the municipal law is not ambiguous, nevertheless, upon the proper construction of the municipal law, *regard may be had by a decision-maker exercising a discretion under that law to the international agreement or obligation.*[135] [emphasis added]

Similarly, in *Kioa v Minister for Immigration and Ethnic Affairs*,[136] it was held that the Minister could take into account the probable effects of deporting the parents of a child on that child's welfare. Justice Brennan stated that the decision-maker, in making a decision to deport an individual under the *Migration Act 1958* (Cth), was entitled to have regard to the ICCPR and other relevant treaties.[137] There is a similar pronouncement in *Tabag v Minister for Immigration and Ethnic Affairs*[138] which also involved the deportation of a family member where Justice Woodward stated that the ICCPR provisions 'would act as a reminder, if one were needed, of the importance of the family and the protection of children in our society'.[139]

The discretion conferred by law to certain administrative decision-makers gives them a considerable latitude or elbow room 'to fashion the considerations

---

employed to constrain administrative decision-making in immigration and refugee cases. See Justin Glyn, *Fundamental Rights in Administrative Decision-Making: Peremptory Norms as Objective Standards in Immigration and Refugee Cases* (Presidian Legal Publications, 2009).

133 Branson, above n 121.

134 (1992) 112 ALR 529 at 534–535.

135 *Minister for Foreign Affairs and Trade v Magno* (1992) 112 ALR 529 at 534–535.

136 (1985) 159 CLR 550.

137 (1985) 159 CLR 550, 630.

138 (1982) 45 ALR 705.

139 (1982) 45 ALR 705, 710.

which will be relevant to its exercise'.[140] In *Minister for Aboriginal Affairs v Peko-Wallsend Ltd*,[141] Justice Mason stated that:

> What factors a decision-maker is bound to consider in making that decision is determined by construction of the statute conferring the discretion. If the statute expressly states the considerations to be taken into account, it will often be necessary for the court to decide whether these enumerated factors are exhaustive or merely inclusive. If the relevant factors ... are not expressly stated, they must be determined by implication from the subject matter, scope and purpose of the Act. In the context of judicial review on the ground of taking into account irrelevant considerations, this Court has held that where the statute confers a discretion which in its terms is unconfined, the factors that may be taken into account in the exercise of discretion are similarly unconfined.[142]

Thus, a statute that authorises the exercise of discretion ought to be examined. Normally, a statute expressly enumerates the relevant considerations to be taken into account and the guidelines that will assist the decision-maker.[143] A statute may list the relevant considerations either in an exhaustive fashion or that they are merely inclusive. Even if they are enumerated exhaustively, the relevant considerations may be couched in broad or general terms which then require the aid of interpretive rules of construction.

In the planning context, broad considerations such as community interest, liveability, sustainability, pleasantness, or other general planning considerations do not readily lend themselves to easy application, and thus the local councils must construe them using settled rules of statutory construction. Construing these planning considerations is an opportunity for local councils to employ international human rights standards to inform their decision-making processes. When the statute that authorises the exercise of discretion does not list the relevant considerations, the discretion on the part of the administrative decision-maker is wider. In *Sean Investments Pty Ltd v MacKellar*,[144] Justice Deane stated that '[w]here relevant considerations are not specified, it is largely for the decision-maker, in the light of matters placed before him by the

140 Peter Bayne, 'Human Rights and Administrative Law' (1991) 17 *Commonwealth Law Bulletin* 320, 322.

141 [1986] HCA 40; (1986) 162 CLR 24 (31 July 1986).

142 Ibid., [15].

143 McMillan and Wiliams, above n 120, 71.

144 (1981) 38 ALR 363, at 375.

parties, to determine which matters he regards as relevant'.[145] This wider discretion is also an opportunity to make use of international human rights standards to inform the administrative decision-making process.

Aside from an express grant of administrative discretion, Catherine Branson identifies *other* possible instances when discretion is conferred to administrative decision-makers, including in the making of "decisions that require consideration of what is 'fair' or 'just' or 'reasonable' in the circumstances."[146] She explained that:

> Indeed, since no administrative decision should be made capriciously, it may be that all decisions which call for an element of judgment and where the factors to be taken into account are not exhaustively specified are decisions to which *consideration of human rights are potentially legitimate*.[147] [emphasis added]

In the above sense, therefore, the authority of local councils to allow or reject proposed structures is replete with discretion. As analysed in later chapters, the guidelines prescribed in many planning regulations are open-ended which allows local councils to impose additional requirements or conditions if they so wish. Second, the guidelines governing the external appearance or the 'out-of-character'-ness of proposed structures are subjective and imprecise. Finally, the planning statutes themselves are orientated in such a way that local councils enjoy a great degree of flexibility in planning decisions owing to their perceived knowledge of local or community needs. Therefore, local planning is an area where human rights considerations can potentially be used to inform the exercise of discretion.

There are several examples that illustrate administrative decision-making in Australia being informed by international human rights standards. The reasoning in these cases may be extended to local planning as a subject matter of administrative law. For example, in *Schoenmakers v Director of Public Prosecutions*,[148] the Federal Court considered the appeal of a man who was refused bail. When he appealed, he had already been detained for eleven months pending his extradition to another country. The issue was whether there were special circumstances justifying his release from remand. Justice French considered what he referred to as 'broader community standards' which favoured the grant of bail. In assessing

145 Ibid.

146 Branson, above n 121.

147 Ibid.

148 (1991) 30 FCR 70.

'broader community standards', he stated that 'it can never be regarded as anything other than a special circumstance that a person should have to spend a year in prison unconvicted of any offence'.[149] He then cited Article 9 of the ICCPR which protects the right of an individual against arbitrary detention. According to him, Article 9 of the ICCPR,

> serves as an indication of the value placed by Australia, as part of the international community, on the liberty of the individual and the presumption in favour of that liberty. That presumption must, of course, give way to specific statutory provisions. But where those provisions do, as in the case of the Extradition Act, allow for normative judgments ... then the presumptions arising under the common law and in relevant international instruments may be taken into account.[150]

In the above ruling, an unincorporated international human rights norm (that is, Article 9 of the ICCPR which guarantees the right against arbitrary detention) was employed to inform the exercise of discretion. The wide latitude in determining what constituted 'broader community standards' has paved the way for the application of an unincorporated international human rights norm. A similar approach can be used in construing broad or general planning considerations.

The case of *Chaudhary v Minister for Immigration and Ethnic Affairs*[151] involved an appeal from a decision denying applications for permanent residence made by the appellant on behalf of himself, his wife and two children. One of the children is a severely handicapped child. While temporarily residing in Australia, the child benefitted from the facilities of a special school and made significant improvement. Because of the decision, she faced the possibility of returning to her country of citizenship where equivalent facilities were not available. The Full Court ruled that the decision-maker had failed to take relevant considerations into account and stated that:

> we think a more realistic meaning [of Australia's interests], than is suggested by a mere concentration upon economics.... True national interest has a concern for Australia's name in the world, and *may at times involve a measure of generosity*. Certainly, it is in Australia's best interests to be seen as civilized and compassionate ... and as willing to accept some of the responsibilities of a leading country in our area of the Pacific....

149 (1991) 30 FCR 70 at 74.

150 (1991) 30 FCR 70 at 75.

151 (1994) 49 FCR 84 (Wilcox, Burchett and Foster J.J.).

> Nor could an assessment of where Australia's interests lay in the present matter ignore the negative impact in our region of a decision to put material cost so far ahead of *human values in relation to a gravely disabled child* who has now been resident here for a number of years, and is likely not only to be denied whatever chances of progress she has, but also to be condemned to regression, if thrown back on the limited resources of Fiji.[152] [emphasis added]

Again, in the above ruling, the determination of 'where Australia's interests lay' conferred the administrative decision-maker a wide degree of latitude. Such leeway was the opportunity for decision-maker concerned to consider 'generosity', and 'human values in relation to a gravely disabled child' into his or her decision-making process.

In *Walsh v Department of Social Security*,[153] a husband and wife were sentenced to three and four months imprisonment, respectively, for social security fraud under the *Social Security Act 1991* (Cth). They appealed to the Supreme Court of South Australia. Justice Perry ruled that, although the sentences were within the sentencing discretion of the lower court, the fact that the sentences would result in three young children being without their parents for several months needed to be considered. In this case, the sentencing law itself expressly provides that the probable effects of the sentencing to one's family or dependants must be factored into the sentencing decision. Justice Perry referred to Australia's international human rights obligations under the ICCPR and the Convention on the Rights of the Child which 'emphasise the protection of the family as the natural and fundamental group unit of society and the need to ensure the child such protection and care as may be necessary for his or her well-being'.[154] He stated that these treaties 'underscore the importance of the [sentencing provisions of the law], which, where possible, should be construed and applied consistently with them'.[155] He stated further that:

> It appears to me that, bearing that provision in mind, either the learned sentencing Magistrate failed to pay sufficient regard to the effect upon the appellants' three young children of a custodial sentence imposed upon both parents, or, on the basis of the additional material which has been placed before me for the purposes of the appeal, recognition of the

152 (1994) 49 FCR 84 at 87–88.
153 (1996) 67 SASR 143.
154 Ibid.
155 Ibid.

> need to have regard to the dependant children, should result in intervention by way of appeal in a form appropriate to ensure that the welfare of the children is adequately protected.[156]

The above cases demonstrate the wide latitude that exists for administrative decision-makers to infuse human rights considerations into their decision-making processes. Arriving at just, fair or reasonable decisions is facilitated by according weight to the relevant human interests or values which, in these cases, found their direct expression in international human rights standards, albeit unincorporated ones.

The impact of an unincorporated international human rights norm upon administrative decision-making was the central issue in the controversial case of *Minister of State for Immigration and Ethnic Affairs v Teoh*.[157] The main issue in this case involved the question of whether Australia's ratification of the Convention on the Rights of the Child could 'give rise to a legitimate expectation that the decision-maker will exercise that discretion in conformity with the terms of the Convention'.[158] The majority of the High Court answered this question in the affirmative. It ruled that Australia's ratification of the convention became the basis for an expectation that a decision-maker will act in conformity with it which, in effect, amounts to giving domestic effect to an unincorporated treaty. The majority stated that:

> ratification by Australia of an international convention is not to be dismissed as a merely platitudinous or ineffectual act, particularly when the instrument evidences internationally accepted standards to be applied by courts and administrative authorities in dealing with basic human rights affecting the family and children. Rather, ratification of a convention is a positive statement by the executive government of this country to the world and to the Australian people that the executive government and its agencies will act in accordance with the Convention. That positive statement is an adequate foundation for a legitimate expectation, absent statutory or executive indications to the contrary, that administrative decision-makers will act in conformity with the Convention and treat the best interests of the children as "a primary consideration."[159]

---

156 Ibid., 22.

157 (1995) 183 CLR 273.

158 Ibid., 288.

159 Ibid., 291.

The *Teoh* ruling stated that individuals like Mr Teoh could legitimately expect that administrative decision-makers will not simply give due regard to unincorporated human rights conventions (that is, the minimum obligation) but instead 'will act in conformity' with them. What sparked the legal uproar over the *Teoh* ruling was the *additional* obligation that, by virtue of a legitimate expectation, administrative decision-makers will act in accordance with an unincorporated treaty.[160]

The doctrine of legitimate expectation as enunciated in *Teoh* was re-assessed in the case of *Minister for Immigration and Multicultural and Indigenous Affairs; Ex parte Lam*[161] where the court held that a legitimate expectation merely calls for the observance of procedural due process (that is, 'natural justice') but it does not create any substantive rights as the *Teoh* ruling seemed to suggest. If an administrative decision-maker anticipates that his or her decision will infringe a human right recognised in an unincorporated treaty, an individual or group who stands to be adversely affected by that decision should be given an opportunity to be heard why that decision should not be taken. Rather than creating substantive rights, a legitimate expectation only encompasses the idea that international human rights norms 'can found an expectation which is legitimate and which should not therefore be disappointed without according natural justice to the person concerned'.[162] In the case of *Untan v Minister for Immigration and Multicultural and Indigenous Affairs*,[163] the Full Federal Court reiterated the 'procedural' nature of the benefit or advantage which can be derived from a legitimate expectation.

Notwithstanding the qualification to the *Teoh* ruling made in subsequent cases like *Lam* and *Untan*, it is necessary to bear in mind that there is one principle recognised in *Teoh* (as well as in the other cases cited above) that remains unaffected and unscathed by these later cases. The *Teoh* case remains good authority on the capacity of administrative decision-makers to take into account human rights considerations in their decision-making processes, even if those human rights find direct expression only in unincorporated human rights

160 Successive Australian administrations sought to cancel the legal ramifications of the *Teoh* ruling by making statements that there was no intention to give rise to any legitimate expectation and by proposing legislation designed to eradicate its legal effect. See Debeljak, 'Does Australia Need a Bill of Rights?', above n 13, 50–51; However, it was only South Australia which enacted a law nullifying the *Teoh* ruling. See *Administrative Decisions (Effect on International Instruments) Act 1995* (SA).

161 (2003) 214 CLR 1.

162 Bayne, above n 140, 322.

163 (2003) FCAFC 69.

treaties. 'To take into account' does not necessarily mean that they are obliged to satisfy human rights claims (that is, to give direct effect to them). It simply means that administrative decision-makers, in exercising their powers and functions, need to be cognisant of international human rights standards in addition to the other considerations or factors already mentioned by their enabling statutes. If human rights considerations outweigh other considerations, then decision-makers should apply human rights not because they are complying with the provisions of unincorporated human rights instruments but because they are rendering just, fair or reasonable decisions as administrative law guides them to do.

4.4 Conclusion

This chapter has highlighted an uneven state of affairs when it comes to the legal protection of religious freedom across Australia. Such protection may indeed be described as 'patchy'. Victoria and the ACT incorporated international standards on religious freedom into their respective jurisdictions and accorded them different means of application including, but not limited to, judicial enforceability – that is, allowing claims of violations of religious freedom to be adjudicated in the courts. By virtue of incorporation, the international standards on religious freedom exist in Victoria and the ACT. Although their means of application may have certain weaknesses, as pointed out in the discussion, such weaknesses do not diminish their juridical existence in those jurisdictions. They have successfully crossed the 'dualist' barrier; and they are part of the law in those jurisdictions. In addition, most Australian states and territories, except New South Wales and South Australia, have legal protection against discrimination based on religion or belief in different areas, including the provision of government services which encompass local land use and planning. Religious groups which are victims of direct or indirect forms of discrimination in their applications to build, extend or renovate places of worship can invoke this legal protection to seek redress.

The discussion in this chapter points to the conclusion that the vehicle with the best potential to transport international human rights standards on religious freedom into the Australian jurisdiction and to give them domestic application is the system of administrative law and jurisprudence which allows, in fact encourages, the infusion of such standards into the administrative decision-making processes. In particular, this chapter demonstrated that local councils in Australia are either legally mandated, or at least expected, to take into consideration the international human rights standards pertaining to religious freedom in their planning decisions. Being administrative bodies, the local councils can and should infuse their planning decision-making process, especially when it involves proposed places of worship, with considerations of religious freedom norms including most relevantly the right to establish and maintain places of worship.

This chapter completes the analysis of the applicable law relevant to this book's motivating question – that is, the international human rights standards on religious freedom, including the right to establish and maintain places of worship. Using case studies as a backdrop for discussion, the next three chapters are an empirical investigation of the functioning of the local planning system in Australia in an effort to evaluate its compatibility, or otherwise, with such standards. These group of chapters put to the real test, so to speak, the applicable law whose provenance, meaning and applicability have been analysed in Chapters 2, 3 and 4, respectively.

PART 3

Evaluating Compliance with the Law

CHAPTER 5

'Amen versus Amenity'

The Protection of the Physical Amenity of an Area and its Impact on the Right to Establish and Maintain Places of Worship

5.1 Introduction

This chapter is the first of three chapters that analyse how the international standards on religious freedom are being complied with in the local planning processes in Australia. Through the use of case studies, these chapters collectively make a case that the principles and concepts that underpin the local planning processes in Australia, as they currently stand, tend to impede the spatial and structural aspect of the right to freedom of religion or belief – that is, the ability of religious groups to appropriate sufficient physical space for their worship and other needs. Such impediment experienced by religious groups is inconsistent with the international standards of the right to freedom of religion or belief, particularly the right to establish and maintain places of worship.

In these three chapters, the conformity of the local planning processes with the afore-mentioned right is evaluated in the context of three local planning objectives, namely, the protection of 'physical amenity', the preservation of 'visual amenity' and the enforcement of 'specific design controls'.[1] The chapters demonstrate that these planning objectives run the risk of colliding with the state's obligation to respect the right of religious groups to establish and maintain places of worship. It bears stressing that it is the Australian local planning system itself which is being evaluated in this book vis-à-vis the international standards on the right to freedom of religion or belief. The commonality of the regulatory tools used in the local planning processes across Australia and the concepts and principles underpinning them makes such a system-wide evaluation possible. The respective chapters on physical amenity, visual amenity and specific design controls are aimed at demonstrating that the local planning processes in Australia are predisposed to infringing the international standards on religious freedom, including the right to establish and maintain places of worship.

This chapter is divided into three parts. The first part discusses the concept of 'amenity' in local planning and unpacks its main components including its physical and visual aspects. The second part analyses planning controversies involving proposed places of worship where issues involving inadequate

1 These planning objectives are analysed in Chapters 5, 6 and 7, respectively.

 | DOI 10.1163/9789004289345_006

parking, excessive vehicular traffic, generation of noise, and similar tangible 'dis-benefits' to a locality played a pivotal part in planning decisions rejecting a development application. Using nine case studies, this chapter examines the decisions of local councils as regards these 'physical amenity' issues and their implications to the constituent elements of the right to freedom of religion or belief, including the right to establish and maintain places of worship. Finally, this chapter concludes that the local councils in Australia, in their zealous aim of protecting the physical amenity of local areas, are likely to infringe important elements of the right to freedom of religion or belief, including the right to establish and maintain places of worship.

5.2 Distinguishing between 'Physical Amenity' and 'Visual Amenity' in Local Planning

In assessing any development application for any proposed structure, local councils consider its likely impact upon the 'amenity' of an area. Planning scholar Leslie Stein noted that amenity 'is always the foremost consideration in the determination of a development application'.[2] However, eluding a precise definition, amenity encompasses a whole gamut of considerations that can potentially produce effects which are detrimental to the convenience of local residents.[3] Thus, considerations that deal with the 'bulk, scale, height and character of the development, floor area, car parking, traffic impact, noise, architectural form, location and availability of public transport, minimum width block, site coverage and landscape'[4] are all taken into account when evaluating any proposed development or use of land. There is no standard definition of amenity in Australian local planning. However, a number of common elements are encompassed by the concept as shown, for instance, by the following explanation by the New South Wales Land and Environment Court in *New Century Developments Pty Limited v Baulkham Hills Shire Council*[5]:

> The concept of 'amenity' is wide and flexible, transcending the merely physical content. The following passage ... attempts to articulate the

---

2 Leslie Stein, *Principles of Planning Law* (Oxford University Press, 2008), 188.

3 David L. Smith, *Amenity and Urban Planning* (Granada Publishing Limited, 1974), 11–29.

4 John Skennar, 'Sydney, A City Growing Within: The Establishment of Buddhist Centres in Western Sydney' (Centre for Cultural Research, University of Western Sydney: Post-Suburban Sydney Conference 2005), 5.

5 [2003] NSWLEC 154 (30 July 2003).

> notion: 'The wide-ranging concept of amenity contains many aspects that may be very difficult to articulate. Some aspects are practical and tangible such as traffic generation, noise, nuisance, appearance, and even the way of life of the neighbourhood. Other concepts are more elusive such as the standard or class of the neighbourhood, and the reasonable expectations of a neighbourhood'. 'Amenity' may embrace the effect of a place on the senses, as well as the residents' subjective perception of their locality. Knowing the use to which a particular site is, or may be, put may affect one's perception of amenity.[6]

In a similarly broad fashion, the concept of amenity has been explained as follows:

> Amenity is an elusive concept. It has its usual meaning of pleasantness, but also has a wider ambit. It has a physical (or tangible) component, which could include character and appearance of building and works, proximity to shopping facilities, quality infrastructure and absence of noise, unsightliness or offensive odours. It has been said to embrace all the features, benefits and advantages inherent in the environment in question.[7]

From the above explanations, it may be inferred that the concept of amenity has a composite character which consists of two primary elements, namely: (i) the material or tangible convenience offered by a locality including, for example, the smooth flow of vehicular traffic, the adequacy of parking spaces, or the tranquillity of a neighbourhood, and (ii) the visual satisfaction derived by looking at the physical landscape including, for example, the beauty of Victorian houses lining a street, the congruence of buildings with equal bulk and height, or the predominantly green landscape of an agricultural area; or stated otherwise, it is the absence of unsightliness. The former, which is referred to in this book as 'physical amenity', is more or less quantifiable based on objective criteria; while the latter, sometimes referred to by planning scholars and practitioners as 'visual amenity',[8] is subjective and often eludes precise measurement. These two primary elements of amenity and their intersection with religious freedom norms are analysed separately in this book.

---

6 Ibid., [53]–[54].

7 Victorian Government Solicitor's Office, Client Newsletter, 'What is Amenity?' (August 2008), 1.

8 Stein, above n 2, 193–195.

5.3 Resolution of Physical Amenity Issues and How it Impinges on the Right to Freedom of Religion or Belief

Using case studies, this chapter analyses concrete examples of how local councils in Australia perform their function of protecting the 'physical amenity' of localities in the context of development applications for the construction, extension or renovation of places of worship. The following sections analyse physical amenity issues arising from such applications such as inadequate parking spaces, excessive vehicular traffic, generation of noise or odour, and similar tangible 'dis-benefits' to an area where a place of worship is proposed. The resolution of these issues by the local councils is examined, particularly as regards its implications to the constituent elements of the right to freedom of religion or belief, including the right to establish and maintain places of worship.

5.3.1 *When Claims of Negative Impact upon the Physical Amenity are Unfounded*

Planning decisions that allow or refuse particular development or use of land are made with the aim of ensuring, among other things, that proposed structures like places of worship will not cause inadequate parking, excessive traffic, unreasonable noise, foul odour and similar tangible 'dis-benefits' to a locality. Local councils may refuse an application to build a place of worship when, in their assessment, the proposed religious structure will lead to any of these undesired outcomes upon the physical amenity of an area. As shown below, the inadequacy of parking spaces, the exacerbation of vehicular traffic, the generation of noise or odour, and similar adverse effects upon an area's physical amenity are staple grounds for objections against proposed places of worship. Thus, local councils are confronted with the task of resolving claims of adverse impact upon the physical amenity. The first case study illustrates how such a task – seemingly simple and straightforward at first – may be accomplished in a manner which is consistent (or otherwise) with the dictates of the right of religious groups to establish and maintain places of worship.

Case Study 5(a)
New Century Developments Pty Limited, Applicant
Baulkham Hills Shire Council, New South Wales

In October 2002, the applicant lodged a development application for the construction of a single storey building for use as a place of worship with 62 parking spaces.[9] The proposal contained three hall areas and ancillary rooms.

---

9 *New Century Developments Pty Limited v Baulkham Hills Shire Council* [2003] NSWLEC 154 (30 July 2003).

It was to be used as a mosque by a local Muslim community. The proposed hours of operation were Monday thru Friday from 8 am to 9.45 pm, and Saturday and Sunday from 9 am to 9.45 pm. The maximum number of people using the facility would be up to 110 attending services twice per week, and up to 250 persons on three occasions per year.[10] Outside these times, it would be used for individual prayer, counselling, Sunday school, funerals and weddings and administration. The application was advertised and 5,181 submissions were received, of which all except 11 submissions opposed the application.[11] In December 2002, the Baulkham Hills Shire Council rejected the application on the grounds that, among others, the proposed structure would create parking and traffic problems in the area, generate unreasonable noise and destroy the area's flora and fauna. The applicant appealed to the New South Wales Land and Environment Court.

During the appeal, the Baulkham Hills Shire Council presented a town planner as a witness who stated, among others, that '[t]he congregation of people from outside the area raised questions of the introduction of traffic that has no other reason to be there [and] the potential for the generation of noise and other nuisance effects'.[12] Some local residents objected that the proposal would impact on the flora and fauna on the subject site. In response, the applicant submitted a technical study prepared by an expert on traffic and parking management which concluded that there would be no traffic or parking problem as a result of the proposal.[13] The applicant also submitted a report prepared by an acoustic expert which concluded that the noise generated by the proposed mosque would not be audible from adjacent residences at any time.[14] Finally, the applicant submitted an assessment done by an environmental expert who concluded that the site is already highly developed and that it does not provide a habitat, nor will the removal of trees impact on any threatened species or ecological communities.[15]

The New South Wales Land and Environment Court reversed the local council's decision and ruled that the proposed mosque would not have an adverse impact on the physical amenity of the area. The Court explained the local councils' task of assessing objections based on alleged negative effect upon the area's physical amenity, stating that:

> the consent authority must not blindly accept the subjective fears and concerns expressed in the public submissions. Whilst such views must be

10 Ibid., [7]–[9].
11 Ibid., [6].
12 Ibid., [31].
13 Ibid., [40].
14 Ibid., [44].
15 Ibid., [47].

> taken into consideration, there must be evidence that can be objectively assessed before a finding can be made of an adverse effect upon the amenity of the area. Whilst the court is clearly entitled to have regard to the views of residents of the area, those views will be accorded little, if any, weight if there is no objective, specific, concrete, observable likely consequence of the establishment of the proposed use.
>
> A fear or concern without rational or justified foundation is not a matter which, by itself, can be considered as an amenity or social impact... Where there is no evidence to support a rational fear it will be irrelevant that members of the community may have modified their behaviour arising from such an unjustified fear.
>
> It follows that in forming an opinion on the probable impact of a proposed development on the amenity of an area, tangible or otherwise, a court would prefer views from residents which are based upon specific, concrete, likely effects of the proposed development.[16]

Consistent with the above ruling, any claim by local residents (or finding by a local council) that the operation of a proposed place of worship will negatively impact the physical amenity of an area ought to be strictly scrutinised to ensure they are not specious. The veracity of any claims or findings must be proven on the basis of expert evidence. Questions about traffic condition, parking availability, noise generation and similar factual issues are usually beyond the expertise of local councils. Therefore, deference to traffic, parking, acoustic or other experts is required to establish the veracity of claims regarding negative effects of a proposed religious structure upon the physical amenity of an area. Local councils should not simply yield to unfounded or bare claims of traffic congestion, excess off-street parking, noise, or waste problems.

In *Telstra Corporation Ltd v Hornsby Shire Council*,[17] the New South Wales Land and Environment Court similarly held that:

> an evaluation must be made of the reasonableness of the claimed perceptions of adverse effect on the amenity of the locality, and that involves the identification of evidence that can be objectively assessed to ascertain whether it supports a factual finding of an adverse effect on the amenity of the locality....
>
> Our findings, including those in relation to the issues of... traffic on Forum Drive South, are based on the expert evidence; the evidence of the

16 Ibid., [61]–[63].

17 [2006] NSWLEC 133; (2006) 146 LGERA 10.

> neighbouring residents where based on objectively assessable and specific likely effects or impacts of the proposed development.[18]

In rendering planning decisions, a deference to the conclusions of experts on traffic, parking, noise or similar physical amenity issues is consistent with the observance of the principle of non-discrimination based on religion or belief. It ensures that any refusal of an application to build a place of worship is not motivated by discriminatory or intolerant attitudes towards any religious group (or towards religion in general) but such a refusal is actually supported by 'objective, specific, concrete, observable likely consequence of the establishment of the proposed use'.[19] Therefore, the deference to experts in resolving physical amenity issues in planning controversies flows from and is a logical dictate of the application of the principle of non-discrimination based on religion or belief which forms part of the substantive content of the right to establish and maintain places of worship, as discussed in Chapter 3.

While a proposed place of worship may be refused by local councils because of its unreasonable adverse impact upon an area's physical amenity, it is important to ensure that such a justification is not a subterfuge for any discriminatory intent. On their face, local planning regulations may appear neutral but they may be selectively enforced for discriminatory purposes against disfavoured religious groups.[20] It is usually the members of a migrant community that are particularly vulnerable to discrimination based on their religion or belief.[21] Their vulnerability is largely explained by the difficulties associated with being transplanted to a foreign environment, the linguistic and cultural barriers and the economic displacement they experience as newly arrived members of society.[22]

Consistent with the principle of non-discrimination based on religion or belief, local councils should satisfy themselves of the existence of any alleged adverse impact upon the physical amenity by resorting to expert evidence. Such a reliance aims to prevent unwarranted bias or favour towards any party, whether for or against the construction of a proposed place of worship. It is an effective means of ensuring that the non-discrimination guarantee is fully

---

18 Ibid.

19 *New Century Developments Pty Ltd v Baulkham Hills Shire Council* [2003] NSWLEC 154 [61].

20 Susan Thompson, 'Planning and Multiculturalism: A Reflection on Australian Local Practice' (2003) 4(3) *Planning Theory & Practice* 275, 276.

21 Donovan Storey, Salut Muhidin and Peter Westoby, 'Planning for Social Inclusion in a Multicultural Urban South East Queensland' (2010) 47(3) *Australian Planner* 142.

22 Ibid.

observed in the planning application process. The non-religious discrimination principle assumes greater relevance in controversies involving the construction of non-Christian places of worship in Australia where the state is called upon to mediate between a local majority population (who wields political influence and who may be opposed to new religious structures) and a minority religious community (who usually lacks such influence).[23]

The next case study illustrates a stark departure from the above dictate of relying on experts to help resolve physical amenity issues. The local council failed to give proper consideration, much less credence, to the conclusion of acoustic experts and rejected the daily use of a mosque because of its alleged adverse impact on the material amenity of a local area, including the quietness and tranquillity of the place. The local council disregarded expert evidence that the daily operation of a mosque would not bring about an excessive noise level which was a crucial issue in dispute.

Case Study 5(b)
Anthony Mundine and Hazem El Masri Association, Applicant
Canterbury Council, New South Wales

In August 2008, Anthony Mundine and Hazem El Masri Association (AMHMA) lodged a development application with the Canterbury Council in New South Wales for the conversion of its existing building into a mosque.[24] Anticipating that the practice of the call to prayer (*adhān*) will not be allowed by the local council, the applicant decided not to include it in its application. In October 2009, the council approved the application but with the conditions that the mosque could only be used three days per week (Wednesdays, Thursdays and Fridays), must not have more than 25 persons inside the mosque at any one time, and only during restricted hours of operation.[25]

The applicant expressed its disappointment about the restrictions placed on the operation of the proposed mosque. An officer of AMHMA stated that 'Muslims have been neglected and ignored. Our prayer takes about 15 minutes and it's very silent and then everybody goes home. The [local council's] recommendations are not feasible and we think these restrictions are very unfair'.[26]

23 See especially, Kevin Dunn, 'Repetitive and Troubling Discourses of Nationalism in the Local Politics of Mosque Development in Sydney, Australia' (2005) 23(1) *Society and Space* 29–50; Nahid Kabir, *Muslims in Australia: Immigration, Race Relations and Cultural History* (London: Kegan Paul, 2005), 180–206.

24 Development Application No. DA/486/2008, Canterbury Council, New South Wales.

25 Joanne Vella, 'Mosque Approved with Muslim backlash', *The Express*, 19 October 2009.

26 Ibid.

One resident was upset with the decision to restrict the use of the mosque and said, 'I think the council is trying to tell us how to pray'.[27] One local council member, who supported the application for the daily use of the mosque, stated that the 'Muslim community prays seven days a week and the hours [prescribed by the local council] do not meet the requirements of the applicants'.[28]

In August 2010, while the construction of the mosque was ongoing, AMHMA lodged a second development application and pressed for the daily use of the mosque from 4.30 am to 11 pm.[29] Knowing fully well that the call to prayer would only jeopardise the application, AMHMA did not bother to seek the local council's permission for it just like in its first application. The second application was supported by an expert assessment conducted by acoustics engineers who had determined that the likely noise level generated by the normal, daily use of the mosque would be acceptable because it falls 'within [the range of] each of the nominated noise criteria'.[30] The new application generated conflicting views from the public, including a petition signed by 562 individuals (including non-local residents) opposing the daily use of the mosque and another petition signed by 77 local residents supporting it.[31]

In October 2010, the Canterbury Council rejected the second application.[32] Responding to the charge that the application was railroaded, Mayor Robert Furolo stated that the daily use of the mosque from 4.30 am to 11 pm would adversely impact the convenience and comfort of the local residents and that the Council's decision was based solely on planning grounds.[33] On the issue of noise generation, the local council has determined that it would be at an unreasonable level during the proposed hours of operation, especially the Friday midday prayers. However, this finding by the local council was not supported by any expert evidence and, therefore, the acoustics report submitted by AMHMA showing the level of noise to be within a reasonable range remained unrefuted. It is worth noting that the issue is not even the negative impact of the call to prayer (*adhān*) upon the peace and quiet of the area (to be discussed in Section 5.3.3), but merely the alleged noise to be generated by the daily use of the mosque.

In the preceding case study, the Canterbury Council failed to satisfy the dictate of the non-discrimination guarantee in the planning application process

27 Ibid.

28 Ibid.

29 Development Application No. DA-456/2010, Canterbury Council, New South Wales.

30 Koikas Acoustics, 'Acoustic Assessment Place of Worship', 12 July 2010.

31 Joanne Vella, 'Application to Run Ludgate St Mosque Seven Days a Week', *The Express*, 12 October 2010.

32 Development Application Decision, Canterbury Council, 22 October 2010.

33 Joanne Vella, 'Council Says no to Daily Worship at Roseland Mosque', *The Express*, 18 October 2010.

that physical amenity questions must be resolved using competent and expert evidence. The failure of the Canterbury Council to give due weight to the acoustic expert's report was contrary to the demands of the non-discrimination principle in planning application processes: first, the alleged negative effect upon the physical amenity of a place must be real and not simply imagined. Subjective fears of local residents which are not supported by evidence are not a sufficient basis for rejecting an application. Second, adverse impact upon the material amenity of the neighbourhood must be clearly demonstrable in fact. Claims that a proposed place of worship will exacerbate traffic conditions, cause excess off-street parking, or generate excessive noise are easy to allege but are more difficult to prove. The burden of proof is on the part of the objectors to substantiate claims of adverse impact upon the physical amenity.

On such factual issues, local councils should render a decision which is evidence-based and not simply a capitulation to unfounded assertions raised by objectors. Claims that the operation of places of worship will adversely affect the physical amenity of an area should be treated as issues of fact, which are best resolved through competent evidence. In the above case study, the professional assessment of acoustics experts that the noise level to be generated by the daily use of the mosque would fall within the 'acceptable range' should have received a proper consideration by the Canterbury Council. The same may be said about the issue of traffic congestion – that is, it must be objectively determined. A bare allegation that the operation of a place of worship will cause an overflow of cars in local streets will not suffice as a justification to reject a proposed place of worship. Consistent with the demands of the non-discrimination guarantee in the planning application process, the findings of traffic engineers on whether or not a proposed place of worship poses traffic congestion or traffic safety issues must receive due consideration by local councils.

5.3.2 *When 'Religious Need' is not Considered Relevant in Resolving Physical Amenity Issues*

Even if the allegation of an adverse impact upon the physical amenity of an area is supported by expert evidence, that factor alone should not automatically lead to a refusal of an application to construct, extend or renovate a place of worship. While that factor must be considered by local councils, it should not trump all other relevant considerations, most especially a religious community's need for prayer facilities. As discussed in Chapter 2, the duty to respect the right to freedom of religion or belief obligates the state to allow the greatest possible exercise of religious manifestation. It requires that local councils should enable the realisation of the applicant's religious interest in having an adequate prayer facility. The importance of that religious interest flows from the symbiotic relationship between the right to establish and maintain places of worship and the other constituent elements of the right to freedom of religion or belief as analysed in Chapter 2. The next case study explains why a religious group's pressing need for a place of worship is a relevant consideration in local planning decisions.

Case Study 5(c)
Jehovah's Witnesses, Applicant
Gold Coast City Council, Queensland

In December 2002, the members of a Jehovah's Witnesses group lodged a development application with the Gold Coast City Council to construct a place of worship which was to have two auditoriums and associated libraries, meeting rooms, a separate caretaker's residence and 100 parking spaces.[34] The proposed building was a single storey with a gross floor area of over 1,000 square metres. It was relatively modest, low design and looked like a large residential dwelling.[35] The applicant had an existing place of worship which was too small to sufficiently accommodate its members who used it as a venue for worship activities and religious instruction.[36]

In September 2005, the application was rejected by the Gold Coast City Council on the grounds that, among others, unacceptable impacts upon the physical amenity of the area would result from the size and scale of the proposed structure. The applicant appealed the decision to the Queensland Planning and Environment Court. A local neighbourhood association, the Friends of Currumbin Association Inc, joined the local council in opposing the appeal.[37]

During the appeal, the expert witnesses called by the local council failed to identify any unacceptable impact on the physical amenity as a result of the size and scale of the proposed place of worship.[38] For example, the evidence of the lighting and noise experts showed that there were no unacceptable impacts in the areas they addressed.[39] While there would be an increase in traffic on a nearby major road, the traffic engineer concluded that the estimated

---

34 *Steensen v Gold Coast City Council* [2007] QPEC 48 (8 June 2007) [4].
35 Ibid.
36 Ibid., [8].
37 Ibid., [1].
38 Ibid., [35].
39 Ibid., [39].

vehicular flow was within acceptable limits for a road with its dimensions.[40] The Queensland Planning and Environment Court held that the local council erred in refusing to grant the application. The Court stated that:

> Even if meaningful conflict with either planning scheme had been found there are planning grounds which would readily overcome the conflict. *The most compelling of these is need – the need for a conveniently located place of worship to advance and promote religious, social and cultural wellbeing for this religious group.* The evidence showing details of the numbers and location of worshippers confirms there is a large population of this religious community in this part of Queensland, pressing this need.
>
> The evidence ... was persuasive that there is 'a latent and unsatisfied demand on the part of persons affected by the planning scheme which is not being met nor being adequately met by the scheme in its present form'. The group has searched long and hard for an alternative to its [existing] premises, which are too small. This site is convenient to the congregations which use it; has good access from the road network; is of sufficient size to ensure the Kingdom Hall can be appropriately landscaped in a way which both provides an attractive amenity for those in the congregation, and for the benefit of the community at large; and, provides all other appropriate, convenient and safe facilities for the group.[41] [emphasis added]

Based on the Court's reasoning quoted above, a religious group's need for a place of worship may, in appropriate cases, obligate local councils to disregard a proposal's inconsistencies with relevant planning instruments and approve the application to build a place of worship. 'Religious need' is an appropriate planning ground that must be factored in the decision-making equation of local councils. As observed by Stein, if a particular use is needed in a community, 'it is seen from a planning point of view as a use whose existence would be in the public interest, and therefore could be considered to *override* the amenity concerns of adjoining neighbours'.[42] [emphasis added] Stein added that a use may override amenity concerns especially if a use is 'public in nature'.[43] The same significance was ascribed to 'religious need' in *Bethel New Life*

40 Ibid.

41 Ibid., [40]–[41].

42 Stein, above n 2, 208.

43 Ibid., 212.

Christian Fellowship Inc v Greater Dandenong City Council[44] where the Victorian Civil and Administrative Tribunal stated that:

> planning is to recognise social needs by providing land for a range of accessible community resources including cultural facilities, and that land use and development planning must support the development and maintenance of communities with adequate safe and physical and social environments for their residents through the appropriate location of uses and developments and quality of urban design. I consider that the proposal is supported in all of these respects, and in particular it would help meet a social need in this community.[45]

In a similar vein, in *Kotku Education and Welfare Society Inc v Brisbane City Council,*[46] the Queensland Planning and Environment Court stated that:

> It is clear this religious group has a latent and unsatisfied demand for a place of religious observance which reflects its ethnic and cultural background. City Plan does not appear to make adequate provision for minority religious groups, like this one. Unlike the position which arose in the *Baptist Union* case, the congregation does not already have a satisfactory and useable, albeit too small, facility available to it – and, it seems, has encountered great difficulty in finding one. This small group would certainly be advantaged by approval, as would the community in general if important matters involving religious and cultural tolerance, and the encouragement of diversity, are taken into account. These factors all press the conclusion that, notwithstanding the small size of the appellant group, it is entitled to raise the question of need, and, indeed, has established it exists to a high degree.[47]

In the above-quoted decisions by appellate tribunals, the priority given to 'religious need' as a consideration in local planning decisions suggests that local councils should exhaust all means to either remove or minimise the potential adverse impact of a proposed religious structure upon an area's physical amenity. Refusing an application should be the last resort, after local councils have attempted, in good faith and in consultation with the applicant religious

---

44 [2009] VCAT 1778 (27 August 2009).

45 Ibid., [36].

46 [2004] QPEC 68 (5 November 2004).

47 Ibid., [60].

community, all practical measures to remove or minimise such adverse impact upon the physical amenity.

However, despite the significance of 'religious need' as a planning consideration, it is given little weight by some local councils in Australia which sometimes rigidly enforce facially-neutral planning regulations. The consequence of such rigid enforcement of planning regulations has been noted by Donovan Storey *et al.* who stated that "in the attempt to practice planning as a 'rational regulatory' exercise, planning has often excluded migrant populations."[48] Laura Beth Bugg made a similar point when she stated that, by choosing a purportedly neutral stance, some local councils 'act only on issues of land use, while avoiding the question of whether there was value to recognising the particular claim of a religious minority group to stake its claim to city space'.[49] Aiming to avoid the charge of being biased, some local councils unjustifiably cling to the façade of neutrality being offered by the rigid application of the black-letter provisions of planning regulations. In resolving planning disputes involving places of worship, they inflexibly rely on facially neutral and generally applicable provisions of planning instruments. Such a stance of 'technical rationality', while giving the appearance of equal and uniform enforcement of planning rules to all members of society, and regardless of their secular or religious objectives, is inconsistent with the state's duty to respect the right to establish and maintain places of worship.

In *Case Study 5(b)* discussed above, the mayor of the Canterbury Council, responding to the charge that the development application was railroaded, denied that religious discrimination had been a factor in the local council's decision. He stated that the rejection of the application for the daily use of the mosque was a simple enforcement of planning rules, and it was exclusively based on planning grounds as this would adversely impact the convenience of local residents.[50] It is worth noting the mayor's particular invocation of planning rules as though it automatically and effectively counters any charge of religious discrimination. By his statement, he was actually revealing his subconscious state of mind in what he believed to be his role in these controversies – that is, as an impartial decision-maker who exclusively relies on the black-letter provisions of facially neutral planning instruments that

48 Storey *et al.*, above n 21, 146.

49 Laura Beth Bugg, 'Religious Freedom and the Right to the City: Local Government Planning and the Rejection of Islamic Schools in Sydney, Australia' (Workshop Paper, Twelfth Berlin Roundtables: Religious Pluralism, Irmgard Coninx Stiftung, 7–11 April 2010), 8.

50 Joanne Vella, 'Council Says no to Daily Worship at Roseland Mosque', *The Express*, 18 October 2010.

prescribe rules on parking, traffic, noise, frontages, setbacks, bulk, height, colour and similar factors, but *not* the 'religious need' of the applicant.

The next case study illustrates how a local council can overly emphasise strict compliance with planning regulations designed to protect an area's physical amenity, while according very little consideration to the pressing 'religious need' of an applicant religious group to have an adequate place of worship. Which of these factors deserved greater emphasis was the main issue in the appeal.

Case Study 5(d)
Chabad House of Malvern Toorak Inc, Applicant
Stonnington City Council, Victoria

The applicant lodged a development application with the Stonnington City Council to extend its existing synagogue and to reduce the previously imposed car parking condition.[51] The synagogue used 30 parking spaces provided by its onsite parking and a nearby parking lot. It is located in an area where there is a substantial Jewish population and the proposed extension was aimed at satisfying their need for an accessible place of worship.[52] The synagogue is situated in a zone where places of worship are allowed to be constructed subject to conditions from the local council.[53] The applicant was aware that the proposed expansion of its synagogue would likely increase the demand for kerbside parking in the surrounding area. Citing its parking regulations applicable to the area, the Stonnington City Council refused the application on the main ground that the proposed synagogue would exacerbate the insufficiency of parking spaces in the surrounding streets. The applicant appealed this decision to the Victorian Civil and Administrative Tribunal.

On appeal, the main issue was whether the impact that the proposed synagogue might have on the amenity of the surrounding residential area (and in particular the physical amenity of enjoying sufficient kerbside parking spaces available in nearby streets) would outweigh the community benefit of having a synagogue with sufficient capacity to accommodate its members. The Tribunal held that the increase demand in parking spaces as a result of the synagogue's expansion (which is 30 parking spaces, by its estimate) is not so significant as to warrant refusal of a permit, given that the synagogue provides

51 *Chabad House of Malvern Toorak Inc v Stonnington City Council* [2001] VCAT 1448 (6 July 2001) [2].

52 Ibid., [10].

53 Ibid., [10].

a significant social benefit for many other members of the local community.[54] Recognising the applicant's religious need, the Tribunal held that:

> Synagogues have to be adjacent to residential areas. It appears from the Responsible Authority and respondent objectors' submissions that their answer is to keep such facilities as small as possible so that impacts are small in scale also. The respondent objectors submitted for example that no expansion should be allowed beyond that already permitted, namely no more than 80 on the Sabbath and 120 to 180 persons on High Holy days. This is despite the fact that the local Jewish community, within reasonable walking distance of Chabat House, comprises substantially more than these numbers.
>
> I have not been persuaded that to hold numbers to the limits advocated by the [local council and objectors] is a fair or reasonable planning outcome. The social and economic effects of such a finding would be significant for the local Jewish community – it would mean that those within walking distance would be restricted in their attendances. It would also prevent the celebration of festive days with the whole local community in attendance. *This social impact must be balanced against the policy guidance of not impacting on the amenity of residential areas by, among other things, reducing the availability of kerbside parking*.[55] [emphasis added]

The rigid reliance of the Stonnington City Council on its parking guidelines led to its decision to refuse the synagogue's extension. Its undue focus on the inability of the applicant to meet the parking guidelines blinded it from realising that the increase in parking demand of 30 parking spaces could be 'comfortably accommodated within the area given the fact that the site fronts Glenferrie Road'[56] where parking spaces are not always difficult to find as determined by the Tribunal. A strict reliance on the black-letter provisions of planning instruments usually leads to a refusal of a development application, notwithstanding the clear 'religious need' that a proposed structure would satisfy. Also realising this grave outcome, the Queensland Planning and Environment Court stated in *Steensen v Gold Coast City Council*[57] that:

> the relevant principles include an approach to construction which best achieves the apparent purposes and objects of the [planning] schemes; …

54 Ibid., [31].

55 Ibid., [13]–[14].

56 Ibid., [31].

57 [2007] QPEC 48 (8 June 2007).

> reading them broadly, and not pedantically, and mindful that strategic plans set out broad desired objectives, not every one of which must be completely met before a proposal can be approved; and, remembering that they are not drawn with the precision of an Act of Parliament and statements of intent, or aims or objectives within them are not intended to provide anything more than guidance for the task of balancing the relevant facts, circumstances and competing interests in order to decide whether a particular use should be rejected as inappropriate.[58]

From the above, it may be extrapolated that the provisions of planning instruments are mere guidance to aid local councils in decision-making, and planning instruments 'should be read and applied in a practical common sense way, rather than in an overly technical way. They should be interpreted in a way which will best achieve their evident purpose'.[59] They should not be mechanically enforced with a pedantic rigor so as to lose sight of the necessity to balance the 'religious need' of an applicant with protecting the physical amenity of an area. Taking into account 'religious need' in the decision-making process of planning authorities is consistent with respecting the right to freedom of religion or belief, and it promotes the greater exercise of religious manifestation. Therefore, the 'religious need' consideration is a window of opportunity for local councils to inform their administrative decision-making with the international human rights standards on religious freedom, including the right to establish and maintain places of worship, as discussed in Chapter 4.

5.3.3 *When the Unique Worshipping Practices or Pattern of Religious Groups are Overlooked or Ignored in Resolving Physical Amenity Issues*

Different religions prescribe different forms of worshipping practices. While some require worshipping in community with co-believers, others emphasise an individualistic orientation such as meditation. While some religious groups require daily attendance in places of worship, others prescribe attendance only on particular days and times. While some perform worship activities by singing alongside a live band performance, others require relatively quiet hymns and chants like the Buddhists,[60] or complete silence during communal

58 Ibid., [48].

59 *Baptist Union of Queensland v Brisbane City Council* [2002] QPEC 41 [11].

60 See generally, David L. Gosling, 'Buddhism: India and Southeast Asia' in John Bowker (ed), *Cambridge Illustrated History of Religions* (Cambridge University Press, 2002), 72–89.

prayer like the Quakers.[61] The differences in worshipping practices are many and reflect theological differences, but all are manifestations of religious belief in worship which are protected.

Problems arise when planning regulations are enforced uniformly and without regard to the unique worshipping practices of individual religious groups. In *Case Study 5(b)*, the local council capped the maximum number of mosque attendees to 25 persons at any given time on the basis of a prescribed ratio between the building's floor area and number of occupants.[62] This decision did not properly consider that Muslims pray side-by-side with each other in a manner that maximises the available physical space.[63] Hassan Mourad described the prescribed manner of praying for Muslims inside a mosque (the '*salat*') which illustrates how the use of space is maximised:

> Assuming that more than one individual is partaking, *salat* are performed in parallel rows, following the movements of a leader, known as the Imam, all facing towards the Kabba in Mecca. Physically, the rows indicate the main spatial direction to which a mosque or prayer hall should correspond. Since worship is relatively simple, mosques require minimal furniture, for example, not necessitating the use of chairs, pews and the like.[64]

Thus, the ratio between floor area and number of occupants used by the local council in *Case Study 5(b)* as the justification for limiting the maximum number of mosque attendees is purely arbitrary and based on ethno-centric assumptions of what constitutes 'comfort' – that is, one that requires a wider personal territorial space. It does not take into account, as it should, the unique worshipping practice of Muslims that does away with that space, a practice that points to the value of egalitarianism in Islamic belief.

Similarly, planning guidelines on traffic, parking and noise emission are sometimes enforced in a 'colour-blind' manner which fails to appreciate the unique worshipping practices of individual religious groups. Different worshipping practices have a direct bearing on how religious groups use their

---

61 See especially, Daniel Steinbock, *Making Silence Together: Collaboration in the Silent Gatherings of Quakers* (PhD Thesis, Stanford University, August 2012), 1–146.

62 Vella, 'Mosque Approved with Muslim Backlash', above n 25.

63 Hassan Mourad, *The Development and Land Use Impacts of Local Mosques* (Undergraduate Thesis, Faculty of the Built Environment, Planning and Urban Development Program, University of New South Wales, 2006) 31.

64 Ibid.

places of worship which, in turn, affects the impact on an area's physical amenity. The failure of local councils to consider each religious group's unique worshipping practices sometimes results in a finding that the area's physical amenity is or is likely to be adversely affected, and thus justifies refusing an application to build, extend or renovate a place of worship. The next three case studies further illustrate this.

Case Study 5(e)
Vietnamese Buddhists Nuns Association
Greater Dandenong City Council, Victoria

The applicant, the Vietnamese Buddhists Nuns Association, lodged a development application with the Greater Dandenong City Council in 2004 for the construction of a two-storey building containing a hall to be used for worship activities, a patriarch hall, a refectory and a general hall, with onsite parking spaces.[65] The proposed building was to be used as a temple for Buddhist nuns. It was expected that three to four nuns would reside in the temple and, several times a day, would 'carry out prayer and chanting practices as well as meditation and there could be up to 30 people attending prayer sessions on a daily basis'.[66] The application was advertised and elicited 22 objections from the public, but not from the immediate neighbours of the site.[67] The objections related mainly to insufficient car parking, heavy traffic and noise. In particular, one objector expressed concern about the likely noise from the proposed temple and the change it would bring into the community that was residential in character.[68] The application had been referred to the local council's traffic and drainage engineers who concluded that the proposal would be satisfactory, subject to conditions.[69] However, the local council disregarded the conclusions of its own engineers[70] and decided to refuse the development application on the ground that the proposed temple would have an unreasonable impact on the amenity of the neighbourhood, including its likely generation of an unacceptable level of noise. The applicant appealed the decision to the Victorian Civil and Administrative Tribunal.

65 *Ferencz Baranyay Architects v Greater Dandenong City Council* [2005] VCAT 934 (20 May 2005) [5]–[6].
66 Ibid., [12].
67 Ibid., [9].
68 Ibid., [15].
69 Ibid., [9].
70 Ibid., [9].

The Tribunal reversed the local council's decision and stated that 'it flies in the face of the factual evidence and advice not only of the applicant's experts but also [the local council's] own experts'[71] that the proposed temple would not adversely impact the physical amenity of the surrounding area. The Tribunal gave credence to a Buddhist abbot who was presented as a witness on behalf of the applicant and testified as to the activities likely to occur within the proposed temple. Agreeing with this witness, the Tribunal stated that:

> the nuns did not attract the larger numbers of people who attended monasteries and their activities are different to the extent that they place less emphasis on catering for larger numbers of people at their services. In any event because Buddhism does not require compulsory attendance at his temples the numbers are generally much smaller than those encountered by Christian and Jewish denomination.
>
> ...
>
> While I have not attended a Buddhist facility in Australia I have certainly had experience with them in parts of Asia such as Thailand and Vietnam. What impressed me most with them was the quietness. Any chanting was low and not discernible outside the buildings. I failed to see how an increased activity on four occasions a year is going to cause any detriment to the surrounding area. It must be remembered that a significant amount of the time spent by Buddhists particularly their religious in temples is in meditation which by nature is a silent act.[72]

In the foregoing case, the local council failed to consider the unique worshipping practice of Buddhists which consists primarily of devotional meditation and relatively low level recitations, hymns and chants. It also failed to take into account that, in Buddhism, temple attendance is not mandatory and that communal worship is not religiously prescribed in the same manner as in Islam, Judaism or Christianity. Such a failure led the local council to arrive at a finding that the operation of the proposed Buddhist temple would generate excessive noise. The application may not have been rejected had the local council been aware of, and appropriately considered, these facts.

The foregoing case study also illustrates the effective deployment of noise complaints to exclude the religious 'other' from using the public sphere. For the local objectors, the operation of the proposed Buddhist temple would pose as an audible intrusion into their locality's tranquillity. However, such an objection

---

71 Ibid., [29].

72 Ibid., [13] and [26]–[27].

was not supported by the facts and was occasioned only by the lack of understanding of the manner in which Buddhists use physical space in their devotional practices. As Peter Edge stated, 'planners need to consider the doctrines and practices of the religious group in question, rather than apply some general idea of what religious groups do'.[73]

Noise complaints are particularly successful in preventing the use of the call to prayer (*adhān*) by Muslims in Australia. In fact, it may be stated that there is a *de facto* ban against the call to prayer across Australia. In *Case Study 5(b)* above, the applicant did not even bother to seek the local council's permission for the use of the call to prayer because it knew fully well that the call to prayer would only jeopardise its application. Similarly, in *Case Study 6(f)* in the next chapter, the applicant Muslim group decided that the call to prayer would be done inside the building and would not be heard from outside the property, thus defeating the call to prayer's original meaning and purpose. In some Australian localities, there is a tendency to regard sounds coming from religious newcomers as a type of noise, and thus should be muted or dampened in order to protect an area's physical amenity. But this has repercussions beyond the protection of amenity because it also offers an important indication of whether minority religious groups have attained genuine acceptance in the Australian localities where they find themselves in. Who has the right to make religious 'noise' freely may ultimately be equated with who does or does not belong in society.

In the next case study, the Greater Dandenong City Council committed the same failure to take into account a religious group's unique worshipping practices which led to the rejection of a proposed upgrading of a place of worship.

Case Study 5(f)
Dandenong Islamic Society Inc, Applicant
Greater Dandenong City Council, Victoria

In July 2004, the Dandenong Islamic Society Inc lodged a development application with the Greater Dandenong City Council for the upgrading of its mosque which was serving the Turkish community in Dandenong.[74] The site where the mosque is located contained a significant range of local institutional uses, including a school, hospital, recreation centre and other places of worship.[75]

---

73 Peter Edge, *Legal Responses to Religious Difference* (Kluwer Law International, 2002), 328.

74 *Dandenong Islamic Society v Dandenong City Council* [2005] VCAT 2501 (28 November 2005) [3].

75 Ibid., [1].

In July 2005, the Dandenong City Council refused the development application on the grounds that, among others, the proposal provided inadequate car parking in an area where there is already an increased demand for short-term parking during business hours on Mondays to Fridays. The local council relied on the specific guidelines (Clause 52.06) contained in the Dandenong Planning Scheme which governs onsite-parking for places of worship.[76] The guidelines set a benchmark of 0.3 parking spaces for each seat or square metre of floor area, whichever is higher.[77] The proposal failed to satisfy the required number of parking spaces under this benchmark. The applicant appealed the decision of the council.

During the appeal, the Victorian Civil and Administrative Tribunal found that the key issue with the proposal was the adequacy of the proposed car parking arrangements. The Tribunal held that the level of on-site car parking in the proposal was acceptable and the proposal should not be refused on parking grounds. In particular, it took notice of a crucial fact about the worshipping patterns of Muslims which the Dandenong City Council had failed to properly take into account in its decision. The Tribunal stated that:

> Most critically, it seems to us a major "plus" for the proposal that the typical peak parking demand period is the middle of the day on each Friday. At this time we expect that many local residents will have driven their cars off to work and/or be less likely to have visitors drive to see them at home, compared to a weekend situation (say with Christian churches that have a Sunday morning peak worship period). While we acknowledge that there is already some demand for business hours local on-street parking from the other nearby institutional uses, we nevertheless consider that the local street work has the capacity in the middle of each Friday to readily accommodate considerable extra on-street parking as a result of worshippers attending at the mosque.... In relation to the likely higher parking demand during the month of Ramadan, we acknowledge this is an issue but ultimately this is only one of 12 months in the year and we see the impacts here as being within acceptable parameters.
>
> ...In terms of what is appropriate and fair in this case, we consider this existing pattern points to a greater degree of flexibility in considering here whether 41 on-site spaces is acceptable. In other words, one might rhetorically ask how many existing places of worship across Melbourne would be forced to close if every one of them was strictly expected to provide on-site parking to satisfy the bulk of their peak parking demand.[78]

76 Ibid., [22]–[24].

77 Ibid.

78 Ibid., [52]–[53].

The Greater Dandenong City Council's uniform enforcement of the Dandenong Planning Scheme provisions governing parking spaces for places of worship did not adequately appreciate, as it should have, the unique worshipping pattern of Muslims and the activities inside a mosque – that is, the peak of mosque attendance takes place only during Friday midday prayers. This means that the parking demand on other days and times would be significantly lower. In *Islamic Education and Welfare Association of Dandenong v Casey City Council*,[79] it was stated that:

> As occurs at places of worship involving other religions, there would be peak days (that can be likened to Christmas and Easter in the Christian Church) but that does not provide a basis for refusal in itself... In our view, the situation of one or two peak days is also not a basis to require on-site parking when such a facility would be severely underutilised for most of the rest of the year.[80]

Based on the above decision, resolving physical amenity issues, including claims of inadequate parking, must take into account the unique worshipping practices or patterns of applicant religious groups. To do otherwise is to invite the possibility of imposing stricter requirements that religious groups may find difficult to comply with. Reversing a local council's finding of inadequate parking spaces in a mosque proposal, the New South Wales Land and Environment Court in *Afgan Community Support Association v Blacktown City Council*[81] also recognised certain peculiarities of mosque attendance when it stated that:

> The Friday afternoon prayer session is outside peak hour traffic volumes and avoids the peak generation periods for the Blacktown High Schools. The demand for parking is similar to that which currently exists and occurs when many residents of nearby properties are at work and there is adequate on street parking available.[82]

Similarly, the practice of orthodox Jews of not using motorised vehicles during their principal day of worship (the Sabbath) is a relevant factor in assessing the demand for parking spaces for a synagogue. In *Chabad House of Malvern Toorak*

---

79 [2004] VCAT 1850 (16 September 2004).

80 Ibid., [55].

81 [2008] NSWLEC 1357 (4 July 2008).

82 Ibid., [28].

Inc v Stonnington City Council,[83] the Victorian Civil and Administrative Tribunal stated that:

> an orthodox synagogue represents something of a conundrum in this respect. Off-street parking may cater for day to day – that is weekday religious observance and administration – but on the principal day of worship, namely the Sabbath which extends from Friday evening to Saturday evening, a car park is not a facility which members of the congregation are in a position to use.[84]

Furthermore, in *Chabad*, it was recognised that car parking demand is typically much lower for a synagogue than other places of worship because the facility is usually close to much of the congregation, encouraging walking; congregations often involve or encourage family groups; and the strict observance of the Jewish faith dictates that motor vehicles not be used on the Sabbath and most High Holy Days.[85]

The above examples of unique worshipping practices or patterns must be factored in by local councils in assessing the adequacy of a proposal's car parking arrangements. To disregard them on the basis of a 'colour-blinded' or uniform application of rules may lead to the imposition of a requirement for more parking spaces than are actually needed by a religious group. Thus, in a similar case in Canada, it was observed that 'institutional uses are sometimes submitted to fairly stringent requirements as regards parking spaces, while in reality many congregations have only a limited number of members (or members who do not drive to their place of worship)'.[86] In *Case Study 5(f)* above, the administrative appeals tribunal accorded sufficient weight to the applicant's worshipping practices or pattern which became the basis for the decision imposing fewer car parking requirements. A different outcome occurred in the next case study.

Case Study 5(g)
Mimar Architects Pty Ltd, Applicant
Hobsons Bay City Council, Victoria

The applicant, Mimar Architects Pty Ltd, lodged a development application with the Hobsons Bay City Council in 2006 for the construction of a mosque

83 *Chabad House of Malvern Toorak Inc v Stonnington City Council* [2001] VCAT 1448 (6 July 2001).
84 Ibid., [12].
85 *Lennon v Glen Eira City Council* [2004] VCAT 1345 (14 July 2004) [68].
86 Annick Germain and Julie Gagnon, 'Minority Places of Worship and Zoning Dilemmas in Montreal' (2003) 4(3) *Planning Theory & Practice* 295, 305.

and a multi-purpose space or court.[87] The proposal involved the construction of a two-storey building and 24 car parking spaces[88] which would serve the Muslim community in Hobsons Bay, Victoria. A large number of local residents opposed the proposal principally because of alleged insufficient car parking spaces to service the facility.[89] Agreeing with the objectors, the Hobsons Bay City Council refused the development application. The applicant appealed to the Victorian Civil and Administrative Tribunal.

During the appeal, the applicant's expert witness submitted that the proposal provides on-site parking for all its daily activities, except Friday midday prayers.[90] At that time, however, sufficient car parking is available on a nearby major road to service the ultimate desired attendance of 80 persons, while relying only on non-residential frontages. The applicant's expert witness pointed out that peak attendance in the facility would only occur for a short period of time because there is little social activity before and after daily prayers.[91] The shortfall in parking during Friday midday prayers was agreed by the experts of both parties to be 13 to 15 parking spaces, based on an expected attendance for Friday midday prayers of up to 80 persons.[92] Despite the agreed finding of the experts that the shortfall was only 13 to 15 parking spaces, the Tribunal affirmed the ruling of the Hobsons Bay City Council that the proposal failed to meet the car parking demands associated with its regular activities without an unreasonable impost on the available public parking supply. The Tribunal stated that:

> In terms of the evidence before us, the pivotal issue revolves around Friday services. However, we do not think that regular activity can simply be separated from the number of occasions over celebratory days when greater overflow parking would occur to accommodate 100 to 200 persons. A limited number of peak days occur in the Christian Church (Easter and Christmas). By contrast, the proposal relies on around 50% or more of the non-residential frontages each Friday over a year, plus two days for Eid, plus Ramadan that extends over 30 days. Numerically, if operating at the capacity requested, this could mean on-street spaces are used more than 20% of days in one year.
>
> We do not consider it appropriate to allow one use to absorb so much of the available resource for such extended periods. Even though the

87 *Mimar Architects Pty Ltd v Hobsons Bay City Council* [2007] VCAT 1184 [1].

88 Ibid., [6].

89 Ibid., [2].

90 Ibid., [21].

91 Ibid., [22].

92 Ibid., [23].

> times of day involved with the peak periods vary from morning, lunchtime and evening, we find this over-steps reasonable reliance on the public resource having regard to the manner in which other land uses operate.[93]

The Tribunal's decision above reveals its lack of full understanding of the worshipping practice or pattern of Muslims. In particular, the Tribunal was mistaken in considering that Muslims are religiously required to go and pray inside a mosque during all the Ramadan days in a manner similar to the religiously obligatory Friday midday prayers when religious attendees arrive and leave a mosque *en masse*.[94] On the contrary, during the Ramadan, attendance in a mosque is merely recommended especially during the 8.00 in the evening prayer (*taraweeh*) when there are less road users and parking demand; it is not religiously obligatory in the same manner as the Friday midday prayers. During the Ramadan, what is faith-dictated is that Muslims abstain as far as practicable from worldly pleasures. Therefore, it is erroneous to regard the Ramadan days as 'celebratory days' which are usually associated with a flurry of activities and the consequent generation of noise, excessive traffic and increased parking demand.

It also bears stressing that the Tribunal's finding that the shortfall of 13–15 car spaces would unreasonably take up a public resource (that is, the available on-street parking) was based on the express comparison it made between Christian and Muslim worship practices or patterns. It found that the use of the mosque would generate a greater demand for parking spaces over a one-year period than that of a Christian church over the same period. Such a comparison illustrates the hidden bias which is sometimes deeply ingrained in societies with a Christian majority where activities of minority religious groups are scrutinised using a Christian 'lens'. In such societies, the state regulation of religious activities is sometimes undertaken while employing Christian standards and benchmarks of what constitutes reasonable or unreasonable imposts on the amenity of a place. The long-term effect of such state regulation is to stifle the activities of non-Christian religious groups, which places it in a direct conflict with the state's duty to allow the greatest possible exercise of religious freedom.

---

93 Ibid., [26]–[27].

94 For the significance of the Friday midday prayers in Islam, see Ruth Gavison and Nahshon Perez, 'Days of Rest in Multicultural Societies: Private, Public, Separate?' in Peter Cane, Carolyn Evans and Zoö Robinson (eds), *Law and Religion in Theoretical and Historical Context* (Cambridge University Press, 2008), 195–196.

5.3.4 *When the Protection of the Physical Amenity Produces a Restrictive Effect upon Religious Exercise*

Sometimes, the conditions imposed by local councils when they approve a development application to build, extend or renovate a place of worship directly restrict the right to manifest one's religion or belief. For example, in *Case Study 5(d)*, it was suggested by some local objectors that the operation of the synagogue be controlled 'in more minute detail'[95] as to the days and hours of operation in order to preserve the adequacy of kerbside parking in the surrounding streets. The Tribunal discounted such a suggestion and stated that:

> The social and economic effects of such a [limit on the days and hours of operation of the synagogue] would be significant for the local Jewish community – it would mean that those within walking distance would be restricted in their attendances. It would also prevent the celebration of festive days with the whole local community in attendance.
>
> ...
>
> While it might be open to control days and hours of operation and attendance levels in more minute detail than is proposed in this determination I am of the view that to do so would be *to unacceptably fetter the flexibility of this place of worship to cater for changing needs*.[96] [emphasis added]

The following case study illustrates how the conditions imposed by a local council on the operation of a place of worship can have a restrictive effect, in the real and physical sense, on a religious community's freedom to worship. These conditions had a significant adverse impact upon religious exercise because they effectively forced a religious group to modify its worshipping practices or patterns.

Case Study 5(h)
Wat Sangharatanaram Inc, Applicant
Gold Coast City Council, Queensland

In December 2007, Wat Sangharatanaram Inc, a Buddhist religious association whose members were mostly Thai immigrants, lodged a development application with the Gold Coast City Council for a permit to construct a temple and an

95 *Chabad House of Malvern Toorak Inc v Stonnington City Council* [2001] VCAT 1448 (6 July 2001) [31].

96 Ibid., [14] and [31].

associated structure on its property in Nerang, Queensland.[97] The association proposed the construction of a 15-metre high Buddhist temple with a traditional Thai architectural design and an auxiliary residence for its monks.[98] Under the proposal, the temple would cater for a maximum of 300 worshippers. The Gold Coast City Council received two petitions containing the signatures of 44 individuals who were opposed to the construction.[99] In addition, the council received several letters from local residents expressing their opposition, citing the potential adverse impact of the proposed temple upon the locality including excessive traffic, inadequate parking and the tranquillity of the area.[100]

In March 2010, the Gold Coast City Council approved the application, but subject to conditions that, in the applicant's view, would hinder the manifestation of their beliefs. Despite the conditions, the applicant did not appeal the local council's decision.[101] The conditions included the following:

(i) The proposed Place of Worship shall be limited to a maximum of eighty (80) persons attending the subject site at any given time except during major events or days of special significance in line with the Holy Buddhist Calendar;
(ii) The major events or days of special significance shall not exceed six per year. A 'management plan' has to be approved by the local council for every such event or day. The plan must contain plans for the traffic management, vehicle access, parking, noise management, and hours of operation.[102]

The decision of the Gold Coast City Council, which was anchored on the need to protect the physical amenity of the area, capped the number of religious ceremonies, events or festivities ('major events or days of special significance in line with the Holy Buddhist Calendar') to six per year. It subjected a significant part of the Buddhists' exercise of the right to manifest their religious beliefs to a system of prior administrative approval. The practical effect of such

97 Melinda Marshall, 'Row over Gold Coast Buddhist Temple', *Local Gold Coast News*, 5 March 2010.
98 Ibid.
99 Ibid.
100 See, e.g., Letter of Greta Lewis to the Gold Coast City Council, 25 November 2008; Letter of IR and JA Gardner to the Gold Coast Council, 17 November 2008.
101 Acceptance of Decision Notice for Development Application, 5 May 2010.
102 Decision Notice to Applicant, Place of Worship, 26 March 2010.

a decision was to ban such religious ceremonies, events or festivities unless a permit was secured, in advance, from the local council. Thus, the Buddhist organisation could not hold such religious ceremonies, events or festivities without a pre-approved 'management plan'. Worse, the council's decision did not specify any guidelines or standards of traffic management, vehicle access, parking, noise management, and hours of operation. Thus, the result was that the exercise of freedom of worship was subject to the whim or caprice of the local council. W Cole Durham observed the danger of such unfettered discretion conferred upon local planning authorities in general when he stated that:

> [t]his gives them the flexibility and power to make reasonable adaptations, but it also means they are open to behind-the-scenes pressures and sources of discrimination that can be all too easily masked. The result can be that the rules are administered in ways that make it difficult or impossible to establish places of worship that meet the needs of religious communities.[103]

The Gold Coast City Council's decision was problematic not because of the vagueness of the guidelines or standards but the utter lack of them. In this situation, non-existent standards attract the danger that the local council would discriminate against the applicant under the pretext of enforcing planning regulations. Such being the case, every application to hold 'major events or days of special significance in line with the Holy Buddhist Calendar' is subjected to the whim, caprice and unfettered discretion of the local council. Emphasising the importance of specifying such standards especially in an enforcement order issued by planning authorities, Edge noted that:

> If the religious interests of residents are to be given proper weight in the planning process, those responsible for enforcement should inform the residents what is acceptable in their situation, especially where the objectionable conduct consists of an increase in the volume of a use of a property, generally referred to as intensification ... To leave the border between acceptable and unacceptable behaviour undefined in an enforcement order is to expose religious activity to a chilling effect, one felt especially by those most eager to obey the law.[104]

---

103 W. Cole Durham, 'Places of Worship: Enhancing Implementation of a Core Right' (Introductory Remarks for Session III of the Supplementary Human Dimension Meeting on Freedom of Religion or Belief, Vienna, Austria, 9–10 July 2009), 3.

104 Peter Edge, *Religion and Law: An Introduction* (Ashgate, 2006), 128–129.

The situation then becomes one of unguided discretion on the part of local planning authorities which runs counter to one of the requirements of permissible limitations to the right to manifest one's religion or belief under Article 18(3) of the ICCPR – that is, the limitation must be 'prescribed by law', to be analysed in detail in Chapter 8. As observed by Roman Podoprigora, '[t]he wider the discretionary authority, the more it is possible for those who wield the authority to conceal the true reasons for their decisions'.[105]

That prior administrative approval must be secured before certain religious ceremonies, festivities or gathering can be performed is inconsistent with the right to freedom of religion or belief. Like other fundamental human rights, the right to worship is not dependent on state consent or authorisation. It is an inherent entitlement of an individual or a religious group, and not a mere privilege to be granted by the state. Being an entitlement that *inheres* in every human being, the default position of state authorities should be to allow the free exercise of the right to worship and restrict the same only when any of the grounds for permissible limitations under Article 18(3) of the ICCPR are shown to be attendant.

As many of the case studies in this chapter illustrate, the exercise of discretion by local councils is reviewable by the respective administrative appeals tribunals in the Australian states and territories. On many occasions, initially 'bad' planning decisions by local councils are overturned by such tribunals as part of the existing administrative review process in Australia. Such process is crucial in the protection of human rights, in general, and the right to freedom of religion or belief, in particular, because it allows for the possibility that an administrative decision-maker (exercising appellate jurisdiction) may inform his or her decision-making with human rights considerations, as analysed in Section 4.3.3.

However, it is important to note that not every applicant religious group has the required resources to institute appellate proceedings to seek a reversal of local planning decisions. Especially for start-up religious groups and those with small membership, the high costs of legal as well as expert services may present an insurmountable hurdle in availing administrative review. As discussed in Section 4.3.3, local councils as administrative decision-makers themselves have the opportunity – in the first instance – to inform their planning decisions with human rights considerations, including the right to freedom of religion or belief. This represents an available legal avenue to constrain or circumscribe an otherwise unguided exercise of discretion in local planning as exemplified by the above case study.

---

105 Roman Podoprigora, 'Freedom of Religion and Belief and Discretionary State Approval of Religious Activity' in Tore Lindholm, W. Cole Durham, Jr and Bahia G. Tahzib-Lie (eds) and Elizabeth A. Sewell and Lena Larsen (associate eds), *Facilitating Freedom of Religion or Belief: A Deskbook* (Martinus Nijhoff Publishers, 2004), 425, 439.

5.3.5 *When the Protection of the Physical Amenity Results in Religious Discrimination or Intolerance*

Objections against a proposed place of worship may not only come from local residents but also from other religious groups which already have an established presence in a locality. In such a situation, the observance of the principle of non-discrimination based on religion or belief by local councils acquires greater significance. In *Canterbury Municipal Council v Moslem Alawy Society Ltd*,[106] Justice McHugh stated that:

> Australian courts should be slow to adopt an interpretation of a legislative instrument which would have the effect of preventing the use of premises in a neighbourhood by some of those who wish to practice their religion while at the same time allowing others to practice their religion in the same neighbourhood. The preservation of religious equality has always been a matter of fundamental concern to the people of Australia and finds its place in the Constitution, s 116.[107]

However, religious equality in the eyes of state authorities is sometimes a difficult aim to achieve in a society with diverse religious demographics. In such a society, it sometimes occurs that places of worship of different religious groups are located close to each other, thus forming a so-called 'church belt'. In this context, physical amenity problems such as inadequate parking spaces, congested traffic and excessive noise are magnified and present a more difficult challenge on the part of local councils whose planning decisions must at all times strictly observe a 'religious equality' stance in the event of inter-religious disputes. The next case study illustrates how a physical amenity issue in a planning application may pit one religious group against another. The official action of the local council reveals the difficulty in implementing religious equality.

Case Study 5(i)
Hamerkas Shelanu Inc, Applicant
Glen Eira City Council, Victoria

The applicant, Hamerkas Shelanu Inc, lodged a development application with the Glen Eira City Council in 2003 to construct additions to its existing building for the purpose of a Jewish community centre which would comprise a synagogue and crèche as well as facilities for Hebrew language and Jewish

106 (1985) 1 NSWLR 525.

107 Ibid., 543–544.

education classes.[108] The applicant's existing building was on a site located on a main arterial road and beside another place of worship, the St John's Uniting Church which has an on-site parking for 15 cars.[109] The applicant's building was previously used for a 30-bed nursing home, and that use of the property had enjoyed shared parking arrangements with the Uniting Church, until the building was proposed to be converted into a synagogue.[110]

The proposed synagogue would provide for religious services with the main services on Saturdays (10 am to 2 pm) accommodating up to 100 people. Up to 15 people would also participate in daily prayer sessions within the centre in the early morning (7 am to 7.45 am). On Friday evenings, it was expected that up to 30 people would attend a half-hour evening service at dusk (6 pm–6.30 pm). The applicant also proposed building office spaces for its rabbi and his assistant and, as required, for teachers and others working in its educational programs.[111]

Under the applicant's proposal, there was no provision for on-site parking.[112] The applicant submitted a Traffic and Parking Management Plan, developed in consultation with the local council staff, which only relied on kerbside parking in several local streets adjacent to non-residential frontages (so as not to affect the local residents' parking).[113] However, the kerbside parking in these local streets was also being used by members of the Uniting Church whenever its own 15 onsite parking spaces were occupied.

In January 2004, the Glen Eira City Council approved the applicant's proposal on the condition that it secured an 'agreement with the adjacent [Uniting] Church to ensure some availability of parking'.[114] The Uniting Church did not agree to any parking arrangement with the applicant.[115] The applicant and some local residents appealed the local council's decision to the Victorian Civil and Administrative Tribunal.

During the appeal, the applicant argued that, in assessing its proposal's parking arrangements, the Tribunal must consider the fact that there are sufficient kerbside parking spaces in several local streets identified in its Traffic and Parking Management Plan.[116] However, taking notice of the fact that

108 *Lennon v Glen Eira City Council* [2004] VCAT 1345 (14 July 2004) [12].
109 Ibid., [4].
110 Ibid., [6].
111 Ibid., [14]–[18] and [21].
112 Ibid., [23].
113 Ibid., [72].
114 Ibid., [23].
115 Ibid., [78].
116 Ibid., [72].

members of the Uniting Church are already using those kerbside parking spaces, the Tribunal was not persuaded.[117] The Tribunal held that the decision of the local council must be set aside and no permit issued. On whether the applicant was justified in relying on the use of the kerbside parking in the local streets, the Tribunal stated that:

> *Obviously, that would impact on others, such as those associated with activities at the Uniting Church who would be forced to other locations.* Taking into account this evidence, I am not satisfied that the conditions are workable in practice.[118] [emphasis added]

In addition, the Tribunal appeared to prioritise non-religious establishments in the locality like supermarkets and shops in the allocation and use of the available kerbside parking when it stated that:

> off-street car parks in the wider area are associated with supermarkets and shops that also generate parking demands and whose needs may increase in time given the re-development of retail premises in the business precincts. It seems to me that the proposal seeks too much on a site that does not provide for any of its parking needs.[119]

Two noteworthy observations can be made about this case. First, the Glen Eira City Council effectively relinquished to another religious group the power to decide whether or not the applicant's proposal to convert its existing building into a synagogue would be approved. In effect, 'state authority is delegated to religious leaders' which, as Roman Podoprigora argued, constitutes an 'impermissible delegation of authority'.[120] This is the practical effect of the condition that the applicant must first secure an agreement with the Uniting Church to devise a shared parking arrangement. It is a complete abdication of the state's duty to observe the principle of non-discrimination based on religion or belief. Podoprigora has also observed this type of impermissible delegation of authority in other countries, when he stated that:

> situations in which state authority is delegated to religious leaders are unusual. Nonetheless, such problems do tend to recur, particularly when

117 Ibid.

118 Ibid.

119 Ibid., [74].

120 Podoprigora, above n 105, 437.

> they take *non-obvious forms.* A religious association that wishes to perform public worship must sometimes obtain permission from the official or state-recognized church, even when not otherwise required by law.[121] [emphasis added]

In the preceding case study, the delegation of authority to the Uniting Church was 'non-obvious' but the practical effect was the same – that is, it was completely up to the Uniting Church whether or not to give consent to a shared parking arrangement with the applicant. Thus, the outcome of the latter's application was also dependent on the decision of the Uniting Church.

Second, the Tribunal effectively favoured the Uniting Church over the applicant in the allocation and use of the kerbside parking spaces in the local streets, a use which the Tribunal itself ironically characterised as part of the 'public realm'.[122] In *Chabad House of Malvern Toorak Inc v Stonnington City Council*,[123] the Tribunal also characterised kerbside parking spaces as part of the public realm when it agreed with the 'submission that kerbside parking is a *public resource* and not something owned per se by abutting residents, although obviously they are the greatest beneficiaries'.[124] [emphasis added] The Tribunal's actions again contravened the principle of non-discrimination based on religion or belief. The above case study exemplifies the type of discrimination in local planning processes in Australia referred to by Carolyn Evans who stated that '[t]here is reason, however, to believe that sometimes formally neutral planning decisions hide some degree of religious discrimination'.[125] Edge also observed that, in general, local planning rules sometimes give undue favour towards established religions or beliefs when he stated that:

> Even if planning law is not used as a tool to limit the growth of a particular religious community, it can still be used to discriminate between religious groups. An obvious example is where a particular religious group is treated under special planning rules, perhaps on the basis of its longer presence in the territory of the State, or a special connection with the State.[126]

121 Ibid.

122 *Lenon v Glen Eira City Council*, above n 108, [78].

123 [2001] VCAT 1448 (6 July 2001).

124 Ibid., [23].

125 Carolyn Evans, 'Religion and the Secular State in Australia', in Javier Martinez-Torron and W. Cole Durham (General Reporters), *Religion and the Secular State/La religion et l'État laïque* (The International Center for Law and Religion Studies, 2010), 87, 94.

126 Edge, *Religion and Law: An Introduction,* above n 104, 122.

In enforcing planning regulations meant to protect an area's physical amenity, local councils must ensure that such regulations are not used for ulterior purposes to favour or hinder a particular religion or belief. Religious equality should underlie such regulations.

Sometimes, planning regulations may also be imposed in *bad faith* to disadvantage a particular religious group. In *Church of Jesus Christ v Casey City Council*,[127] the local council was the vendor of the land upon which a Mormon church was proposed to be constructed. The sale of the land was subject to the condition that the Mormon religious group obtain a planning permit. During the negotiation for the sale, the contracting parties clearly understood that a Mormon church was intended for the site. However, after the development application was lodged by the Mormon group, the Casey City Council rejected it on the main ground that the proposed church was in the wrong zone. Reversing its earlier position, the local council found that the proposed Mormon church was not an appropriate non-residential use in a residential area[128] and that '[t]he proposal is unsuitably located having regard to traffic considerations and would tend to generate traffic hazards'.[129] The decision reeks of bad faith because the local council was in fact 'initially pro-active in the selection of this site against other sites in the area'.[130]

In addition, local planning processes may provide fertile ground for expressing religious intolerance. In *Case Study 5(a)*, several objections were raised against the construction of the proposed mosque. Underlying these objections was a suspicion or fear of Muslims who were regarded as 'outsiders' who were not welcome in the community. For example, an objector in that case stated that the 'congregation of people from outside the area' is responsible for:

– the introduction of traffic that has no other reason to be there
– the potential for the generation of noise and other nuisance effects, e.g. with large numbers of people exiting the site at night
– the 'presence' of an activity that is unrelated to the community in which it sits.[131]

---

127 [2001] VCAT 322 (28 February 2001).

128 Ibid., [1].

129 Ibid., [2].

130 Ibid., [9].

131 *New Century Developments Pty Limited v Baulkham Hills Shire Council* [2003] NSWLEC 154 (30 July 2003) [31].

Underneath such an objection is an intolerant attitude towards Muslim Australians which is disguised as a legitimate planning objection and channelled into the local planning process. Such an 'us-versus-them' attitude is laundered or sanitised to make them acceptable (or, at least, less objectionable) in the local planning discourse. Worse still, the indifference of some local councils has provided such expressions of intolerant attitude with a semblance of legitimacy.

The presence of a place of worship (particularly a mosque) in a locality is sometimes deliberately associated with gang violence or street crime. Again, in *Case Study 5(a)*, local residents expressed the opinion that it had already resulted in anti-social behaviour when the house and roadway on the site had been painted with graffiti. They felt that the proposed mosque was the 'trigger for these actions'.[132] Some local residents stated that this type of antisocial behaviour 'had not occurred before in their community, were abhorrent to their community and caused them to fear for their safety'.[133] They stated that if the proposed mosque was approved, 'these acts of antisocial behaviour would continue to occur in their community and thereby have an adverse social impact'.[134] Along the same line is the fear that, once a mosque is allowed in a locality, it will become a 'hotbed of terrorism'.[135] Scott Poynting *et al.* pointed out that the refusals of applications to build mosques are tied to a larger 'moral panic' about Muslims in Australia, in which Islam is unjustifiably linked with 'criminality, terrorism, lack of civilisation and lack of humanity'.[136] Such panic is spread by representing suburbs with a significant Muslim population 'as sites of criminality and gang warfare – the breeding grounds for a culture of violence as well as for intergenerational and intercultural disrespect'.[137]

It has also been claimed that, once their places of worship are allowed in a locality, Muslims, Hindus, Sikhs, Buddhists or other minorities would start taking over the entire locality, thus displacing current residents. A resident who objected to the construction of a mosque stated that '[Muslims] will take over the whole neighbourhood if they open the mosque'.[138] Local residents of

---

132 Ibid., [36].

133 Ibid.

134 Ibid.

135 Padraic Murphy, 'Cairns Muslims Win Fight for Mosque', *The Australian*, 27 June 2008.

136 Scott Poynting, Greg Noble, Paul Tabar and Jack Collins, *Bin Laden in the Suburbs: Criminalising the Arab Other* (Sydney Institute of Criminology, 2004), 50.

137 Graeme Turner, 'The Cosmopolitan City and Its other: the Ethnicizing of the Australian Suburb' (2008) 9(4) *Inter-Asia Cultural Studies* 568, 575.

138 Barclay Crawford, 'New planning rules target Muslims', *The Sunday Telegraph*, 14 November 2010.

Bankstown in New South Wales expressed concern that their area has been 'taken over by Lebanese' and that Muslim migrants are all over the area.[139] This same objection is sometimes couched differently, as when objectors try to sow panic among local residents of the possibility of change in the population structure if the construction of a place of worship is allowed. For example, a chief town planner based his recommendation that a proposed mosque be rejected precisely upon this sort of fear, stating that:

> A 'Place of Worship' becomes a focal point and *the larger its catchment the greater the effect will be in changes in the social and population structure of the locality.* The mosque is nearly double in size to that erected in Lakemba and indications are that it would operate in a similar manner, i.e. a regional place of public worship ... the most appropriate recommendation should be one of refusal.[140] [emphasis added]

The above objections which were suggestive of religious intolerance or discrimination have been laundered or sanitised by co-mingling them with planning objections concerning physical or visual amenity concerns that appeared legitimate on the surface. In a similar case, Susan Thompson observed that certain 'community opposition ... is grounded in racist attitudes but delivered as legitimate town planning objections'.[141] Leonie Sandercock and Beverly Kliger made the same observation in a study on the local planning processes in three Melbourne localities in 1997, stating that:

> There are a number of questions stemming from these cases and complaints that need to be addressed. First, is the planning system, through its residential zoning regulations, an (albeit unintentional) ally of residents' prejudice? The answer would seem to be Yes, in that *these regulations provide the channel through which racial hostility can be masked as something else, and thereby legitimised.*[142] [emphasis added]

A local planning process that tolerates local residents' prejudice against minority groups is inconsistent with the principle of non-discrimination based on

---

139 Bugg, above n 49, 4.

140 Kevin Dunn, 'Representations of Islam in the Politics of Mosque Development in Sydney' (2001) 92(3) *Royal Dutch Geographical Society* 291, 299.

141 Susan Thompson, 'Planning and Multiculturalism: A Reflection on Australian Local Practice' (2003) 4(3) *Planning Theory & Practice* 275, 276.

142 Leonie Sandercock and Beverly Kliger, 'Multiculturalism and the Planning System: Part One' (1998) 35(3) *Australian Planner* 127, 131.

religion or belief. It has been observed that '[i]t is a cause for concern that the planning system gives voice and apparent legitimacy to certain complaints [against proposed places of worship] which are clearly a manifestation of racial prejudice'.[143] Rather than giving them an appearance of legitimacy, or worse, according them believability, local councils should recognise their depravity as soon as objectors attempt to channel them into the local planning processes.

5.4 Conclusion

There is a common theme that runs throughout this chapter – that is, the local councils in Australia, in their zealous aim of protecting the physical amenity of localities, have the potential to infringe elements of the right to freedom of religion or belief, including the right to establish and maintain places of worship. If they are unaware of the profound impact of their local planning decisions on religious freedom, then the risk becomes even greater. In several ways, this chapter has illustrated that ever present risk in the Australian local planning processes.

First, unfounded claims of negative impacts upon the physical amenity of an area have been accorded credence by some local councils, which led to the rejection of applications to construct proposed places of worship. Second, in some of the case studies featured in this chapter, 'religious need' did not receive the consideration it rightfully deserves in planning decisions involving places of worship. Third, the unique worshipping practices or patterns of religious groups are sometimes overlooked or ignored by local councils in resolving physical amenity issues, oftentimes resulting in rejections of proposed places of worship. Fourth, restrictive effects upon the exercise of religious manifestation are sometimes produced by planning decisions that gave too much weight to physical amenity concerns even if, on balance, they are not unreasonable. Finally, the protection of physical amenity of an area may produce a religiously discriminatory outcome, or may lead to the channeling of religiously intolerant attitudes in the local planning processes and giving them a semblance of legitimacy.

This chapter contributes to answering the primary research question identified in Chapter 1 – that is, Are the local planning processes in Australia consistent

---

143 Leonie Sandercock and Beverly Kliger, 'Multiculturalism and the Planning System: Part Two' (1998) 35(4) *Australian Planner* 223, 225.

with the international standards on religious freedom, including the right of religious groups to establish and maintain places of worship? Based on the foregoing analysis of local planning decisions involving physical amenity issues, it may be concluded that the international standards on religious freedom, including the right to establish and maintain places of worship, are susceptible to being infringed by the local planning processes in Australia. Such processes have the tendency to engender violations of the right to establish and maintain places of worship, and are therefore inconsistent with it.

The next chapter analyses another typical ground for refusing development applications to construct, extend or renovate places of worship in Australia – that is, the 'out of character-ness' of proposed places of worship with the surrounding area or locality. Like the protection of physical amenity, the preservation of visual amenity offers an important vantage point from where to assess the conformity of local planning processes in Australia with the right to freedom of religion or belief, in general, and the right of religious groups to establish and maintain their places of worship, in particular. Like the present chapter, the next sheds light on the book's primary research question.

CHAPTER 6

'Beauty is in the Eye of the Worshipper'

The Preservation of the Visual Amenity of an Area and its Impact on the Right to Establish and Maintain Places of Worship

6.1 Introduction

This chapter continues the analysis of the engagement of religious groups with the local councils in Australia in their applications to build, extend or renovate places of worship. In this chapter, the focus is on the other primary component of the concept of amenity in Australian local planning – that is, 'visual amenity' which is the feeling of pleasure or satisfaction that an area evokes as a result of factors including, for instance, the congruence of building designs, the evenness of the height and bulk of structures, the harmony of colours, and the general aesthetic character of an area.[1] As the case studies in this chapter illustrate, a proposed place of worship may be assessed by a local council as likely to damage or harm the 'visual amenity' of its surrounding area and therefore the application for its construction should be rejected.

This chapter is in three parts. First, it discusses the concept of 'visual amenity' and unmasks its highly subjective nature. The categorisation ascribed to a proposed structure as being 'out of character' with an area is carefully scrutinised. What does 'character' mean? Is the area whose visual amenity is to be preserved comprised of the street, block, neighbourhood or the entire suburb? Second, this chapter analyses nine case studies involving proposed places of worship where alleged 'intrusions' upon an area's visual amenity played a pivotal part in planning decisions. It examines the decisions of local councils as regards these visual amenity issues and their conformity with the international standards on religious freedom, including the right to establish and maintain places of worship. In the process, this chapter unmasks the purported neutrality of the local planning system in Australia by demonstrating that the majority's Anglo-Celtic culture is actually embedded in local planning regulations, thus rendering the system *inherently* discriminatory against non-Christian religions or beliefs in Australia. Finally, this chapter concludes that the right to establish and maintain places of worship is highly vulnerable to being infringed by a regulatory system which is geared towards the preservation of the visual

1 David L. Smith, *Amenity and Urban Planning* (Granada Publishing Limited, 1974), 11–29; See the discussion in Section 5.2 on the distinction between physical and visual amenities.

 | DOI 10.1163/9789004289345_007

amenity of Australian localities – a planning concept which is laden with imprecision, arbitrariness and subjectivity.

6.2 'Visual Amenity' and its Subjective Nature

Proposals to construct places of worship are sometimes rejected by local councils on the ground that they are likely to produce an adverse impact upon an area's visual amenity. Expressed in various ways, such a ground has been cited by local councils to justify rejections of applications to build, extend or renovate places of worship. For example, proposed places of worship have been determined to be: 'inappropriate having regard to the character of the area'[2]; inconsistent with the 'nature of the locality and the neighbourhood character'[3]; has 'an adverse impact on the rural character and appearance of the area'[4]; 'not in keeping with the predominantly residential area'[5]; not 'an acceptable response to the streetscape and neighbourhood context'[6]; against 'the neighbourhood character of the area'[7]; has an adverse 'impact on the visual outlook and character of the area'[8]; inconsistent with the 'residential character of the area'[9]; or spoils the 'agricultural nature of the valley'.[10] Such determinations of a negative impact upon an area's visual amenity ultimately arise from an individual's subjective feelings when his or her aesthetic sensibility is somehow offended by a structure, which he or she considers different, alien or even exotic, and is proposed to occupy physical space alongside structures that the individual regards as normal, pleasant or beautiful.

In Australian local planning practice, 'visual amenity' is typically defined as:

> a measure of the visual quality of a site or area experienced by residents, workers or visitors. It is the collective impact of the visual components which make a site or an area pleasant to be in. [T]he term assumes a

---

2 *City Gospel Trust v Nillumbik Shire Council* [2010] VCAT 517 [11].

3 Ibid., [15].

4 *Victory Worship Centre v Cardinia Shire Council* [2009] VCAT 810 [2].

5 *Highfield Gospel Trust v Devonport City Council* [2010] TASRMPAT 135 (6 July 2010) [7].

6 *Wheeler v Kingston City Council (Correction)* [2012] VCAT 1094 (24 August 2012) [46].

7 *Blackburn Community Church v Whitehorse City Council* [2004] VCAT 2623 (20 December 2004) [78].

8 *City Gospel Trust v Nillumbik Shire Council* [2010] VCAT 517 [12].

9 Padraic Murphy, 'Cairns Muslims Win Fight for Mosque', *The Australian*, 27 June 2008.

10 Nicolas Perpitch, 'Bias Denied as Swan Valley Mosque Rejected', *The Australian*, 18 December 2009.

> broad context, relating to elements which contribute to the visual pleasantness and character of towns, localities and neighbourhoods rather than any site specific considerations.[11]

Using visual amenity as a standard, local councils evaluate the appearance of proposed structures vis-à-vis the relevant area's general character or nature. Those which are determined to be 'intrusive' against the visual amenity are rejected. As the case studies in this chapter illustrate, determining whether a proposed religious structure is 'out of character' with an area is not as simple and straightforward as may first appear. Allegations of impairment of the visual amenity are highly subjective claims which do not lend themselves to easy resolution. As planning scholar Leslie Stein noted:

> Visual amenity is about perception, matters of taste, memory, and ascribing a benefit to beauty, which has deep, psychological roots. It is illustrative of the ability of the general concept of amenity to absorb intangible matters that draw from the source of psychological well-being and are not capable of measurement.[12]

As analysed below, the subjectivity of the concept of visual amenity places it in a direct collision course with the right to establish and maintain places of worship. Both have overlapping areas that may in fact be repugnant to each other. Thus, while the former seeks to preserve the existing external appearance or beauty of the built environment, the latter welcomes and in fact encourages new religious structures that may not necessarily be in visual harmony with that environment.

The preservation of visual amenity, because of its subjective nature, accords local councils in Australia with a greater degree of discretion than does the protection of the physical amenity. The previous chapter demonstrated that physical amenity issues are largely amenable to being measured by technical experts who, in turn, may be relied upon by local councils. It is argued that the deference to technical experts in resolving physical amenity issues significantly reduces the likelihood of bias or favour towards a particular religious group, thus respecting the principle of non-discrimination on the basis of religion or belief. In contrast, the wider discretion involved in resolving visual amenity issues increases that likelihood. Therefore, the preservation of visual

---

11 Maroochy Shire Council, Queensland, Strategic Plan (2000), Volume 2, Chapter 7 'Visual Amenity'.

12 Leslie Stein, *Principles of Planning Law* (Oxford University Press, 2008), 194–195.

amenity has a profound implication upon religious freedom in Australia. As further observed by Stein:

> An analysis based on amenity is perhaps the least objective or most open-ended enquiry of any planning consideration ... Yet, amenity remains the key determinant because it is a melting pot of matters from which, it is hoped, the true character of the area can be discovered. The particular ingredients in that melting pot are pulled out to serve either the developer's interest or those of the planning authority or residents, without any systematic approach.[13]

In determining a proposed structure's impact upon visual amenity, there are three sequential questions that need to be answered by local councils.[14] First, the character or nature of the area must be understood by 'defin[ing] the baseline qualities that are worthy of preservation'.[15] Second, the likely impacts of a proposed structure upon the visual amenity of an area must be reasonably ascertained. Third and finally, the degree of those impacts must somehow be measured to determine if they are nonetheless acceptable or reasonable under the circumstances.[16] These three questions call for a value judgment on the question of beauty or pleasantness in the physical landscape. However, as analysed below, it is the value judgment of the dominant Anglo-Celtic culture that usually finds its way into what the 'character' or 'nature' of the area means. This chapter analyses how such a dominant culture-defined concept of visual amenity hinders the ability of religious groups in Australia, especially the non-Christian religions or beliefs, to fully exercise their right to establish and maintain places of worship.

6.3 Preservation of 'Visual Amenity' and How it Impinges on the Right to Establish and Maintain Places of Worship

The following sections analyse case studies involving proposed places of worship where alleged damage or harm upon an area's visual amenity played a pivotal part in planning decisions. They examine the decisions of local councils as regards visual amenity issues and their conformity with the international

13 Ibid., 189–190.

14 Ibid., 197.

15 Ibid.

16 Ibid.

standards on religious freedom, including the right to establish and maintain places of worship.

6.3.1 *When Visual Amenity Is Based on an Incorrect Determination of an Area's Character or Nature*

As shown below, the excessive bulk and height of buildings, their obtrusive colours, their 'exotic' appearance and similar aesthetic-based complaints are staple grounds for objection against proposed places of worship. Thus, like in physical amenity issues, local councils are confronted with the task of determining the veracity of these allegations of adverse impact upon the visual amenity of a place.

The preservation of an area's visual amenity *assumes* several things. First, it is assumed that a particular area possesses a recognisable and consistent 'character' or 'nature' which is worthy of being preserved by planning authorities. Stein noted that "[w]hen qualities are condensed into a combined aesthetic description, then that description becomes the 'character' of the locality."[17] It is against this character that any proposed development is evaluated as to whether it blends with it or contradicts it. But such an assumption does not always hold true because an area may in fact consist of different or even opposing structural elements incapable of being lumped together into just one character or nature. What is more plausible is that an area possesses a clearly predominant character or nature. Second, even if an area has a predominant character or nature, it may in fact be in transition into another character or nature.[18] Usually driven by demographic factors, the changing character or nature of an area must be considered in ascertaining its true character or nature. Third and finally, the boundaries of an area that separate it from other areas are also assumed.[19] These boundaries are not always clearly delineated or demarcated. Thus, the relevant 'area' may be a street, a block, a precinct, a neighbourhood, or even an entire suburb or locality. Different stakeholders in a planning controversy may have different understandings of the relevant area's scope and limits. Thus, an immediate neighbour may emphasise the protection of the streetscape as the relevant area (in order to spare his or her property from a

---

17 Ibid., 195.

18 See, e.g., the claim of the applicant religious group in *Baptist Union of Queensland v Brisbane City Council & Anor* [2002] QPEC 41 [96].

19 Stein, above n 12, 206–207. The imprecision of the boundaries of the relevant locality or area is apparent in Stein's suggestion that it is 'equated with a 'neighbourhood' or a distinct zone for which there are particular planning goals, even though in particular cases a smaller area may be affected, or the area affected may go beyond a zone or even over a border of the municipality'. Stein, above n 12, 207.

perceived visual intrusion by a proposed place of worship), but an applicant religious group may regard the whole precinct consisting of diverse uses as the relevant area (in order to bolster its position that a proposed place of worship is consistent with that existing diversity of uses). It has been noted that:

> [t]he concept of locality is flexible and is not confined by establishing a quadrilateral bounded by four streets. It requires a separate determination in each case to be able to ascribe the weight to be given to the evidence of experts or residents in relation to the area.[20]

Therefore, the assumptions used to contain and capture the meaning of 'visual amenity' are prone to imprecision, arbitrariness and subjectivity. The categorisation of an area as a distinct 'area' and as having a recognisable and consistent character or nature must always be raised as factual issues in a local planning process. The foregoing assumptions must be tested and not simply be accepted as gospel truth. When a character or nature is incorrectly ascribed to an area (assuming it is a distinct area), there is a greater likelihood that it may lead to incorrect planning decisions, including the likely rejection of proposed places of worship as exemplified by the case studies below.

The first case study illustrates an unfounded claim of a negative impact upon an area's visual amenity. The claim was based on the erroneous assumption that the subject area was made up of uniform and harmonious structures whose aggregate appearance is worthy of being preserved when, in fact, the area was comprised of diverse structures.

Case Study 6(a)[21]
Hamerkas Shelanu Inc, applicant
Glen Eira City Council, Victoria

The applicant, Hamerkas Shelanu Inc, lodged in 2003 a development application with the Glen Eira City Council to extend its existing building for the purpose of a Jewish community centre which would comprise a synagogue, crèche and rooms for Hebrew language and Jewish education classes.[22] The applicant's building was located on a main arterial road (Glen Huntly Road) running through the City of Glen Eira.[23] It was located between a business

20 *Tempora Pty Ltd v Shire of Kalamunda* (1994) 10 SR (WA) 296, 305.

21 Also featured as *Case Study 5(i)* in Chapter 5.

22 *Lennon v Glen Eira City Council* [2004] VCAT 1345 (14 July 2004) [12].

23 Ibid., [5].

precinct and a neighbourhood centre.[24] A tram line runs along the road on which it was located with a tram stop near the front of the subject land. On the north and south side of the road are mixed structures of substantial 'form of massing'.[25]

In January 2004, the Glen Eira City Council approved the applicant's proposal subject to certain conditions.[26] Unsatisfied with those conditions, the applicant appealed the council's decision to the Victorian Civil and Administrative Tribunal. During the appeal, one of the main issues pertained to the proposal's alleged negative impact upon the area's visual amenity because of the 'scale and mass of the works and design detailing'[27] of the proposed building. In some of the submissions, there were also objections to the 'architectural detailing, such as the domes'.[28] In its decision,[29] the Tribunal found that the proposal would not negatively impact the visual amenity of the surrounding area, stating that:

> It seems to me that the built form character of the neighbourhood within which the subject land lies essentially comprises a spine of relatively intense development along Glen Huntly Road ... Furthermore, it is also apparent that there is significant diversity in the height, bulk and style of buildings fronting Glen Huntly Road in the immediate vicinity of the subject land. This is because buildings in the vicinity of the subject land reflect diversity in land use including the nursing home itself, medium density housing (both older and newer development), a church, local shops and former dwellings now used as medical centres ...
>
> Having regard to the above, I consider that the development of a two storey building, generally in the form proposed, is not at odds with the diverse built form character and pattern of development found along Glen Huntly Road. The building will present itself as an institution, however, I do not see what is wrong with this particularly given that the existing building presents itself in much the same way. The proposed building will clearly be larger than what exists, but again, I do not consider this to be inappropriate given that the subject land is located on

24 Ibid., [7].

25 Ibid., [44].

26 Ibid., [23].

27 Ibid., [41].

28 Ibid., [44].

29 The Tribunal reversed the local council's decision based on the sole ground that the applicant's proposal did not provide adequate parking spaces.

> Glen Huntly Road where development is more intense.... I consider that the proposed development will not be out of place within a neighbourhood context where properties along Glen Huntly Road are developed in a relatively intense manner and there is significant diversity in the built form.[30]

The Tribunal in effect held that the allegation of adverse impact upon the visual amenity was a nebulous claim because there already exists in the subject area an intense and diverse set of developments and uses, such that the proposed synagogue would in no way cause a visual degradation of that area. In terms of the area's visual amenity, the proposed building would simply add to the area's diversity of structures and thus would not cause any harm. The objectors ascribed a different 'character or nature' to the subject area which did not accurately reflect its true appearance.

The above case study demonstrates the relative ease in putting forth a claim of a negative impact upon the character or nature of an area because of the highly subjective nature of the concept of visual amenity. It is a matter of taste or preference which people may not share in common. More worryingly, the above case study illustrates how precarious proposals to build places of worship are in a subjectivity-ridden local planning process because, at any stage, the relevant decision-maker may have a preference or taste which is opposed to that of the applicant.

The next case study illustrates another unfounded claim of a negative impact upon an area's visual amenity. The subject area was a mix of different developments and, therefore, its existing character was no longer 'pristine' as the objectors claimed.

Case Study 6(b)
Blackburn Community Church of Christ, applicant
Whitehorse City Council, Victoria

The applicant, the Blackburn Community Church of Christ, lodged a development application with the Whitehorse City Council in 2004 to construct a 'Place of Assembly including a new 500 seat auditorium, ancillary meeting rooms and ancillary café and to extend the existing Place of Worship with ancillary offices, and car parking'.[31] The existing buildings on the site were

30 *Lennon v Glen Eira City Council*, above n 22, [42].

31 *Blackburn Community Church of Christ v Whitehorse City Council* [2004] VCAT 2623 (20 December 2004) [9].

used as a place of worship, meeting rooms and an administration office. The site was surrounded by residential land uses to the north, west and south. There were also numerous non-residential uses within approximately one kilometre of the site including the Blackburn Primary and High Schools, Blackburn Road Shopping Centre, the North Blackburn Square Shopping Centre, an Anglican church and a Sikh temple.[32] Other non-residential uses in the area included a Telstra exchange, Blackburn North Bowling Club and other primary schools.[33]

The Whitehorse City Council approved the application subject to certain conditions. Not satisfied with these conditions, the applicant appealed the local council's decision to the Victorian Civil and Administrative Tribunal. During the appeal, objectors complained of the proposal's alleged negative impact upon the 'Neighbourhood Character/Impact on Streetscape'.[34] The Tribunal found that the 'stand-out issue' in the case was the proposal's inadequate parking provision. It decided to give the applicant an opportunity to modify its proposal in order to address the concern of inadequate parking. On the issue of the alleged negative impact upon the neighbourhood character or streetscape, the Tribunal stated that:

> The proposed redevelopment of the Church buildings and car parking will … generally sit comfortably within the neighbourhood character of the area. Given the range of other institutional uses which already exist in the area, and in particular the apparently "George Orwell inspired" appearance of the Telstra exchange across Surrey Road, clearly this is not a "pristine residential area" but one where a combination of residential and non-residential built form already exists.
>
> The proposed redevelopment of the Church buildings and car parking will sit comfortably with the relevant streetscape. It was common ground at the hearing that as the new built form is concentrated towards the rear of subject land, there will be no significant change to the Surrey Road streetscape. Although there were submissions made that the landscaping provided at the front of the proposed new car park is inadequate, the existing streetscape of this part of Surrey Road is already somewhat "hard edge" (notably the Telstra exchange) and I consider the proposed car parking frontage is acceptable.[35]

32 Ibid., [51].

33 Ibid., [77].

34 Ibid., [74].

35 Ibid., [78].

In the above case study, the objectors' claim of adverse impact upon the visual amenity was based on a wrong assumption that the subject area was 'a pristine residential area'[36] when in fact it was not. The presence of diversified structures within a kilometre of the site gave the relevant area a 'mixed' character or nature; not a pristine residential character as suggested by the objectors. An alleged visual impost of proposed places of worship must be evaluated vis-à-vis the correctly ascribed character or nature of their surrounding environment. When the assumed character or nature of an area is not challenged or questioned, there is a greater likelihood that it may lead to unreasonable planning decisions, including the likely rejections of proposed places of worship.

In addition, the one-kilometre radius that the Tribunal identified appeared to be the relevant 'area' in its determination (although at times it referred to the 'streetscape' which is smaller). In contrast, the objectors had in mind a larger area that encompasses the contiguous residential neighbourhoods beyond the one-kilometre radius in order to bolster their contention that the proposal would disrupt the area's alleged residential character. These different conceptions of the scope of the relevant area further illustrate the imprecision, arbitrariness and subjectivity involved in identifying visual amenity. The assumed extent and limit of a supposed 'area' or 'locality' must not simply be accepted as truth; they must be challenged or questioned in planning applications involving places of worship, lest an incorrect determination of an area's character or nature leads to rejection of proposed places of worship.

6.3.2 *When the Preservation of Visual Amenity Results in 'Aesthetic Intolerance' against Non-Christian Religions or Beliefs*

Aiming to preserve an area's visual amenity, local councils may refuse an application to build a place of worship when, in their assessment, a proposed religious structure will spoil the visual satisfaction that an area elicits from residents, visitors or the public. As explained below, local councils – because of their heavy reliance on ethnocentric assumptions of beauty or pleasantness in the physical environment – may be predisposed to rejecting proposed non-Christian places of worship whose distinct architecture is steeped in religious tradition. There is therefore a greater likelihood that local councils may infringe the full exercise by religious groups of their right to establish and maintain places of worship. Local councils' obsession with preserving an area's existing character or nature (whether validly identified or not) may hinder the establishment of new religious structures which have their own faith-inspired architectural designs or styles. This may lead, in turn, to a failure to satisfy a pressing 'religious

36 Ibid.

need' for adequate physical spaces where religious groups can exercise their right to manifest their religious or other beliefs.

That a proposed Hindu temple is 'out of character' with its surrounding area, and thus impairs visual amenity, was a pivotal factor in the local council's decision to refuse the development application in the next case study.

Case Study 6(c)
Shree Swaminarayan Temple Trust, applicant
Hills Shire Council, New South Wales

In March 2009, the Shree Swaminarayan Temple Trust, a Hindu religious organisation, lodged a development application with the Hills Shire Council for the construction of a Hindu temple and a 60-space car park on its two-hectare property in Nelson, New South Wales.[37] A temple trustee, Dinesh Jadva, stated that one of the reasons why their organisation chose the site was its 'the tranquil ambience' which is well suited for their members' acts of worship and meditation.[38] Harry Walia, a chapter president of the Global Organisation of People of Indian Origin, said that 'the proposed development would provide a central worship place for the growing number of Hills district Hindus' which, according to his estimation, numbered around 4,000.[39] The site's proximity to different modes of public transportation (that is, a bus service and a railway station) was another important consideration in selecting the site. The public transport would make it accessible to Hindu worshippers while significantly lessening the adverse impact on vehicular traffic conditions in the area.[40]

In May 2009, a public consultation was held in relation to the proposed Hindu temple. Several members of the applicant attended the consultation and emphasised that '[t]he proposed development is rural, approved for a place of worship and is unlikely to interfere with the economic well-being of any business or with the health of the surrounding community'.[41] On the other hand, John Higman, speaking on behalf of a neighbourhood association, stated that a Hindu temple is simply out of place in 'a small, rural suburb that did not even have town water, sewerage or roadside guttering'.[42] A local resident, Mark Panos, expressed a similar opinion that, while he respects Hinduism and its

37 Development Application No. 1178/09/HA, 12 March 2009.
38 Claire Thompson, 'Temple of Division', *Hills Shire Times*, 12 May 2009.
39 John Blair, 'Temple at Odds with Residents', *Rose Hill Times*, 2 June 2009.
40 John Blair, 'Temple or Club, Box Hill Says No', *Hills Shire Times*, 26 May 2009.
41 Justin Vallejo, 'Sydney Rejects Religious Temples', *The Daily Telegraph*, 1 February 2008.
42 Ibid.

adherents, his particular neighbourhood is not the best place for a Hindu temple. Mr Panos stated that, 'We would love to have these people in our community. However, there are many other blocks close by that would be more appropriate'.[43] The other objections raised involved the alleged unreasonable hours of operation of the religious facility, its poor waste water management plan, the temple's sheer bulk and scale, and that the temple would spoil the tranquillity of the area.[44] In December 2009, the Hills Shire Council refused the development application. The local council stated that one of the grounds for the refusal was that the proposed temple 'has not been designed having regard to and will unacceptably impact on the rural character of the surrounding area'.[45]

In the foregoing case study, the local council's emphasis on preserving the 'rural character of the surrounding area' connotes a static conception of beauty and pleasantness of a place. Such a conception is averse to change when change is warranted by changes in the religious demographic profile of the locality. It effectively excluded the applicant religious group (who has a growing number of members in the same area) from expressing, in architectural built form, its own standard of beauty and pleasantness. In basing its decision on the need to preserve the 'rural character of the surrounding area', the Hills Shire Council endorsed a particular version of what the area *ought to* look like. It therefore made a subjective determination of the external appearance that the area should project to its residents, visitors and other users. Such a determination illustrates the malleable nature of the concept of visual amenity in local planning.

When the interpretation of a subjective concept like visual amenity is conferred to local councils, there is a danger of endorsing one version of visual pleasantness while suppressing other versions. Massimo Leone described the objections against places of worship for being 'out of character' with the surrounding environment – and thus negatively impacting visual amenity – as 'aesthetic intolerance' which 'is probably the most common and also the most effective [objection] in this kind of legal controversies'.[46] Commenting on similar instances of 'aesthetic intolerance' in the

---

43 Thompson, above n 38.

44 Blair, above n 39.

45 The Hills Shire Council, Notice to Applicant of Determination of a Development Application, 14 December 2009.

46 Massimo Leone, 'Legal Controversies about the Establishment of New Places of Worship in Multicultural Cities: A Semiogeographic Analysis', in Anne Wagner and Jan Broekman (eds), *Prospects of Legal Semiotics* (Springer, 2010), 217, 225.

United Kingdom, Ceri Peach and Richard Gale observed that the cause of the problem is 'a system of planning the principles of which were enshrined in law some years prior to the development of large diaspora communities. The planning system was never designed to be responsive to such culturally diverse social change'.[47]

The proposed Hindu temple in the above case study was precipitated by the demographic changes that took place in Nelson, New South Wales and nearby localities. The influx into these places of individuals and their families who adhere to the Hindu faith has created a legitimate demand for an accessible and suitable place of worship. In a sense, the local planning process failed to keep up with the demands of a changed demographic landscape. As observed by John Skennar, '[p]lanning law and protocols can seem static and even abstract in contemporary multicultural society where existing instruments are held rigidly over the communities that they are intended to serve'.[48] Satisfying people's legitimate needs, including the need to respect their right to manifest their religion or belief, ought to be the determinant of change in the built environment. After all, structures or edifices ultimately serve, and must be subordinate to, human needs.

In addition to a claim that a proposed Buddhist temple destroys the visual amenity of an area, the next case study illustrates how such a claim may be commingled with expressions of religious intolerance which are then channelled into the local planning process, thereby giving them a semblance of legitimacy.

Case Study 6(d)[49]
Wat Sangharatanaram Inc, applicant
Gold Coast City Council, Queensland

In December 2007, Wat Sangharatanaram Inc, a Buddhist religious association, lodged a development application with the Gold Coast City Council to construct a temple and a residence for monks on its property in Nerang, Queensland.[50] The association proposed construction of a 15-metre high Buddhist temple

47 Ceri Peach and Richard Gale, 'Muslims, Hindus and Sikhs in the New Religious Landscape of England' (2003) 93(4) *The Geographical Review* 469, 486.

48 John Skennar, 'Sydney, A City Growing Within: The Establishment of Buddhist Centres in Western Sydney', in Cristina Rocha and Michelle Barker (eds), *Buddhism in Australia: Traditions in Change* (2011), 86.

49 Also featured as *Case Study 5(h)* in Chapter 5.

50 Melinda Marshall, 'Row over Gold Coast Buddhist Temple', *Local Gold Coast News*, 5 March 2010.

with a traditional Thai architectural design.[51] One of the main objections against the proposed Buddhist temple complex was its alleged incompatibility with the character of the Nerang area. For example, local objectors complained about the '[d]ozens of colourful flags and banners that seem to often adorn the road frontages of these premises giving a *cheap look* to the area'. [emphasis added].[52] Also raising a similar objection, the owner of the adjacent property stated that:

> The architecture of the Buddhist Temple is significantly intrusive at a maximum height of approximately 16 m above ground level – equivalent to a 5 storey building... The intrusiveness is accentuated by the bright orange coloured roof tiles, which are an essential feature of Thai temple architecture. Hence although the temple would be a striking building in a South East Asian setting (equivalent to a church with a tall spire in a traditional English village), it is out of character in western Nerang.[53]

Some members of the Gold Coast City Council also opposed the proposed Buddhist temple. Councillor Peter Young questioned the 'cultural relevance' of the proposed temple in the Nerang community. Mr Young stated that the proposed temple 'is culturally relevant in a Buddhist community. It is not culturally relevant in Nerang. What has not been taken into account is the cultural elements of the Nerang community'.[54] Another councillor, Susie Douglas, stated that people might mistakenly believe that Nerang is a Buddhist community if the proposed Buddhist temple were approved. She expressed the concern that 'It's going to become such a landmark and it will influence the way people think about the area, in that it will become a Buddhist community'.[55]

Robert Fraser, the treasurer of the applicant religious group, defended the proposed Buddhist temple by stating that 'Buddhist temple roofs were traditionally tall to remind worshippers to show reverence. Anybody who's travelled to Thailand would understand that this is a symbol of Thai Buddhism and we would like people to recognise that'.[56] Other members of the group stated

51 Ibid.

52 Letter of IR and JA Gardner to the Gold Coast City Council, 17 November 2008.

53 Letter of Peter Hobson to the Gold Coast City Council, 2 December 2008.

54 Marshall, above n 50; This particular argument on the need to protect the 'cultural identity' of a majority population against the intrusion of 'alien' or 'exotic' structures is further analysed in Section 8.3.2.

55 Ibid.

56 Marshall, above n 50.

that the size and height of the proposed Buddhist temple was crucial in order to establish its 'presence in keeping with Buddhist traditions ... [and should not] be confused as a statement of bigness or monumentalism, but as an expression of warmth, of invitation, all-embracing oneness, harmony with spirituality and physicality intertwined'.[57]

In March 2010, the Gold Coast City Council approved the application, subject to strict conditions concerning the construction and operation of the temple. In the applicant's view, such conditions hindered the manifestation of their belief. Despite the conditions, the applicant did not appeal the council's decision.[58] The conditions included[59]: (i) the reduction of the overall size and floor area of the proposed Buddhist temple allowing only a maximum of 80 persons attending the subject site at any given time, except during major events or days of special significance in line with the Buddhist calendar; and (ii) that the Buddhist temple and its associated structures must not be painted in highly reflective, bright or obtrusive colours. In particular, the proposed bright red and golden colours of the temple's façade were disapproved. However, the suggestion made by Councillor Young to reduce the height of the temple by 20 percent (from 15 to 12 metres) was rejected by the local council after hearing cultural explanations.[60]

Like the proposed Buddhist temple in Nerang in the above case study, the architectural contributions of minority groups in the physical landscape, are entitled to protection by local planning regulations because such groups have an established existence in many Australian localities. However, as observed by Susan Thompson, local planning regulations are predominantly Anglo-centric and '[r]arely do they include expressions of immigrant community history despite the fact that many of these groups have had a long and important presence in local areas across the country'.[61] In a multi-religious society like Australia, one of the challenges of the local planning system is how to satisfy the need of various religious groups to express their identities in the built environment.[62]

In the above case study, a local resident called into question the 'cultural relevance' of the Buddhist temple in Nerang, Queensland when it is common

57 Greg Stolz, 'Buddhist Temple in Nerang Gets Go-Ahead under Strict Conditions', *The Courier-Mail*, 23 March 2010.

58 Acceptance of Decision Notice for Development Application, 5 May 2010.

59 Decision Notice to Applicant, Place of Worship, 26 March 2010.

60 Stolz, above n 57.

61 Susan Thompson, 'Planning and Multiculturalism: A Reflection on Australian Local Practice' (2010) 4(3) *Planning Theory & Practice* 275, 276.

62 Peach and Gale, above n 47, 487.

knowledge that hundreds of Buddhist adherents are bona fide and long established residents of that area. Other local objectors had no qualm suggesting that the adornments of the proposed Buddhist temple would give 'a cheap look to the area'.[63] In these controversies, the local councils need to frame the relevant issues and elevate the level of public discourse into one which shuns religious intolerance and discrimination. To be indifferent about them, under a pretext of observing neutrality in the planning process, is to confer intolerant and discriminatory attitudes a semblance of legitimacy and thus invite further infringements of religious freedom.

When a local council determines the 'out of character-ness' of a proposed place of worship, it is actually engaged in the process of architectural review whose aim is to protect the 'visual compatibility of areas that possess a common architectural design or harmonious visual pattern'.[64] This is done through the use of planning regulations that seek to regulate the qualitative features of buildings. However, planning regulations that seek to preserve the visual amenity of an area are not neutral. Rather, they embody the dominant cultural values of Anglo-Celtic Australia and tend to overlook the cultural contributions of minority groups. Planning expert Leonie Sandercock observed that 'culturally diverse cities and regions are a challenge to planning systems, policies and practices … [where] difference comes to be seen as a problem'.[65] She lamented the fact that the values and norms of the dominant culture ultimately manifest themselves in planning policies and practices that effectively subdue minority groups, thus resulting in their cultures' diminished presence in the overall physical landscape of a locality.[66]

It is a common assumption that local planning regulations are underpinned by impartial norms that are uniformly applied to all individuals and groups in society.[67] But this is only what appears on the surface. Planning regulations that 'reproduc[e] the dominant ideologies of their communities have set out very particular set of prescriptions about what does and does not belong'.[68]

63 Letter of IR and JA Gardner to the Gold Coast Council, 17 November 2008.

64 Angela Carmella, 'Houses of Worship and Religious Liberty: Constitutional Limits to Landmark Preservation and Architectural Review' (1991) 36 *Villanova Law Review* 401, 430.

65 Leonie Sandercock, 'When Strangers Become Neighbours: Managing Cities of Difference' (2000) 1(1) *Planning Theory and Practice* 13, 15.

66 Ibid.

67 Leonie Sandercock and Beverly Kliger, 'Multiculturalism and the Planning System: Part One' (1998) 35(3) *Australian Planner* 127, 129.

68 Laura Beth Bugg, 'Religious Freedom and the Right to the City: Local Government Planning and the Rejection of Islamic Schools in Sydney, Australia' (Workshop Paper, Twelfth Berlin Roundtables: Religious Pluralism, Irmgard Coninx Stiftung, 7–11 April 2010), 7.

Deeply embedded in local planning regulations are the cultural values of the dominant social group. Hence, it is the majority group's lifestyle, ways of thinking and perceptions of beauty or ugliness that are sought to be preserved by the local planning system. Commenting on the Australian context, Leonie Sandercock and Beverly Kliger noted that planning regulations 'embody the values and norms of the dominant Anglo-Celtic culture at the expense of all other cultural groups… [W]e need to pay attention to the cultural biases inscribed in planning'.[69] They further commented that:

> Assigning value to particular styles and designs of streetscapes and precincts privileges the values of one culture – the dominant Anglo-Celtic – over all others. Clearly it is this dominant culture's heritage that is being valued when heritage and conservation strategies give protection to Victorian terraces, Edwardian cottages, Federation houses, Californian bungalows (rather than to Greek, Italian or Cambodian modifications of them, or to altogether different preservation strategies).[70]

Therefore, infused with an ethnocentric bias, local planning regulations in Australia perpetuate a static conception of beauty and pleasantness, and exclude other such conceptions which are usually steeped in religious traditions.

In the next case study, an appellate court held that a mosque, while different from its surrounding structures, did not impair an area's visual amenity but actually complemented it. This lends support to the notion that a local council's conception of beauty or pleasantness in the built environment need not be static. Rather, it can be made to conform to the right to establish and maintain places of worship which encourages new religious structures even though their architectural designs or styles may be incongruous with existing and long-established structures.

Case Study 6(e)
Kotku Education and Welfare Society Inc, applicant
Brisbane City Council, Queensland

In May 2003, the applicant Kotku Education and Welfare Society Inc, a Muslim religious organisation composed mainly of Turkish immigrants, lodged a

69 Leonie Sandercock and Beverly Kliger, 'Multiculturalism and the Planning System: Part Two' (1998) 35(4) *Australian Planner* 223, 227.

70 Ibid., 223.

development application with the Brisbane City Council to construct a Turkish-style mosque and a cultural centre on its property.[71] Several local residents opposed the application on the ground that 'the size and features' of the proposed mosque would constitute "discordant elements when compared with the existing 'rural residential' nature of local development, which they cherish."[72] They further alleged that the proposed mosque would be 'just too big and out of character for the site that has been chosen. It will unduly impact on our lives in many ways, and on the environment and character of the area'.[73] One of the local objectors explained that the proposed Turkish-style mosque and its associated structures:

> whilst of architectural interest, are out of character with other structures in the area – which are residential dwellings, many also having backyard sheds and chook houses in keeping with the nature of the area. Despite attempts to ultimately block views of the structures with planting trees, the buildings will still be quite easily visible, particularly from Tinchborne Street.[74]

The Brisbane City Council failed to make a timely decision on the application as prescribed in its internal rules. The applicant deemed this inaction a refusal and filed an appeal to the Planning and Environment Court of Queensland. During the appeal, it was argued that the proposal was consistent with one of Brisbane's strategic directions of "encouraging social and cultural diversity, and a wide social and cultural 'mix'."[75] In 2004, the Court upheld the applicant's appeal and allowed the construction of the mosque and cultural centre. As to the objection that the proposed mosque would be 'out of character' with the existing appearance of the area, Judge Alan Wilson stated that "[a]ll these buildings (and the formal garden) are in a 'Turkish' style, featuring colours and intricate patterns of Turkish origin, quite different from the nearby houses but on any view interesting and pleasing."[76] His Honour added that:

> While the [proposed mosque's] architecture is exotic, it is of a very high standard and the fact of difference does not ... make it inherently undesirable or necessarily detrimental to the amenity of the area. Even the

71 *Kotku Education and Welfare Society Inc v Brisbane City Council* [2004] QPEC 068.

72 Ibid., [5].

73 Ibid., [5].

74 Ibid., [42].

75 Ibid., [19].

76 Ibid., [7].

> most jaundiced eye would concede it is no less attractive than some of the residential development that has taken place, and the only fair conclusion is that ... it will ultimately be, while different, nevertheless attractive and pleasing.[77]

The learned judge's description of the proposed Turkish-style mosque as 'attractive and pleasing' is based on his own subjective perception of external beauty and pleasantness. His Honour further stated that '[t]he fact this development involves buildings in an architectural style quite different from, and a little larger than, the established residences does not mean it will detract from the appearance or amenity of the area, or the streetscape'.[78] Judge Wilson's reasoning supports the conclusion that the concept of visual amenity need not be constrained by a static conception of beauty or pleasantness in the built environment.

In a sense, the subjectiveness of visual amenity is both its blessing and its curse. Being a malleable one, the concept of visual amenity can be made to conform to, or be compatible with, other societal interests such as fostering religious diversity. It can be conceived of as being *inclusive* of other versions of beauty or pleasantness in the built environment. Such inclusiveness is the vital key to harmonise the local councils' traditional role of preserving visual amenity with the equally important obligation of respecting the right to establish and maintain places of worship. The malleability of the concept itself is the key to harmonising the seemingly contradictory thrusts of, on one hand, local planning regulations that seek to preserve the appearance of streetscapes and, on the other hand, the right to establish and maintain places of worship that values the flourishing of 'alien', 'foreign' or 'exotic' religious structures.

6.3.3 *When the Preservation of Visual Amenity 'Domesticates' Places of Worship*

The preservation of visual amenity through the local planning processes has another negative consequence which involves the 'domestication' of the architectural designs of religious structures. This takes place when places of worship, whose appearance is steeped in religious tradition, are directed by local councils to conform to a preferred common standard of appearance. In *Highfield Gospel Trust v Devonport City Council*,[79] the applicant religious group had no choice but to propose in the first instance a place of worship which was 'simple in style and residential in form'[80] or risk a refusal by the local council

77 Ibid., [43].
78 Ibid., [32].
79 [2010] TASRMPAT 135 (6 July 2010).
80 Ibid., [1].

whose planning instruments seek to maintain the subject locality's suburban character which 'primarily consists of larger family homes set in well maintained and spacious garden settings'.[81] The proposed place of worship (which was eventually approved) was described as:

> the built form of the proposal can on no view of it be said to be inconsistent with [the suburban character] categorisation. The proposed church is *designed to appear domestic in both scale and external appearance.* Its built form and siting, particularly given the fact that it is well set back from the road, will not be intrusive in the least.[82] [emphasis added]

The 'domestication' effect is felt most acutely by non-Christian religious groups in Australia as they are required to conform or assimilate, or risk rejection of their applications to build, extend or renovate places of worship. As planning scholar Samantha Ngui observed:

> Requiring developments to blend into the surrounding area is a form of spatial assimilation. Churches already dominate the surrounding area and so Christian groups are not called to assimilate to the existing landscape. It is [the] religious minorities who are called to assimilate or face likely exclusion from the area.... Spatial assimilation is incompatible with the neutrality principle which requires that no particular religious group receive preferential treatment.[83]

With the next three case studies as a backdrop of discussion, the planning regulations' 'domestication effect' on places of worship is further analysed. Unfortunately, for many religious groups (especially non-Christian ones), resisting such an effect usually results in the rejection by local councils of their applications to build, extend or renovate their religious structures.

Case Study 6(f)
Islamic Education and Welfare Association of Dandenong, applicant
Casey City Council, Victoria

In August 2003, the applicant lodged a development application with the Casey City Council to construct a mosque on its property located in Narre

81 Ibid.
82 Ibid., [22].
83 Samantha Ngui, *Freedom to Worship: Frameworks for the Realisation of Religious Minority Rights* (PhD Thesis, University of New South Wales, 2008), 104.

Warren North, Victoria.[84] Under the proposal, the applicant intended to build a two-storey building 'with traditional Islamic architectural themes, such as a central dome, arched windows and minarets'.[85] The proposed mosque has an overall height up to the top of the dome and minaret of approximately 11 metres.[86] Its general shape viewed from above is like 'two overlapping diamonds, centrally linked and enclosed with a covered perimeter walkway'.[87] It has a total useable floor area of 1,516 square metres. However, in accordance with the recommendations of a planning committee organised by the local council, the floor area of the proposed mosque was reduced by 20 percent.[88]

The proposed mosque is intended to be used by Muslims of Fijian Indian background. It is also envisaged to be used as a community centre to provide assistance to new migrants with a similar background, and to provide religious instruction to children on Sundays. In terms of the intensity of use, there would be Friday midday prayers which it was anticipated would be attended by about 90 persons. On special religious occasions, however, the number of people using the mosque could reach up to 270 persons.[89] No sound amplification device was proposed as the call to prayer (*adhān*) would be done inside the building and would not be heard from outside the property.[90]

The Casey City Council refused the application on the grounds that, among others, the proposed mosque and associated works were inappropriate in terms of urban design and neighbourhood character considerations. In reaching this decision, the local council considered the proposed mosque's architectural design which was allegedly incongruent with the surrounding structures. The applicant appealed the local council's decision to the Victorian Civil and Administrative Tribunal, which reversed it. On the proposed mosque's 'exotic' architectural features, the Tribunal ruled that:

> We consider that the proposed scale of the building is consistent with other religious facilities in the area, as shown on photographs tendered by

84 *Islamic Education and Welfare Association of Dandenong v Casey City Council* [2004] VCAT 1850 (16 September 2004) [6].

85 Ibid., [7].

86 Ibid., [8].

87 Ibid., [7].

88 Ibid., [7].

89 Ibid., [10].

90 Ibid., [10].

> Mr Chow. Most of the other religious facilities in the area have idiosyncratic architecture. We agree with Mr Chow that is appropriate that for *a mosque should look like a mosque.*
>
> The proposed building is substantial. However, we accept Mr Janif's evidence that that is a reflection of its proposed use. A large "mosque" area is required *so that traditional postures can be performed as part of prayers.* Separate areas, denoted as areas for "activity centre and Sunday classes," are large *because there is a need to split up groups by sex and age.* As noted by Mr Janif, the proposed building is also of substantial size as it is for the glory of God.
>
> We accept Mr Chow's submission that respect for local character should be considered in terms of building scale, setbacks from boundaries and landscaping intentions. Our finding is that the proposed building is an appropriate response in those terms.[91] [emphasis original]

The Casey City Council's decision suggests that places of worship should assimilate with the general character of their surrounding areas. It was an attempt at spatial assimilation which is usually directed at minority religious groups whose structures reflect their own architectural tradition. Usually inspired by their fundamental religious beliefs, such structures are sought to be 'homogenised' by planning instruments that give a high value to preserving an area's visual amenity. Commenting on the 'homogenisation' of places of worship, Ngui observed that:

> Planning rules on amenity dictate that a place of worship must be compatible with the local area. This is often a particular challenge for religious minorities who seek to employ a particular architectural style in an already established order. There is a clear assertion that places of worship which are identifiably non-Christian are not acceptable.[92]

Furthermore, specifically with respect to mosque proposals, it has been observed that local councils would most likely approve "design alterations that 'de-Islamised' the appearance of a mosque or Islamic centre. Buildings were termed 'cultural centres' and if they did not look like mosques they were deemed more acceptable to the local scene."[93]

---

91 Ibid., [45]–[47].

92 Ngui, above n 83, 102.

93 Nahid Kabir, *Muslims in Australia: Immigration, Race Relations and Cultural History* (Kegan Paul, 2005), 198.

In the foregoing case study, the Tribunal's statement that 'a mosque should look like a mosque' is an apt recognition of the nexus between a place of worship's architectural design and fundamental religious beliefs.[94] To standardise the appearance of a mosque in order to make it conform to the character of a place, whether that character is hard fact or a nebulous claim, is to devalue the religious beliefs of others that are sought to be expressed in built form. Massimo Leone posed a relevant question: 'if the coexistence of Christian Australians and Muslim Australians is a value, how can the coexistence of Christian and Islamic architectures be not a value?'[95] In relation to a rejected mosque proposal in Brisbane, Queensland, Leone observed that:

> on the one hand, the 2000 City Plan has as one of its Desired Environmental Outcomes (DEO) "to promote social and cultural diversity, and non-discriminatory access to public and private development"; on the other hand, the same City Plan has as one of its DEO "the protection of landscapes that enhance amenity and character in rural and semi-rural areas, and sympathetic development which complements surrounding character and style in both urban and rural areas." According to the first DEO, the establishment of a new Turkish styled mosque in semi-rural Brisbane should be welcomed, while according to the second DEO it should be contrasted.[96]

For religious groups, the failure to heed the 'assimilating' demand of visual amenity preservation usually leads to rejection of a proposed place of worship. The next case study illustrates how the height and form of a proposed place of worship can render it, in the eyes of a local council, 'out of character' with the surrounding area and therefore should not be allowed as originally put forward.

Case Study 6(g)
Uniting Church in Australia (Coromandel Parish), applicant
City of Happy Valley, South Australia

The applicant, the Uniting Church in Australia (Coromandel Parish), lodged a development application with the City of Happy Valley Council in 1996 to

94 See further discussion in Chapter 7 about the nexus between physical structures and religious beliefs.

95 Leone, above n 46, 226.

96 Ibid.

build a place of worship in its property.[97] It proposed to build a hall complex consisting of an auditorium with 550 seats and facilities such as a kitchen, foyer, toilets, a small reception room and an entrance canopy.[98] There was an existing building (formerly used as a Baptist church) and a dwelling on the site. Under the proposal, both these structures would be incorporated as part of the hall complex. On-site parking for 222 cars was also proposed. Many local residents and the Coromandel Valley Community Association Inc opposed the use of the site as a place of worship in the manner proposed.

The City of Happy Valley Council refused the application on the grounds that, among others, '[t]he intensity and scale of the proposed development is considered to be out of character with the existing locality'.[99] The applicant appealed this decision to the Environment, Resources and Development Court of South Australia. During the appeal, a witness for the local council stated that "[t]he overall height of the structure and expansive roofed area has no comparison to any 'residential' form within the locality... As such, the proposed building introduces a number of built form elements not evident in the locality at present nor 'envisaged' by the Development Plan."[100] The witness added that the proposed place of worship 'will represent a significant departure from any other form of development either existing in or envisaged in the zone'.[101] The Court reversed the decision of the local council and granted the application. On the issue of whether the proposed building's overall height and expansive roof adversely impacts the surrounding area, the Court stated that:

> We agree with [the council's witness] that the overall height of the proposed auditorium and the roof form proposed therefor find no parallel in any of the residential development within the locality. *However, to say that the proposed building does not resemble nearby dwellings is to say no more than that it is not a residential use of land.* It is unlikely that forms of development, such as churches or schools, which serve a neighbourhood or wider residential area, will be of a scale or form comparable to that of the residential development nearby, albeit that their materials, colours, form and siting should be in sympathy with that development.
>
> In the subject instance, whilst we acknowledge that opinions may differ as to the architectural qualities of the proposal, its design, siting,

97 *Uniting Church v Happy Valley City Council and Gilbert* [1997] SAERDC 409 (30 June 1997).

98 Ibid.

99 Ibid.

100 Ibid.

101 Ibid.

> materials and scale will, in our view, achieve a degree of harmony with surrounding development...[102] [emphasis added]

Thus, the overall height and roof form of the proposed place of worship, although different from neighbouring houses, should not be a ground for its refusal. The Court suggested that it is unreasonable to argue that places of worship and houses, although allowed to be constructed in the same zone, ought to be similar in terms of architectural design. The Court's decision rejected the local council's attempt to tame or domesticate architectural designs which are different from the established and accepted form. Refusing to be so tamed or domesticated, religious groups are often faced with the possibility of not being able to satisfy their need for a place of worship.

In *Wheeler v Kingston City Council*,[103] the appellate tribunal stated that:

> The church is a large building of a design, scale, height, siting and mass that quite obviously set it apart from the dwellings that characterise the streetscape and neighbourhood. *This is neither unusual nor unacceptable.* Places of worship are typically established within residential neighbourhoods and, due to the nature of their function and use, do not emulate the domestic residential architecture of the surrounding dwellings.[104] [emphasis added]

In a similar vein, in *Taraborelli v Casey City Council*,[105] the appellate tribunal stated that:

> The new church building is the most significant and contentious aspect of the proposal in built form terms. Religious facilities do not have to look like houses. They can be large. It is self-evident that a church in the Russian Orthodox style will look different to the existing dwellings and the simple low rise church building already on the review site.

These decisions further support the conclusion that the 'spatial assimilation' being carried out through planning regulations as a means of preserving an area's visual amenity should be rejected. The liturgical function and use of places of worship are inextricably intertwined with their architectural

---

102 Ibid.

103 *Wheeler v Kingston City Council* (*Correction*) [2012] VCAT 1094 (24 August 2012).

104 Ibid., [46].

105 [2011] VCAT 2013 [18].

designs,[106] and therefore such places should not be required to emulate the appearance of residential dwellings. The next case study illustrates how a proposed place of worship's substantial size, in relation to nearby residential properties, prompted a local council to reject it.

Case Study 6(h)
City Gospel Trust, applicant
Nillumbik Shire Council, Victoria

The applicant, the City Gospel Trust, lodged a development application with the Nillumbik Shire Council in 2009 for the construction of a place of worship for its Melbourne congregation.[107] It proposed to build a single-storey building constructed in brick and timber reflecting a contemporary design.[108] The maximum height of the building would be 7.5 metres. It was to be built approximately 17 metres from the boundary.[109] It was also proposed that 384 car parking spaces would be provided on the premises. Capable of accommodating up to 2,000 persons, the proposed building was 'of substantial size'[110] in relation to the residential properties in its vicinity. It would be used for a range of activities including prayer meetings, bible studies and administrative meetings. The number of persons attending these activities would vary: from about 50 persons attending a prayer activity on Sunday mornings, to approximately 700 persons during bible studies held thrice a week, and about 1,200 persons during larger prayer gatherings once a month.[111]

The site was surrounded by residential neighbourhoods. To the south of the site, there was new residential estate which was made up of individual 1,000-square metre lots, many of which had been developed with single or double storey houses.[112] To the west and east of the site, there were large residential properties as well as smaller residential suburban-sized lots.[113]

The Nillumbik Shire Council refused the application on the ground that 'the proposed building is inappropriate having regard to the character of the area; the scale and intensity of the proposed use of the land is significant and

106 See also the discussion in Section 7.2.
107 *City Gospel Trust v Nillumbik Shire Council* [2010] VCAT 517.
108 Ibid., [8].
109 Ibid., [9].
110 Ibid., [16].
111 Ibid., [6].
112 Ibid., [3].
113 Ibid., [4].

excessive'.[114] The local residents supported the council's decision because of the alleged inappropriateness of the proposed building in a residential area and, owing to its large size, its 'impact on the visual outlook and character of the area'.[115] The applicant appealed the council's decision to the Victorian Civil and Administrative Tribunal which reversed the decision and allowed the construction of the proposed building. On the issue of the building's huge size in relation to nearby residential properties, the Tribunal stated that:

> There is no doubt that the form of the development is quite different to the housing located to the south and south east. It would be nonsense to suggest otherwise. However, what needs to be understood is that if the purpose of the zone contemplates the establishment of non-residential uses in residential areas, a consequence of this is that a development form that departs from the traditional housing forms must also be contemplated.
>
> In this regard I refer to the comments of my colleagues in *De Nova Group Pty Ltd v Boroondara City Council* when they said:
>
> It must be acknowledged that the proposed building is a large building, significantly larger than any other nearby residential buildings. Does this mean that such a building is inappropriate in a residential environment such as this? Schools, churches, public halls, kindergartens, hospitals and nursing homes are all uses which can be found within a residential zone. [W]e are of the view that the proposal is not inappropriate in a planning sense merely because what is proposed is a large building. What needs to be resolved is the question of whether or not this proposed large building unreasonably impacts on the amenity of its immediate neighbours, or on the streetscape.[116]

The Tribunal emphasised that, as long as non-residential uses are allowed in a residential area, it may be expected that the non-residential structures like places of worship may 'depart from the traditional housing forms'.[117] It is not reasonable to require them to emulate the appearance of residential dwellings. In the above case study, the substantial size per se of a proposed religious

114 Ibid., [11].
115 Ibid., [12].
116 Ibid., [37]–[39].
117 Ibid., [37].

structure, which is necessitated by the need to cater to a large number of worshippers, cannot be made the basis for rejecting the proposal. The issue of whether a proposed place of worship unreasonably impacts on the amenity of the surrounding neighbours, or on the streetscape must be resolved by delving beyond the simple question of the building's size alone.

6.3.4 *When the Preservation of Visual Amenity Results in Discrimination Based on Religion or Belief*

The visual amenity of an area is the embodiment of the aesthetic taste of a majority population. In Australia, the preservation of visual amenity is underpinned by an Anglo-Celtic version of the Australian dream neighbourhood. As planning scholar Laura Beth Bugg observed:

> while Australian anti-discrimination … legislation and frameworks make discoursive space for the inclusion of religious minorities, urban planning policy at the local government level restricts or denies religious minority groups a right to the city. This is done through land-use ordinances that establish boundaries of acceptable activity, behaviour, and development, *which inscribe hegemonic Anglo-Australian values onto the landscape.* [This] serves to exclude religious minority groups from the physical landscape. This not only creates spatial cleavages, but also restricts religious freedom by prohibiting the full exercise of religious practice.[118] [emphasis added]

Based on this view, a local planning process that seeks to preserve one version of visual amenity is *inherently* discriminatory. It tends to favour those places of worship which conform to the existing Anglo-Celtic standards in Australia's built environment. The tall and pointed spires of a Christian church, for example, will most likely be ascertained as visually compatible with the 'agricultural' nature of a locality; or the cross and bell tower of a Catholic Church visually attuned with the 'residential' character of an area. There is a strong likelihood that both places of worship will not occasion objections based on a potential negative impact upon the visual amenity. On the other hand, a mosque's imposing dome and minaret or a conspicuous Buddha monument will most likely occasion objections for being visually intrusive on the character of an area. Ngui has aptly observed that:

> The application of amenity rules works to advantage Christian groups who already dominate the religious landscape and who do not challenge

118 Bugg, above n 68, 2.

> the religious landscape on a visual level. This transgresses both the libertarian principle and the neutrality principle by limiting the free practice of religion and demonstrating a preference for a particular religious group.[119]

Therefore, local planning processes that seek to preserve the visual amenity of Australian localities promote an *institutional* bias which tends to favour Christian places of worship and to disfavour non-Christian ones. These planning processes themselves, because of their adherence to an Anglo-Celtic version of beauty or pleasantness in the physical environment, breed a discriminatory outcome. What is occurring is a form of *indirect discrimination* based on religion or belief.[120] In *Derksen v The Netherlands*,[121] the Human Rights Committee stated that the principle of non-discrimination:

> prohibits both direct and indirect discrimination, the latter notion being related to a rule or measure that may be neutral on its face without intent to discriminate but which nevertheless results in discrimination because of its exclusive or disproportionate adverse effect on a certain category of persons.[122]

In a more detailed manner than the Committee's statement above, the UN High Commissioner for Human Rights explained that:

> indirect discrimination occurs when a neutral measure has a disparate and discriminatory effect on different groups of people and that measure cannot be justified by reasonable and objective criteria. Indirect discrimination recognizes that treating unequals equally can lead to unequal results which can have the effect of petrifying inequality. Combating indirect discrimination is an important means of dealing with the institutional and structural biases – often unintentional and unperceived – that result in discrimination and that act as impediments to the achievement of equal human rights for all.[123]

---

119 Ngui, above n 83, 102.

120 For a discussion on the difference between direct and indirect forms of discrimination, see Section 4.3.2.

121 Human Rights Committee, *Views*: *Communication No. 976/2001*, UN Doc CCPR/C/80/D/976/2001 (1 April 2004) ('*Derksen v The Netherlands*').

122 Ibid., para 9.3.

123 *Analytical Study of the High Commissioner for Human Rights on the Fundamental Principle of Non-discrimination in the Context of Globalization*, UN Doc. E/CN.4/2004/40 (15 January 2004), para 12.

Thus, there are three elements that concur to produce indirect discrimination. First, there is a measure, regulation or rule that is facially 'neutral' – that is, applied uniformly to all subjects. The requirement that a proposed structure must not be 'out of character' with an area is applied to all development applications to construct places of worship. In turn, the 'out of character-ness' of a proposed structure is measured against a uniform standard of beauty or pleasantness in the built environment. Second, the subjects of regulation are 'unequals' which means that they are not similarly situated in one or more respects. Flowing from theological differences, the architectural designs or styles of places of worship are different, as would be expected. The bright, golden domes are innate to a Sikh *gurdwara*, in the same manner as the tall and slender minarets are intrinsic to a mosque. Third, the uniform application of the measure, regulation or rule produces 'a disparate and discriminatory effect on different groups of people' and that measure, regulation or rule 'cannot be justified by reasonable and objective criteria'. Measured against a uniform standard of beauty or pleasantness in the built environment, proposed non-Christian places of worship are more likely to be found as 'out of character' with the nature of an area compared to those places of worship that have a familiar or accustomed appearance because of their long established presence in Australia's towns and cities. Hence, a church's tall bell tower or a spire will most likely be allowed but not an equally tall Islamic minaret or Buddhist pagoda. This study of Australian local planning processes reveals that all three elements of indirect discrimination are present via practices that seek to preserve an area's visual amenity.

In Australia, proposals to build non-Christian places of worship will most likely encounter difficulties that are occasioned by a regulatory framework that places too much weight on Anglo-Celtic standards of beauty and pleasantness in the built environment. As a consequence, there is an ever present danger that the right of religious groups to establish and maintain places of worship may be infringed. The next case study shows a somewhat rare exception to what has been described above. It illustrates how the preservation of an area's visual amenity may produce a discriminatory outcome even against a long established religious group in Australia.

Case Study 6(i)
Roman Piotrowski, applicant
Greater Dandenong City Council, Victoria

The applicant lodged two development applications with the Greater Dandenong City Council in 1999.[124] The first application was for the construction

124 *Willrath v Greater Dandenong City Council* [2000] VCAT 2124 (31 October 2000).

of a Catholic church building having the capacity to accommodate 430 persons, with an area of 760 square metres and 139 car parking spaces.[125] The second application sought approval to use an existing building with an area of 150 square metres as a chapel to accommodate 200 persons and with 60 car parking spaces.[126] Both religious structures were proposed to be built on the subject land which was located along Greens Road which is a primary arterial road.

Opposite the subject land was a Turkish mosque which, at the time of the appeal, was being constructed, having previously secured a planning permit from the local council. When completed, the mosque would be set back 75 metres from Greens Road. In addition, immediately beside the subject land was a Buddhist temple which, at the time of the appeal, was also under construction. When completed, the Buddhist temple would be set back 55 metres from Greens Road while its car parking would be set back 35 metres.

The Greater Dandenong City Council approved the applications for the construction of the proposed Catholic church and chapel. Local residents appealed this decision to the Victorian Civil and Administrative Tribunal. During the appeal, the Tribunal found that the main issue was the 'visual bulk' of the proposed buildings.[127] The Tribunal held that the proposed chapel should be allowed, but the proposed church building should be rejected because of its visual impact from Greens Road. It stated that 'the monolithic or single form design of the building, coupled with only a 30m setback would, I believe, result in this building sitting prominently in what is otherwise a mostly open landscape'.[128] In terms of visual impact, the Tribunal compared the proposed Catholic church building with the Turkish mosque and the Buddhist temple complex which were then under construction in the immediate vicinity of the subject land. It stated that:

> At the time of my inspection construction of Stage One of the next door, Buddhist Temple was underway. Although currently set back 70 m from Greens Road, I appreciate that the ultimate development will extend to within 55 m of the frontage. I regard this latter setback however as substantially greater than the 30 m setback proposed for the subject land. The Buddhist complex also has a far less imposing scale and built form mass, being comprised of a series of attached, single storey polygonal

125 Ibid., [1].
126 Ibid., [1].
127 Ibid., [3].
128 Ibid., [60].

> shaped pavilions or rotundas, rather than being one substantial and imposing built form element.
>
> Stage Two of the mosque development, almost opposite the subject land, which is certainly of an imposing design and of a substantial scale, is at least proposed to be set back a significant distance from Greens Road. It is also set at somewhat of an angle to the road. Car parking is proposed to the front of this building. This however is to be set back between 35 and 55 m from the road, with landscaping to the front. I find the proposed church would be more prominent within the Greens Road view corridor than even this quiet substantial development.[129]

In the above case study, the Tribunal faulted the proposed Catholic church building's 'monolithic or single form design', but at the same time acknowledged the proposed Turkish mosque's 'imposing design and substantial scale'. Moreover, the Tribunal cited the proposed Catholic church's inadequate setback from the road (of only 30 metres) as the main reason for its rejection, but did not see any visual amenity problem with the 35-metre setback of the mosque's car parking (whose substantial size and lighting were also visually prominent from Greens Road). In a largely vacant area like Greens Road, it seems likely that the five-metre difference would be of little significance.

This case study illustrates how a high degree of subjectivity in the local planning process, specifically in preserving an area's visual amenity, can lead to a discriminatory result. The proposed Catholic church building, Turkish mosque and Buddhist temple were the subject of separate development applications, and their merits were heard on separate occasions. However, since their visual impact stood to harm or intrude into the *same* visual amenity (that is, they were to be built in the same area along Greens Road), it is reasonable to expect that these religious structures would be assessed using a common or uniform visual standard. Although the Tribunal viewed the Buddhist temple complex as 'far less imposing', all three religious structures are substantial developments on their respective sites. The proposed Catholic church building, Turkish mosque and Buddhist temple were intended to cater to a large number of attendees ranging from 430 to 1,200 persons. In an area which is generally flat and *without* any other buildings in the immediate vicinity, all three religious structures would be visually prominent from Greens Road from most angles. Therefore, the rejection of the proposed Catholic church building runs counter

129 Ibid., [60], [62].

to logic and common sense when the Turkish mosque and Buddhist temple complex – both substantial scale developments – were allowed.

6.4 Conclusion

The case studies in this chapter illustrate the constraints faced by religious groups as they engage with the local planning processes in Australia. They are indicative of the discourses employed by religious groups, local objectors and local councils in planning disputes involving visual amenity issues. This chapter revolves around one central theme – that is, the right of religious groups to establish and maintain places of worship is highly prone to being infringed by local planning processes that are geared towards the preservation of the visual amenity of localities, even though the concept is imprecise, arbitrary and subjective. Planning regulatory tools that aim to preserve the visual amenity of localities effectively subdue other versions of beauty or pleasantness in the built environment while promoting the traditional or 'familiar' versions. Such tools tend to disadvantage proposed places of worship with non-familiar architectural designs or appearance.

The tension between the preservation of visual amenity and the right to establish and maintain places of worship is exemplified in the case studies. The former is part of the traditional role of local councils as protector of the convenience, cleanliness, pleasantness and orderliness of local areas; while the latter involves facilitating the building of structures that adequately satisfy the needs of religious groups, even though they may be visually regarded as strange, exotic or 'alien' edifices. The local councils are at the very fulcrum of these two competing interests or values, although they tend to place greater importance on visual amenity concerns than on religious freedom, as the case studies illustrate. The state's duty to respect the right to establish and maintain places of worship demands a different approach on the part of local councils in resolving issues arising from a religious building's purported impact against the visual amenity of an area. Such an approach should not be dominated by a heavy reliance upon a concept that perpetuates the hegemony of a dominant culture and that excludes the religious 'other' from Australia's localities, neighbourhoods or streets.

Complementing the analysis in this chapter, the next chapter analyses another type of planning regulatory tool which is also designed to preserve an area's visual amenity, and its repercussions to the right to freedom of religion or belief. Such regulatory tool is composed of specific design controls imposed on proposed structures, including regulations on height, area, bulk, colour, road setbacks, screening elements and similar qualitative attributes. What are the implications to religious freedom when local councils disallow certain structural features of places of worship? Can places of worship be 'hidden' from the public view without infringing religious freedom norms? Can religious groups be compelled to vary architectural designs that embody their core religious beliefs? Using case studies as backdrop for discussion, the next chapter analyses these important issues.

CHAPTER 7

'The Devil is in the Details'

Specific Design Controls on Places of Worship and State Encroachment on Religious Expression and Exercise

7.1 Introduction

The previous chapter discussed the rejection of applications to build, extend or renovate places of worship that were found to be 'out of character' with a locality or area.[1] Using this general aesthetic standard, local councils evaluate a proposed place of worship's visual compatibility with an assumed general scenery or landscape of a locality. This chapter complements this analysis by exploring the use of *specific* design controls imposed on proposed religious edifices. Local councils impose these controls in order that the putative harm posed by a proposed religious building against the character of a locality or area may be prevented, or at least minimised. As illustrated in this chapter, specific design controls include regulations on colour, area, height, size, bulk, road setbacks, screening elements, and similar qualitative attributes of proposed places of worship or their particular structural features like domes, spires, roofs or windows.

This chapter analyses the ramifications for the right to freedom of religion or belief when the appearance of proposed places of worship or their particular structural features are subjected to design controls imposed by a secular authority. Design controls may adversely impact the right to freedom of religion or belief in two major ways. First, they have the potential to impinge on the freedom of religious expression – that is, the ability of religious communities to express and communicate their religious beliefs through their built structures. Such expression or communication of beliefs may be vital to a religious group's prescribed manner of worship, observance, practice or teaching. Second, design controls can pose a real obstacle (in the physical sense) to a group's freedom of religious exercise – that is, their liturgy or the actual conduct of rituals, ceremonies and other kinds of worship. Both ramifications are assaults against the *forum externum* of the right to freedom of religion or belief.

This chapter is divided into three parts. The first part analyses the direct connection between the belief system of religious groups and the design of

1 See discussion in Section 6.3.

 | DOI 10.1163/9789004289345_008

their places of worship. Using seven case studies as backdrop for discussion, the second part examines how this nexus may be severed by local planning processes which subject the construction of places of worship to rigid design controls that result in alterations in their faith-dictated appearance, both in the structures' interior and exterior components. The third part concludes that, consistent with a state's obligation to respect the right of religious groups to establish and maintain places of worship, local planning processes must be respectful of the symbiotic relationship between the architecture of religious structures and their expressive and liturgical functions.

7.2 The Manifestation of Religious Beliefs in Physical Structures

Religious beliefs, like any other type of belief, exist in the realm of the *forum internum* – that is, one's inner thought or conscience. They are transmitted between individuals, and hence cross the realm of the *forum externum*, only when they are expressed in some form or another. Hence, for example, a Catholic priest who delivers his sermon from a pulpit is engaged in the transmittal of religious beliefs; and so too does a group of Buddhist monks who chant hymns and songs while performing a religious ceremony. In these examples, the transmittal of religious beliefs is readily observable not only because of the presence of the speaker and the audience, but also because of the verbal message being imparted.

However, not all transmittal of religious beliefs occurs in a direct and obvious manner. Communication of religious beliefs can also be accomplished in more subtle and indirect ways such as through artistic works, such as architecture which is regarded as 'a form of symbolic expression, which, like other forms of art, demonstrates various political, social, or religious ideas'.[2] In particular, religious architecture is comprised of those structures designed and constructed at the behest of religious communities and intended by them to be centres of their worship activities.[3] '[T]hrough its shapes, symbols, decorations, ornamentations and monumentality', religious architecture is anchored on 'a strong intention to communicate a particularized message about a group's religious beliefs'.[4] In its internal and external architecture, a place of worship

2 Thomas Pak, 'Free Exercise, Free Expression, and Landmarks Preservation' (1991) 91(7) *Columbia Law Review* 1813, 1836.

3 Anne Fornerod, 'The Places of Worship in France and the Public/Private Divide', in Silvio Ferrari and Sabrina Pastorelli (eds), *Religion in Public Spaces: A European Perspective* (Ashgate, 2012), 322, 324.

4 Pak, above n 2, 1840.

may be rich with symbols that express fundamental theological beliefs. Therefore, the religious edifice itself becomes the spatial expression of core religious tenets.

A religious community's claims as to the divine existence, and humanity's relationship with it, are usually expressed through the physical features of their place of worship. This nexus is apparent in the embodiment of core religious principles in the physical features that make up most places of worship. For religious communities, the choice of architectural design is not random but faith-dictated. For example, the place of worship of the adherents of the Baha'i religion must have nine sides (that is, a nonagon) to reflect their devotion to the 'glory of God' which is translated as '*baha*' which, in their belief system, has a numerical value of nine.[5] On the other hand, the relative simplicity and austerity of the interior of Protestant churches are a reflection of their firm abhorrence to idolatry.[6] There is therefore a direct association between the belief system of a religious community and the physical structure of its place of worship. Angela Carmella described this symbiotic linkage in the following way:

> Ecclesiastical architecture has always been inextricably linked with basic religious choices made by worshipping communities. In both its functional and visual aspects, the house of worship reflects and influences all dimensions of a religious community's life – its primary theological principles, its liturgical practices, its faith renewal movements, its doctrinal development, its missional goals and its identity. The purpose of the structure is a religious one; religious choices are embodied in it; those choices in turn shape the individual and communal religious experience ...[7]

For this analysis, the physical features of a place of worship may be divided into three distinct features, namely: the façade, interior worship area and associated structures. The façade includes all characteristics that give a place of worship its qualitative external appearance including its height, bulk, shape, contour, size, orientation, colour, texture, external ornamentation and similar characteristics. It is the part of the religious structure that proclaims to the community at large not only the presence of a religious group but also the

5 'Abdu'l-Bahá, *The Promulgation of Universal Peace* (Bahá'í Publishing Trust, 1982), 71.

6 See especially, Sergiusz Michalski, *Reformation and the Visual Arts: The Protestant Image Question in Western and Eastern Europe* (Routledge, 1993), 169–194.

7 Angela Carmela, 'Houses of Worship and Religious Liberty: Constitutional Limits to Landmark Preservation and Architectural Review' (1991) 36 *Villanova Law Review* 401, 404–405.

particular religious message it is designed to convey, affirm and propagate. In a manner of speaking, the façade is a canvass where views about the divine and the physical world are painted. It is therefore an expression of fundamental religious choices. For example, the gold-coloured tips (or *shikhara*) on Hindu temple domes represent the mythological 'Mount Meru' which is the residence of the principal deities in the Hindu religious tradition.[8] Hindus believe that these deities have their own celestial kingdoms in 'Mount Meru' where their devotees will reside with them when they eventually die, while awaiting their reincarnation into the next life.[9] Like a Hindu temple, a Muslim mosque is accentuated by features that are littered with religious allusions. The five-pointed star represents the five pillars of Islam[10] which are the five duties that all Muslims must obey,[11] while the crescent moon circumscribing the five-pointed star represents the guiding light of Allah.[12] Together, they are the most iconic of Islamic religious symbols.

Interior worship spaces such as the altar in a Catholic church or the interior of a Buddhist temple are where the main, and usually the most religiously important, rite or ceremony takes place. They are necessarily different for each religion or belief which reflects theological differences. Their design is the spatial manifestation of how a religious community views itself in relation to its god and how such a god should be properly worshipped. Thus, for example, a mosque's interior worship area has to be designed pointing to a geo-spiritual focus. Prayers inside a mosque are performed in parallel rows while the worshippers face towards Mecca in Saudi Arabia. This geo-spiritual focus on a sacred place directly affects the construction of a mosque's interior worship space. It must be built with the correct orientation to Mecca even though such orientation does not run parallel to an area's street or building lines. On the other hand, the interior worship space of a Buddhist temple reflects the priority placed by Buddhist teachings on individual meditation. It is comprised of a shrine room where a statue of the Buddha, in different sculptural versions such as standing, sitting, walking or reclining position, can be found. Done as

---

8 I W Mabbett, 'The Symbolism of Mount Meru' (1983) 23(1) *History of Religions* 64–83.

9 Ibid.

10 Malek Chebel, *Symbols of Islam* (Assouline Press, 2001), 17–18.

11 These five duties are the belief that Allah is the only god and that Muhammad is his final prophet; the conduct of prayers five times a day; fasting during the holy month of Ramadan; the giving of *'zakat'* or a percentage of one's yearly accumulated wealth to the poor; and the pilgrimage to Mecca, Saudi Arabia at least once in one's lifetime. See Jamila Hussain, *Islam: Its Law and Society* (Federation Press, 2003), 14–15.

12 Chebel, above n 10, 17–18.

personal acts of devotion, offerings of incense and flowers are made to show reverence to the Buddha.

The egalitarian nature of religious communities, the intercessional roles of religious officials (and thus the importance of a religious establishment), a worshiper's relationship with a divine being and other religious views are all given material representation in the way the interior worship areas are designed. Referring to the manner in which worshippers pray inside a church, John Janzen described the 'rituals of congregational life', which according to him, 'offer[s] the most fitting focus for an understanding of the congregational built form'.[13] The built form, in other words, follows how the community of worshippers understands itself and its relationship with its god or gods.

An associated structure is any physical feature which is not physically attached to a place of worship itself, but nevertheless performs an important religious function. For example, a minaret, a pagoda, a bell tower and a lotus pond are physical features which are structurally independent from the main place of worship. Because they are physically detached from the place of worship itself, their importance is sometimes undervalued because acts of worship can still be performed without them. However, far from being religiously useless auxiliary structures, they contribute to the overall religious experience of worshippers, in as much as they evoke emotive or poignant responses from them. Like the façade and the interior worship spaces, associated structures also convey, affirm and propagate core religious beliefs. The presence of these structures completes the worshippers' overall religious experience because of the emotional or affective response they generate from them. John Costonis described religious structures as possessing 'semiotic' properties and they 'function as signs, conveying cognitive and emotional meanings'.[14] Thus, the serene and tranquil atmosphere they help provide is deliberate in order to produce an intense religious or spiritual connection between the worshippers and their objects of faith.

In summary, a place of worship's external façade, interior worship area, and associated structures are all vessels that contain expressions of religious beliefs. Through them, individually and collectively, a religious group conveys, affirms, teaches and propagates its fundamental theological doctrines concerning the divine existence and mankind's relationship with it. The next section analyses the ramifications to the right to freedom of religion or belief when the nexus

13 John Janzen, 'Form and Meaning in Central Kansas Mennonite Buildings for Worship' (1999) 73(2) *The Mennonite Quarterly Review* 323, 326.

14 John Costonis, 'Law and Aesthetics: A Critique and a Reformulation of the Dilemmas' (1982) 80 *Michigan Law Review* 355, 392.

between physical structures and the religious beliefs they embody is broken through the intervention of local planning processes, specifically through the enforcement of specific design controls on proposed places of worship.

7.3 The Curtailment of Religious Expression and Religious Exercise through Specific Design Controls on Proposed Places of Worship

When a secular authority (in this instance, the local councils) exercises the power to approve or deny faith-dictated designs of proposed places of worship, it raises two issues that are vital to the right to freedom of religion or belief. First, there is an immediate impact on a religious community's freedom of religious expression through its architecture – that is, its ability to affirm, convey and propagate its religious beliefs through its built structures. The practical effect is that local councils suppress certain religious beliefs from being expressed through built structures while allowing other religious beliefs. As discussed below, such interference is accomplished through the use of specific design controls such as prescriptions on colour, area, height, size, bulk, road setbacks, screening elements, and similar qualitative attributes.

Second, there is a direct impact on the ability of a religious group to fully exercise its right to manifest religion or belief because of spatial or structural constraints and limitations imposed by design controls. As analysed below, it may be that the colour, area, height, size, brightness, bulk and similar qualitative attributes of places of worship are religiously mandated, and may be indispensable to the conduct of religious rituals, ceremonies and other types of worship. Therefore, altering these seemingly innocuous attributes of places of worship likewise alters the exercise of religious manifestation itself.

Thus, religious expression and religious exercise may be curtailed by the imposition of specific design controls on proposed places of worship. Such curtailment takes place in three distinct but sometimes overlapping contexts, namely: (1) prohibiting the construction of particular features of a place of worship, (2) hiding places of worship from public view, and (3) truncating or scaling back their prominent or distinguishing features. In these contexts, a religious group's expression of its religious beliefs as embodied in the structures themselves is curtailed, and that religious exercise which is tied to, or dependent on, physical structures is restricted. Both repercussions are limitations on important elements of the right to freedom of religion or belief as guaranteed by international human rights law. Employing case study analyses, these three contexts are discussed below.

7.3.1 *When Important Structural Features of Places of Worship Are Not Allowed to Be Constructed*

The first case study involves a local council's rejection of a proposed place of worship on the ground that its most important liturgical feature – a baptismal pond – was allegedly incompatible with the character of the locality. The consequence to the applicant religious group's exercise of religious manifestation is highlighted.

Case Study 7(a)
Sabian Mandaean Association in Australia Ltd, applicant
Wollondilly Shire Council, New South Wales

In December 2007, the applicant Sabian Mandaean Association in Australia Ltd, lodged a development application with the Wollondilly Shire Council in New South Wales for a place of worship comprising of 'a baptismal pond with terrace seating for 300 people covered with shade cloth, car parking for seventy cars and a toilet, shower and change room block'.[15] The applicant was a religious group which follows the teachings of Saint John the Baptist. The nature of their religious ceremonies requires the use of running water, including during rites such as baptisms and marriages.[16] As initially proposed, the baptismal pond would have free flowing water pumped from and then returned to the Nepean River. The surface area of the pond would be approximately 320 square metres and the pond would have an average depth of 0.9 metres.[17] A stretched shade cloth was proposed over the seating area attached to timber posts with a maximum height of 8.4 metres.[18] The provision of on-site parking for 70 cars was also proposed. The local council received a considerable number of submissions which opposed the application on the grounds that the proposed baptismal pond was incongruous with the rural character of the area and would likely cause flooding, soil erosion and the instability of the river bank.

In December 2008, the local council rejected the development application on the grounds that the proposed baptismal pond would likely have negative environmental consequences to the Nepean River and would have adverse visual impact with the rural character of the area.[19] The applicant appealed to

15 *The Sabian Mandaean Association in Australia Ltd v Wollondilly Shire Council* [2009] NSWLEC 94 [1].
16 Ibid., [2].
17 Ibid., [2].
18 Ibid., [2].
19 Ibid., [42].

the New South Wales Land and Environment Court.[20] While the appeal was pending, the applicant provided significant amendments to its proposal, including the reduction of the size of the proposed baptismal pond to accommodate a maximum number of 100 persons and the reduction of the parking facilities to only 25 spaces.[21]

Relying on the conclusions of experts, the Court held that the proposed baptismal pond would not cause any flooding, soil erosion or instability of the river bank.[22] On the issue of whether the proposed baptismal pond would have a negative impact upon the rural character of the area, the Court accepted the following expert's conclusion:

> The baptism pond has been amended in terms of its seating capacity and location, the height and size of the shade cloth and the pond size have been reduced. The seating is not proposed to be cut into the embankment which runs parallel to the river. This means the previous mounding has been removed and the seating has been reduced from 300 to 100. The sail structures have also been amended where the number of structures has been reduced to reflect the reduction in seating. The new location has also allowed the height of the sails to be reduced.
>
> [T]he use of appropriate dark colours such as greys, blacks and earthy tones for the sails, the sail posts and seats would ensure that these elements blend within the current setting. In addition, the structures/works proposed are not of a size, height or scale that would stand out. Accordingly it is considered that the visual impact of this amendment is acceptable.[23]

In the above case study, the proposed baptismal pond is inextricably tied with the applicant's core religious tenet of following their religious patron, Saint John the Baptist. This is an example of what Peter Edge observed that, 'in some [religious] traditions particular forms of sacred space are essential for particular religious activities, or for structured community worship'.[24] The local council's decision to disallow the construction of the baptismal pond directly restricted the applicant's exercise of its fundamental belief due to spatial constraints. Without such a baptismal pond, the applicant's religious observances or practices requiring the use of running water (which is a central tenet in the

20 Ibid., [3].
21 Ibid., [5].
22 Ibid., [17]–[21].
23 Ibid., [43].
24 Peter Edge, *Religion and Law: An Introduction* (Ashgate, 2006), 123.

applicant's belief system) could not be performed in the religiously prescribed manner. Without that crucial structure, the Sabian Mandaeans in this case study could not adequately perform their religiously mandated acts of worship, observance or practice. The local council's decision to disallow its construction has incapacitated them from fully enjoying their freedom of religious exercise.

In an analogous situation, the prohibition against the installation of a kitchen (called a *langar*)[25] inside a Sikh *gurdwara* directly interferes with the right to manifest religious beliefs in worship, observance and practice. The interior worship space of a Sikh *gurdwara* prominently features a *langar* immediately beside the actual prayer area.[26] It reflects the symbolic importance of the sharing of food in the Sikh faith.[27] Disallowing the construction of a *langar* would directly interfere with the religious observance and practice of sharing of food which is deeply rooted on the egalitarian character of a Sikh religious community.

Design controls that affect the principal worship spaces, as illustrated by the above examples, can directly restrict the exercise of the right to freedom of religion or belief. Such restrictive effect may be very severe including, for instance, leaving a religious community without a choice but to alter its religious ritual or ceremony as a result of spatial or structural limitations. Therefore, when features such as a baptismal basin, a kitchen or other structures which are indispensable in religious worship, observance and practice are disallowed or removed from design proposals, the interference with the freedom of religious exercise is immediate and severe. Design controls that affect such features are not innocuously regulating the colour, area, height, size, shape, brightness, bulk and similar qualitative attributes of places of worship; but rather they are directly impinging on the freedom of religious exercise itself. Referring to the inability of a Christian religious group to redesign its church's interior worship space due to design controls imposed by a municipality in the United States, Richard Babcock and David Theriaque commented that:

> It takes no stretch of imagination to realize the extent of the governmental interference to the practice of a religion that occurs when a religious organization is prohibited from physically arranging the interior of its

---

25 Ceri Peach and Richard Gale, 'Muslims, Hindus and Sikhs in the New Religious Landscape of England' (2003) 93(4) *Geographical Review* 469, 478.

26 Ibid.

27 William Owen Cole and Piara Singh Sambhi, *The Sikhs: Their Religious Beliefs and Practices* (Sussex Academic Press, 1995), 63–66.

> own property in the manner it desires. Such a prohibition interferes with conduct that is central to the practice of the religious organization.[28]

The next case study involves a local council's view of a minaret as being visually intrusive or disruptive against the character of an area which led to its decision to reject a proposed mosque renovation. A minaret is an elevated structure used by Muslims to signal their prayer times. Like a baptismal pond and a Sikh *langar*, a minaret is religiously significant to its proponents such that its prohibition may restrict the exercise of religious freedom.

Case Study 7(b)[29]
Dandenong Islamic Society Inc, applicant
Greater Dandenong City Council, Victoria

In July 2004, the Dandenong Islamic Society Inc lodged a development application with the Greater Dandenong City Council for the renovation of its mosque which was serving the Turkish community in Dandenong, Victoria.[30] In July 2005, the local council refused the development application on the grounds that, among others, the proposed renovation of the mosque would be 'unacceptably out of character through its bulk and siting with the locality'.[31] One of the local council's objections was 'that the proposed improvements are too big/bulky for the site, leading to unacceptable visual bulk in terms of the likely views of the proposed new buildings on the site from the public realm'.[32] In particular, the local council found that the proposed 'high minaret' of the renovated mosque would be inappropriate 'in terms of neighbourhood character for a site located on the edge of a residential area'.[33]

The applicant appealed the local council's decision to the Victorian Civil and Administrative Tribunal. Finding that the mosque's renovation would not produce any unacceptable impact upon the traffic and parking conditions in the surrounding area, the Tribunal allowed the proposal. With respect to the

28 Richard Babcock and David Theriaque, 'Landmarks Preservation Ordinances: Are the Religion Clauses Violated by Their Application to Religious Properties?' (1992) 7(2) *Journal of Land Use and Environmental Law* 165, 197.

29 Also featured as *Case Study 5(f)* in Chapter 5.

30 *Dandenong Islamic Society v Dandenong City Council* [2005] VCAT 2501 (28 November 2005) [3].

31 Ibid., [4].

32 Ibid., [28].

33 Ibid., [28].

alleged damage or harm to the area's visual amenity posed by the proposed minaret, the Tribunal stated that:

> In terms of neighbourhood character issues, we accept that the proposed new mosque building (especially the proposed minaret) will be a noticeable and somewhat different visual feature in the neighbourhood. However, we consider that this does not necessarily make the proposed mosque incompatible with the existing neighbourhood character. Bearing in mind that the subject land is on the edge of the residential area and that there are other large institutional buildings along Cleeland Street, we consider that the existing neighbourhood character is somewhat more mixed and "hard edge," and that therefore there is sufficient flexibility with the local neighbourhood character for the proposed mosque and associated buildings to sit comfortably in their location.... [H]aving a new mosque that becomes a local landmark is not necessarily a bad thing in a residential area.[34]

This case study illustrates a usually controversial aspect in a mosque proposal – that is, when local councils prohibit the construction of Islamic minarets which are considered religiously significant by Muslims.[35] While minarets do not, strictly speaking, structurally form part of a mosque, their construction is an intrinsic part of the manifestation of the religious faith of Muslims and thus they come under the mantle of protection of the right to freedom of religion or belief.

While some non-Muslims may consider minarets as non-essential to worship itself (for instance, it has been argued that the Muslims can still pray even without the minarets),[36] this is not how Muslims view these structures. In this regard, it is the Muslims' view of minarets that should prevail. This is because the religious significance of minarets forms part of the Islamic religious doctrine which *only* the Muslims themselves – and certainly not the state nor

---

34 Ibid., [32].

35 Titus Burckhardt, *Art of Islam: Language and Meaning, Commemorative Edition* (World Wisdom, Inc, 2009), 87–90.

36 For example, it has been claimed that 'a ban on building minarets would not prevent Muslims from freely developing and living a religious belief nor from practising and spreading their religion. The ban on minarets would not therefore compromise the real essence of the fundamental right to freedom of religion'. See Vincenzo Pacillo, '*Stopp Minarett*? The Controversy over the Building of Minarets in Switzerland: Religious Freedom versus Collective Identity', in Silvio Ferrari and Sabrina Pastorelli (eds), *Religion in Public Spaces: A European Perspective* (Ashgate, 2012), 337, 345.

other religions – can define. The choice to designate a place or a structure as sacred or religiously significant is part of the non-regulable *forum internum* of the freedom of religion or belief which is an absolute human right. That choice belongs to the religious community concerned, and its truth or veracity cannot be assessed by others. An assessment made by others as to the propriety of assigning religious significance to certain structures is a direct interference – an affront – against the right to hold religious convictions of one's own choice.

In Chapter 2, it was demonstrated that the legal protection of the *forum internum* extends beyond its traditional conception of safeguarding the right to maintain or change one's religion or belief, and also encompasses the right not to be compelled, in any manner, to act or behave in contradiction with one's religion or belief. Thus, for example, an individual cannot be compelled to salute a flag if it contravenes his or her inner beliefs, nor can a religious group be forced to perform worship activities different from those prescribed in its religious tenets. In the same manner, in building places of worship, religious groups may not be compelled by planning authorities to vary architectural design choices – which are embodiments of core religious beliefs – without encroaching upon the realm of the *forum internum*.

In 2009, the construction of minarets in Switzerland was submitted to the voters in a referendum.[37] The outcome of the electoral exercise was an amendment to the Swiss constitution which bans the construction of minarets in Switzerland. Responding to this development, the Special Rapporteur on freedom of religion or belief stated that a 'ban on the minarets amounts to an undue restriction of the freedom to manifest one's religion and constitutes a clear discrimination against members of the Muslim community in Switzerland'.[38] In addition, Switzerland's decision to hold the referendum did not sit well with the Human Rights Committee which, in its Concluding Observation on the report submitted by Switzerland that year, stated that:

> The Committee is concerned about the referendum initiative aimed at prohibiting the construction of minarets and about the discriminatory

---

37 For a complete account of the events leading to the amendment of the Swiss constitution which bans the construction of minarets all throughout Switzerland, see especially, Pacillo, above n 36, 337–352; See also Lorenz Langer, 'Panacea or Pathetic Fallacy? The Swiss Ban on Minarets' (2010) 43(4) *Vanderbilt Journal of Transnational Law* 863.

38 Office of the High Commissioner for Human Rights, *Switzerland: UN Expert on Religious Freedom Regrets Outcome of Vote to Ban Construction of Minarets* (2009) <http://www.ohchr.org/en/NewsEvents/Pages/DisplayNews.aspx?NewsID=9649&LangID=e> at 7 October 2014.

> advertising campaign which accompanies it. It notes that the State party does not support this referendum initiative which, if adopted, will bring the State party into non-compliance with its obligations under the Covenant (arts. 2, 18, 20). The State party should strenuously ensure respect for freedom of religion and firmly combat incitement to discrimination, hostility and violence.[39]

Although the Human Rights Committee dealt with the construction of minarets and not places of worship per se, the underlying issue was the propriety of subjecting the enjoyment of the freedom of religious manifestation to a popular vote in a society which has a Christian majority. The Committee, through the above pronouncement, sought to guard religious freedom from any impairment as a result of measures countenanced by the majority of the population. Like all human rights, the right to freedom of religion or belief, including its important element of the right to establish and maintain places of worship, ought to be immune from the vagaries of popular sentiment.

Religious freedom, along with all fundamental freedoms guaranteed in international human rights instruments, must be placed above and beyond the reach of the changing tides of popular opinion. The rationale for this position goes into the very essence of the 'universality' principle of human rights which affirms that every human being enjoys certain fundamental freedoms and entitlements that are inherent and inalienable.[40] As human rights expert Paul Sieghart noted, the main trait that distinguishes human rights from other rights is "their universality: according to classical theory, they are said to 'inhere' in every human being by virtue of [one's] humanity alone."[41] By virtue of this universality principle, the manifestation of religious freedom cannot be made contingent upon the preference of the majority population determined through referenda, plebiscites or other forms of electoral exercise. Because places of worship are integral to religious manifestation, submitting the construction of such places or their particular features to a referendum is tantamount to allowing the majority to decide whether the minority may exercise its own religious freedom.

Continuing the analysis of instances when 'liturgical' features of places of worship are disallowed by local councils, the next two case studies illustrate

---

39 Human Rights Committee, *Concluding Observation on the Report of Switzerland*, UN Doc CCPR/C/CHE/CO/3 (3 November 2009), para 8.

40 Louis Henkin, 'The Universality of the Concept of Human Rights' (1989) *Annals of the American Academy of Political and Social Science* 506, 10–16.

41 Paul Sieghart, *The International Law of Human Rights* (Oxford University Press, 1983), 75.

the indispensability of certain objects, articles or icons in the exercise of the right to manifest religious beliefs. The negative impact on the right to freedom of religion or belief caused by the failure of local councils to appreciate this linkage is underscored.

Case Study 7(c)
Greek Orthodox Archdiocese of Australia Consolidated Trust, applicant
Mornington Peninsula Shire Council, Victoria

In March 2000, the Greek Orthodox Archdiocese of Australia lodged a development application with the Mornington Peninsula Shire Council for the construction of a parish hall that would extend its existing church building.[42] The local council received submissions from local residents opposing the proposed extension on ground of its substantial size and the 'increased frequency and scale of events and the proposed hours of operation, given the proximity of residential properties'.[43] In February 2001, the local council rejected the development application. The applicant appealed the council's decision to the Victorian Civil and Administrative Tribunal.

During the appeal, the presence of an important religious icon inside applicant's church building was objected to by some local residents. According to them, the approval to use the said building as a place of worship was "made on an understanding that the icon of '*Panagia Kamariani*' was not to be housed in the Church."[44] The applicant confirmed that the icon is indeed inside its church building and it intended to transfer it to the new parish hall when it is completed. One of the objectors complained about the 'icon attract[ing] a large number of persons from outside the Parish … [and] that these attendances are to the extent that the Church (and Hall) operates as a regional facility'.[45]

The Tribunal held that the proposed extension to applicant's church building would not cause any traffic congestion, inadequate parking or noise and, therefore, its construction should be allowed subject to certain conditions.[46] On the issue of the religious icon '*Panagia Kamariani*' being housed in the church building, the Tribunal found that 'there is no permit condition

42 *Harrison v Mornington Peninsula Shire Council* [2001] VCAT 2010 (23 October 2001).

43 Ibid., [25].

44 Ibid., [36]; The '*panagia kamariani*' is an icon depicting the Virgin Mary and was discovered in ancient Greece after the Virgin Mary allegedly appeared in a Greek family in three apparitions.

45 Ibid., [36].

46 Ibid., [70], [81] and [91].

disallowing'[47] the icon, contrary to the allegation of one of the objectors. The Tribunal stated that:

> We indicated that we were aware that an icon is within the Church and accept that significant numbers of people may attend the Church to venerate it. We did not consider that receipt of further evidence in relation to the provenance of the icon would be of assistance in determining whether or not to allow a Parish Hall on the subject site.[48]

In the above case study, the local council rejected the proposed parish hall because of the likelihood that the use of the site as a place of worship would further intensify primarily due to the presence of a 'significant religious icon' within the site. Some local residents wanted to remove the icon because it attracted more worshippers to the site, thus impacting the area's physical amenity.

The Religion Declaration, one of the foundational instruments that built religious freedom in international law, as discussed in Chapter 2, recognises the indispensability of certain articles, materials, or other objects in the conduct of religious ceremonies or rituals. It declares that religious organisations have the freedom '[t]o make, acquire and use to an adequate extent the necessary articles and materials related to the rites or customs of a religion or belief'.[49] As analysed in Chapter 3, such freedom is subsumed under the right to establish and maintain places of worship, to the extent that some religious articles and materials indispensably form part of religious edifices.[50] Thus, maintaining a religious statue, an altar, a baptismal basin or font, a cross, a *migrab*, a kitchen, and other physical symbols or structures is part and parcel of religious freedom. Without them, the conduct of certain religious manifestations in worship, practice or observance will be impossible. This is especially true for religious manifestations that are performed 'in community with others'. The Human Rights Committee also recognised this indispensability of symbols or structures when it stated in General Comment 22 that the freedom to manifest religion or belief:

> extends to ritual and ceremonial acts giving direct expression to belief, as well as various practices integral to such acts, including the building of

47 Ibid., [38].
48 Ibid., [39].
49 Religion Declaration art 6(c).
50 See discussion in Section 3.3.4.

> places of worship, the use of ritual formulae and objects, the display of symbols, and the observance of holidays and days of rest.[51]

In the next case study, another crucial object of belief – a Buddha statue – was at the centre of a planning controversy when it was ordered to be removed by the local council as a result of significant local opposition.

Case Study 7(d)
Khmer Krom and Australian Buddhist Association Inc, applicant
Liverpool City Council, New South Wales

In 2003, the Khmer Krom and Australian Buddhist Association Inc lodged a development application with the Liverpool City Council in New South Wales to renovate its temple and thereby 'formalise' its existing use as a place of worship.[52] The application was met with opposition from local residents who complained about the alleged damage or harm caused by the temple to the area's physical and visual amenity. It was reported that the "local response to the proposal was aggressive and damning including references to 'frightening the horses and being an eyesore', (in an environment where heavy haulage vehicles are parked and lay rusting in the landscape)."[53] The local council required the preparation of a master plan that showed the temple's long-term impact upon the area. After complying with all the requirements imposed by the local council, the application was approved and construction began. The applicant Buddhist association, however, 'was forced to remove the five-metre high golden Buddha (the eyesore), from the site'.[54]

The removal of the Buddha statue was a direct impingement on religious worship, observance and practice because a Buddha statue – and what it represents and evokes on the part of the worshipper – occupies a central part in Buddhist spiritual beliefs. Without that crucial object of faith, worshipers cannot adequately perform their religiously mandated acts of worship. Its removal incapacitated them from enjoying their freedom of religious exercise. A Buddhist temple without a Buddha statue does not satisfy the requirements

51 General Comment 22, para 4.

52 John Skennar, 'Sydney, A City Growing Within: The Establishment of Buddhist Centres in Western Sydney', in Cristina Rocha and Michelle Barker (eds), *Buddhism in Australia: Traditions in Change* (2011), 86, 90.

53 Ibid.

54 Ibid.

of that particular belief. In fact, from the perspective of Buddhist adherents, it is not a proper Buddhist temple at all.[55]

To summarise, local councils should accord religious organisations the greatest leeway possible in the design of proposed places of worship, especially their structural features which serve a *liturgical* function – that is, those which are used in the performance of a religious ceremony or ritual. For example, in Italy, the liturgical function of Christian bells is appropriately considered by state authorities in regulating their use, as observed by Tymen van der Ploeg:

> In Italy there are several rules that may apply to bell-ringing ... [which] distinguish between the ringing of bells not directly connected with worship and that directly connected with worship. The 'non-worship' use of bells is subject to the same rules of any other noise emission. The ringing of bells connected to a Roman Catholic service is considered to be an expression of the free exercise of the Catholic religion ... There are many cases where the court argued that the sound of bells, as long as it is for liturgical use, is something that should not be regulated in terms of noise pollution and public health. The regulation of the ringing of bells, in this case, is the responsibility of the ecclesiastical authority.[56]

Thus, using an analogous reasoning, and with respect to structural features that serve a liturgical function, local councils should exercise the minimum regulation possible so as not to interfere with religious exercise itself. To do otherwise is to condition, directly or indirectly, the exercise of the right to manifest religious beliefs upon governmental approval and the attendant risk of subjecting such exercise on the whim, caprice or partiality of local planning authorities. Such discretionary state approval of religious exercise is inconsistent with the fundamental essence of religious freedom as guaranteed in international human rights law.

7.3.2 *When Places of Worship Are Hidden from Public View*

Aside from their functional uses as venues for religious and socio-cultural activities, places of worship proclaim to the public a religious community's

---

55 For a comprehensive discussion of the significance of Buddha statues and their different positions (for example, reclining, sitting down, arms up or down, etc.), see generally Carol Stratton, *What's What in a Wat: Thai Buddhist Temples Their Purpose and Design* (2010) 1–104.

56 Tymen van der Ploeg, 'Places of Worship: Between Public and Private: A Comparison between Bulgaria, Italy and the Netherlands', in Silvio Ferrari and Sabrina Pastorelli (eds), *Religion in Public Spaces: A European Perspective* (Ashgate, 2012), 353, 365.

'symbolic public presence and open practice of their faith'.[57] Annick Germain and Julie Gagnon noted that 'places of worship seek to affirm the collective identity of their membership in public space, either through choice of location or architectural features'.[58] Especially for minority religious communities which may have encountered opposition before they could successfully build a place of worship, such a building is their collective 'assertion of their negotiated terms of belonging'[59] within their adopted societies. Therefore, places of worship are also meant as religious symbols to be 'displayed' in the public space. There is a strong intention to communicate religious messages using places of worship as the medium.

However, despite the significance of places of worship as religious symbols, some local councils in Australia require that they be hidden from public view, either totally or partially. This 'hiding' strategy is resorted to in order to prevent or minimise their alleged harm to an area's visual amenity. It is accomplished in one of two ways as the case studies will show: (i) by the imposition of mandatory setbacks from the road, or (ii) by putting up screening elements such as tall trees and fences that are designed to hide a religious structure from public view. In particular, non-Christian places of worship or their particular structural features are sometimes regarded as 'eyesores' that must be blocked from the public sight. The 'hiding' solution reveals how little value some local planning authorities ascribe to the architectural designs of places of worship which, as discussed above, are steeped in religious tradition, and negates their important symbolic function.

For example, the use of mandatory setback from the road was employed in order to hide places of worship in a Western Australian suburb. In December 2009, the City of Swan in Perth rejected a development application by the Bosnian Muslim community to construct a mosque.[60] The then mayor, Charlie Zannino, explained that the proposed mosque did not comply with the provisions of planning regulations that require new buildings to fit in with the agricultural nature of the valley which is well regarded for its vineyards and

57 Laura Beth Bugg, 'Religious Freedom and the Right to the City: Local Government Planning and the Rejection of Islamic Schools in Sydney, Australia' (Workshop Paper, Twelfth Berlin Roundtables: Religious Pluralism, Irmgard Coninx Stiftung, 7–11 April 2010), 2.

58 Annick Germain and Julie Gagnon, 'Minority Places of Worship and Zoning Dilemmas in Montreal' (2003) 4(3) *Planning Theory & Practice* 295, 306.

59 Peach and Gale, above n 25, 487.

60 Nicolas Perpitch, 'Bias denied as Swan Valley mosque rejected', *The Australian*, 18 December 2009.

restaurants. He stated that '[i]t is a fairly large building, with two storeys, and a minaret at 21 metres on a small block. It would have stood out'.[61] Prior to this decision, the City of Swan local council had approved the construction of a Buddhist temple and a Pentecostal Dream Builders church because 'they had been built on large blocks and set well back from the road, *virtually out of sight'*. [emphasis added].[62]

The imposition of mandatory setbacks upon proposed places of worship are inconsistent with the international human rights standard that such places are also vehicles for religious expression, as discussed in Chapter 3. When places of worship are deliberately hidden from public view as illustrated in the above examples, there is an immediate curtailment of a religious community's freedom of religious expression through its architecture – that is, its ability to convey, affirm and propagate their religious beliefs through built structures. Because places of worship are designed to be seen by the public, hiding them from public view devalues their worth as vehicles of religious expression. Mandatory setbacks aim to silence the religious messages that are conveyed through the religious structures themselves.

Places of worship, in a real sense, celebrate a religious community's arrival and acceptance into the community. The link between the freedom of religion or belief and the freedom of speech is apparent. Explaining the complementary relationship of the two freedoms, Carolyn Evans states that:

> If freedom of religion were to disappear overnight from the various treaties, constitutions, and statutory bills of rights in which it is currently found, much that is currently protected as religion could equally be covered as a manifestation of freedom of expression. While religion certainly has its contemplative internal dimension, *most religions are also communicative in a variety of ways*. Religious individuals may pray together, sing or chant, read from holy works, teach their children, write religious works of various kinds, preach, protest, and proselytize – all examples of free speech as well as the free exercise of religion.[63] [emphasis added]

To Evans' enumeration above can be added the construction of places of worship which is both an exercise of the right to manifest one's religion or belief and an exercise of freedom of expression. As explained in Section 7.2 above, places

61 Ibid.

62 Ibid.

63 Carolyn Evans, 'Religion and Freedom of Expression', in John Witte, Jr and M. Christian Green (eds), *Religion & Human Rights: An Introduction* (Oxford University Press, 2012), 188.

of worship have a communicative function because they announce the presence of a religious group in the larger community and, equally important, they convey particularised religious messages through their unique structural features. Local councils' imposition of mandatory setbacks effectively subdues the communication of these messages to the public. Forced to be constructed as far as possible from the public view, a church's cross, a mosque's crescent moon and star, or a Buddhist temple's pagoda lose their effectiveness as communicative devices.

The next case study illustrates another way of 'hiding' places of worship from the public view. It is accomplished through the installation of screening elements such as trees, plants or fences that literally block the public's view of a religious building.

Case Study 7(e)
The Macedonian Orthodox Church & Cultural Community
Gold Coast Inc, applicant
Gold Coast City Council, Queensland

The applicant lodged a development application with the Gold Coast City Council in May 1994 for the construction of a church with a gross floor area of 1,055 square metres and a maximum height of 29 metres.[64] The plans submitted by the applicant showed that the building would incorporate Orthodox Church design features. Land uses in the subject locality were predominantly rural residential. After several hearings, the applicant submitted a revised proposal showing a reduced floor area of 580 square metres and a maximum height of 24 metres excluding a cross [65] which the local council still found objectionable. After the Gold Coast City Council failed to decide on the application within the statutory period, the applicant appealed the council's deemed refusal to the Queensland Planning and Environment Court.

During the appeal, the pivotal issue was the height of the proposed building which included towers and domes. The applicant contended that the height should be permitted to reach at least 17 metres allegedly because 'theological reasons exist which would not permit a building of [a lower] height to be consecrated'.[66] On the other hand, the local council contended that the height

64 *The Macedonian Orthodox Church & Cultural Community Gold Coast Inc v Gold Coast City Council* [2000] QPEC 2 (14 January 2000).

65 Ibid.

66 Ibid.

should be limited to 12 metres. Some local residents argued that a height of 7.5 to 10 metres was more appropriate. Agreeing with the local council, the Queensland Planning and Environment Court held that 'it is appropriate to restrict the impact upon the visual amenity of residents in the locality by limiting the height of the church building to 12 metres'.[67] In addition to reducing the height of the proposed church, the Court also ordered that its towers and domes must be 'hidden' from public view, stating that:

> In my view, the construction of a 17 metres high building as proposed by the appellant would adversely impact on the visual amenity of nearby residents. *However, this impact can generally be satisfactorily reduced by existing and proposed landscaping measures to ensure that only broken occasional views of the bell-tower or domes will be visible* if the height of the church is limited to 12 metres. I do not accept that landscape measures can adequately soften views of the bell-towers and domes if the building is constructed to a height of 17 metres.[68] [emphasis added]

A similar 'hiding' strategy using 'landscaping measures' was employed by the Kalamunda Shire Council in Western Australia in December 2010 when it caused an applicant to lodge a revised development application which substantially reduced the height and bulk of a proposed Hindu temple. According to its architect, the reduced height would make it 'of comparative size to nearby buildings and, although different, it would express the identity and culture of the people using the building'.[69] The architect described the reduced height of the domes to be at the same level as the trees surrounding the complex and the proposed multi-storey structure as within the limits prescribed by the building code.[70] In December 2010, the Kalamunda Council approved the application subject to 12 conditions which included that, in addition to the reduced size of the proposed structure:

> d) *The applicant is to install and maintain mature screen planting on the southern, eastern and western boundaries* and within the rear parking area to the satisfaction of the Director Planning and Development Services.

---

67 Ibid.

68 Ibid.

69 Kaitlyn Offer, 'Krishna Temple to Expand', *In My Community*, 28 December 2010.

70 Ibid.

> e) Provision of a colours and textures schedule to the satisfaction of the Director of Planning and Development Services.[71] [emphasis added]

As illustrated in the above examples, when local councils order the 'hiding' of places of worship from public view through the use of screening elements, both the right to manifest one's religion or belief and the freedom of expression are restricted. They undermine these two fundamental freedoms by preventing architectural religious expressions from being imparted by religious groups *and* from being received by their intended audience. Anat Scolnicov noted that '[t]he degree of protection accorded to religious speech should not be any less than that accorded to other kinds of political speech. For the same reason, the right to religious freedom must include a right to receive religious speech'.[72] Therefore, the aggrieved parties or 'victims' whose rights are violated in situations like these are 'those who impart the speech and those who wish to receive the speech'.[73]

In effect, by employing these 'hiding' strategies, the state assumes the role of a censor who classifies and screens what are acceptable and unacceptable forms of architectural religious expression. Planning scholars Ceri Peach and Richard Gale also observed the same 'hiding' decisions being used by local planning authorities in Birmingham in the United Kingdom, stating that:

> [t]he mosque is hidden behind shops, and its dome and minaret cower beneath the roofline of neighbouring older houses. Trees screen the site. The local planning authority supported the development with the argument that the site was well chosen to minimise impact on the general public. Translated from planning-speak, this means that local White people will not see it.[74]

The tall screening trees, plants or fences that literally block religious messages from being imparted and reaching their intended recipients limit the ability of religious communities to inform the public at large about their faith. In the same manner, hiding the iconic features of places worship is tantamount to censorship of the specific religious ideas that they are meant to communicate to the public for purposes of informing them about the faith.

---

71 Shire of Kalamunda, Western Australia, Minutes Ordinary Council Meeting (20 December 2010) 12.

72 Anat Scolnicov, *The Right to Religious Freedom in International Law: Between Group Rights and Individual Rights* (Routledge, 2011) 194.

73 Ibid., 195.

74 Peach and Gale, above n 25, 482.

7.3.3 *When Distinguishing Features of Places of Worship Are 'Toned Down'*

Local councils employ another strategy to make places of worship more 'acceptable' to objectors. It is done by toning down their prominent and distinguishing features in terms of their size, height, bulk and colour. The size of a mosque's domed roof, the height of a Hindu *mandir* or the colours of a Buddhist pagoda, for instance, are toned down in order to lessen the perceived incongruity they provide to the visual harmony of an area. However, as analysed below, many such alterations in the structural features of places of worship have a corresponding impact upon the religious beliefs that are intended to be conveyed, affirmed or propagated. The next case study illustrates how a local council's order to scale back a prominent feature of a synagogue had a corresponding impact upon that feature's liturgical function.

Case Study 7(f)[75]
Chabad House of Malvern Toorak Inc, applicant
Stonnington City Council, Victoria

In 2000, the applicant lodged a development application with the Stonnington City Council to extend its existing synagogue.[76] The Stonnington City Council refused the application on the main ground that the proposed extension would exacerbate the inadequacy of parking spaces in the surrounding streets. The applicant appealed to the Victorian Civil and Administrative Tribunal. During the appeal, one of the main issues was the alleged adverse impact of the synagogue's extension upon the area's visual amenity. The local council and some local objectors argued that 'the two storey additions [to the synagogue] – which include a row of clerestory windows above the proposed multi-purpose and expanded ladies' gallery area – represented an excessive amount of visual bulk'.[77] The clerestory windows allegedly did not "achiev[e] architectural and urban design outcomes that 'contribute positively to local urban character and enhance the public realm while minimising detrimental impact on neighbouring properties'."[78] As a result of these objections, and in order to avoid risking a refusal, the applicant lodged a revised application that included a substantial reduction of the clerestory windows' dimension. As regards the visual impact of these modified windows, the Tribunal stated that:

75 Also featured as *Case Study 5(d)* in Chapter 5.

76 *Chabad House of Malvern Toorak Inc v Stonnington City Council* [2001] VCAT 1448 (6 July 2001) [2].

77 Ibid., [29].

78 Ibid., [28].

> [t]hese plans substantially reduce the visual impacts of the clerestory windows – making the clerestory more consistent with the general architectural theme of the building. It would be fair to say that with this change the contest in relation to the built form scale of the building reduced considerably. Following my inspection of the premises I am satisfied that the new addition will be in no way out of character with the surrounding area which includes some quite substantial two storey dwellings at the entrance to Embling Road.... In general terms I find the whole complex sits comfortably within the Glenferrie Road streetscape.[79]

As originally proposed, the synagogue's clerestory windows were large and gave the proposed building a bulky appearance. The windows were intended to be large in order to allow more light to illuminate the interior main worship space of the synagogue. In the Jewish faith, the light that enters a synagogue has a special religious significance. It has been stated that in Judaism 'Light is a religious symbol'[80] which reflects a firm belief that 'Israel is called a light to the nations (Isaiah 43:6)'.[81] As Jewish scholar Lee Levin noted, '[p]roviding light for the synagogue came to be considered a meritorious duty.... Windows were the main source of light (e.g., *Bar'am*), and buildings with clerestory windows were designed to provide an even greater amount of light'.[82] In Jewish belief, the synagogue's lighting is intended to create an atmosphere of devotion. Therefore, in the above case study, the originally proposed clerestory windows of the synagogue were intended to serve a religious purpose. The local council's decision to reduce the size of the windows in order to minimise their purported 'detrimental impact on neighbouring properties' did not innocuously regulate the external appearance of the synagogue. Rather, the decision interfered with and impaired the religious function that those windows were meant to accomplish or satisfy. Having been substantially reduced in size, the clerestory windows could not allow more *'bar'am'* or divine light or illumination to enter the synagogue.

The next case study illustrates another local council's attempt to tone down a proposed mosque's bulk which, in turn, is attributable to its large interior worship space. The applicant argued that a large interior worship space is in fact necessitated by the religiously prescribed posture or manner of praying in Islam.

---

79 Ibid., [30].

80 The Great Synagogue Sydney, *Symbolism in the Synagogue* (2010) <http://www.greatsynagogue.org.au/Traditions/SynagogueSymbolism.aspx> at 23 October 2014.

81 Ibid.

82 Lee I. Levin, *The Ancient Synagogue: The First Thousand Years* (Yale University Press, 2005), 359.

Case Study 7(g)[83]
Islamic Education and Welfare Association of Dandenong, applicant
Casey City Council, Victoria

In August 2003, the applicant lodged a development application with the Casey City Council to construct a mosque on its property in Narre Warren North, Victoria.[84] Under the proposal, the applicant intended to build a two-storey building 'with traditional Islamic architectural themes, such as a central dome, arched windows and minarets'.[85] The proposed mosque had an overall height up to the top of the dome and minaret of approximately 11 metres[86] and a total useable floor area of 1,516 square metres.

In accordance with the recommendations of the local council's planning office, the floor area of the proposed mosque was reduced by 20 percent.[87] However, despite a favourable recommendation from the planning committee, the Casey City Council refused the application on the grounds that, among others, the proposed mosque was inappropriate in terms of neighbourhood character considerations. In reaching this decision, the local council considered the proposed mosque's substantial size or bulk which was allegedly incongruent with the surrounding structures. The applicant appealed the local council's decision to the Victorian Civil and Administrative Tribunal. On the proposed mosque's size or bulk, the Tribunal ruled that:

> The proposed building is substantial. However, we accept Mr Janif's evidence that that is a reflection of its proposed use. A large "mosque" area is required *so that traditional postures can be performed as part of prayers.* Separate areas, denoted as areas for "activity centre and Sunday classes," are large because there is a *need to split up groups by sex and age.* As noted by Mr Janif, the proposed building is also of substantial size as it is *for the glory of God.*
>
> We accept Mr Chow's submission that respect for local character should be considered in terms of building scale, setbacks from boundaries and landscaping intentions. Our finding is that the proposed building is an appropriate response in those terms.[88] [emphasis added]

---

83 Also featured as *Case Study 6(f)* in Chapter 6.

84 *Islamic Education and Welfare Association of Dandenong v Casey City Council* [2004] VCAT 1850 (16 September 2004) [6].

85 Ibid., [7].

86 Ibid., [8].

87 Ibid., [7].

88 Ibid., [44]–[47].

In faulting the proposed mosque's bulk or size, the Casey City Council failed to appreciate the direct relationship between physical space and Islamic beliefs. In particular, the mosque's size or bulk is determined by its interior worship space which, in turn, is directly influenced by how Muslims perform the '*salat*'. The Tribunal took into account the unique worshipping practice of Muslims inside a mosque when it stated that:

> for religious reasons prayers are only conducted in the area denoted as "mosque." In that area worshippers must be clean and without shoes. There may be some circulation through the adjoining hallways but those areas are not used for prayers. Furthermore, a mat area of approximately 1.44 square metres is required for each adult. That area is needed to perform prayer postures and there are markings on the floor to regularise the arrangement. As noted by Mr Janif, the arrangement has not changed in over 1,400 years. A plan supplied by Mr Janif indicates that the mosque area is thus capable of accommodating 143 males (marginally more if children are attending).[89]

The planning committee's recommendation to reduce the size or bulk of the mosque, while ostensibly made to preserve the evenness of structures in the area, had the further repercussion of depriving the mosque of a large expanse of interior worship area which was needed in order to perform the faith-dictated manner of worship among Muslims. This case study illustrates how spatial limitations can affect the very conduct of religious rites or ceremonies. The 'toning down' of the proposed mosque's size or bulk failed to recognise the symbiotic relationship between the mosque's interior worship area and the religiously prescribed manner of praying in Islam.

A similar 'toning down' strategy was employed by the local council in *Case Study 6(d)*, discussed in Chapter 6, concerning the substantial size and bright colours of a proposed Buddhist temple complex. The local council was persuaded by local objectors who complained about the temple's substantial height and that '[t]he architecture of the Buddhist Temple is significantly intrusive ... The intrusiveness is accentuated by the bright orange coloured roof tiles, which are an essential feature of Thai temple architecture'.[90] In response to these objections, it was argued that the huge size of Buddhist temples and statues is an intrinsic part of Buddhist spiritual beliefs. In the end, the local

---

89 Ibid., [73].

90 Letter of Peter Hobson to the Gold Coast City Council, 2 December 2008.

council approved the construction of the Buddhist temple complex under strict conditions, one of which was that the '[b]uildings and structures must not be painted in highly reflective, bright or obtrusive colours'.[91] In another proposed Buddhist temple in Leumeah, New South Wales, the applicant religious group 'felt the need to step back from a traditional Thai architectural style, as they were concerned it might not get approval'.[92] According to the leader of the Buddhist monks, 'If that fear was not there we may have done it better'.[93]

Altering a place of worship's structural features (such as the bright orange roof of a Buddhist temple) does not innocuously regulate a building's external appearance in order to preserve an area's visual amenity. Rather, it distorts the particularised religious messages which those features are meant to convey. The colours of proposed places of worship are deliberately chosen in order to communicate certain religious claims both to the worshippers and to the public at large. In Buddhism, white is the symbol of purity while bright orange is a symbol of warm hospitality, both of which are important values in Buddhist teachings.[94] In Hinduism, the bright golden tip of its domes symbolises a mythological mountain where principal Hindu deities reside together with the souls of their devotees.[95] If bright gold is the religiously prescribed colour of these domes, changing it to something else via specific design controls which proscribe 'intrusive' colours constitutes an interference with the expression of a religious belief. When planning authorities attempt to alter these symbols, including those seemingly inconsequential colours, they are literally treading on sacred grounds.

A *combined* strategy of hiding a place of worship and truncating its features was employed in a development application to construct a Buddhist temple in Sellicks Hill, South Australia. The applicant group, the Nan Hai Pu Tuo Temple of Australia Inc, lodged a development application, in February 2009, to construct a complex consisting of temple buildings, a 35-metre high pagoda, residence for

---

91 Greg Stolz, 'Buddhist Temple in Nerang Gets Go-Ahead under Strict Conditions', *The Courier-Mail*, 23 March 2010.

92 John Skennar, 'Sydney, A City Growing Within: The Establishment of Buddhist Centres in Western Sydney' (Centre for Cultural Research, University of Western Sydney: Post-Suburban Sydney Conference, 2005), 4.

93 Ibid.

94 Paul Hansen, Colour Symbolism Represented in Buddhist Traditions (2003) <http://www.people.vcu.edu/~djbromle/color03/colorsymbolisminbuddhismPaul.htm> at 25 October 2014.

95 Mabbett, above n 8, 64–83.

its monks, an 18-metre high silver Buddha statue, memorial garden, lotus pond and a parking lot on its property.[96] As part of the application process, the Buddhist group was required to submit a report in accordance with a set of mandatory design guidelines that included the following:

> 4.4 DESIGN/VISUAL AMENITY
> 4.4.1 Describe the visual impact of the proposed development on the immediate locality, taking into account its height, scale and massing, when viewed from various vantage points including from Sellicks Beach, the Sellicks Hill escarpment and Aldinga Beach.
> ...
> 4.4.3 Describe the architectural elevation treatments for visible building elements, having regard to the prominent nature of the site and the need to integrate with and complement the existing landscape.
> ...
> 4.4.7 Provide details of the landscape plan showing any screening elements.
> 4.4.8 Provide details of the construction materials, surface treatments and colours for the proposed development.[97]

Detailed prescriptions on architectural design, such as the above example, make it difficult for religious groups to follow their own faith-dictated designs. Instead, they are compelled to surrender their designing prerogative – an activity where religious beliefs are the raw materials that inspire architectural expression – to local councils. By so doing, local councils become enmeshed in the process of deciding what religious tenets are worthy of expression and the appropriate manner of expressing them in architectural built form.

In this situation, an excessive entanglement between a secular authority and religious organisations is created, thus undermining the autonomy of religious organisations in the choice of beliefs worthy of expression. The state cannot arrogate this task unto itself because it amounts to intervening in the exclusive domain of religious communities to assign the relative significance of their religious beliefs and express in architectural form only those they deem important. It would be absurd for a religious organisation to express in

96 Jai Bednall, '$15 million Buddhist temple for Sellicks Hill', *Southern Times Messenger*, 6 January 2009.

97 Department of Planning and Local Government, Guidelines for the Preparation of a Development Report for the Nan Hai Pu Tuo Temple at Sellicks Hill, South Australia (June 2009), 9–10.

built form all of its religious beliefs. In determining the hierarchical importance of religious beliefs, it is the view of religious communities that should matter and not the views of the state. This is because the religious significance attached to architectural structures forms part of their religious doctrine which *only* they themselves – and not the state – can define. The choice of what religious beliefs to express, communicate or teach to others is part of the *forum internum* of the freedom of religion or belief which is absolute under international human right law. That choice belongs to the religious community concerned and its truth cannot be assessed by others. An assessment made by others is a direct interference – an affront – against the fundamental right to hold religious convictions of one's own choice.

By toning down their distinctive features, the expressive intent that is embodied in these religious structures is thereby diluted and, at times, may even be distorted. Directing the domes of a Hindu temple to be painted with a colour other than a bright gold, for example, destroys their intended symbolism of eternal life with Hindu deities. Similarly, allowing the construction of a Buddhist pagoda but only with four layers (instead of the religiously mandated five) to prevent it from 'standing out' from the surrounding structures distorts its spiritual symbolism. When the external appearance of places of worship is controlled by the state, it is also controlling the religious messages they are meant to convey, affirm, propagate or teach. While the stated aim is the preservation of the visual harmony of a place, the practical effect is the intrusion in the exclusive province of religious communities to determine what beliefs are worthy of expression.

The respective spheres of the secular and the religious are not always separate. In fact, there are many situations when the two are entangled. There is no better vantage point to observe this entanglement than to explore controversies involving the construction of places of worship in Australia. Emboldened by a secular objective, local councils encroach upon religious prerogatives in the choice of symbols and designs that reflect religious beliefs and the manner of expressing them in architectural built form. This encroachment is made possible by the wide discretion conferred upon the local councils and the subjective concept of 'visual amenity' that they seek to preserve.

The state, acting through local councils, cannot arrogate unto itself a choice which, consistent with religious autonomy, is reserved to religious communities themselves by virtue of their right to freedom of religion or belief. When religious doctrine is translated into a form of expression, genuinely and in good faith, (in this case, as architectural designs of places of worship), it is incumbent upon the state – on the basis of its duty to respect the right to freedom of religion or belief – to ensure that local planning processes give religious communities the greatest freedom possible in deciding how best to use their property in accordance with their religious or other beliefs.

7.4 Conclusion

There is a direct connection between the belief system of a religious community and the design of its places of worship. This nexus is apparent in the embodiment of core religious principles in the structural features that make up a place of worship. For religious communities, the choice of architectural design is not random but faith-dictated. Religious architecture has always been inextricably linked with basic religious choices or claims. In both its functional and visual aspects, a place of worship reflects all the dimensions of a religious community's life – its primary theological principles, its liturgical practices, its doctrinal development, its religious identity. Religious choices are therefore embodied in the religious building itself.

The use of specific design controls by local councils may interfere with two aspects of religious freedom. First, they may break up the nexus between physical structures and the fundamental theological beliefs they are meant to affirm, convey or propagate. Second, they may restrict religious exercise when spatial limitations affect the very conduct of religious rites or ceremonies. Like the broad criteria of 'out of character-ness' of a structure from its surrounding area which was analysed in the previous chapter, specific design controls that prescribe a structure's height, size, bulk, area, colour, setbacks, screening elements, and similar qualitative attributes seek to preserve a particular version of a dream neighbourhood. But whose version? And at what expense?

This chapter has illustrated how specific design controls, whose aim is to protect the majority's aesthetic sensibility, may impede the right of religious expression and religious exercise. Both aspects of the right to freedom of religion or belief become vulnerable to being violated by local planning processes whose functioning is heavily influenced by a planning philosophy that an Australian neighbourhood should be made up of neatly aligned houses, buildings with even height and bulk, structures with familiar designs and complementary colours, and frontages with recognisable features.

A planning regulatory framework that hinders religious expression and exercise is inconsistent with the right to freedom of religion or belief. Consistent with a state's duty to respect this right, local planning processes must be respectful of the direct association between the architectural designs of religious structures and: (i) their expressive or communicative function, and (ii) their indispensable role in performing religious ceremonies and rituals – that is, their liturgical function. An awareness of this nexus should inform and guide local planning decisions instead of simply endorsing the majoritarian version of the dream Australian neighbourhood – which is a version that entails the muting of religious expression and limiting religious exercise. This chapter corroborates the main argument raised in the two previous chapters that, as they currently stand, the concepts and principles that underpin the local planning processes across Australia engender the risk of violating the international human rights standards on religious freedom, including the right to establish and maintain places of worship.

PART 4

Implications and Conclusion

CHAPTER 8

A Balancing Exercise under International Human Rights Law

The Right to Establish and Maintain Places of Worship vis-à-vis Legitimate Planning Objectives

8.1 Introduction

Apart from its internal realm (*forum internum*) which is absolutely protected, all the other constituent elements of the right to freedom of religion or belief, including the right to establish and maintain places of worship, may be validly restricted by the state. The rationale behind 'limitations clauses'[1] is the fact that most human rights when claimed by individuals or groups 'do not exist in isolation from communal goals, aims, and interests of others co-existing in political and legal life'.[2] Therefore, limitations clauses are meant to serve as balancing mechanisms in order that the state can weigh the relative significance of human rights vis-à-vis other societal interests. This chapter dissects the limitations clause provided in Article 18(3) of the ICCPR which is the limitations clause *specifically* applicable to the right to manifest one's religion or belief. It demonstrates that the restrictions to the right to establish and maintain places of worship which are caused by the enforcement of local planning regulations are extremely difficult to be justified on the basis of Article 18(3). This analysis bolsters the finding that the Australian local planning system tends to restrict the structural aspect of the right to freedom of religion or belief, in a manner which is inconsistent with international human rights law.

This chapter is in three parts. First, the requirements of a 'permissible limitation' under Article 18(3) of the ICCPR are analysed, and their application in the

1 As analysed in Section 2.3, 'limitations clauses' identify the narrow circumstances under which a state may validly restrict the exercise of the right to freedom of religion or belief. See especially, T. Jeremy Gunn, 'Permissible Limitations on the Freedom of Religion or Belief' in John Witte, Jr and M. Christian Green (eds), *Religion and Human Rights: An Introduction* (Oxford University Press, 2012) 254, 255.

2 Basak Cali, 'Balancing Human Rights? Methodological Problems with Weights, Scales and Proportions' (2007) 29 *Human Rights Quarterly* 251, 256.

 | DOI 10.1163/9789004289345_009

particular context of restrictions against the right to establish and maintain places of worship is illustrated. The aim is to ascertain whether such restrictions satisfy the requirements that they must be: (i) 'prescribed by law', (ii) 'necessary to protect public safety, order, health, or morals or the fundamental rights and freedoms of others', and (iii) 'directly related and proportionate to the specific need on which they are predicated'.[3] Second, this chapter illustrates that the societal interests that underpin the protection of amenity in local planning may in fact be 'translated' into human rights claims themselves. This paves the way for a balancing exercise between the right to establish and maintain places of worship and two of the most important human rights claims underpinning the protection of amenity, namely, (i) the right of local residents to the peaceful or quiet enjoyment of their property and (ii) the right of a majority population to its 'cultural identity' as expressed in the streetscape. Finally, this chapter concludes that the requirements of Article 18(3) of the ICCPR are formidable for local councils to satisfy, considering the strict interpretation that should be accorded to the grounds of public safety, order, health, or morals or the fundamental rights and freedoms of others. A planning regulatory framework which assigns a central role to the problematic concept of amenity engenders, and even attracts, restrictions against the right to establish and maintain places of worship that are difficult to justify on the basis of Article 18(3) of the ICCPR.

8.2 Permissible Limitations to the Right to Establish and Maintain Places of Worship under Article 18(3) of the ICCPR

With respect to the right to freedom of religion or belief, the relevant limitations clauses are Article 29(2) of the UDHR which is a generic limitations clause that applies to all the rights recognised therein[4]; Article 18(3) of the ICCPR which is a right-specific limitation clause applicable only to the right to freedom of religion or belief[5]; and Article 1(3) of the Religion Declaration which is

3 General Comment 22, para 8.

4 Article 29(2) of the UDHR provides that: 'In the exercise of his rights and freedoms, everyone shall be subject only to such limitations as are determined by law solely for the purpose of securing due recognition and respect for the rights and freedoms of others and of meeting the just requirements of morality, public order and the general welfare in a democratic society'.

5 Article 18(3) of the ICCPR provides that: 'Freedom to manifest one's religion or beliefs may be subject only to such limitations as are prescribed by law and are necessary to protect public safety, order, health, or morals or the fundamental rights and freedoms of others'.

a verbatim reaffirmation of Article 18(3) of the ICCPR.[6] Among these clauses, it is Article 18(3) of the ICCPR which states *the* law on the permissible limitations on the right to freedom of religion or belief. This is because it was intended to refine the broadly conceived limitations clause in Article 29(2) of the UDHR and thus embodies the later expression of the legislative will of the international community as regards the subject. For example, it may be noticed that the 'general welfare' ground which is 'probably the vaguest limitation ground of all'[7] is present in Article 29(2) of the UDHR but is omitted in Article 18(3) of the ICCPR. Furthermore, Article 18(3) of the ICCPR provides a tailored and specific limitations clause which is applicable only to the right to freedom of religion or belief. Being a built-in limitation to the right to freedom of religion or belief, it therefore constitutes the *lex specialis* which must prevail over general provisions like Article 29(2) of the UDHR.[8] Meanwhile, Article 1(3) of the Religion Declaration is a verbatim reproduction of Article 18(3) of the ICCPR which is 'taken to bear identical meaning'.[9]

Article 18(3) of the ICCPR states that:

> Freedom to manifest one's religion or beliefs may be subject only to such limitations as are prescribed by law and are necessary to protect public safety, order, health, or morals or the fundamental rights and freedoms of others.

The operation of Article 18(3) is triggered only when there is a 'limitation'[10] on the right to religious manifestation. The first issue, therefore, is to determine what constitutes a 'limitation' of such a right. Specifically, and relevant to the main problem

---

6 Article 1(3) of the Religion Declaration provides that: 'Freedom to manifest one's religion or beliefs may be subject only to such limitations as are prescribed by law and are necessary to protect public safety, order, health, or morals or the fundamental rights and freedoms of others'.

7 Cornelis De Jong, *The Freedom of Thought, Conscience and Religion or Belief in the United Nations (1946–1992)* (Hart-Intersentia, 2000) 93.

8 This rule of treaty construction is encapsulated in the Latin phrase '*lex specialis derogat legi generali*'. See especially, Mark E. Villiger, *Customary International Law and Treaties* (Martinus Nijhoff Publishers, 1985), 36.

9 Paul Taylor, *Freedom of Religion: UN and European Human Rights Law and Practice* (Cambridge University Press, 2005), 293.

10 The provisions of the ICCPR interchangeably use the terms 'limitation' [Articles 5(3) and 18(3)] and 'restriction' [Articles 12(3), 19(3), 21 and 22(2)]. It was observed that 'neither the text of the Covenant, nor the *travaux préparatoires* support such an interpretation' which differentiates between the two terms. See especially, Alexandre Kiss, 'Commentary by the Rapporteur on the Limitation Provisions' (1985) 7(1) *Human Rights Quarterly* 15.

raised in this book, the first question is – When is there a limitation against the right to establish and maintain places of worship? Chapter 3 demonstrated that the right to establish and maintain places of worship is a distinct human rights norm composed of nine separate sub-elements,[11] each of which may be infringed by state authorities or non-state actors which, in turn, engenders the state's duty to protect the right. Any such infringement properly constitutes a 'limitation' to the right to establish and maintain a place of worship. The different case studies analysed in Chapters 5, 6 and 7 involved infringements by local councils of one or more sub-elements of the right to establish and maintain a place of worship.

Having determined that the right to establish and maintain a place of worship has been 'limited' in a particular situation, the next issue is the 'permissibility' of such a limitation under Article 18(3) of the ICCPR. To be permissible, a limitation must be: (1) 'prescribed by law', (2) 'necessary to protect public safety, order, health, or morals or the fundamental rights and freedoms of others', and (3) 'proportional to the specific need on which it is predicated'.[12] These requirements may be regarded as a *sequential* three-step process[13] so that, for example, if the first requirement is not satisfied then the limitation may be declared not permissible without the need to assess the limitation against the second and third requirements. These requirements are analysed in the next section in the context of restrictions to the right to establish and maintain places of worship.

8.2.1 *The Limitation must be 'Prescribed by Law'*

As regards the permissibility of limitations to the right to religious manifestation, states have the burden of demonstrating that such limitations comply with the requirements of Article 18(3) of the ICCPR.[14] The onus is upon the state authorities whose action restricted the freedom of worship to demonstrate

11 As discussed in Chapter 3, the nine elements are: (1) the right to a legal entity status, (2) the right to acquire or possess real property for religious use, (3) the right to be free from 'bureaucratic' or 'administrative obstacles' in obtaining permit to build places of worship, (4) the right to 'make, acquire and use the necessary articles and materials related to the rites or customs of a religion or belief', (5) the right to express religious or other beliefs in physical structures, (6) the right to access, use and peaceful enjoyment of places of worship, (7) the right to 'solicit and receive voluntary financial and other contributions from individuals and institutions' for purposes of establishing or maintaining a place of worship, (8) the right to physical protection of places of worship, and (9) the right to be free from discrimination based on religion or belief in the local planning process.

12 General Comment 22, para 8.

13 Gunn, above n 1, 259–262.

14 Bahiyyih Tahzib, *Freedom of Religion or Belief: Ensuring Effective International Legal Protection* (Martinus Nijhoff Publishers, 1996), 170.

that it satisfied all the requirements of permissible limitations in Article 18(3) of the ICCPR. To justify any restriction, a state must be able to identify a permissible limitation allowed under Article 18(3).

Interpreting Article 18(3) of the ICCPR, the Human Rights Committee stated that the '[l]imitations imposed must be established by law and must not be applied in a manner that would vitiate the rights guaranteed in article 18'.[15] The requirement that a limitation must be 'prescribed by law'[16] is in turn composed of three separate conditions.

First, the source of the authority to restrict the right to manifest one's religion or belief (particularly in this case, the right to establish and maintain places of worship) should be either a statutory provision or a regulation which is competently issued by an administrative authority. Kevin Boyle opined that the limitation 'must be based on pre-existing law',[17] and thus limitations that are authorised by laws that have a retroactive application do not satisfy the first requirement. Limitations should not be based on the state authority's bare discretion, caprice or whim.[18] Alexandre Charles Kiss stated that '[i]n every case the objective is to avoid arbitrary restrictions on rights by requiring that the limitation be established by general rule'.[19] Kiss further observed that:

> The condition that a restriction must be provided by law is essentially a formal one: any restriction on recognized rights and freedoms in a state must be by general rule, normally imposed by the legislature; measures taken by the executive authority, such as the police or local administration, are excluded *unless authorized by general legislation*.[20] [emphasis added]

Thus, the general rule allowing the restriction of the right to religious manifestation must be expressed as a legal provision enacted by the legislature or an

15 General Comment 22, para 8.

16 In the different provisions of the ICCPR, the following terms are used: 'prescribed by law', 'provided by law', 'established by law' and 'in conformity with law'. These terms have the same meaning. See Kiss, above n 10, 18.

17 Kevin Boyle, 'Freedom of Religion in International Law' in Javaid Rehman and Susan Breau (eds), *Religion, Human Rights and International Law* (Martinus Nijhoff Publishers, 2007), 23, 43.

18 Gunn, above n 1, 259–260.

19 Alexandre Charles Kiss, 'Permissible Limitations on Rights' in Louis Henkin (ed), *The International Bill of Rights: The Covenant on Civil and Political Rights* (Columbia University Press, 1981), 290, 304.

20 Ibid., 305.

administrative issuance which is 'authorized by general legislation'. Manfred Nowak similarly commented that the restriction 'must be set down in formal legislation or an equivalent unwritten norm of common law in a manner adequately specified for the enforcement organs'.[21] Both written and unwritten law are therefore contemplated. The restriction may also be authorised by regulations competently issued by the executive or administrative authorities pursuant to a legislative delegation. Local planning regulations (in the form of zoning ordinances and the different types of planning controls) will have no difficulty satisfying this first condition because they are issued by local councils pursuant to the authority delegated to them by the relevant state or territory planning statutes.[22]

Second, such legal provision or regulation must be 'sufficiently clear and accessible'[23] which means that those to whom it is applied may consult it in order to determine the scope of any proscribed conduct.[24] Kiss observed that:

> Another meaning of the obligation to adopt limitations only by law is that the restrictive measures are to be clear and accessible to everyone who might be concerned. Adequate information should be available in this regard for citizens: each individual must have the opportunity to know his [or her] rights in order to be able to protect them.[25]

This second condition goes to the very heart of the substantive due process of law which requires that the subjects of a law or regulation (that is, the individuals or organisations to whom the law or regulation is meant to apply) be adequately apprised of any proscribed conduct. For example, 'secret laws or unpublished administrative regulations'[26] do not satisfy this condition.

Finally, and being an offshoot of the second condition, the law or regulation that authorises the restriction on the right to manifest one's religion or belief

21 Manfred Nowak, *U.N. Covenant on Civil and Political Rights: CCPR Commentary* (N.P. Engel, 2005, 2nd revised edition), 425.

22 These are the *Planning and Environment Act 1987* (Vic), *Environmental Planning and Assessment Act 1979* (NSW), *Development Act 1993* (SA), *Planning and Development Act 2005* (WA), *Land Use Planning and Approvals Act 1993* (Tas), and *Planning Act* (NT). In the ACT, planning decisions are made by the Planning and Land Authority pursuant to the *Planning and Development Act 2007* (ACT).

23 Boyle, above n 17, 43.

24 Gunn, above n 1, 260.

25 Kiss, 'Commentary by the Rapporteur on the Limitation Provisions', above n 10, 18.

26 Gunn, above n 1, 260.

'must be written in such a way as to be sufficiently understandable so that a person reading it could know whether or not the actions in question are prohibited'.[27] As a further guarantee of substantive due process, this final condition requires that, by consulting the law or regulation, an individual or organisation may be able to *reasonably foresee* if a conduct would violate it or not. Paul Taylor commented that, in order to satisfy the condition, the law or regulation 'must be formulated with sufficient precision that the consequences of a given action are foreseeable'.[28]

In summary, the above three conditions of the 'prescribed by law' requirement entail that the law or regulation that authorised the limitation to the right to religious manifestation must not 'be vague, unclear, arbitrary, or give[s] unfettered discretion to state authorities'.[29] These conditions essentially aim to constrain the exercise of official discretion, lest it becomes capricious or even despotic. As W Cole Durham noted, "[f]reedom from arbitrary state action is at the core of what is required by the 'prescribed by law' phrase that appears in several of the international limitations clauses. Indeed, it is at the heart of what is meant by the ideal of 'rule of law'."[30]

The 'prescribed by law' requirement requires a case-by-case assessment of the *intrinsic quality* of the particular law or regulation that authorises restrictions on the right to religious manifestation. The assessment must focus on whether or not the law or regulation satisfies the conditions pertaining to source, clarity and foreseeability as discussed above. A bare assertion that a state authority is bestowed by law or regulation with the power to limit the right to religious manifestation is not enough because it may in fact be vague, unclear, arbitrary, or gives unfettered discretion to state authorities. As illustrated in Chapters 5, 6 and 7, development applications to construct, extend or renovate places of worship are evaluated by local councils on the basis of local planning regulations on physical amenity, visual amenity and specific design controls. Depending on the particular facts of each case, such local planning regulations may or may not meet the conditions pertaining to source, clarity and foreseeability.

Local planning regulations protecting an area's physical amenity are usually formulated in a sufficiently clear manner because issues relating to traffic, parking,

---

27 Ibid.

28 Taylor, above n 9, 294.

29 Gunn, above n 1, 260.

30 W. Cole Durham, Jr, 'Facilitating Freedom of Religion or Belief through Religious Association Laws' in Tore Lindholm, W. Cole Durham, Jr and Bahia G. Tahzib-Lie (eds), and Elizabeth A. Sewell and Lena Larsen (associate eds), *Facilitating Freedom of Religion or Belief: A Deskbook* (Martinus Nijhoff Publishers, 2004) 321, 382.

noise and other tangible 'dis-benefits' to a place are more or less quantifiable issues based on objective criteria. For example, planning regulations on parking usually prescribe a minimum number of parking spaces for a place of worship based on anticipated number of attendees. Similarly, planning regulations on acceptable noise level of places of worship usually provide objective (and technical) criteria. Being sufficiently clear, such planning regulations enable a religious group to reasonably foresee whether its proposed place of worship is compliant with these regulations or not. Therefore, planning regulations pertaining to physical amenity are likely to be able to satisfy the source, clarity and foreseeability conditions as discussed above.

By contrast, the conditions of clarity and foreseeability will likely not be satisfied by local planning regulations that are meant to preserve an area's visual amenity. In Chapter 6, visual amenity was shown to be tied to the preservation of an area's 'character' which rests on several subjective and mistake-prone assumptions. It was shown that the assumed 'character' of an area is highly subjective. This subjectivity provides local councils with an almost unfettered discretion when resolving applications to build places of worship (see discussion in Sections 6.2 and 6.3.1). The wider this discretionary authority is, the greater the opportunity for local councils to hide the real motivations behind their planning decisions. Commenting that an unfettered discretion is anathema to the rule of law, French CJ of the High Court of Australia, stated that:

> Planning decisions, whether at the level of large scale regional development, the formulation of particular schemes relating to land use in urban, semi-rural and rural areas, the practical application of such schemes, or the formulation and application of regulations and by-laws – all involve the exercise of public power conferred by law. *Planning, to the extent that it involves the exercise of such power is, like every other field of official decision-making, subject to the rule of law. No official can make a decision which affects the legal rights and interests or liberties of a person or body unless such decision is authorised by law.*[31] [emphasis added]

Thus, a planning regulation that provides that any proposed structure 'must be respectful of the character of the area' or 'should not be out of character with the area' will likely not provide sufficient clarity, nor give individuals or groups the opportunity to reasonably foresee whether or not a proposed structure's

31 Chief Justice Robert French AC, 'Property, Planning and Human Rights' (Planning Institute of Australia, National Congress, Canberra, 25 March 2013), 7.

architectural design is allowed. As analysed in Section 6.2, the determination of an area's 'character' is laden with imprecision, arbitrariness and subjectivity. Therefore, similar planning regulations that are imprecise, arbitrary and subjective will likely fail to satisfy the clarity and foreseeability conditions as discussed above.

In every case involving a restriction on the right to establish and maintain places of worship, there is a need to assess whether or not the relevant local planning regulation, on the basis of which the restriction was made, satisfies the above three conditions pertaining to source, clarity and foreseeability. The assessment requires more than a perfunctory search for an authorising law or regulation. It requires an examination of the intrinsic quality of the provisions to determine whether they are clear enough to be understood, and definite enough to be able to anticipate proscribed conduct.

8.2.2 *The Limitation must be 'Necessary to Protect Public Safety, Order, Health, or Morals or the Fundamental Rights and Freedoms of Others'*

The second requirement for a limitation to the right to establish and maintain places of worship to be permissible under Article 18(3) of the ICCPR is that the limitation must be in furtherance of at least one of the five specifically identified 'legitimating' *grounds*, namely: public safety, public order, public health, public morals or the fundamental rights and freedoms of others. The Human Rights Committee commented that 'paragraph 3 of article 18 is to be strictly interpreted: restrictions are not allowed on grounds not specified, even if they would be allowed as restrictions to other rights protected in the Covenant, such as national security'.[32] Therefore, the list of grounds for permissible limitations on the freedom to manifest one's religion or belief is exhaustive. The *only* possible grounds are public safety, public order, public health, public morals or the fundamental rights and freedoms of others, all of which must be strictly interpreted.[33] If a restriction is based on grounds other than those mentioned in Article 18(3) of the ICCPR, such as the sweeping and far-reaching

---

32 General Comment 22, para 8; In the other rights guaranteed in the ICCPR such as the right to freedom of expression (Article 19), freedom of assembly (Article 21) and freedom of association (Article 22), 'national security' is an available ground for permissibly limiting these rights. See Sarah Joseph, Jenny Schultz and Melissa Castan, *The International Covenant on Civil and Political Rights: Cases, Materials and Commentary* (Oxford University Press, 2004, 2nd edition), 508.

33 General Comment 22, para 8.

concepts of 'the general welfare', 'the common good', or 'necessary in a democratic society', then the restriction will be an impermissible limitation.

Based on the foregoing, in every case involving a limitation on the right to establish and maintain places of worship, there is a need to examine whether or not such a limitation was for the purpose of any of the five legitimate grounds. In other words, it must be examined whether or not the objective of the limitation is "properly directed at the protection of 'public safety', 'order', 'health', or 'morals' or the 'fundamental rights and freedoms of others'."[34] The meaning of these grounds and how they can be invoked by planning authorities in order to legitimately restrict the right to establish and maintain places of worship in a given situation are analysed successively in the following sections.

8.2.2.1 'Public Safety'

In 1984, a group of 31 distinguished experts in international law convened in Siracusa, Sicily in Italy to consider the limitation and derogation provisions of the ICCPR. The result was the Siracusa Principles on the Limitation and Derogation Provisions in the ICCPR (Siracusa Principles).[35] The Siracusa Principles is a set of guiding principles that serve as interpretative tools for the application of the limitation and derogation provisions of the ICCPR. The Siracusa Principles were officially recognised by the former UN Commission on Human Rights.[36] It has been noted that the:

> Siracusa Principles were not only circulated in UN documents and cited in UN and other studies, they are also occasionally referred to as an authoritative source in the committees that carry out supervisory tasks with respect to the implementation of the two international covenants.[37]

The Siracusa Principles 'provide authoritative guidance to the meaning of the terms used in the limitation clauses ... [and] provide some general interpreta-

34 Taylor, above n 9, 301–302.

35 See especially, 'Introduction' (1985) 7(1) *Human Rights Quarterly* 1–14.

36 UN Commission on Human Rights, *The Siracusa Principles on the Limitation and Derogation Provisions in the International Covenant on Civil and Political Rights*, UN Doc E/CN.4/1985/4 (28 September 1984) (*'Siracusa Principles'*).

37 Alex Geert Castermans, Lydia Schut, Frank Steketee and Luc Verhey (eds), *The Role of Non-Governmental Organizations in the Promotion and Protection of Human Rights: Symposium Organized on the Occasion of the Award of the Premium Erasmianum to the International Commission of Jurists* (Leiden, Stichting NJCM-Boekerij, 1990), 65.

tive guidelines for the justification of limitations of ICCPR rights'.[38] Cornelis de Jong also commented that the Siracusa Principles 'may help in developing a better understanding of the precise scope of the various elements of the limitation clause of article 18 of the Covenant'.[39] Therefore, whenever relevant, the Siracusa Principles are referred to in this section in conjunction with the authoritative pronouncements of the Human Rights Committee and relevant commentaries to shed light on the meaning and import of the requirements of Article 18(3) of the ICCPR.

The Siracusa Principles defined the term 'public safety' as the 'protection against danger to the safety of persons, to their life or physical integrity or serious damage to their property'.[40] The human rights guaranteed in the ICCPR may be restricted 'if their exercise involves danger to the safety of persons, to their life, bodily integrity, or health'.[41] Although 'public safety' is a distinct ground, it is usually combined with the grounds of 'public health'[42] in order to provide greater justification for why state authorities are limiting a human right. Manfred Nowak and Tanja Vospernik commented that the ground of 'public safety' requires the demonstration of 'a *specific* danger [which] arises threatening the safety of persons (their life, integrity, or health) or property'.[43] [emphasis added]

In *Singh Bhinder v Canada*,[44] the author alleged that the requirement that he wear a 'hard hat' at work infringed his right to manifest his religion by preventing him from wearing a turban, a religiously prescribed head garment in Sikhism. He argued that the requirement did not constitute a 'public safety' ground. The Human Rights Committee rejected his argument and stated that the requirement that a hard hat be worn is 'a limitation that is justified by reference to the grounds laid down in article 18, paragraph 3'.[45] The Committee

---

38 Human Rights Watch, *Hostile to Democracy: The Movement System and Political Repression in Uganda* (Human Rights Watch, 1999), 21.

39 De Jong, above n 7, 82.

40 Siracusa Principles, principle 33.

41 Kiss, 'Permissible Limitations on Rights', above n 19, 298.

42 Taylor, above n 9, 321.

43 Manfred Nowak and Tanja Vospernik, 'Permissible Restrictions on Freedom of Religion or Belief' in Tore Lindholm, W Cole Durham, Jr and Bahia G. Tahzib-Lie (eds) and Elizabeth A. Sewell and Lena Larsen (associate eds), *Facilitating Freedom of Religion or Belief: A Deskbook* (Martinus Nijhoff Publishers, 2004), 147, 150–151.

44 Human Rights Committee, *Views: Communication No 208/1986,* UN Doc A/45/40 vol. 2 (9 November 1989) (*'Singh Bhinder v Canada'*).

45 Ibid., para 6.2.

added that the 'legislation requiring that workers…be protected from injury and electric shock by the wearing of hard hats is to be regarded as reasonable and directed towards objective purposes that are compatible with the Covenant'.[46] Tahzib criticises this decision because the author's refusal to wear a hard hat could only possibly endanger his own personal safety and not that of his co-workers or the general public.[47] Airing the same criticism, Sarah Joseph and Melissa Castan stated that:

> It is a shame that the [Committee] did not spell out exactly how the limitation conformed to article 18(3). Though the hard hat measure arguably protected Singh's *personal* health and safety, the Committee did not address how his non-compliance with the measure could threaten *public* safety and health.[48] [emphasis original]

Therefore, in evaluating the ground of 'public safety', there must be a clear distinction between forms of religious manifestation that endanger the safety of other persons and those which only affect the safety of the individual exercising the religious manifestation.[49] The danger or risk to the *personal* safety of the individual exercising the religious manifestation may not be a valid ground for limiting that exercise, depending on the particular facts of a case.

In the context of building, extending or renovating places of worship, one possible scenario where construction work could endanger 'public safety', according to the principles set out above, is when it is done with wanton disregard of safety standards in building construction. For example, state authorities would be justified on 'public safety' grounds halting the construction of a church tower if the crane being used was defective and could crash onto a public street, thus posing a danger to the safety of persons, to their life or physical integrity or serious damage to their property. In a similar vein, state authorities would be justified in prohibiting the continued use of a Sikh *gurdwara* if its religiously prescribed *'langar'* (communal kitchen) was found to be worn out, such that it constituted a fire hazard that could endanger temple attendees. Even then, these measures limiting the right to establish and maintain places of worship could only be justified on a temporary basis in order to allow the fixing of the damaged crane so that the construction of the church can resume,

---

46 Ibid.

47 Tahzib, above n 14, 296.

48 Sarah Joseph and Melissa Castan, *The International Covenant on Civil and Political Rights: Cases, Materials, and Commentary* (Oxford University Press, 2013, 3rd edition), 574.

49 Nowak and Vospernik, above n 43, 151.

or the replacing of the worn out *'langar'* so that the *gurdwara* can be put back to public use. It is only in comparable situations where there exists a clear risk to the public that a limitation may be said to be justified on 'public safety' grounds.

By contrast, the negative impacts upon an area's physical amenity posed by a proposed religious structure such as increased traffic, inadequate parking, excessive noise level, or similar 'dis-benefits' to a place (as analysed in Chapter 5) cannot reasonably be considered a danger to 'public safety' as defined above. It would be quite an exaggeration if, for instance, it were to be argued that an increased flow of vehicles within the vicinity of a proposed place of worship during particular days and hours would endanger the 'public safety' of pedestrians or other road users. Neither could inadequate parking spaces or excessive noise coming from a church pose a danger to 'public safety' as properly understood. But prohibiting the construction of a place of worship on a site which is prone to bush fires may perhaps be justified to protect 'public safety'. Thus, the ground of 'public safety' requires more than mere inconvenience or annoyance to people, rather it requires a demonstration of a serious physical danger to their life and limb (as well as property) directly as a result of the construction or use of a place of worship.

The condition that the danger must be specific, as pointed out by Nowak and Vospernik, precludes generalised or blanket claims of danger to public safety. The danger must be shown to be concrete and real; unfounded assertions are not enough. For example, the presence and operation of a mosque in a locality is sometimes erroneously associated with gang violence, street crime or anti-social behaviour as discussed in Section 5.3.5. This kind of unsubstantiated fear and panic over the construction of a place of worship cannot legitimately cause state authorities to invoke the protection of 'public safety' and thereby restrict the right to establish and maintain places of worship on that ground.

8.2.2.2 'Public Order'

There are two competing views on the meaning of the ground of 'public order'. It has been broadly interpreted to mean 'public policy' which is the equivalent of the French legal concept of '*ordre public*'.[50] This interpretation may justify far-reaching limitations to the right to manifest one's religion or belief because the concept of 'public policy' is wide and malleable, and should therefore be rejected. By contrast, 'public order' has been narrowly interpreted as the 'prevention of disorder'[51]

50 De Jong, above n 7, 98.

51 Ibid.

which means the avoidance of public disturbances, riots, confusion or chaos in the streets. Consistent with the rule that the limitation clauses ought to be strictly interpreted, Taylor opined that Article 18(3) of the ICCPR "refers only to 'order' (or in French, *'la protection de l'ordre'*), and not … *'ordre public'* so as to avoid notions of social policy and to position it in line with the phrase 'prevention of disorder'."[52] De Jong similarly opined that the 'prevention of disorder' concept "coincides with the proper meaning of 'public order', but not with its French counterpart '*ordre public*'."[53] To support his opinion, de Jong observed how in comparable articles of the ICCPR the term 'public order' is followed by '(*ordre public*)' to emphasise its broad meaning, but this addition was omitted in Article 18(3).[54] The equally authentic French text of Article 18(3) of the ICCPR does not mention *'ordre public'* but *'la protection de l'ordre'* which, according to Karl Josef Partsch, 'clearly suggests that limitations on freedom to manifest one's religion cannot be imposed to protect *ordre public* with its general connotations of national public policy, but only where necessary to protect public order narrowly construed, i.e., to prevent public disorder'.[55] Nowak supports this view stating that:

> An overview of the various limitation clauses in the Covenant in the authentic languages therefore makes it unmistakeably clear that the term 'public order' in Art. 18(3) has a different meaning than in Arts. 12, 14, 19, 21 and 22. This means that freedom of religion and belief may not be restricted for all of the reasons stemming from the concept of *ordre public* under French civil law but rather only to avoid disturbances to public order in the narrow sense.[56]

The above interpretation is supported by the *travaux préparatoires* of Article 18 of the ICCPR. In order to avoid a broad interpretation of the term 'public order', the British representative during the drafting recommended the formula 'the prevention of disorder' with the explanation that "if 'public policy' could be invoked to restrict freedom of religion, the restrictions could be stringent indeed."[57] This

---

52 Taylor, above n 9, 323.

53 De Jong, above n 7, 98.

54 Ibid., 98–99.

55 Karl Josef Partsch, 'Freedom of Conscience and Expression, and Political Freedoms' in Louis Henkin (ed), *The International Bill of Rights: The Covenant on Civil and Political Rights* (Columbia University Press, 1981), 209, 212–213.

56 Nowak, above n 21, 428.

57 UN Doc E/CN.4/SR. 319 (1952) 12 (United Kingdom), also cited in Anna-Lena Svensson-McCarthy, *The International Law of Human Rights and States of Exception: With Special*

formula was supported by the Lebanese representative who stated that if 'the maintenance of order included action by the courts and enforcement of respect for the general principles governing a society, it was far too broad a basis for limitations of freedom of religion'.[58] Therefore, the narrow meaning ascribed to 'public order' is the correct interpretation. It has been noted that 'public order':

> is often taken to be the most expansive justification for imposing limitations on freedom of religion, since many assume that what is intended is the broad notion of *"ordre public"* in French law used to describe a generalized sense of prevailing public policies. [B]oth the English and French versions of the ICCPR make it clear that in context, the phrase "public order" is *intended to justify incursions on religious freedom only in the narrow sense of preventing public disturbances.*[59] [emphasis added]

However, in *Coeriel et al v The Netherlands*,[60] the Human Rights Committee broadly interpreted the ground of 'public order' when it ruled that state authorities were justified in denying the request of the authors to change their names which is religiously prescribed before they could become Hindu priests. The Committee held that 'the regulation of surnames and the change thereof was eminently a matter of public order and restrictions were therefore permissible under paragraph 3 of article 18'.[61] Nowak and Vospernik have criticised this ruling "because the conduct in question fails to disrupt 'public order' in the narrow sense contemplated by the Covenant."[62] The broad interpretation ascribed by the Human Rights Committee to 'public order' in *Coeriel* would justify far-reaching limitations to the right to manifest religion or belief, which would conflict with the unmistakeable intent of Article 18(3) of the ICCPR as revealed by its *travaux préparatoires*.

In the context of building, extending or renovating places of worship, the state authorities would be justified in limiting the right to establish and maintain

---

Reference to the Travaux Préparatoires *and Case-law of the International Monitoring Organs* (Martinus Nijhoff Publishers, 1998), 152.

58 UN Doc E/CN.4/SR. 319 (1952) 13 (Lebanon).

59 The Oslo Coalition on Freedom of Religion or Belief, *Chapter 6 Manfred Nowak and Tanja Vospernik, Permissible Restrictions on Freedom of Religion or Belief* (2004) <http://www.oslocoalition.org/deskbook_nowak_vospernik.php> at 17 March 2013.

60 Human Rights Committee, Views: Communication No. 453/1991, UN Doc CCPR/C/52/D/453/1991 (9 December 1994) ('Coeriel et al v The Netherlands').

61 Ibid., para 6.1.

62 Nowak and Vospernik, above n 43, 154.

places of worship on the ground of 'public order' only in situations where a proposed place of worship could reasonably be foreseen as likely to cause or provoke public disturbances, riots, confusion or even chaos in the streets. For example, local authorities may be justified in preventing the construction by a religious group of a place of worship on a site which is across from a place of worship owned and used by a rival religious group, with the two groups having a recent history of violent confrontations or clashes. Preventing a confrontation between hostile religious groups under this situation may be justifiable.[63] To allow the construction on that site would likely provoke public disorder within the meaning and intent of Article 18(3) of the ICCPR.

In drafting General Comment 22, the members of the Human Rights Committee were aware of the 'need for sensitivity in the siting of religious buildings',[64] with one member 'emphasis[ing] the need to avoid provocation by building in the vicinity of rival places of worship',[65] while another member mentioned the setting up of a Carmelite convent at the entrance to the former Auschwitz concentration camp where thousands of Jews were murdered.[66] Therefore, outside a situation where a proposed place of worship would most likely provoke a public disorder as illustrated by the example in the preceding paragraph (and analogous situations), the right to establish and maintain places of worship does not easily yield to the 'public order' ground under Article 18(3) of the ICCPR.

8.2.2.3 'Public Health'

The inclusion of the 'public health' ground in Article 18(3) of the ICCPR did not engender any dispute or discussion during the drafting of this provision.[67] This was because public health 'corresponds to a relatively clear and accepted concept and is not likely to be a focus of controversy'.[68] The Siracusa Principles state that:

> Public health may be invoked as a ground for limiting certain rights in order to allow a state to take measures dealing with a serious threat to the health of the population or individual members of the population. These

63 Ibid., 151.
64 Taylor, above n 9, 242.
65 Ibid.
66 Ibid.
67 Kiss, 'Permissible Limitations on Rights', above n 19, 302–303.
68 Ibid., 303.

> measures must be specifically aimed at preventing disease or injury or providing care for the sick and injured.[69]

Based on the above understanding of the term, limitations based on 'public health' grounds may involve collective measures as well as measures aimed at the protection of the health of individuals. In both cases, the threat to their health must be serious or grave enough as to endanger *other* members of the population, and not just the religious actor or actors involved in the religious exercise. The former may include measures to counter an epidemic; while the latter may involve measures applicable only to certain individuals who may spread communicable diseases. For example, state authorities may be justified in preventing a religious group from burying their dead in a cemetery (which is also a site of religious importance) without proper sanitation and other health requirements. In the same manner, as Nowak observed, '[w]hen a mandatory State measure (e.g., vaccination duty) is necessary in the interest of public health – i.e., the health of others – contrary religious convictions may certainly be restricted'.[70] Although some religions prescribe their members to avoid immunisations, the state may be justified in limiting this particular religious belief on the basis of an overriding interest of the community – that is, the prevention of communicable diseases. In one case in the United Kingdom,[71] an appellate court found as legitimate, on 'public health' grounds, the slaughter of a temple bull which was tested positive for bovine tuberculosis, over the objection of a religious group that regarded the bull as an object of worship. The court found that the danger of transmitting the animal's disease justified the limitation on the group's freedom to manifest its religious belief.

Therefore, as can be gleaned from the above examples, the 'public health' ground consists of two elements, namely: (i) the gravity or seriousness of the health risk and (ii) the religious manifestation's adverse health effect on others beyond the religious actor or actors involved in the religious exercise. In their analysis of limitations to the right to manifest one's religion or belief on the basis of 'public health' considerations, Heather Payne and Norman Doe concluded that:

> On the one hand, therefore, laws are used to limit freedom of religion when a religious activity may result in harm to the health of those not involved in the religious activity in question: for example, restrictions on

69 Siracusa Principles, principle 25.

70 Nowak, above n 21, 429.

71 *R (Suryananda) v Welsh Ministers* [2007] EWCA Civ 893.

> religious practice in the production of food and prohibitions on parental refusal (on religious grounds) of lifesaving medical treatment for children fall into this category because fulfilment of the religious practice may cause harm to others.
>
> Conversely, there are no legal restrictions on religious practice, or else there are exemptions from legal restrictions on it, when a religious practice causes no obvious harm to the physical health of others, or else is likely to cause harm only to the person carrying on that religious practice. For example, exemptions for the religious use of peyote [a type of drug usually used for religious rituals by native American Indians], respect for adult refusal of medical treatment on religious grounds, and religious exemptions from the use of crash helmets, may be understood to fall into this category, as the religious practice causes no direct harm to the health of others.[72]

Applying the above conditions of the 'public health' ground in the context of building, extending, renovating or using places of worship, the state authorities would be justified in limiting the right to establish and maintain places of worship on the ground of 'public health' only in situations where there exists a serious or grave threat to the health of a community or a large section of it (that is, the health risk must be a *public* risk[73]). Thus, for instance, a place of worship to be constructed using materials laden with asbestos or other hazardous materials may be validly rejected by state authorities on the basis of protecting the 'public health'. Similarly, state authorities may be justified in temporarily preventing a Sabian Mandaean group from using a poorly maintained baptismal pool in its religious ceremonies to ensure that it does not become a breeding place for malaria-carrying mosquitoes. Like in these examples, the gravity or seriousness of the health risk to the public must be objectively demonstrated. Hence, for example, a claim that church attendees usually leave garbage in the vicinity of a place of worship after a church service (which certainly inconveniences the neighbours) does not approximate the required degree of gravity or seriousness of the health risk, as illustrated in the above examples.

For a limitation to be permissible based on the ground of 'public health', it must be shown that there is a direct *causal link* between the serious health risk,

72 Heather Payne and Norman Doe, 'Public Health and the Limits of Religious Freedom' (2005) 19 *Emory International Law Review* 539, 554–555.

73 Joseph and Castan, above n 48, 574.

on one hand, and the construction, extension, renovation or use of a place of worship, on the other, such that restricting the latter is a suitable measure to address the former. For example, in *Toonen v Australia*,[74] the Human Rights Committee held that the criminalisation of homosexual conduct cannot be considered a reasonable measure to achieve a public health objective. The Committee stated that:

> [a]s far as the public health argument of the Tasmanian authorities is concerned, the Committee notes that the criminalization of homosexual practices cannot be considered a reasonable means or proportionate measure to achieve the aim of preventing the spread of AIDS/HIV ... Secondly, the Committee notes that no link has been shown between the continued criminalization of homosexual activity and the effective control of the spread of the HIV/AIDS virus.[75]

Finally, like limitations based on the ground of 'public safety', the limitations based on 'public health' can only be temporary in nature until the serious or grave health risk is addressed.

8.2.2.4 'Public Morals'

Every limitation clause in the ICCPR includes 'public morals' or 'public morality' as a possible ground for limiting the rights recognised therein.[76] However, the jurisprudence of the Human Rights Committee demonstrates that the protection of 'public morals' has never been invoked by states as a stand-alone ground. 'Public morals' appears to be the weakest of the grounds for permissible limitation of the rights recognised in the ICCPR, including the right to freedom of religion or belief. This is largely explained by the vagueness and subjectivity of the concept of 'public morals' itself. Even during the drafting of Article 18(3) of the ICCPR, the term 'public morals' was criticised by the Philippine delegate for its vagueness and subjectivity.[77] It has also been described

---

74 Human Rights Committee, *Views: Communication No. 488/1992*, UN Doc CCPR/C/50/D/488/1992 (31 March 1994) (*'Toonen v Australia'*); Although the case involved the right to privacy under Article 17 of the ICCPR, it is illustrative of the Committee's understanding and application of the ground of 'public health'.

75 Ibid., para 8.5.

76 ICCPR, arts 12(3), 14(1), 18(3), 19(3), 21 and 22(2).

77 Commission on Human Rights, 6th sess, UN Doc E/CN.4/353/Add.3 (Philippines); See especially, MJ Bossuyt, *Guide to the* Travaux Préparatoires *of the International Covenant on Civil and Political Rights* (Martinus Nijhoff Publishers, 1987) 102.

as 'definitely the least clear and most controversial of all the legitimating grounds for justifying restrictions'[78] on the right to manifest one's religion or belief.

Kiss attempted to define 'public morals' as comprising those principles 'which are not always legally enforceable but which are accepted by a great majority of the citizens as general guidelines for their individual and collective behaviour'.[79] However, this definition is problematic because it assumes that there is *fixed* sense of right or wrong which the 'great majority of the citizens' commonly share. There is no such thing, but only the relativeness and fluctuating notion and content of public morality which changes depending on the moral question involved. Thus, for example, views on abortion, gambling, prostitution or other issues may radically differ from one political, social or religious community to the next, and they vary over time. According to de Jong, even on the assumption that 'there are commonly held morals, they are likely to be too vague',[80] such that their practical use as a ground for restricting human rights would be problematic. This notwithstanding, the Human Rights Committee stated that:

> the concept of morals derives from many social, philosophical and religious traditions; consequently, limitations on the freedom to manifest a religion or belief for the purpose of protecting morals must be based on principles not deriving exclusively from a single tradition.[81]

The consequence of the above statement is that the protection of 'public morals' cannot be anchored on the precepts of an official state religion or even the predominant religion of a country.[82] Therefore, when invoked by state authorities as a ground for restricting the right to manifest one's religion or belief, 'public morals measures should reflect a pluralistic view of society, rather than a single religious culture'.[83] In actual practice, however, what is perceived as morally right and wrong is heavily influenced by the predominant religious views of a society.

It would be extremely difficult for state authorities to legitimately restrict the right to establish and maintain places of worship on the ground of protecting

---

78 Nowak and Vospernik, above n 43, 159.

79 Kiss, 'Permissible Limitations on Rights', above n 19, 304.

80 De Jong, above n 7, 97.

81 General Comment 22, para 8.

82 Taylor, above n 9, 327.

83 Joseph, Schultz and Castan, above n 32, 510.

'public morals' given the concept's vagueness and subjectivity, as discussed above. The difficulty does not arise from the question of how physical structures could possibly offend 'public morality' but in the determination of what 'public morality' precisely is. For example, it would be difficult for state authorities to justify the removal of two statues in a Rastafarian place of worship that depict Jesus Christ and Bob Marley sporting tattoos and smoking cigarettes on the ground that tattoos are 'immoral' and that smoking is a 'sin'. Neither can state authorities validly restrict the right of a group that practices the *'wicca'*[84] religion to build a place of worship on the ground that the belief in and practice of witchcraft are 'evil'. The concept of 'public morals' is so nebulous that state authorities are highly susceptible to the charge of imposing their own biases or prejudices if they anchor their rights-restricting actions on the basis of this ground.

8.2.2.5 'The Fundamental Rights and Freedoms of Others'

Article 18(3) of the ICCPR is unique for its inclusion of 'the fundamental rights and freedoms of others' as a ground for permissible limitation on the right to manifest one's religion or belief. The placement of the adjective 'fundamental' which describes the 'rights and freedoms of others' is deliberate. Other limitations clauses in the ICCPR merely state 'the rights and freedoms of others' without the qualification 'fundamental'.[85] Similarly, the generic limitations clause of the UDHR simply speaks of 'securing due recognition and respect for the rights and freedoms of others'.[86] Partsch stated that 'the special character and high value of the freedom to manifest one's religion [or belief] may explain the differences in Article 18(3)'.[87] On the significance of this difference in legal terminology, the Special Rapporteur on freedom of religion or belief similarly commented that:

> [Article 18(3)] allows for restrictions only in very exceptional cases. In particular the fact that it mentions the protection of "*fundamental* rights and freedoms" of others as a ground for restriction indicates a stronger protection than for some other rights whose limitation clauses refer simply

---

84 The 'wicca' religion 'regards itself as the recovery of an ancient European religion whose practitioners use rituals and techniques to recover power, especially within themselves, to change their lives for the better'. See especially, John Bowker, 'New Religions' in John Bowker (ed), *Cambridge Illustrated History of Religions* (Cambridge University Press, 2002), 305, 307.

85 See, e.g., ICCPR arts 12, 21 and 22.

86 UDHR art 29(2).

87 Partsch, above n 55, 212.

> to the "rights and freedoms of others" (e.g. article 12, 21 and 22).[88] [emphasis original]

Therefore, forms of religious manifestation in worship, observance, practice and teaching (including the right to establish and maintain places of worship) should not be restricted by the state based on the need to protect the human rights of others that are not considered 'fundamental'. Taylor opined that "[i]f the 'rights and freedoms of others' are to be the legitimate basis of State restrictions on the manifestation of religion, they must be 'fundamental'."[89] This suggests that the right to manifest one's religion or belief is not commensurate with any ordinary right but, in fact, enjoys a greater degree of protection from international human rights law. De Jong similarly opined that "the addition of the term 'fundamental' requires from States a careful weighing between the freedom to manifest one's religion or belief and *only the more important* rights of others."[90] [emphasis added] Durham agreed with this view and stated that:

> Consistent with the general recognition that only high order state interests should override a right as fundamental as freedom of religion or belief, limitation clauses for freedom of religion or belief have been drafted very narrowly. Indeed, in many respects, the limitations allowed in connection with freedom of religion or belief are narrower than those allowed with respect to other fundamental rights.[91]

This view, of course, begets the crucial question of the hierarchy of human rights under international human rights law – that is, on what basis can a human right be considered as more important than another? Several key guidelines (which are independent from each other) may assist in illuminating the issue.

First, in any comparison of the relative importance of a human rights vis-à-vis another, the analysis cannot ignore the existence of the 'non-derogable' rights contemplated in Article 4 of the ICCPR. Explaining the nature of such rights, Kiss stated that:

---

88 *Interim Report of the UN Special Rapporteur on Freedom of Religion or Belief*, UN Doc A/60/399 (30 September 2005), paras 62–63.

89 Paul Taylor, 'Religion and Freedom of Choice' in John Witte, Jr and M. Christian Green (eds), *Religion and Human Rights: An Introduction* (Oxford University Press, 2012) 170, 171.

90 De Jong, above n 7, 91.

91 Durham, above n 30, 359.

> certain rights recognized by the Covenant *have a special character and are therefore entitled to greater protection than the others.* According to Article 4, no derogation may be made in time of public emergency from Articles 6, right to life; 7, prohibition of torture; 8(1) and (2), prohibition of slavery; 11, prohibition of imprisonment for contractual debt; 15, non-retroactivity of criminal legislation; 16, recognition as a person before the law; and 18, right to freedom of conscience, religion and thought. These... rights and freedoms form the hard core of the rights recognized by the Covenant and *it is normal that they should be given special consideration should a conflict arise with other rights and freedoms.*[92] [emphasis added]

Based on the foregoing, the protection of a human right which does not approximate the 'special character' of the non-derogable rights enumerated above cannot prevail over the right to freedom of religion or belief (including its *forum externum* limb) which is non-derogable. It is also noteworthy that the rights enumerated in Article 4 of the ICCPR are those that have attained (or are at least close to attaining) the status of *jus cogens* or peremptory rules of international law[93] which are at the top of the hierarchy of international law norms. Thus, any conflict between them and other human rights occupying a lower position in the hierarchy should be resolved in favour of the former. The *jus cogens* or peremptory rules of international law include but are not limited to the right against torture, the right against *ex post facto* laws, the right to self-determination of peoples, the prohibition against genocide or slavery, and the right against racial discrimination.[94]

Second, there is also a view that the 'fundamental' character of rights may be determined by looking primarily at a state's domestic legal system, especially its constitutional setup. Nowak, for example, is of the opinion that:

> In contrast to human rights, the term "fundamental rights" points primarily toward national law and describes in general those subjective rights that, in comparison to other rights, are more strongly protected (usually at the level of the constitution) with special national remedies

92 Kiss, 'Commentary by the Rapporteur on the Limitation Provisions', above n 10, 22.

93 For a discussion on the emergence of *jus cogens* norms under international law, see especially Antonio Cassesse, 'For an Enhanced Role of *Jus Cogens*' in Antonio Cassesse (ed), *Realizing Utopia: The Future of International Law* (Oxford University Press, 2012) 158–171.

94 Antonio Cassese, *International Law* (Oxford University Press, 2005, 2nd edition), 198–204; Ian Brownlie, *Principles of Public International Law* (Oxford University Press, 2003, 6th edition), 488–490.

> (often a so-called constitutional complaint to the supreme court or an independent constitutional court). This means that States parties are entitled to limit freedom of religion or belief in order to protect those rights of others that have the character of fundamental rights and freedoms in their legal system.[95]

Nowak's view contemplates domestic legal systems which have separate and hierarchical regimes between rights guaranteed in the countries' fundamental law (that is, a constitutional instrument) and rights guaranteed by ordinary legislation, and any conflict between the two sets of rights are resolved in favour of the former. Based on this view, the right to manifest one's religion or belief cannot be legitimately restricted by the state on the ground of protecting a human right recognised only by ordinary legislation. However, if the restriction is on the ground of protecting a constitutional right, then it is a permissible limitation, provided that all the other requirements of Article 18(3) are satisfied.

Johan van der Vyver similarly described the relative importance of certain constitutional rights over other rights when he stated that:

> Many constitutional systems founded on a bill of rights proclaim the preeminence of certain constitutional rights. In probably every constitutional system there is in fact a certain basic *Grundnorm*, determined by the historical circumstances and political structure of the country concerned, which permeates the entire spectrum of rights protected.[96]

Such *Grundnorms* include, for example, the protection of the right to human dignity in the German constitutional system; the freedoms of speech, of the press, and religion (the so-called First Amendment freedoms) in the American constitutional system; and the protection of human dignity, equality and freedom in the South African constitutional setup.[97] In these legal systems, such *Grundnorms* prevail over ordinary or statutory rights in the event of a conflict.

Third, the Siracusa Principles contemplate a potential clash between human rights that are recognised in the ICCPR and those that are recognised elsewhere. It provides that:

---

95 Nowak, above n 21, 430.

96 Johan van der Vyver, 'Limitations of Freedom of Religion or Belief: International Law Perspectives' (2005) 19 *Emory International Law Review* 499, 508.

97 Ibid.

> [t]he scope of the rights and freedoms of others that may act as a limitation upon rights in the Covenant extends *beyond* the rights and freedoms recognized in the Covenant.
>
> When a conflict exists between a right protected in the Covenant and one which is not, *recognition and consideration should be given to the fact that the Covenant seeks to protect the most fundamental rights and freedoms.* In this context especial weight should be afforded to rights not subject to limitations in the Covenant.[98] [emphasis added]

The first paragraph above makes it clear that the rights and freedoms which are recognised elsewhere but not in the ICCPR may also limit the human rights recognised in the ICCPR, including the right to freedom of religion or belief. However, the second paragraph requires that a balancing rule should be followed in such an eventuality – that is, the balancing exercise must give 'recognition and consideration' that the ICCPR-recognised human rights are intended to be of priority over those that are not included in the Covenant. Hence, for example, and following the Siracusa Principles, the protection of the human right to property which is not recognised in the ICCPR,[99] cannot override the right to freedom of religion or belief guaranteed in Article 18 of the Covenant.

Employing these three independent guidelines, the analysis in Section 8.3 below focusses on the underlying societal interests beneath the protection of an area's physical amenity (as discussed in Chapter 5) and the preservation of an area's visual amenity through broad and specific design controls (as discussed in Chapters 6 and 7, respectively), both of which are the typical justifications cited by local councils in rejecting proposed places of worship. These underpinning societal interests may in fact be translated as human rights claims themselves. In other words, their essence may be encapsulated and expressed as human rights, and thus allow a human rights-balancing exercise under Article 18(3) of the ICCPR between the right to establish and maintain places of worship and such societal interests (now translated as human rights themselves). The analysis in Section 8.3 below is guided by the foregoing discussion on the meaning and import of the ground of 'the fundamental rights and freedoms of others' as a permissible limitation to the right of religious manifestation.

---

98 Siracusa Principles, principles 35–36.

99 The human right to property is discussed in greater depth in Section 8.3.1 below.

8.2.3 *The Limitation must be 'Directly Related and Proportionate to the Specific Need on Which it is Predicated'*

The third and final requirement if a limitation to the right to manifest one's religion or belief is to be legitimate is the notion of 'proportionality'. The Human Rights Committee stated that even in situations where the restrictions against the freedom to manifest one's religion or belief are 'prescribed by law' and are based on the grounds of 'public safety, order, health, morals or the fundamental rights and freedoms of others' (the first two requirements discussed in Sections 8.2.1 and 8.2.2, respectively), they must still be 'directly related and proportionate to the specific need on which they are predicated'.[100] The third requirement therefore requires two conditions be satisfied: the *suitability* of the governmental action with the societal interest being pursued, and the *commensurability* between the severity of the restriction against the right to religious manifestation and the importance of the societal interest sought to be advanced by the governmental action.

First, there must be a direct and rational relationship between the societal interest and the particular action chosen by the state in order to pursue it. The two cannot be unrelated to each other. Lorenz Langer stated that a proper analysis 'will have to consider suitability because it will be impossible to assess the proportionality of means and ends if there is no rational connection between the two'.[101] Second, referring to the requirement of 'proportionality' in limiting human rights in general, Gunn explained that:

> there should be a proportionate correlation between the seriousness of the harm that the State seeks to prevent when imposing the restriction on the manifestation of religion and the severity of the infringement on the liberty that the restriction imposes.[102]

Both tests of suitability and proportionality must be satisfied for limitations to the right to religious manifestation to be permissible under international human rights law. Hence, for example, if state authorities decided to deport a visiting '*imam*' because a rival religious group threatened that it would bomb the mosque where he was being hosted, the governmental action has no rational connection with the aim of protecting public safety and order, and thus it failed the test of suitability in this instance. However, if the state authorities

---

100 General Comment 22, para 8.

101 Lorenz Langer, 'Panacea or Pathetic Fallacy? The Swiss Ban on Minarets' (2010) 43(4) *Vanderbilt Journal of Transnational Law* 863, 889.

102 Gunn, above n 1, 263.

decided to close down the mosque for one day to determine and eliminate the bomb threat, the governmental action is justifiable on its face, on the ground of protecting public safety and order. But if the mosque remains closed for a month, the restriction is no longer 'proportionate to the specific need' on which it was predicated. Thirty days is an unreasonably long period for the authorities to determine and eliminate the threat. Gunn further explained that:

> the doctrine of proportionality, when applied to limitations of rights, identifies the importance of the State action, such as a statute, against the importance of the infringement of the rights. But, in its narrower sense, it is used to describe the process of either "weighing" the various interests against each other, or to find a "fair balance of interests." But, essentially, proportionality in human rights analysis considers whether the State action is sufficiently important to justify limitations on protected rights.[103]

Therefore, the principle of proportionality prohibits governmental action that results in a restriction to the right to religious manifestation *in excess of* what is needed to accomplish a legitimate objective (that is, public safety, public order, public health, public morals or the protection of the fundamental rights and freedoms of others). In other words, the burden to religious manifestation must not be excessive, relative to such objectives. Proportionality analysis requires a balancing test between the communal good being sought by restricting the right to religious manifestation and the consequent harm to those individuals or groups whose right to religious manifestation is curtailed. Proportionality analysis seeks to prevent a restriction to the right to religious manifestation which would clearly outweigh the aim of the governmental action. In addition, it requires that any such restriction should minimise, as far as possible, the consequent diminishing of religious liberty.

As illustrated in Chapters 5, 6 and 7, planning decisions can, in varying degrees of severity, restrict the right to establish and maintain places of worship. An example of a severe restriction is an unjustified rejection by a local council of a proposed place of worship. It is severe because, by its very nature, it is a complete denial of the right to establish and maintain places of worship.[104]

---

103 T. Jeremy Gunn, 'Deconstructing Proportionality in Limitations Analysis' (2005) 19 *Emory International Law Review* 465, 470.

104 Reported to have occurred in other countries, another complete negation of this right is 'the destruction of places of worship or assembly without the consent of the religious community concerned'. See De Jong, above n 7, 393.

Another severe restriction is an unjustified disallowance of particular features of places of worship that serve liturgical purposes, thus directly impacting religious exercise. On the other hand, lesser-degree forms of restriction to the right to establish and maintain places of worship include variances in the architectural design of proposed places of worship including height, bulk, colour and other qualitative attributes (which do not affect liturgy), normal delays in obtaining planning permits, or planning conditions as to the days and hours of operation of a religious building. Noting the various types of restrictions against the right to establish and maintain places of worship and their degrees of severity, Durham stated that:

> the types of problems that arise and the contexts in which they arise are extremely varied. Sometimes land use restrictions are used to exclude particular religious groups from a city altogether. Sometimes they push religious groups to unattractive locations that are difficult for their members to reach. Sometimes they impose staggering costs. Sometimes complex problems arise because of changes in liturgy or shifts in the demography of a particular religious community.[105]

Done on a case-by-case basis, a proper 'proportionality' analysis should therefore take into account the above differences in the degree of severity of the restriction, and must assess their commensurability with the objective of the governmental action in question. For example, if the governmental action involves a severe restriction – for example, the rejection of a proposed place of worship or a disallowance of an important religious icon inside a church, it may only be justified by an equally compelling governmental objective. Therefore, the most severe forms of restrictions to the right to establish and maintain places of worship may be considered as 'permissible limitations' under Article 18(3) of the ICCPR if, and only if, the state authorities can demonstrate that the communal interest sought to be achieved is of paramount significance.

Other permutations of this 'proportionality' rule may be stated as follows:

> To the extent that a state restriction prevents a great harm and the infringement on the liberty is slight, the restriction presumably is justifiable.... On

105 W. Cole Durham, 'Places of Worship: Enhancing Implementation of a Core Right' (Introductory Remarks for Session III of the Supplementary Human Dimension Meeting on Freedom of Religion or Belief, Vienna, Austria, 9–10 July 2009), 3.

> the other hand, if the State's interest is low and the infringement on liberty is high, the State action presumably is not justifiable.[106]

The principle of proportionality is sometimes not observed in situations where proposed places of worship are rejected on physical amenity concerns despite a clear demonstration of the applicant's pressing 'religious need' which is a relevant planning consideration as discussed in Chapter 5. For example, in *Case Study 5(g)*, the local council and the appellate tribunal both justified the rejection of a proposed mosque that could have catered to the entire Muslim population of Hobsons Bay, Victoria by pointing to the proposal's parking shortfall of 13 to 15 spaces, which was allegedly an unreasonable impost on the available public parking supply. In this case, the state's interest in ensuring that the public parking supply would not be burdened by an additional 13 to 15 spaces was low, while the rejection of the mosque constituted an infringement on religious liberty which was high. Therefore, the test of proportionality as applied to restrictions to the right to establish and maintain places of worship requires a consideration of the societal or communal good that the state is pursuing, and weighing it with the importance of the religious activity being curtailed. Such a test does not have a uniform outcome when applied to all restrictions to the right to establish and maintain places of worship, but must be carried out on a case-by-case basis.

8.3 Legitimate Planning Objectives Versus the Right to Establish and Maintain Places of Worship

This section ties up two hitherto separate analyses made thus far in this book: on one hand, the analysis made in Chapters 5, 6 and 7 pertaining to the protection of amenity in local planning and, on the other hand, the analysis made in Section 8.2.2.5 above regarding 'the fundamental rights and freedoms of others' as a ground for permissible limitation to the right to manifest one's religion or belief. The singling out in this discussion of the ground of 'fundamental rights and freedoms of others' is necessitated by two interrelated reasons.

First, as shown in the preceding sections, the other four grounds for the limitation of the right to manifest religion or belief (that is, public safety, public order, public health and public morals) are narrow grounds that, except in extreme cases, do not squarely fit the physical or visual amenity concerns used

106 Gunn, above n 1, 263.

by local councils to justify restrictions against the right to establish and maintain places of worship. In other words, if local councils point to physical or visual amenity concerns to justify restrictions against the right to establish and maintain places of worship, it would be difficult for them to validly argue that such concerns constitute the ground of public safety, public order, public health or public morals (except in extreme examples illustrated in Sections 8.2.2.1 to 8.2.2.4). Therefore, having eliminated these four grounds, there is a need to determine whether the protection of an area's physical or visual amenity could possibly constitute the last remaining ground in Article 18(3) of the ICCPR – that is, the protection of 'the fundamental rights and freedoms of others'. The relevant question is: Does the the protection of an area's physical or visual amenity implicate a fundamental right or freedom of others?

Second, and extending the argument above, the protection of an area's physical and visual amenity is actually underpinned by human rights claims, albeit they are usually not articulated as such in planning controversies. In other words, underneath the protection of physical and visual amenity, there lie unstated human rights claims. This approach of 'converting' amenity concerns into human rights claims allows a human rights-balancing exercise under Article 18(3) of the ICCPR between a religious group's right to establish and maintain places of worship, on one hand, and the protection of physical and visual amenity (now expressed as human rights themselves), on the other. Carolyn Evans recognised the need for this balancing exercise when she stated that, '[i]n the application and interpretation of the right to religious freedom and belief, there is an inevitable balancing act with other human rights'.[107] Such balancing act may also apply in planning controversies. As French CJ of the High Court of Australia stated, a planning process 'often involves the determination of what the public interest requires and the resolution of tensions between the public interest and the legitimate interests of individuals, groups and organisations within the community'.[108]

For this purpose, Article 18(3) serves as a built-in balancing mechanism to weigh the relative significance of the right to establish and maintain places of worship and the human rights claims that underpin the protection of amenity. The issue therefore is: Is the protection of physical and visual amenity directed towards the protection of a 'fundamental right or freedom of others' such that

---

107 Carolyn Evans, 'Balancing Religious Freedom Rights and Other Human Rights' in Paula Gerber and Melissa Castan (eds), *Contemporary Perspectives on Human Rights Law in Australia* (Thompson Reuters, 2013), 475, 481.

108 French, above n 31, 4.

a restriction against the right to establish and maintain places of worship based on amenity protection would be a permissible limitation under Article 18(3) of the ICCPR?

The following sections demonstrate a balancing exercise between the right to establish and maintain places of worship, on one hand, and two human rights claims that directly underpin the protection of amenity, on the other. Two such claims are (1) the right of local residents to the peaceful or quiet enjoyment of their property, and (2) the right of a majority population to protect its 'collective identity' as expressed in the streetscape. It is against these two rights that the right to establish and maintain places of worship should be measured, while carefully employing the balancing directive of Article 18(3) of the ICCPR.

8.3.1 *Right of Local Residents to the Peaceful or Quiet Enjoyment of Their Property*

Chapter 1 discussed that the overriding objective of local planning is to bring about the general convenience that a locality can offer its residents, visitors and other users. It does so, as illustrated in Chapters 5, 6 and 7, by preventing or addressing the negative impacts of proposed or existing structures upon the physical and visual amenity of an area. Thus, for example, a resident who drives his or her car uninterruptedly in local streets and regularly finds an available kerbside parking space could be regarded as 'enjoying' his or her property more as compared to another resident of a busy and crowded locality who is denied these tangible 'amenities'. Similarly, an owner of a house located in a street with neatly aligned structures which have a fairly uniform height and bulk could be considered as visually 'enjoying' his or her house more as compared to another owner whose dwelling is situated in a busy and crowded neighbourhood with mixed or discordant structures. From the viewpoint of local residents, therefore, the protection of their area's physical and visual amenity safeguards their human right to the peaceful enjoyment of their property. It is in this sense that the protection of amenity is actually a *derivative* of the human right to property. Article 17 of the UDHR recognises 'property' as a distinct human entitlement, stating that:

(1) Everyone has the right to own property alone as well as in association with others.
(2) No one shall be arbitrarily deprived of his property.[109]

---

109 UDHR art 17.

The right to the peaceful enjoyment of property is one of the essential attributes of the human right to property, the two others being 'the right to exclude others and the right to dispose of property'.[110] The 'right to exclude' may be equated with the ability to control who uses or enjoys one's property; while the 'right to dispose of' means the right to transfer or pass on property (or part of it) to another person through agreements (for example, a contract of sale or lease) or by operation of law (for example, intestate succession).[111] On the other hand, the 'right to peaceful or quiet enjoyment of property' means that the owner or lawful possessor of the property can expect and demand that other persons will not impair the condition of his or her property and will not interfere with the reasonable comfort and convenience of his or her occupation of the property.[112] These three main attributes are traditionally considered as the most essential components in the 'bundle of rights'[113] which collectively exist and are referred to as property.

However, as illustrated in the case studies analysed in Chapter 5, the right of local residents to the peaceful or quiet enjoyment of their property may conflict with a religious group's right to establish and maintain a place of worship. As observed by Samantha Knights:

> There may be a tension between the right of organized religions to establish places of worship and to act in accordance with religious doctrine, and the right of the local community as a whole to peaceful enjoyment of property. The ringing of church bells, the call to prayer broadcast through speakers from the minarets of mosques, and the celebration of religious festivals may all interfere with the rights of local residents to peaceful enjoyment of their homes.[114]

Thus, in a situation of genuine conflict between the two rights, there is a need to assess the significance of the right of local residents to the peaceful or quiet enjoyment of their property, and compare it with the right of a religious group to establish and maintain a place of worship. Such an assessment and comparison are central to balancing these conflicting human rights.

110 Theo RG van Banning, *The Human Right to Property* (Intersentia, 2002), 18.
111 Ibid.
112 Ibid.
113 Ibid.
114 Samantha Knights, *Freedom of Religion, Minorities and the Law* (Oxford University Press, 2007), 66.

The human right to property recognised in Article 17 of the UDHR is unlike the other human rights recognised in the UDHR which were elaborated in later human rights instruments, especially in the ICCPR and the International Covenant on Economic, Social and Cultural Rights (ICESCR).[115] Such elaboration has cemented their legal status as norms of international law. In contrast, the human right to property was not included in either the ICCPR or the ICESCR, and remains stagnant as a broadly formulated human right in the UDHR. Commenting on the failure of efforts to cement the status of the right to property at the international level, Gudmundur Alfredsson stated that:

> The most notable failure is the outright absence of the right in both the [ICCPR and ICESCR]. Notwithstanding several proposals, no such article was adopted. In lengthy debates there was disagreement on practically every aspect of the topic, including such issues as the scope of property, conformity with State laws, expropriation and other allowable limitations, due process of law, compensation and indeed the very inclusion of the right.[116]

Theo van Banning attributed the non-inclusion of the human right to property in the ICCPR and the ICESCR to 'the absence of international agreement as to the exact content of property rights at the time of the drafting of these instruments'.[117] Such non-inclusion has effectively stunted the normative growth of the right to property at the international level.

Although Banning observed the presence of 'property-related rights' in the ICCPR and the ICESCR (such as the right of peoples over their natural wealth and resources, right to social security, and the right not to be discriminated against on the ground of property), he regards these as an incomplete and fragmented protection of the human right to property.[118] He stated that those 'provisions do not provide protection for the right to property *as a whole*'.[119] [emphasis added] In contrast, as Banning also observed, the right to property's

115 *International Covenant on Economic, Social and Cultural Rights,* opened for signature 16 December 1966, 999 UNTS 3 (entered into force 3 January 1976) (*'ICESCR'*).

116 Gudmundur Alfredsson, 'Article 17' in Asbjorn Eide, Gudmundur Alfredsson, Goran Melander, Lars Adam Rehof and Allan Rosas (eds), *The Universal Declaration of Human Rights: A Commentary* (Scandinavian University Press, 1992), 255, 259.

117 Banning, above n 110, 5.

118 Ibid., 45.

119 Ibid.

inclusion in the European Convention on Human Rights[120] has 'led to a better understanding of and a large degree of consensus on the content of the right to property and has contributed to a good protection in Europe of a right which plays such an important role in individual lives and in the global economy'.[121] Such better understanding, consensus and protection did not occur at the international level.

Aside from the UDHR, the human right to property is also recognised in a couple of international human rights instruments. First, the International Convention for the Elimination of All Forms of Racial Discrimination guarantees the right of every person to equality before the law without distinction as to race, colour or national or ethnic origin, including the enjoyment of 'the right to own property alone as well as in association with others' and the 'right to inherit'.[122] Second, the Convention on the Elimination of All Forms of Discrimination against Women recognises the right to property in a provision that guarantees equal right for both spouses to ownership, acquisition, management, administration, enjoyment and disposition of property.[123] In both instances, however, the protection accorded to the right to property was merely incidental to the main issue or problem addressed by each instrument, namely, racial discrimination and discrimination against women. They were not substantive elaborations of the right to property per se, which have thus remained conceptually under-developed as an international human rights norm.

Therefore, at the international level,[124] the human right to property cannot be said to have attained a 'fundamental character' such that its protection can be considered a ground for the permissible limitation of the right to manifest

---

120 *Protocol No. 1 to the European Convention for the Protection of Human Rights and Fundamental Freedoms,* adopted 20 March 1952, 213 UNTS 262, ETS 9 (entered into force 18 May 1954) art 1.

121 Banning, above n 110, 45.

122 *International Convention for the Elimination of All Forms of Racial Discrimination,* adopted 21 December 1965, 660 UNTS 195, reprinted in 5 ILM 352 (1966) (entered into force 4 January 1969) art 5.

123 *Convention on the Elimination of All Forms of Discrimination against Women,* adopted 18 December 1979, 1249 UNTS 13, reprinted in 19 ILM 33 (1980) (entered into force 3 September 1981) art 16.

124 In contrast, in regional human rights instruments, the human right to property has received varying degrees of elaboration. It is recognised in varying degrees in regional human rights conventions like the American Convention on Human Rights (Article 21), the African Charter on Human and People's Rights (Article 14), and Protocol I to the European Convention of Human Rights (Article 1).

one's religion or belief under Article 18(3) of the ICCPR. In particular, the right to peaceful enjoyment of property 'may be reduced, for instance, for reasons of public interest or if the interests of others deserve a priority above the interests of the owner [or possessor]'.[125] Under international human rights law, the right to property does not occupy a prioritised position in the catalogue of recognised human rights, and thus cannot override a human right which enjoys a 'privileged status'[126] such as the right to freedom of religion or belief. The protection accorded to property, a human right which is not of a 'fundamental character', cannot therefore prevail over the right to freedom of religion or belief (including its *forum externum* limb) which, in contrast, is a fundamental freedom in international human rights law. In the hierarchy of international human rights norms, religious freedom occupies a relatively higher status – that is, more 'fundamental' – than the right to property. When placed in a balancing scale, *ceteris paribus*, the right to religious freedom is more significant than the right to property.

Furthermore, the human right to property cannot be considered 'fundamental' even by following Nowak's suggestion that the determination of the fundamental character-ness of a right may be done by examining a state's constitutional document to identify 'those subjective rights that, in comparison to other rights, are more strongly protected ... with special national remedies',[127] nor by following Van der Vyver's suggestion to look for the 'basic *Grundnorm*, determined by the historical circumstances and political structure of the country concerned, which permeates the entire spectrum of rights protected'.[128] Australian constitutional law does not accord any privileged status to the right to property in the sense which approximates a specially protected right or a '*Grundnorm*' contemplated by Nowak and Van der Vyver, respectively.

The Australian Constitution provides that the Commonwealth Parliament has the power to enact laws with respect to 'the acquisition of property on just terms from any State or person for any purpose in respect of which the Parliament has power to make laws'.[129] This constitutional provision operates both as a clause that confers the Commonwealth with the power to acquire property, and as a guarantee that such acquisition can only be made 'on just terms'. Thus, the right to property is protected by the Australian Constitution to

125 Banning, above n 110, 19.
126 Nowak and Vospernik, above n 43, 147.
127 Nowak, above n 21, 430.
128 Van der Vyver, above n 96, 508.
129 Australian Constitution s 51(xxxi).

the extent that acquisition of property for public purposes by the Commonwealth should be on 'just terms'.[130] With respect to acquisition of property for public purposes by the state or territory governments (or their agencies), the payment of 'just terms' to the owners of acquired properties is mandated, not by the state constitutions, but by the relevant statutes in each of the states and territories.[131] However, the foregoing constitutional and statutory provisions mandating the payment of 'just terms' for any taking of property do not elevate the right to property to the status of a specially protected right or a *'Grundnorm'* in the sense envisaged by Nowak and Van der Vyver, respectively, in the hierarchy of values or interests recognised in Australian domestic law. Finally, while the right to property is 'valued and protected in the legal tradition of the common law, which is part of the Australian legal tradition',[132] the right to property is recognised in the common law alongside other rights of individuals or groups and does not occupy any sort of privileged position in relation to them.

Daniel Conkle explained the underlying rationale for the privileged treatment of the right to freedom of religion or belief when he stated that:

> [r]eligious beliefs, by their very nature, form a central part of a person's belief structure, his inner self. They define a person's very being – his sense of who he is, why he exists, and how he should relate to the world around him. A person's religious beliefs cannot meaningfully be separated from the person himself: they are who he is. The essential identity of a person and his religious beliefs means that these beliefs often will be grounded on intense convictions.[133]

Agreeing with this reasoning, Peter Edge commented that 'for many religious adherents their religious beliefs, practices, and identity occupy a position of special importance in their life'.[134] Therefore, the right to freedom of religion or

130 For an illustration of acquired property in consideration of 'just terms', see *Wurridjal v Commonwealth* (2009) 237 CLR 309; and where a claim to be paid in 'just terms' was unsuccessful, see *Tobacco Plain Packaging Case jt International sa v Commonwealth* (2012) 86 ALJR 1297; (2012) 291 ALR 669.

131 See, e.g., *Land Acquisition (Just Terms Compensation) Act 1991* (NSW) s 37; *Land Acquisition and Compensation Act 1986* (Vic) s 30; *Acquisition of Land Act 1967* (Qld) s 18; *Land Administration Act 1997* (WA) s 202; *Land Acquisition Act 1969* (SA) s 22; *Land Acquisition Act 1993* (Tas) s 24; *Lands Acquisition Act 1994* (ACT) s 42; *Lands Acquisition Act 1978* (NT) s 59.

132 French, above n 31, 1.

133 Daniel Conkle, 'Toward a general theory of the establishment clause' (1988) 82 *Northwestern University Law Review* 1115, 1164–1165.

134 Peter Edge, *Religion and Law: An Introduction* (Ashgate, 2006) 7.

belief enjoys a fundamental status because it goes to the very core of a person's identity. However, this 'self-identity' rationale cannot be used to similarly argue that the right to freedom of religion or belief is more fundamental than another human right which underpins the protection of amenity – that is, the right of the majority group in society to its own cultural identity. As analysed in the next section, the latter is also 'fundamental' because, like religious belief, cultural identity is also a significant part of an individual's being – his or her inner self.

8.3.2 *Right of a Majority Population to Its 'Cultural Identity' as Expressed in the Streetscape*

As analysed below, the maintenance of 'cultural identity' is an important element of the much broader right to enjoy one's culture. An invocation of this right in the context of local planning was illustrated in *Case Study 6(d)* where, it will be recalled, a member of the Gold Coast City Council objected to the proposed Buddhist temple by questioning its 'cultural relevance' in the community. The councillor argued that the proposed Buddhist temple 'is culturally relevant in a Buddhist community, [but] it is not culturally relevant in Nerang, [Queensland]. What has not been taken into account is the cultural elements of the Nerang community'.[135] By making these assertions, the councillor essentially invoked the right of the majority population to preserve its 'cultural identity' as expressed in the 'streetscape' – that is, the landscape, scenery, vista, or view of the street – and called for its legal protection against a perceived intrusion by the proposed 'alien' or 'exotic' religious structure.

This particular argument merits close analysis because it is symptomatic of the many objections raised against the construction of places of worship belonging to religious minorities in Australia. It reflects an ostensible tension between two substantive human rights, namely: the right of a religious minority to establish and maintain places of worship and the right of the majority population to preserve its 'cultural identity' as expressed in the streetscape. Vincenzo Pacillo has similarly observed this kind of tension in the context of the minaret controversy in Switzerland,[136] when he stated that:

> Western European countries have strong ties to a solid architectural tradition and they have always been committed to preserving a natural

135 Melinda Marshall, 'Row over Gold Coast Buddhist temple', *Local Gold Coast News*, 5 March 2010.

136 See discussion in Section 7.3.1.

> landscape that is perceived as an existential dimension. To build a minaret in such a context creates considerable axiological tension *between the demands of minority religious groups and the identity values of the majority of the population.* It therefore requires the local authorities to perform a complex balancing act, at least in Switzerland, though this situation does not appear to be different in other European legal systems.[137] [emphasis added]

Pacillo contends that there is a clash between the demands of minority religious communities and the identity values of the majority population. In this collision, Pacillo concludes that 'collective cultural identities ... can oppose the claims of groups that have arrived more recently'.[138]

However, a close analysis of the right to enjoy one's culture using the lens of international human rights law reveals that there is *no* genuine conflict of rights involved in this situation. The clash between the right to establish and maintain places of worship, on one hand, and the right of the majority population to its cultural identity, on the other, is specious. The appearance of this clash was the result of a misinterpretation of the meaning and import of the right to preserve one's 'cultural identity' as expressed in the streetscape. Properly construed, such a right is perfectly reconcilable with the right to establish and maintain places of worship, as analysed below.

Under international human rights law, the logical starting point for an analysis of the legal significance of the right to enjoy one's culture begins with Article 27(1) of the UDHR which provides that:

> *Everyone has the right freely to participate in the cultural life of the community,* to enjoy the arts and to share in scientific advancement and its benefits. [emphasis added]

This provision was closely echoed in Article 15(1)(a) of the ICESCR which provides that '[t]he States Parties to the present Covenant recognize the right of everyone [t]o take part in cultural life'.[139] The Committee on Economic, Social

137 Vincenzo Pacillo, '*Stopp Minarett?* The Controversy over the Building of Minarets in Switzerland: Religious Freedom versus Collective Identity' in Silvio Ferrari and Sabrina Pastorelli (eds), *Religion in Public Spaces: A European Perspective* (Ashgate, 2012), 337, 341.

138 Ibid., 350.

139 ICESCR art 15(1)(a); Meanwhile, in the Australian domestic jurisdiction, the right to enjoy one's culture is recognised in Section 19 of the *Charter of Human Rights and Responsibilities 2006* (Vic) and Section 27 of the *Human Rights Act 2004* (ACT).

and Cultural Rights (ESCR Committee),[140] through its General Comment 21,[141] elaborated on the meaning and import of Article 15(1)(a) of the ICESCR. First, the ESCR Committee explained that the term 'everyone' denotes an individual or a collective. In other words, cultural rights may be exercised by a person: '(a) as an individual, (b) in association with others, or (c) within a community or group, as such'.[142] Second, the ESCR Committee described the concept of 'culture' as 'a broad, inclusive concept encompassing all manifestations of human existence'.[143] The Committee further stated that:

> culture, for the purpose of implementing article 15(1)(a), encompasses, *inter alia*, ways of life, language, oral and written literature, music and song, non-verbal communication, religion or belief systems, rites and ceremonies, sport and games, methods of production or technology, *natural and man-made environments*, food, clothing and shelter and the arts, customs and traditions.[144] [emphasis added]

This pronouncement by the ESCR Committee makes clear that the 'natural and man-made environments', including the physical or built environment, are an indispensable part of culture which comes within the protective scope of Article 15(1)(a) of the ICESCR. Man-made environments include all types of developments done on the natural surroundings. Thus, sidewalks, parks, neighbourhoods, precincts, locales, streets and the appearance of these places are part of the man-made environment.

---

140 The ESCR Committee is the main UN body that monitors the compliance of States Parties with their obligations under the ICESCR. Its members are 18 independent experts who are elected for four-year terms on the basis of equitable geographic representation. In terms of international human rights standards setting, the Committee's functions are largely the same as that of the Human Rights Committee. See especially, Philip Alston and Ryan Goodman, *International Human Rights: The Successor to International Human Rights in Context: Law Politics and Morals* (Oxford University Press, 2013) 286–287.

141 ESCR Committee, *General Comment 21: Right of everyone to take part in cultural life (art. 15, para. 1 (a), of the International Covenant on Economic, Social and Cultural Rights)*, UN Doc E/C.12/GC/21 (21 December 2009) (*'General Comment 21'*).

142 General Comment 21, para 9.

143 Ibid., para 11; The ESCR Committee explained that: 'Cultural rights are an integral part of human rights and, like other rights, are universal, indivisible and interdependent. The full promotion of and respect for cultural rights is essential for the maintenance of human dignity and positive social interaction between individuals and communities in a diverse and multicultural world'. See General Comment 21, para 1.

144 Ibid., para 13.

One of the necessary conditions for the realisation of the right to enjoy one's culture, according to the ESCR Committee, is the availability of 'cultural goods and services' for everyone. The Committee explained that:

> *Availability* is the presence of cultural goods and services that are open for everyone to enjoy and benefit from, including libraries, museums, theatres, cinemas and sports stadiums; literature, including folklore, and the arts in all forms; *the shared open spaces essential to cultural interaction, such as parks, squares, avenues and streets;* nature's gifts, such as seas, lakes, rivers, mountains, forests and nature reserves, including the flora and fauna found there, which give nations their character and biodiversity; intangible cultural goods, such as languages, customs, traditions, beliefs, knowledge and history, as well as values, which make up identity and contribute to the cultural diversity of individuals and communities.[145] [emphasis added]

Thus, 'the shared open spaces essential to cultural interaction, such as parks, squares, avenues and streets' are cultural goods that must be made 'available' to everyone – that is, the majority and minority groups in society – as flowing from their right to enjoy their culture. To leave no doubt, the ESCR Committee further stated that 'article 15, paragraph 1(a) of the Covenant also includes the right of minorities and of persons belonging to minorities to take part in the cultural life of society, and also to conserve, promote and develop their own culture'.[146] Therefore, while the majority population is justified in anchoring its claim to preserve its cultural identity as expressed in the streetscape on the right to enjoy culture, minority groups have an equal right to enjoy this same 'cultural good' by virtue of Article 15(1)(a) of the ICESCR itself and, equally importantly, on the strength of Article 27 of the ICCPR which also guarantees *inter alia* the right of religious minorities 'to enjoy their own culture'.[147] In summary, the streetscape is a common cultural good to be enjoyed by all groups in society.

The ESCR Committee also accords one particular 'cultural good' with a special emphasis, stating that:

> Of all the cultural goods, one of *special value* is the productive intercultural kinship that arises where diverse groups, minorities and communities can freely share *the same territory*.[148] [emphasis added]

145 Ibid., para 16(a).

146 Ibid., para 32.

147 See discussion on Article 27 of the ICCPR in Section 2.2.2.

148 General Comment 21, para 16(a).

The Committee's reference to 'territory' can only mean physical territory or space that individuals and groups inhabit and where they interact with each other such as neighbourhoods, locales, squares, parks, streets or sidewalks. Such physical spaces may be viewed as a free and accessible canvas on which all groups, whether the majority or minority, can paint their respective cultural and religious identities.

The legal entitlement that safeguards the right of the majority to enjoy its culture is *the same* legal entitlement that guarantees the right of minorities to enjoy their own. Therefore, the visibility of minority religions in the streetscape (in the form of sufficient places of worship) is not to be regarded as a diminution of the majority's 'cultural identity' as expressed in that streetscape. Religious minorities have as much entitlement to access and to leave their imprint on the streetscape as anyone else. By making an imprint upon the streetscape through their religious structures, minority religious groups do *not* preclude the majority from similarly leaving their own mark and claiming their own share of the public space. Thus, there being no real conflict, minority places of worship and the cultural elements of the majority can coexist side by side with each other, while contributing to a diversified streetscape. This is only logical because, if the coexistence of people of different creeds is an acknowledged value in a multi-religious society like Australia, then the coexistence of their respective imprints upon the built environment must also be a value.

Going back to the 'cultural' objection raised against the proposed Buddhist temple in Nerang, Queensland in *Case Study* 6(*d*), it may be stated that such an objection is flawed, in so far as it demanded the exclusion of the proposed Buddhist temple from Nerang's streetscape. The Buddhist community in Nerang has a long established presence in the locality. Its religious and social festivities, distinct businesses, restaurants and signages have left indelible imprints in the physical landscape of Nerang. These too are an inseparable part of the cultural elements of the locality. Leonie Sandercock and Beverly Kliger asked the crucial question: 'Must heritage become frozen in aspic, untouchable by subsequent generations and cultures with different needs?'[149] The answer is no because minority religious groups, like the Buddhists in Nerang, also have a legitimate claim for the promotion and protection of their own cultural legacy by the local planning process.

The 'streetscape', as a common cultural good, squarely corresponds to one of the three types of spaces in Silvio Ferrari's deconstruction of the 'public

149 Leonie Sandercock and Beverly Kliger, 'Multiculturalism and the Planning System: Part Two' (1998) 35(4) *Australian Planner* 223.

sphere'.[150] He contends that an understanding of the type of space and the role of different actors in that space is crucial in analysing the legal regulation of religious activities.[151] According to Ferrari, the public sphere is made up of three distinct but sometimes overlapping spaces, namely, the 'common space', 'political space', and 'institutional space'.[152]

The common space is comprised of physical locations that individuals or groups enter or access in order to go about their daily activities or functions.[153] In the common space, individuals or groups have no express or implied agenda of influencing others, airing grievances, nor shaping public policy, but simply live out their existence *as themselves*. For example, a Sikh man who wears a turban waiting to catch a bus may be said to be in a common space and simply 'being' himself. Similarly, a Muslim woman who wears a *burqa* while buying groceries is in a common space and simply 'being' herself. Underneath these religious garments are persons who are simply practising their religion. Ferrari further comments that the common space is:

> the physical space that people have to enter to meet their basic needs: in this sense it is inescapable. This space is not accessed with the intent to participate in a political debate but simply to get to work or to buy what is needed for daily life.... From a normative point of view this common space must be kept as accessible as possible to avoid segregating in their homes people who do not feel able to enter it without manifesting their religion or belief.[154]

On the other hand, the political space is 'the space of debate and discussion where the public discourse takes shape'.[155] A public square where a rally or demonstration is being held or a sidewalk where campaign leaflets are being handed out to passers-by may be characterised as a political space. Finally, the institutional space is 'the place where coercive deliberations, which are compulsory for all, are taken'.[156] The courtroom, legislative halls, local council session

150 For a discussion of the different areas of the 'public sphere' and the regulation of religious manifestations taking place in them, see especially Silvio Ferrari, 'Religion in the European Public Spaces: A Legal Overview' in Silvio Ferrari and Sabrina Pastorelli (eds), *Religion in Public Spaces: A European Perspective* (Ashgate, 2012) 139, 149–154.

151 Ibid., 149.

152 Ibid., 149–150.

153 Ibid.

154 Ibid.

155 Ibid., 150.

156 Ibid., 151.

halls, and administrative tribunals are institutional spaces which are both places for debate and discussion, and for making binding decisions for all. Thus, institutional spaces are the physical embodiment of the state – that is, they are part of the state apparatus. Being such embodiment, there is a greater rationale for regulating the presence of religion in institutional spaces in order to prevent the perception that the state is supporting one particular religion. As discussed below, the same rationale does not apply to the regulation of the common spaces which do not embody nor represent the state.

Using Ferrari's taxonomy of spaces in the public sphere, the 'streetscape' forms part of the common space where state regulation should be at the barest minimum and exercised only when an activity 'creates real and actual difficulties to an orderly enjoyment of the common space'[157] by others. The common space should be the freest space when individuals or groups use it simply to *exist and live* as they are – that is, when they use it to engage in innocuous activities that are indispensable to their very being and which only concern or affect them, and not others. Anat Scolnicov has referred to 'the intrinsic right of each cultural (or religious) group to exist with equal respect'.[158] Such respect for individual or group identities, including religious ones, is maximised when the common space is made freely accessible by the state to everyone and immunised from unnecessary legal regulation. Van der Vyver has emphasised:

> the truism that the law is not always a feasible instrument to curtail social evils. The focus of the law in matters of religion should remain confined to acts that are clearly and widely recognized as decidedly criminal, or which in the public interest evidently require administrative regulation. Beyond those confines, legal proscription must be avoided.[159]

Carolyn Evans has similarly noted how religious freedom is sometimes best protected when the state refrains from regulation, stating that:

> Another approach to protecting rights is for the government to leave certain areas free from regulation … Rather than requiring religions to seek permission to exercise their rights or giving those rights express forms of

157 Ibid., 150.

158 Anat Scolnicov, *The Right to Religious Freedom in International Law: Between Group Rights and Individual Rights* (Routledge, 2011), 46.

159 Van der Vyver, above n 96, 511.

> protection, the government decides not to intervene in particular areas. By leaving an area unregulated, governments leave individuals and groups free to decide how best to live their lives and pursue their interests. Sometimes the best protection that a government can give to religious freedom is to simply leave people free to make their own decisions about religious issues.[160]

In the above sense, the streets and the view from the streets – that is, the scenery, vista or landscape – should be left alone by the state as much as possible. They are part of the common space that everyone should be able to access freely, and where they can express religious identities without fear that they may be sanctioned if they do so. Anne Fornerod made a similar point when she stated that:

> [i]t would be 'of fundamental importance that the public space remains hospitable to the religious preferences of its inhabitants: the visible presence of a plurality of religions and beliefs *in the streets, squares and in the schools, hospitals and so on* is indispensable for the pluralism on which a democratic society is based'.[161] [emphasis added]

Thus, in the common space, an individual should be free to wear appropriate clothing which is prescribed by his or her religion even if it may be different from those worn by everybody else.[162] In the same manner, a religious group should be free, as much as possible, to build a place of worship in accordance with a faith-inspired architectural design even though it is different from the surrounding structures and leaves a unique imprint upon the scenery, vista or landscape of the area. In other words, the 'streetscape' must be made favourable to the greatest possible exercise of religious manifestation, in all its forms including the building of appropriately designed places of worship.

---

160 Carolyn Maree Evans, *Legal Protection of Religious Freedom in Australia* (Federation Press, 2012), 107.

161 Anne Fornerod, 'The Places of Worship in France and the Public/Private Divide', in Silvio Ferrari and Sabrina Pastorelli (eds), *Religion in Public Spaces: A European Perspective* (Ashgate, 2012), 322.

162 See generally, Silvio Ferrari and Rinaldo Cristofori (eds), *Law and Religion in the 21st Century* (Ashgate, 2010), 291–332; Anastasia Vakulenko, *Islamic Veiling in Legal Discourse* (Routledge, 2012).

8.4 Conclusion

This chapter illustrated that the actual scope of the right to establish and maintain places of worship is determined by an analysis of its permissible restrictions under Article 18(3) of the ICCPR. It is only then that its true capacity to benefit religious groups can be completely grasped. The stringent requirements of Article 18(3) attest to the 'privileged' position that the right to religious freedom – including its structural aspect – enjoys in the catalogue of international human rights norms. Thus, in situations of conflict with other human rights, the right to freedom of religion or belief does not easily yield to opposing human rights including those that underpin the objectives of local planning.

International human rights law does not proscribe local planning regulations per se, but it subjects them to a critical assessment when they result in any restriction of the right to religious manifestation, including the building, extension or renovation of places of worship. Such critical assessment involves an examination, on a case-by-case basis, of whether planning decisions involving places of worship do satisfy the requirements of permissible limitations under Article 18(3) of the ICCPR. The onus is upon state authorities whose actions have restricted the manifestation of religion or belief to prove that their actions are consistent with Article 18(3) of the ICCPR. This chapter has shown that restrictions against the right to establish and maintain places of worship occasioned by the planning system's focus on the protection of amenity are difficult to justify on the basis of the grounds of 'public safety, order, health, morals or the fundamental rights and freedoms of others'. Such restrictions are more likely to be impermissible under Article 18(3) of the ICCPR.

This chapter also illustrated that certain human rights claims lie beneath the protection of amenity. Two such claims are measured vis-à-vis the right to establish and maintain places of worship. First, in a human rights balancing exercise, the right of local residents to the peaceful or quiet enjoyment of property tends to capitulate in favour of the 'fundamental' right of religious groups to establish and maintain places of worship. Thus, in local planning controversies pitting property rights against religious freedom, the latter has a decided advantage when placed on a balancing scale. Second, the right of the majority population to preserve its 'cultural identity' as expressed in the streetscape was demonstrated to be in *harmony* with the right of religious groups to establish and maintain places of worship. The seeming clash between the two 'fundamental' rights was shown to be the result of an erroneous interpretation of the right to enjoy one's culture which, under a close analysis, reveals inherent or built-in protections for cultural or religious minorities.

CHAPTER 9

Conclusion

The End of the Journey

9.1 Introduction

> The advent of new communities and the introduction of different, minority religions, in greater numbers than previously, present Australian society with new challenges. They will require fresh legal responses; from the branches of Executive Government and administration, from the courts and from the legislature.[1]

Michael Kirby, former Justice of the High Court of Australia, made the above observation almost two decades ago. He was right in anticipating that changes in the religious demographic profile of Australia would necessitate, as he puts it, 'fresh legal responses' from all branches of the Australian government, if they are to be responsive to the needs of a diverse society. This book has demonstrated that one particular segment of Australian law – the system of local planning – has failed to keep pace in this regard by continuously clinging to anachronistic regulatory tools that hinder the spatial and structural aspect of the right to freedom of religion or belief. This study suggests that the local planning system is functioning under the assumption that Australia is still culturally and religiously homogenous. Twenty-first century Australia is vastly different.

The infusion of international human rights norms, particularly those pertaining to the right to freedom of religion or belief, into the Australian local planning system could have been its 'fresh legal response' to the demands of 21st-century Australia. Unfortunately, however, this human rights-inspired overhaul of Australian local planning has not yet materialised, and the principles and concepts that underpin the discipline continue to be, as planning scholar Susan Thompson convincingly described, 'culturally exclusive, inequitable and unwilling and/or unable to accommodate different ways of being in urban space'.[2] Religious freedom norms have barely infiltrated the local

---

1 Michael Kirby, 'Australian Interfaith and Its Problems' (Speech delivered at the First National Congress of the Interfaith Association of Australia, Macquarie University, 19 November 1996), 1–2.

2 Susan Thompson, 'Planning and Multiculturalism: A Reflection on Australian Local Practice' (2001) 4(3) *Planning Theory & Practice* 275, 277.

 | DOI 10.1163/9789004289345_010

planning system in Australia. The result is the paradox that, while religious diversity is formally celebrated and extolled in Australia, the important spatial and structural aspect of that diversity – that is, the ability of religious groups to fully exercise their right to establish and maintain places of worship – tends to be constrained by the local planning processes. As revealed in the analysis in Chapters 5, 6 and 7, this constraining effect is the result of the enforcement of planning regulatory tools which are underpinned by, and thus promote, the majority population's Anglo-Celtic standards of convenience and beauty in the built environment.

In this final chapter, the salient findings of the previous chapters are summarised. This is followed by a discussion of the contribution that this study makes to the existing body of knowledge and its wider significance to the understanding of the interaction between law and religion.

9.2 Summary of Findings

By analysing the incremental contributions of each of the international human rights instruments guaranteeing religious freedom, Chapter 2 demonstrated that a distinct right to establish and maintain places of worship has been carved out from the core nucleus of the right to freedom of religion or belief. Being part of a coherent whole, the right to establish and maintain places of worship enjoys the same international legal guarantees that protect religious freedom. The key principles underlying the international legal protection of religious freedom have been demonstrated to have a direct positive bearing on the protective capacity of the right to establish and maintain places of worship, and vice versa. Such a symbiotic relationship fortifies the legal protection of the spatial and structural aspect of religious freedom.

Chapter 3 explained how the status of the right to establish and maintain places of worship as a distinct human rights norm was solidified by demonstrating how it has received its own substantive contents through the process of international human rights standard-setting. It demonstrated how the bare and austere manner in which the right was articulated in Article 6(a) of the Religion Declaration could be compensated by resorting to and synthesising the pronouncements of human rights authorities that have a direct influence on international standard-setting pertaining to religious freedom. This same technique can also be employed in order to increase understanding of other vague or imprecise elements of the right to freedom of religion or belief. Like its 'parent' human right, the right to establish and maintain places of worship has a composite character, comprising distinct but related elements all operating concertedly to achieve one goal – that is, to ensure that the spatial or structural requirements of religious manifestation are adequately met. The analysis has left no doubt as to the existence and status of the right to establish and maintain places of worship in the corpus of international human rights law.

Chapter 4 demonstrated how international standards on religious freedom, including the right to establish and maintain places of worship, can successfully cross two formidable 'barriers' in order to be of beneficial use to rights-holders. The first barrier pertains to Australia's strictly 'dualist' approach to the relationship between domestic and international law which relegates the enforceability of human rights norms exclusively to the international sphere. In order to bring the rights home, so to speak, the process of incorporation by ordinary legislation was the chosen route in Victoria and the Australian Capital Territory (ACT), both of which have enacted human rights Acts. Most state and territory jurisdictions have legal provisions that guarantee the principle of non-discrimination (including on the basis of religion or belief), which largely parallel the non-discrimination principle found in international human rights law. Meanwhile, showing great promise and potential, the reception of international human rights norms into the administrative decision-making processes may hold the key in producing planning decisions that respect the structural aspect of religious freedom. This potential is evident in many of the case studies examined in Chapters 5, 6 and 7 when administrative appeals tribunals, in reviewing local councils' planning decisions, took into account the 'religious need' for places of worship as a relevant consideration, which often led to planning outcomes which were favourable to religious groups. Being administrative bodies, the local councils can and should similarly infuse their planning decision-making processes with considerations of religious freedom norms.

The second barrier pertains to the opposability of international human rights norms against the local councils in Australia. The relevant issue is this: Can a set of standards existing and enforceable in the international sphere be employed to evaluate the actions of state authorities in the lowest tier of government in Australia? In the human rights Acts of Victoria and the ACT, the local councils squarely fall within the meaning of 'public authorities', and are thus considered duty-bearers of human rights obligations, including the right to freedom of religion or belief. They carry the mandatory obligations not to breach human rights and to treat them as 'relevant considerations' in their planning decisions. Outside Victoria and the ACT, administrative law doctrines allow local councils to inform their planning decisions with human rights considerations, including the right to freedom of religion or belief. While this is only discretionary on the part of local councils outside Victoria and the ACT, this represents an opportunity for religious groups to urge local councils to assess applications to construct, extend or renovate places of worship from the perspective of human rights law. In other words, there is an available legal avenue if the local councils genuinely want to employ human rights considerations in their local planning decisions.

Chapters 5, 6 and 7 are the book's centre of gravity. These chapters delved into an extensive analysis of the issues that arise in connection with applications to construct, extend or renovate places of worship in Australia and their resolution by local councils. The findings point to the conclusion that the local planning system in Australia tends to hinder the ability of religious groups to fully exercise their right to establish and maintain places of worship. That religious groups face this kind of hindrance – brought about by the state apparatus that exercises the 'power of control' over the built environment – is inconsistent with the international human rights standards pertinent to the right to freedom of religion or belief. The analysis suggests that the local planning system in Australia follows a regulatory framework which is more predisposed towards a rigid control approach rather than a facilitative approach. The former subdues religious expression and exercise; while the latter fosters the greatest possible exercise of religious freedom by individuals and groups.

Chapter 5 demonstrated that, in resolving physical amenity issues, local planning processes in Australia may potentially infringe critical elements of the right to freedom of religion or belief, including the right to establish and maintain places of worship. First, exaggerated or false harms to an area's physical amenity have sometimes been given credence by local councils, thus leading to rejections of proposed places of worship. Second, in some of the case studies, 'religious need' has not received sufficient consideration in planning decisions involving places of worship. Third, the unique worshipping practice or pattern of religious groups is sometimes overlooked or ignored by local councils in resolving physical amenity issues, oftentimes resulting in rejections of proposed places of worship. Fourth, restrictive effects upon the exercise of religious manifestation are sometimes produced by planning decisions that give disproportionate weight to physical amenity concerns compared to 'religious need' considerations. Finally, the protection of an area's physical amenity has sometimes produced religiously discriminatory outcomes or has sometimes led to the channelling of intolerant attitudes in the local planning processes.

Chapter 6 revealed how the right to establish and maintain places of worship becomes prone to being infringed by planning processes that are geared towards preserving an area's visual amenity, even though this concept is imprecise, arbitrary and subjective. First, the character of an area is sometimes erroneously determined by local councils, thus leading to rejections of proposed places of worship. Second, the preservation of an area's visual amenity has sometimes resulted in 'aesthetic intolerance' against non-Christian religious architecture, thus resulting in the rejection of proposed places of worship. Third, it has also sometimes resulted in the 'domestication' of the appearance of places of worship with profound impact upon their effectiveness as vehicles of religious expression. Finally, the preservation of visual amenity has sometimes resulted in discrimination based on religion or belief.

Chapter 7 revealed how the use of specific design controls by local councils – again, in order to preserve an area's visual amenity – can directly interfere with two important aspects of the right to freedom of religion or belief. First, design controls have sometimes impinged on the ability of religious communities to express and communicate their religious beliefs through their built structures. Such expression or communication of beliefs may be vital to a religious group's prescribed manner of worship, observance, practice or teaching. Second, design controls have sometimes caused spatial obstacles to a religious group's freedom of religious exercise – that is, their liturgy or the actual conduct of rituals, ceremonies and other kinds of worship. Both ramifications are assaults on the *forum externum* of the right to freedom of religion or belief.

Thus, the analysis in these three chapters has shown that the right to establish and maintain places of worship is highly susceptible to being infringed in the Australian planning system because of the wide discretion conferred upon local councils to ascertain the impacts of proposed religious structures upon the amenity of local areas. The enforcement of local planning regulations to proposed places of worship therefore typifies a highly problematic state of affairs – that is, anchoring the exercise and enjoyment of a religious freedom norm upon a system of discretionary state approval. The mutual repulsiveness between such a right and administrative discretion is a theme that reverberates throughout the book.

Chapter 8 demonstrated that restrictions against the right to establish and maintain places of worship, in order to be permissible under international human rights law, must successfully run the gauntlet of the strict requirements of Article 18(3) of the ICCPR – that is, the tailor-made 'limitations clause' applicable to the right to manifest one's religion or belief. The narrow interpretation that must be ascribed to such requirements suggests that claims of justified restrictions against the right to manifest one's religion or belief should not be made lightly. And neither should they be accepted readily by administrative or judicial bodies without subjecting them to a rigorous test of compatibility with Article 18(3) of the ICCPR. The rationale for both is the privileged status of the right to freedom of religion or belief under international human rights law. Because of such status, the right to freedom of religion or belief does not easily yield to opposing societal interests in the event of a conflict, including those that underpin the local planning system.

9.3 Contribution to the Body of Knowledge

This work has contributed to the understanding of the legal protection of the spatial and structural aspect of the right to freedom of religion or belief under international human rights law. It has done so by analysing the normative content of one of its constituent elements – that is, the right to establish and maintain places of worship – and by demonstrating its normative force as a distinct human right. The analysis of the symbiotic relationship between the right to establish and maintain places of worship and the other elements of the right to freedom of religion or belief has enabled a fuller grasp of the former's normative potency, compared to when it is considered in isolation. Such a conceptual device has aided the appreciation of the simultaneous and concerted operation of these religious freedom norms in an actual context, thereby augmenting each other's protective capacity in order to benefit rights-holders. Furthermore, aiming to distil their standard-setting value to religious freedom, this work has analysed the relevant pronouncements of the Human Rights Committee and the Special Rapporteur on freedom of religion or belief in order to reveal the conceptual core that makes up the right to establish and maintain places of worship as understood by these human rights authorities. The analysis has helped refine the erstwhile broad conception of the substance of this important religious human right. It has therefore contributed to understanding the process of solidifying the normative status of the right to establish and maintain places of worship.

From a human rights perspective, this work has examined how the respect for the right to freedom of religion or belief is being concretised in the religious physical landscape of Australia – that is, its churches, temples, synagogues, mosques and other places of worship. It has shed light on an aspect of the broader question of whether or not the right to freedom of religion or belief is being adequately protected in Australia. Such a question can now be partially answered, and thus add to the existing body of knowledge about the legal protection of religious freedom in Australia: the principles and concepts that underpin the local planning processes in Australia, as they currently stand, tend to hinder the ability of religious groups to fully exercise their right to establish and maintain places of worship. Such a hindrance experienced by religious groups is inconsistent with the international human rights standards on religious freedom. This overall conclusion has the benefit of the case study analysis in Chapters 5, 6 and 7 which demonstrated the commonality of regulatory tools as well as the principles and concepts employed by the Australian local planning system, and thereby enables a system-wide evaluation and critique using the international standards on religious freedom as points of reference.

The analysis of the impact of places of worship upon the 'streetscape' – that is, the landscape, scenery, vista, or view of the streets – has contributed to the understanding of the "general question concerning the 'visibility of religion' within the structuring of the public life of the State."[3] As Malcolm Evans noted, the existence of places of worship in a community is one of the aspects of the visibility of religion in that community's public sphere.[4] Impediments or constraints to constructing places of worship subdue that visibility. For instance, there is an alarming trend in some European states to prohibit the visibility of religion from public view, purportedly in order to safeguard overriding state interests such as maintaining strict secularity (as in the French prohibition of the wearing of the face-covering *burqa* in the streets[5]) or preserving a nation's cultural identity (as in the Swiss justification for banning the construction of Islamic minarets[6]). Using a distinctly human rights law analysis, this study has made a modest contribution to the existing body of legal scholarship[7] that, on the whole, counters this trend by demonstrating the nature of the streetscape as a 'common cultural good' which should be made accessible to *all* groups in

3 Malcolm Evans, 'Religious Symbols: An Introduction' in Silvio Ferrari and Rinaldo Cristofori (eds), *Law and Religion in the 21st Century: Relations between States and Religious Communities* (Ashgate, 2010), 291, 292.

4 Ibid., According to Evans, the other aspects of the 'visibility' of religion in the public sphere include the wearing of religious clothing, the public display of religious symbols (crucifixes, icons, etc.) and the public observance of religious 'days of rest' or festivals.

5 See especially, Anastasia Vakulenko, *Islamic Veiling in Legal Discourse* (Routledge, 2012), 16–22; Islamic Information and Services Network of Australasia, *The Burqa and Niqab: Uncovering the Facts* (2013) <http://www.iisna.com/home/> at 7 September 2013.

6 Vincenzo Pacillo, '*Stopp Minarett?* The Controversy over the Building of Minarets in Switzerland: Religious Freedom versus Collective Identity' in Silvio Ferrari and Sabrina Pastorelli (eds), *Religion in Public Spaces: A European Perspective* (Ashgate, 2012), 337.

7 See discussion in Section 8.3.2; The following are representative of such legal scholarship: Silvio Ferrari and Sabrina Pastorelli (eds), *Religion in Public Spaces: A European Perspective* (Ashgate, 2012), 1–391; Silvio Ferrari and Rinaldo Cristofori (eds), *Law and Religion in the 21st Century: Relations between States and Religious Communities* (Ashgate, 2010), 291–329; Winfried Brugger and Michael Karayanni (eds), *Religion in the Public Sphere: A Comparative Analysis of German, Israeli, American and International Law* (Max-Planck-Institut für ausländisches öffentliches Recht und Völkerrecht, 2007), 163–252; Malcolm Evans, *Manual of the Wearing of Religious Symbols in Public Areas* (Council of Europe Publishing, 2009).

society. Every religious group in Australia has an equal right to access the streetscape and leave their unique imprint upon it in order to signal their symbolic public presence. No religious group should be denied this access.

The streetscape should be the freest space available for individuals and groups, and their activities in that space should be susceptible to state regulation only in clear instances of infringement of the equal right of others to enjoy that space. If a religious activity occurring in that space does not produce real difficulties upon the ability of other individuals or groups to enjoy that space, then state impediments are unwarranted. By making an imprint upon the streetscape through the building of places of worship, a religious group does not preclude others from similarly leaving their own mark and claiming their own share of the public space. To put a ban against such imprinting upon the streetscape is inconsistent with the right to freedom of religion or belief. This analysis lends support to the argument that banning the visibility of religion from the public view constitutes a breach of international human rights law.

Finally, this research has contributed to the understanding of the richness and multiplicity of the interaction between law and religion. The biblical edict 'Render therefore unto Caesar the things which are Caesar's; and unto God the things that are God's'[8] actually masks several difficulties when applied in concrete disputes involving the exercise of religious freedom in an area where the state has a legitimate interest to protect. A building may be regarded as the 'house of God', literally or figuratively, but the fact remains that it has a temporal and earthly existence which may affect other individuals which, in turn, makes it a legitimate subject of state regulation. Therefore, in building places of worship, the interaction of law and religion is inevitable. The analysis in this book has confirmed that such an interaction tends to be detrimental for religious groups. Like other law-religion interfaces, the interaction between planning law and the right to establish and maintain places of worship in Australia tends to produce a constraining effect upon the latter.

9.4 Wider Significance of the Study

This book has wider significance beyond the Australian jurisdiction because it provides a useful template in assessing the compatibility of local planning processes in other ICCPR states parties with the right to establish and maintain places of worship. The functioning of the local planning processes in other countries (and how they are impacting the ability of religious communities to

8 *The Holy Bible* (*King James Version*) Matthew 22:21.

build places of worship) may similarly be evaluated using the international standards on religious freedom. The structure, methodology and arguments of this study may inform such an endeavour.

Furthermore, the analysis of the grounds for permissible limitations to the right to establish and maintain places of worship has relevance in other limitations clause analysis involving other human rights guaranteed in the ICCPR. As discussed in Chapter 8, the grounds of public safety, order, health and morals (but not the 'fundamental rights and freedoms of others') are also present in the limitations clauses applicable to the other human rights recognised in the Covenant. The meaning and essence of these rights can only be adequately grasped by considering how they can be validly restricted by the state. The same strict construction should be given to the grounds of public safety, order, health and morals, and the same burden of proof should be placed upon state authorities whose acts or omissions have restricted any of these rights recognised in the ICCPR.

This study also has wider significance in terms of understanding the utility of unincorporated international human rights norms in the Australian domestic jurisdiction. Although it focusses only on the right to freedom of religion or belief, the analysis on how it may be transported and accorded domestic application in Australia may similarly be employed with respect to other unincorporated international human rights norms. In particular, this study lends support to the conclusion of other scholars that pertains to the availability of a legal avenue for international human rights norms to penetrate and permeate the administrative decision-making processes in Australia,[9] most of which has the potential to positively or negatively impact the enjoyment of rights by individuals and groups in Australian society. In the absence of a comprehensive and entrenched Bill of Rights in Australia, the penetration of international human rights norms into the administrative decision-making processes – which is mandatory in Victoria and the ACT but discretionary in other jurisdictions – may partially yet effectively compensate for that absence.

Finally, the analysis concerning the availability of the streetscape as a 'common cultural good' applies, with equal validity and force, to other minority groups in society including ethnic, linguistic and gender minorities. Such groups have an equal right to access, enjoy and leave their respective imprints

9 See especially, John McMillan and Neil Williams, 'Administrative Law and Human Rights' in David Kinley (ed), *Human Rights in Australian Law* (Federation Press, 1998), 63; Ryszard Pietrowicz and Stuart Kaye, *Human Rights in International and Australian Law* (Butterworths, 2000), 281; Peter Bayne, 'Human rights and administrative law' (1991) 17 *Commonwealth Law Bulletin* 320.

upon the physical environment, provided that they do not entail any actual difficulty on the part of other individuals or groups to *equally* enjoy that part of the 'public sphere'. The streetscape should be made accessible to other minority groups who wish to express their identities through the architectural built form, and to do so without fear that they would be penalised or sanctioned if they do so.

9.5 Opportunities for Further Research

Several opportunities for further research have come into view as a result of this study. First, the impact of Australian local planning regulations on the use of private residential dwellings as a place of worship is a fertile ground for further study and analysis. Such research could build on this book by similarly employing international human rights standards to inform its investigation. Second, the impact of local planning regulations on the construction of religious schools in Australia (such as Islamic *madrasas*, Buddhist monasteries, or Catholic seminaries and nunneries) is an area of further study which may also build from this work. Is establishing a religious school part of the right to freedom of religion or belief? Does the construction of religious schools also encounter community opposition based on physical and visual amenity concerns? Third, it would also be worthwhile to examine the degree of opposition against different places of worship and, using a comparative approach, ascertain if particular religious groups encounter a greater degree of opposition compared to others. In Australia, is the construction of mosques more objectionable than, say, that of Buddhist temples? If so, what can account for the difference? Finally, the use of streets, street corners, parks, squares and other public spaces in Australia as 'temporary' sacred spaces by certain religious groups (for instance, during religious processions, parades or public re-enactments of religiously significant events) presents another fertile ground for research that may build from this analysis by employing a similar human rights-based evaluation of the local regulations that govern such 'temporary' use of the public space for religious purposes.

9.6 An Epilogue

> The role of religion is paradoxical. It makes prejudice and it unmakes prejudice. While the creeds of the great religions are universalistic, all stressing brotherhood, the practice of these creeds is frequently divisive

> and brutal. The sublimity of religious ideals is offset by the horrors of persecution in the name of these ideals.[10]

Indeed, countries have gone to war because of religion, and human beings have killed others in the name of their deeply held religious convictions. Yet this violent imagery is difficult to reconcile with the values of compassion, neighbourly love and harmony which most religions or beliefs essentially adhere to. The Thirty Years' War was fought largely as a religious conflict between Catholics and Protestants[11]; yet both religions unmistakeably profess their adherence to the 'Golden Rule'[12] or the 'Love Thy Neighbour' precept. Indeed, some fundamental core teachings commonly underlie the major religions of the world,[13] yet religion itself seems to have a paradoxical effect upon human beings. Throughout history, it has divided peoples and pitted them against each other while, at the same time, proclaiming the virtue of solidarity, equality and peace. Sadly, this paradox has not been consigned to the dustbin of history. In modern times, it manifests itself in various forms which range from muted tensions to brutal persecution between religious groups, and the varying types and degrees of religious discrimination and intolerance in between.[14] In societies that formally adhere to pluralism, this paradox may assume subtle forms which are almost imperceptible on the surface. In such societies, state institutions value the 'otherness' of others and every segment of society is

---

10 Gordon W. Allport, *The Nature of Prejudice* (Basic Books, 25th edition, 1988), 444.

11 See especially, Ronald Asch, *The Thirty Years' War: The Holy Roman Empire and Europe, 1618–48* (Saint Martin's Press, 1997).

12 'Do unto Others as You Would Have Them Do unto You'. See Antony Flew (ed), *A Dictionary of Philosophy* (Pan Books /The McMillan Press, 1979); William P. George, 'Looking for a Global Ethic? Try International Law' in Mark W. Janis and Carolyn Evans, (eds) *Religion and International Law* (Martinus Nijhoff Publishers, 2004), 483, 499.

13 For example, Arcot Krishnaswami observed that '[t]he precept that one should love one's neighbor as oneself was part of Christianity even before it had been organized as a Church. The same idea permeates Judaism and Islam, as well as the various branches of Buddhism, Confucianism and Hinduism, and it may also be found in the teachings of many non-religious beliefs'. Arcot Krishnaswami, 'Study of Discrimination in the Matter of Religious Rights and Practices' (1978) 11 *New York University Journal of International Law and Policy* 227, 228.

14 See generally, Paul A. Marshall (ed), *Religious Freedom in the World* (Rowman & Littlefield Publishers, 2008, 2nd edition); See also, U.S. Department of State, Bureau of Democracy, Human Rights and Labor, International Religious Freedom Report for 2013, <http://www.state.gov/j/drl/rls/irf/religiousfreedom/index.htm#wrapper> at 21 October 2014.

supposed to follow suit under pain of legal sanctions. Australia is one such society that formally embraces diversity in all its forms, including religious diversity. Yet despite such a formal policy, it is possible, as illustrated in this book, that a particular area of law which is so critical to the full enjoyment of the right to religious freedom remains impermeable and resistant to pluralist demands.

Bibliography

Books

Ahdar, Rex and Ian Leigh, *Religious Freedom in the Liberal State* (Oxford University Press, 2005).

Alfredsson, Gudmundur, 'Article 17', in Asbjorn Eide, Gudmundur Alfredsson, Goran Melander, Lars Adam Rehof and Allan Rosas (eds), *The Universal Declaration of Human Rights: A Commentary* (Scandinavian University Press, 1992), 255.

Allport, Gordon W., *The Nature of Prejudice* (Basic Books, 25th edition, 1988).

Alston, Philip and Ryan Goodman, *International Human Rights: Text and Materials, The Successor to International Human Rights in Context* (Oxford University Press, 2013).

Asch, Ronald, *The Thirty Years' War: The Holy Roman Empire and Europe, 1618–48* (Saint Martin's Press, 1997).

Aust, Anthony, *Handbook of International Law* (Cambridge University Press, 2nd edition, 2010).

Azmi, Shaheen, Lorne Foster and Lesley Jacobs, *Balancing Competing Human Rights Claims in a Diverse Society: Institutions, Policy, Principles* (Irwin Law Inc, 2012).

Bagaric, Mirko, Peter Faris and Theo Alexander, *Australian Human Rights Law* (CCH Australia Limited, 2011).

Bailey, Peter, *The Human Rights Enterprise in Australia and Internationally* (LexisNexis, 2009).

Bailey, Peter, *Human Rights Law* (Thompson Reuters, 2012).

Bonett, Warren (ed), *The Australian Book of Atheism* (Scribe Publications, 2010).

Bossuyt, M.J., *Guide to the* Travaux Préparatoires *of the International Covenant on Civil and Political Rights* (Martinus Nijhoff Publishers, 1987).

Bowker, John, 'New Religions', in John Bowker (ed), *Cambridge Illustrated History of Religions* (Cambridge University Press, 2002) 305.

Boyle, Kevin, 'Freedom of Religion in International Law', in Javaid Rehman and Susan Breau (eds), *Religion, Human Rights and International Law* (Martinus Nijhoff Publishers, 2007), 23.

Brasch, Nicolas, *Australia's Local Government* (Macmillan Education Australia, 2011).

Brownlie, Ian, *Basic Documents in International Law* (Oxford University Press, 5th edition, 2002).

Brownlie, Ian, *Principles of Public International Law* (Oxford University Press, 6th edition, 2003).

Brownlie, Ian and Guy S. Goodwin-Gill, *Basic Documents on Human Rights* (Oxford University Press, 5th edition, 2006).

Burckhardt, Titus, *Art of Islam: Language and Meaning, Commemorative Edition* (World Wisdom, Inc, 2009).

Carney, Gerard, *The Constitutional Systems of the Australian States and Territories* (Cambridge University Press, 2006).

Cassesse, Antonio, *International Law* (Oxford University Press, 2nd edition, 2005).

Cassesse, Antonio, 'For an Enhanced Role of *Jus Cogens*', in Antonio Cassesse (ed), *Realizing Utopia: The Future of International Law* (Oxford University Press, 2012), 158.

Castermans, Alex Geert, Lydia Schut, Frank Steketee and Luc Verhey (eds), *The Role of Non-Governmental Organizations in the Promotion and Protection of Human Rights: Symposium Organized on the Occasion of the Award of the Premium Erasmianum to the International Commission of Jurists* (Stichting NJCM-Boekerij, 1990).

Chebel, Malek, *Symbols of Islam* (Assouline Press, 2001).

Cole, William Owen and Piara Singh Sambhi, *The Sikhs: Their Religious Beliefs and Practices* (Sussex Academic Press, 1995).

Crawford, James and W. Edison, 'International Law and Australian Law', in K Ryan (ed), *International Law in Australian Law* (Law Book Company, 1984).

Creyke, Robin, 'The Performance of Administrative Law in Protecting Rights', in Tom Campbell, Jeffrey Goldsworthy and Adrienne Stone (eds), *Protecting Rights Without a Bill of Rights: Institutional Performance and Reform in Australia* (Ashgate, 2006), 101.

Crotty, Robert, 'Multiculturalism and Religious Pluralism', in Norman Habel (ed), *Religion and Multiculturalism in Australia: Essays in Honour of Victor Hayes* (Australian Association for the Study of Religion, 1992), 35.

Cumper, Peter, 'Religion, Belief and International Human Rights in the Twenty-First Century', in Sarah Joseph and Adam McBeth (eds), *Research Handbook on International Human Rights Law* (Edward Elgar Publishing, 2010), 467.

De Jong, Cornelis, *The Freedom of Thought, Conscience and Religion or Belief in the United Nations (1946–1992)* (Hart-Intersentia, 2000).

De Jonge, Alice, 'Australia', in Dinah Shelton (ed), *International Law and Domestic Legal Systems: Incorporation, Transformation and Persuasion* (Oxford University Press, 2011), 23.

Debeljak, Julie, 'Does Australia Need a Bill of Rights?' in Paula Gerber and Melissa Castan (eds), *Contemporary Perspectives on Human Rights Law in Australia* (Thomson Reuters, 2013), 37.

Dinstein, Yoram, 'Freedom of Religion and the Protection of Religious Minorities', in Yoram Dinstein and Mala Tabory (eds), *The Protection of Minorities and Human Rights* (Martinus Nijhoff Publishers, 1992), 157.

Diver, Alice and John Thompson, 'Prayers, Planners and Pluralism: Protecting the Rights of Minority Religious Groups', in Javaid Rehman and Susan Breau (eds), *Religion, Human Rights and International Law: A Critical Examination of Islamic State Practices* (Martinus Nijhoff Publishers, 2007), 465.

Dixon, Martin and Robert McCorquodale, *Cases and Materials on International Law* (Oxford University Press, 4th edition, 2003).

Donnelly, Jack, *Universal Human Rights in Theory and Practice* (Cornell University Press, 3rd edition, 2013).

Durham, W. Cole Jr, 'Perspectives on Religious Liberty: A Comparative Framework', in Johan van der Vyver and John Witte, Jr (eds), *Religious Human Rights in Global Perspective: Legal Perspectives* (Martinus Nijhoff Publishers, 1996), 1.

Durham, W. Cole Jr, 'Facilitating Freedom of Religion or Belief through Religious Association Laws', in Tore Lindholm, W. Cole Durham, Jr and Bahia G. Tahzib-Lie (eds) and Elizabeth A Sewell and Lena Larsen (associate eds), *Facilitating Freedom of Religion or Belief: A Deskbook* (Martinus Nijhoff Publishers, 2004), 321.

Durham, W. Cole Jr and Brett G. Scharffs, *Law and Religion: National, International, and Comparative Perspectives* (Aspen Publishers, 2010).

Edge, Peter, *Legal Responses to Religious Difference* (Kluwer Law International, 2002).

Edge, Peter, *Religion and Law: An Introduction* (Ashgate, 2006).

Eide, Asbjorn, 'Minority Protection and World Order: Towards a Framework for Law and Policy', in Alan Philips and Allan Rosas (eds), *Universal Minority Rights* (Institute for Human Rights, Abo Akademi University, 1995), 87.

Evans, Carolyn, 'Religion and the Secular State in Australia', in Javier Martinez-Torron and W. Cole Durham (General Reporters) *Religion and the Secular State/La religion et l'État laïque* (The International Center for Law and Religion Studies, 2010), 87.

Evans, Carolyn, 'Religion and Freedom of Expression', in John Witte, Jr and M. Christian Green (eds), *Religion and Human Rights: An Introduction* (Oxford University Press, 2012), 188.

Evans, Carolyn, 'Balancing Religious Freedom Rights and Other Human Rights', in Paula Gerber and Melissa Castan (eds), *Contemporary Perspectives on Human Rights Law in Australia* (Thomson Reuters, 2013), 475.

Evans, Carolyn and Simon Evans, *Australian Bills of Rights: The Law of the Victorian Charter and the ACT Human Rights Act* (LexisNexis Butterworth, 2008).

Evans, Carolyn Maree, *Legal Protection of Religious Freedom in Australia* (The Federation Press, 2012).

Evans, Malcolm, *Religious Liberty and International Law in Europe* (Cambridge University Press, 1997).

Evans, Malcolm, *Manual of the Wearing of Religious Symbols in Public Areas* (Council of Europe Publishing, 2009).

Evans, Malcolm, 'Religious Symbols: An Introduction', in Silvio Ferrari and Rinaldo Cristofori (eds), *Law and Religion in the 21st Century: Relations between States and Religious Communities* (Ashgate, 2010), 291.

Ferrari, Silvio, 'Religion in the European Public Spaces: A Legal Overview', in Silvio Ferrari and Sabrina Pastorelli (eds), *Religion in Public Spaces: A European Perspective* (Ashgate, 2012), 139.

Ferrari, Silvio and Rinaldo Cristofori (eds), *Law and Religion in the 21st Century* (Ashgate, 2010).

Flew, Antony (ed), *A Dictionary of Philosophy* (Pan Books/The McMillan Press, 1979).

Fornerod, Anne, 'The Places of Worship in France and the Public/Private Divide', in Silvio Ferrari and Sabrina Pastorelli (eds), *Religion in Public Spaces: A European Perspective* (Ashgate, 2012), 323.

Gavison, Ruth, 'Days of Worship and Days of Rest: A View from Israel', in Winfried Brugger and Michael Karayanni (eds), *Religion in the Public Sphere: A Comparative Analysis of German, Israeli, American and International Law* (Max-Planck-Institut für ausländisches öffentliches Recht und Völkerrecht, 2007), 379.

Gavison, Ruth and Nahshon Perez, 'Days of Rest in Multicultural Societies: Private, Public, Separate?' in Peter Cane, Carolyn Evans and Zoö Robinson (eds), *Law and Religion in Theoretical and Historical Context* (Cambridge University Press, 2008).

Glyn, Justin, *Fundamental Rights in Administrative Decision-Making: Peremptory Norms as Objective Standards in Immigration and Refugee Cases* (Presidian Legal Publications, 2009).

Goodhart, Michael, *Human Rights: Politics and Practice* (Oxford University Press, 2013).

Gosling, David L., 'Buddhism: India and Southeast Asia', in John Bowker (ed), *Cambridge Illustrated History of Religions* (Cambridge University Press, 2002), 72.

Griffin, Leslie C., *Law and Religion: Cases and Materials* (Foundation Press, 2007).

Gunn, T. Jeremy, 'Permissible Limitations on Freedom of Religion or Belief', in John Witte, Jr and M. Christian Green (eds), *Religion and Human Rights: An Introduction* (Oxford University Press, 2012), 254.

Hamilton, Marci A., *God vs. the Gavel: Religion and the Rule of Law* (Cambridge University Press, 2005).

Hammer, Leonard M., *The International Human Right to Freedom of Conscience: Some Suggestions for Its Development and Application* (Ashgate, 2001).

Hanna, Kris, 'Freedom of Discrimination on the Basis of Religion', in Paul Babie and Neville Rochow (eds), *Freedom of Religion under Bills of Rights* (University of Adelaide Press, 2012), 365.

Henkin, Louis, *International Law: Politics and Values* (Martinus Nijhoff Publishers, 1995).

Higgins, Rosalyn, *Problems and Process: International Law and How We Use It* (Oxford, Clarendon Press, 1994).

Hussain, Jamila, *Islam: Its Law and Society* (Federation Press, 2003).

Janis, Mark W. and Carolyn Evans (eds), *Religion and International Law* (Martinus Nijhoff Publishers, 2004).

Jayawickrama, Nihal, *The Judicial Application of Human Rights Law: National, Regional and International Jurisprudence* (Cambridge University Press, 2002).

Johnson, William, *Urban Planning and Politics* (Planners Press, 1989).

Joseph, Sarah and Melissa Castan, *The International Covenant and Civil and Political Rights: Cases, Materials, and Commentary* (Oxford University Press, 3rd edition, 2013).

Joseph, Sarah, Jenny Schultz and Melissa Castan, *The International Covenant on Civil and Political Rights: Cases, Materials and Commentary* (Oxford University Press, 2nd edition, 2004).

Kabir, Nahid, *Muslims in Australia: Immigration, Race Relations and Cultural History* (Kegan Paul, 2005).

Keeble, Lewis, *Principles and Practice of Town and Country Planning* (The Estates Gazette, 1959).

Kiss, Alexandre Charles, 'Permissible Limitations on Rights', in Louis Henkin (ed), *The International Bill of Rights: The Covenant on Civil and Political Rights* (Columbia University Press, 1981), 290.

Knights, Samantha, *Freedom of Religion, Minorities and the Law* (Oxford University Press, 2007).

Langlaude, Sylvie, *The Right of the Child to Religious Freedom in International Law* (Martinus Nijhoff Publishers, 2007).

Leone, Massimo, 'Legal Controversies about the Establishment of New Places of Worship in Multicultural Cities: A Semiogeographic Analysis', in Anne Wagner and Jan Broekman (eds), *Prospects of Legal Semiotics* (Springer, 2010), 217.

Lerner, Natan, 'Religious Human Rights under the United Nations', in Johan van der Vyver and John Witte, Jr (eds), *Religious Human Rights in Global Perspective: Legal Perspectives* (Martinus Nijhoff, 1996), 79.

Lerner, Natan, 'The Nature and Minimum Standards of Freedom of Religion or Belief', in Tore Lindholm, W Cole Durham, Jr and Bahia G. Tahzib-Lie (eds) and Elizabeth A. Sewell and Lena Larsen (associate eds), *Facilitating Freedom of Religion or Belief: A Deskbook* (Martinus Nijhoff Publishers, 2004), 63.

Lerner, Natan, *Religion, Secular Beliefs and Human Rights: 25 Years after the 1981 Declaration* (Martinus Nijhoff Publishers, 2006).

Levin, Lee I., *The Ancient Synagogue: The First Thousand Years* (Yale University Press, 2005).

Little, David, 'Studying Religious Human Rights: Methodological Foundations', in Johan van der Vyver and John Witte, Jr (eds), *Religious Human Rights in Global Perspective: Legal Perspectives* (Martinus Nijhoff Publishers, 1996), 45.

Llewellyn, David and H. Victor Conde, 'Freedom of Religion or Belief under International Humanitarian Law and International Criminal Law', in Tore Lindholm, W. Cole Durham, Jr and Bahia G. Tahzib-Lie (eds) and Elizabeth A. Sewell and Lena Larsen (associate eds), *Facilitating Freedom of Religion or Belief: A Deskbook* (Martinus Nijhoff Publishers, 2004), 125.

Machnyikova, Zdenka, 'Religious Rights', in Marc Weller (ed), *Universal Minority Rights: A Commentary on the Jurisprudence of International Courts and Treaty Bodies* (Oxford University Press, 2007), 179.

Marshall, Paul A. (ed), *Religious Freedom in the World* (Rowman & Littlefield Publishers, 2nd edition, 2008).

Martin, Francisco Forrest, Stephen J. Schnably, Richard J. Wilson, Jonathan S. Simon and Mark V. Tushnet, *International Human Rights and Humanitarian Law: Treaties, Cases, and Analysis* (Cambridge University Press, 2006).

Mason, Anthony, 'The Role of the Judiciary in Developing Human Rights in Australian Law', in David Kinley (ed), *Human Rights in Australian Law* (Federation Press, 1998), 26.

Mason, Anthony, 'Human Rights and Courts', in Paul Babie and Neville Rochow (eds), *Freedom of Religion under Bills of Rights* (University of Adelaide Press, 2012), xi.

McCrea, Ronan, *Religion and the Public Order of the European Union* (Oxford University Press, 2010).

McGinley, Gerald and Harry Reicher, 'The Relationship of International Law to Australian Law', in Harry Reicher (ed), *Australian International Law: Cases and Materials* (LBC Casebooks, 1995).

McMillan, John and Neil Williams, 'Administrative Law and Human Rights', in David Kinley (ed), *Human Rights in Australian Law* (Federation Press, 1998), 63.

Michalski, Sergiusz, *Reformation and the Visual Arts: The Protestant Image Question in Western and Eastern Europe* (Routledge, 1993).

Mill, John Stuart, *On Liberty* (United Kingdom, 1859).

Miller, Dale, *The Basic Writings of John Stuart Mill: On Liberty, the Subjection of Women and Utilitarianism* (Modern Library Classics, 1980).

Moeckli, Daniel, Sangeeta Shah and Sandesh Sivakumaran (eds) and David Harris (consultant editor), *International Human Rights Law* (Oxford University Press, 2010).

National Human Rights Consultation Report (Commonwealth of Australia, 2009).

Nowak, Manfred, *U.N. Covenant on Civil and Political Rights: CCPR Commentary* (N.P. Engel, 2nd revised edition, 2005).

Nowak, Manfred and Tanja Vospernik, 'Permissible Restrictions on Freedom of Religion or Belief', in Tore Lindholm, W. Cole Durham, Jr and Bahia G. Tahzib-Lie (eds) and Elizabeth A. Sewell and Lena Larsen (associate eds), *Facilitating Freedom of Religion or Belief: A Deskbook* (Martinus Nijhoff Publishers, 2004), 147.

O'Connell, Mary Ellen, *The Power and Purpose of International Law: Insights from the Theory and Practice of Enforcement* (Oxford University Press, 2008).

O'Neill, Nick, Simon Rice and Roger Douglas, *Retreat from Injustice: Human Rights in Australian Law* (Federation Press, 2nd edition, 2004).

Orakhelashvili, Alexander, *Peremptory Norms in International Law* (Oxford University Press, 2006).

Osiatynski, Wiktor, *Human Rights and Their Limits* (Cambridge University Press, 2009).

Pacillo, Vincenzo, '*Stopp Minarett*? The Controversy over the Building of Minarets in Switzerland: Religious Freedom versus Collective Identity', in Silvio Ferrari and

Sabrina Pastorelli (eds), *Religion in Public Spaces: A European Perspective* (Ashgate, 2012), 337.

Partsch, Karl Josef, 'Freedom of Conscience and Expression, and Political Freedoms', in Louis Henkin (ed), *The International Bill of Rights: The Covenant on Civil and Political Rights* (Columbia University Press, 1981), 209.

Phillips, Estelle M. and Derek S. Pugh, *How to Get a PhD: A Handbook for Students and Their Supervisors* (Open University Press, 3rd edition, 2000).

Piotrowicz, Ryszard and Stuart Kaye, *Human Rights in International and Australian Law* (Butterworths, 2000).

Podoprigora, Roman, 'Freedom of Religion and Belief and Discretionary State Approval of Religious Activity', in Tore Lindholm, W. Cole Durham, Jr and Bahia G. Tahzib-Lie (eds) and Elizabeth A. Sewell and Lena Larsen (associate eds), *Facilitating Freedom of Religion or Belief: A Deskbook* (Martinus Nijhoff Publishers, 2004), 425.

Poynting, Scott, Greg Noble, Paul Tabar and Jack Collins, *Bin Laden in the Suburbs: Criminalising the Arab Other* (Sydney Institute of Criminology, 2004).

Rees, Neil, Katherine Lindsay and Simon Rice, *Australian Anti-discrimination Law: Text, Cases and Materials* (Federation Press, 2008).

Rehman, Javaid, *Islamic State Practices: International Law and the Threat from Terrorism, A Critique of the 'Clash of Civilizations' in the New World Order* (Hart Publications, 2005).

Ritchie, David, 'Principles and Practice of Site Protection Laws in Australia', in David Carmichael, Jane Hubert, Brian Reeves and Audhild Schanche (eds), *Sacred Sites, Sacred Places* (1994), 227.

Ronalds, Chris and Elizabeth Raper, *Discrimination Law and Practice* (The Federation Press, 2012).

Sandberg, Russell, *Law and Religion* (Cambridge University Press, 2011).

Schachter, Oscar, 'The Obligation to Implement the Covenant in Domestic Law', in Louis Henkin (ed), *The International Bill of Rights: The Covenant on Civil and Political Rights* (Columbia University Press, 1981), 311.

Schachter, Oscar, 'The UN Legal Order: An Overview', in Christopher Joyner (ed), *The United Nations and International Law* (Cambridge University Press, 1997), 3.

Scheinin, Martin, 'Article 18', in Asbjørn Eide, Gudmundur Alfredsson, Göran Melander, Lars Adam Rehof and Allan Rosas (eds), *The Universal Declaration of Human Rights: A Commentary* (Scandinavian University Press, 1992), 263.

Scolnicov, Anat, *The Right to Religious Freedom in International Law: Between Group Rights and Individual Rights* (Routledge, 2011).

Shaw, Malcolm N., *International Law* (Cambridge University Press, 6th edition, 2008).

Shelton, Dinah, 'The Promise of Regional Human Rights Systems', in Burns Weston and Stephen Marks (eds), *The Future of International Human Rights* (Transnational Publishers Inc, 1999), 351.

Shelton, Dinah, 'Introduction', in Dinah Shelton (ed), *International Law and Domestic Legal Systems: Incorporation, Transformation and Persuasion* (Oxford University Press, 2011), 22.

Shelton, Dinah and Paolo Carrozza, *Regional Protection of Human Rights* (Oxford University Press, 2nd edition, 2013).

Sieghart, Paul, *The International Law of Human Rights* (Oxford University Press, 1983).

Sisely, Diane, 'Inspired by the Human Rights Act: The Victorian Charter of Human Rights and Responsibilities', in Nicolas Kang-Riou, Jo Milner and Suryia Nayak (eds), *Confronting the Human Rights Act: Contemporary Themes and Perspectives* (Routledge, 2012), 85.

Skennar, John, 'Sydney, A City Growing Within: The Establishment of Buddhist Centres in Western Sydney', in Cristina Rocha and Michelle Barker (eds), *Buddhism in Australia: Traditions in Change* (2011), 86.

Smith, David L., *Amenity and Urban Planning* (Granada Publishing Limited, 1974).

Sproats, Kevin and Roslyn Crichton, 'Regulatory Reforms: Balancing Interests', in Brian Dollery and Neil Marshall (eds), *Australian Local Government: Reform and Renewal* (MacMillan Education, 1997), 247.

Stahnke, Tad, 'The Right to Engage in Religious Persuasion', in Tore Lindholm, W. Cole Durham, Jr and Bahia G. Tahzib-Lie (eds), and Elizabeth A. Sewell and Lena Larsen (associate eds), *Facilitating Freedom of Religion or Belief: A Deskbook* (Martinus Nijhoff Publishers, 2004), 619.

Stein, Leslie, *Principles of Planning Law* (Oxford University Press, 2008).

Steiner, Henry, Philip Alston and Ryan Goodman, *International Human Rights in Context: Law, Politics, Morals* (Oxford University Press, 3rd edition, 2008).

Svensson-McCarthy, Anna-Lena, *The International Law of Human Rights and States of Exception: With Special Reference to the Travaux Préparatoires and Case-law of the International Monitoring Organs* (Martinus Nijhoff Publishers, 1998).

Tahzib, Bahiyyih, *Freedom of Religion or Belief: Ensuring Effective International Legal Protection* (Martinus Nijhoff Publishers, 1996).

Taylor, Paul, *Freedom of Religion: UN and European Human Rights Law and Practice* (Cambridge University Press, 2005).

Taylor, Paul, 'Religion and Freedom of Choice', in John Witte Jr and M. Christian Green (eds), *Religion & Human Rights: An Introduction* (Oxford University Press, 2012), 170.

Temperman, Jeroen, *State-Religion Relationships and Human Rights Law towards a Right to Religiously Neutral Governance* (Martinus Nijhoff Publishers, 2010).

Temperman, Jeroen, 'Religious Symbols in the Public School Classroom', in Jeroen Temperman (ed), *The Lautsi Papers Multidisciplinary Reflections on Religious Symbols in the Public School Classroom* (Martinus Nijhoff Publishers, 2012), 142–176.

The Holy Bible (*King James Version*) (Canterbury Classics/Baker & Taylor Publishing Group, 2013).

Thompson, Susan and Paul J. Maginn, *Planning Australia: An Overview of Urban and Regional Planning* (Cambridge University Press, 2012).

Vakulenko, Anastasia, *Islamic Veiling in Legal Discourse* (Routledge, 2012).

Van Banning, Theo R.G., *The Human Right to Property* (Intersentia, 2002).

Van der Ploeg, Tymen, 'Places of Worship: Between Public and Private: A Comparison between Bulgaria, Italy and the Netherlands', in Silvio Ferrari and Sabrina Pastorelli (eds), *Religion in Public Spaces: A European Perspective* (Ashgate, 2012), 353.

Villaroman, Noel, 'The Right to Establish and Maintain Places of Worship: The Developments of Its Normative Content under International Human Rights Law', in Silvio Ferrari and Sabrina Pastorelli (eds), *Religion in Public Spaces: A European Perspective* (Ashgate, 2012), 295.

Villiger, Mark E., *Customary International Law and Treaties* (Martinus Nijhoff Publishers, 1985).

Willheim, Ernst, 'Australian Legal Procedures and the Protection of Secret Aboriginal Spiritual Beliefs: A Fundamental Conflict', in Peter Cane, Carolyn Evans and Zoë Robinson (eds), *Law and Religion in Theoretical and Historical Context* (Cambridge University Press, 2008), 214.

Williams, George, *A Charter of Rights for Australia* (University of New South Wales Press, 2007).

Articles

Babcock, Richard and David Theriaque, 'Landmarks Preservation Ordinances: Are the Religion Clauses Violated by Their Application to Religious Properties?' (1992) 7(2) *Journal of Land Use and Environmental Law* 165.

Bayne, Peter, 'Human Rights and Administrative Law' (1991) 17 *Commonwealth Law Bulletin* 320.

Benvenisti, Eyal, 'Margin of Appreciation, Consensus, and Universal Standards' (1999) 31 *International Law and Politics* 843.

Bielefeldt, Heiner, 'Freedom of Religion or Belief – A Human Right Under Pressure' (2012) 1(1) *Oxford Journal of Law and Religion* 1.

Burayidi, Michael, 'The Multicultural City as Planners' Enigma' (2001) 4(3) *Planning Theory and Practice* 259.

Cali, Basak, 'Balancing Human Rights? Methodological Problems with Weights, Scales and Proportions' (2007) 29 *Human Rights Quarterly* 251.

Carmella, Angela, 'Houses of Worship and Religious Liberty: Constitutional Limits to Landmark Preservation and Architectural Review' (1991) 36 *Villanova Law Review* 401.

Castan, Melissa and Julie Debeljak, 'Indigenous Peoples' Human Rights and the Victorian Charter: A Framework for Reorienting Recordkeeping and Archival Practice' (2012) 12(2) *Archival Science* 213.

Charlesworth, Hilary, Madelaine Chiam, Devika Hovell and George Williams, 'Deep Anxieties: Australia and the International Legal Order' (2003) 25 *Sydney Law Review* 423.

Clark, R.S., 'The United Nations and Religious Freedom' (1978) 11 *New York University Journal of International Law and Politics* 197.

Conkle, Daniel, 'Toward a General Theory of the Establishment Clause' (1988) 82 *Northwestern University Law Review* 1115.

Cordes, Mark, 'Where to Pray? Religious Zoning and First Amendment' (1986–1987) 35 *University of Kansas Law Review* 697.

Costonis, John, 'Law and Aesthetics: A Critique and a Reformulation of the Dilemmas' (1982) 80 *Michigan Law Review* 355.

Debeljak, Julie, 'Parliamentary Sovereignty and Dialogue under the Victorian Charter of Human Rights and Responsibilities: Drawing the Line between Judicial Interpretation and Judicial Law-Making' (2007) 33 *Monash University Law Review* 9.

Debeljak, Julie, 'Balancing Rights in a Democracy: The Problems with Limitations and Overrides of Rights under the Victorian Charter of Human Rights and Responsibilities Act 2006' (2008) 32 *Melbourne University Law Review* 422.

Dunn, Kevin, 'Representations of Islam in the Politics of Mosque Development in Sydney' (2001) 92(3) *Royal Dutch Geographical Society* 291.

Dunn, Kevin, 'Repetitive and Troubling Discourses of Nationalism in the Local Politics of Mosque Development in Sydney, Australia' (2005) 23(1) *Society and Space* 29.

Edge, Peter, 'The Construction of Sacred Places in English Law' (2002) 14 *Journal of Environmental Law* 161.

Evans, Carolyn, 'Strengthening the Role of the Special Rapporteur on Freedom of Religion or Belief' (2006) 1 *Religion & Human Rights: An International Journal* 75.

Evans, Carolyn, 'Time for a Treaty? The Legal Sufficiency of the Declaration on the Elimination of All Forms of Discrimination and Intolerance' (2007) *Brigham Young University Law Review* 617.

Gerber, Paula, Joanna Kyriakakis and Katie O'Byrne, '*General Comment 16* on State Obligations Regarding the Impact of the Business Sector on Children's Rights: What Is Its Standing, Meaning and Effect?' (2013) 14 *Melbourne Journal of International Law* 1.

Germain, Annick and Julie Elizabeth Gagnon, 'Minority Places of Worship and Zoning Dilemmas in Montreal' (2003) 4(3) *Planning Theory & Practice* 295.

Gray, Anthony, 'Section 116 of the Australian Constitution and Dress Restrictions' (2011) 16(2) *Deakin Law Review* 293.

Gunn, T. Jeremy, 'Deconstructing Proportionality in Limitations Analysis' (2005) 19 *Emory International Law Review* 465.

Henkin, Louis, 'The Universality of the Concept of Human Rights' (1989) *Annals of the American Academy of Political and Social Science* 506.

Janzen, John, 'Form and Meaning in Central Kansas Mennonite Buildings for Worship' (1999) 73(2) *The Mennonite Quarterly Review* 323.

Keetch, Von and Mathew Richards, 'The Need for Legislation to Enshrine Free Exercise in the Land Use Context' (1999) 32 *University of California Davis Law Review* 725.

Kennan, Jim, 'The Role of International Human Rights Law in Australian Law' (2009–2010) 44 *Valparaiso University Law Review* 895.

Kolis, Annette, 'Architectural Expression: Police Power and the First Amendment' (1979) 16 *Urban Law Annual* 273.

Krishnaswami, Arcot, 'Study of Discrimination in the Matter of Religious Rights and Practices' (1978) 11 *New York University Journal of International Law and Policy* 227.

Langer, Lorenz, 'Panacea or Pathetic Fallacy? The Swiss Ban on Minarets' (2010) 43(4) *Vanderbilt Journal of Transnational Law* 863.

Langlaude, Sylvie, 'The Rights of Religious Associations to External Relations' (2010) 32(3) *Human Rights Quarterly* 502.

Laycock, Douglas, 'State RFRAs and Land-Use Regulations' (1999) 32 *University of California Davies Law Review* 755.

Lostal, Marina, 'The Meaning and Protection of Cultural and Places of Worship under the 1977 Additional Protocols' (2012) 59(3) *Netherlands International Law Review* 455.

Mabbett, I.W., 'The Symbolism of Mount Meru' (1983) 23(1) *History of Religions* 64.

Mason, Peter W., 'Pilgrimage to Religious Shrines: An Essential Element in the Human Right to Freedom of Thought, Conscience and Religion' (1993) 25 *Case Western Reserve Journal of International Law* 619.

McLeish, S, 'Making Sense of Religion and the Constitution: A Fresh Start to 116' (1992) 18(2) *Monash University Law Review* 207.

Mortensen, Reid, 'The Unfinished Experiment: A Report on Religious Freedom in Australia' (2007) 21 *Emory International Law Review* 167.

Mutua, Makau, 'Standard Setting in Human Rights: Critique and Prognosis' (2007) 29 *Human Rights Quarterly* 547.

Pak, Thomas, 'Free Exercise, Free Expression, and Landmarks Preservation' (1991) 91(7) *Columbia Law Review* 1813.

Payne, Heather and Norman Doe, 'Public Health and the Limits of Religious Freedom' (2005) 19 *Emory International Law Review* 539.

Peach, Ceri and Richard Gale, 'Muslims, Hindus and Sikhs in the New Religious Landscape of England' (2003) 93(4) *Geographical Review* 469.

Sandercock, Leonie, 'When Strangers Become Neighbours: Managing Cities of Difference' (2000) 1(1) *Planning Theory and Practice* 13.

Sandercock, Leonie, 'Planning in the Ethno-culturally Diverse City: A Comment' (2001) 4(3) *Planning Theory and Practice* 319.

Sandercock, Leonie and Beverly Kliger, 'Multiculturalism and the Planning System: Part One' (1998a) 35(3) *Australian Planner* 127.

Sandercock, Leonie, and Beverly Kliger, 'Multiculturalism and the Planning System: Part Two' (1998b) 35(4) *Australian Planner* 223.

Sohn, Louis, 'The Shaping of International Law' (1978) 8 *Georgia Journal of International and Comparative Law* 18.

Ssenyonjo, Manisuli, 'The Islamic Veil and Freedom of Religion, the Rights to Education and Work: A Survey of Recent International and National Cases' (2007) 6 *Chinese Journal of International Law* 653.

Storey, Donovan, Salut Muhidin and Peter Westoby, 'Planning for Social Inclusion in a Multicultural Urban South East Queensland' (2010) 47(3) *Australian Planner* 142.

Sullivan, Donna, 'Advancing the Freedom of Religion or Belief through the UN Declaration on the Elimination of Discrimination and Intolerance' (1988) 82 *American Journal of International Law* 487.

Temperman, Jeroen, '25th Anniversary Commemoration of the Adoption of the 1981 UN Declaration on the Elimination of Intolerance and Discrimination Based on Religion or Belief – A Report' (2007) 2(1) *Religion & Human Rights: An International Journal* 19–30.

Temperman, Jeroen, 'Are State Churches Contrary to International Law?' (2013) 2(1) *Oxford Journal of Law and Religion* 119–149.

Thanissaro, Phra Nicholas, 'Home Shrines in Britain and Associated Spiritual Values' (2010) 31(3) *Journal of Beliefs & Values* 353.

Thompson, Susan, 'Planning and Multiculturalism: A Reflection on Australian Local Practice' (2003) 4(3) *Planning Theory & Practice* 275.

Turner, Graeme, 'The Cosmopolitan City and Its Other: the Ethnicizing of the Australian Suburb' (2008) 9(4) *Inter-Asia Cultural Studies* 568.

Twomey, Anne, 'Always the Bridesmaid – Constitutional Recognition of Local Government' (2012) 38(2) *Monash University Law Review* 142.

Vakulenko, Anastasia, 'Islamic Headscarves and the European Convention on Human Rights: An Intersectional Perspective' (2007) 16 *Social and Legal Studies* 183.

Van der Vyver, Johan, 'Limitations of Freedom of Religion or Belief: International Law Perspectives' (2005) 19 *Emory International Law Review* 499.

Villaroman, Noel, 'Rescuing a Troubled Concept: An Alternative View of the Right to Development' (2011) 29(1) *Netherlands Quarterly of Human Rights* 13.

Villaroman, Noel, 'Not in My Backyard: The Local Planning Process in Australia and Its Impact on Minority Places of Worship' (2012) 7(3) *Religion & Human Rights: An International Journal* 215.

Wehener, Ann L., 'When a House Is Not a Home but a Church: A Proposal for Protection of Home Worship from Zoning Ordinances' (1993) 22 *Capital University Law Review* 491.

Weil, Prosper, 'Towards Relative Normativity in International Law' (1983) 77 *American Journal of International Law* 413.

Williams, George, 'The Victorian Charter of Human Rights and Responsibilities: Origins and Scope' (2006) 30 *Melbourne University Law Review* 887.

Wills, Ted, 'Religious Landmarks, Guidelines for Analysis' (1992) 53 *Ohio State Law Journal* 211.

Treaties, Resolutions and Other UN Documents

American Convention on Human Rights (*Pact of San José*), signed 22 November 1969, 1144 UNTS 123, OASTS 36, O.A.S. Off. Rec. OEA/Ser.L/V/11.23, doc.21, rev.6 (1979), reprinted 9 ILM 673 (1970) (entered into force 18 July 1978).

Charter on Human and Peoples' Rights, adopted 27 June 1981, CAB/LEG/67/3 rev. 5, 21 ILM 58 (1982), (entered into force 21 October 1986).

Commission on Human Rights Resolution 1986/20, 42 UN ESCOR Supp. (No. 2) at 66, UN Doc E/CN.4/1986/65 (1986).

Convention on the Elimination of All Forms of Discrimination against Women, adopted 18 December 1979, 1249 UNTS 13, reprinted in 19 ILM 33 (1980) (entered into force 3 September 1981).

Declaration on the Elimination of All Forms of Intolerance and of Discrimination Based on Religion or Belief, GA Res 36/55, UN GAOR, 36th sess, 73rd plen mtg, Supp No 51, UN Doc A/RES/26/55 (25 November 1981).

European Convention for the Protection of Human Rights and Fundamental Freedoms, signed 4 November 1950, 213 UNTS 221, ETS 5 (entered into force 3 September 1953).

Human Rights Committee, *Concluding Observation on the Report of Belgium,* UN Doc CCPR/CO/81/BEL (2004).

Human Rights Committee, *Concluding Observation on the Report of Bulgaria,* UN Doc CCPR/C/BGR/CO/3 (19 August 2011).

Human Rights Committee, *Concluding Observation on the Report of the Democratic People's Republic of Korea,* UN Doc CCPR/CO/72/PRK (27 August 2001).

Human Rights Committee, *Concluding Observation on the Report of Georgia,* UN Doc CCPR/C/GEO/CO/3/CRP.1 (19 October 2007).

Human Rights Committee, *Concluding Observation on the Report of Iran,* UN Doc CCPR/C/IRN/CO/3 (29 November 2011).

Human Rights Committee, *Concluding Observation on the Report of Israel,* UN Doc CCPR/C/ISR/CO/3 (3 September 2010).

Human Rights Committee, *Concluding Observation on the Report of Kuwait,* UN Doc CCPR/C/KWT/CO/2 (18 November 2011).

Human Rights Committee, *Concluding Observation on the Report of Luxembourg,* UN Doc CCPR/CO/77/LUX (15 April 2003).

Human Rights Committee, *Concluding Observation on the Report of Maldives,* UN Doc CCPR/C/MDV/CO/1 (31 August 2012).

Human Rights Committee, *Concluding Observation on the Report of the Republic of Moldova,* UN Doc CCPR/CO/75/MDA (5 August 2002).

Human Rights Committee, *Concluding Observation on the Report of Switzerland,* UN Doc CCPR/C/CHE/CO/3 (3 November 2009).

Human Rights Committee, *Views: Communication No. 570/1993,* UN Doc CCPR/C/50/D/570/1993 (8 April 1994) (*'MAB, WAT and J-AYT v Canada'*).

Human Rights Committee, *Views: Communication No. 1207/2003,* UN Doc CCPR/C/84/D/1207/2003 (23 August 2005) (*'Malakhovsky and Pikul v Belarus'*).

Human Rights Committee, *Views: Communication No. 1249/2004,* UN Doc CCPR/C/85/D/1249/2004 (18 November 2005) (*'Sister Immaculate Joseph et al v Sri Lanka'*).

Human Rights Committee, *Views: Communication No. 1474/2006,* UN Doc CCPR/C/91/D/1474/2006 (14 November 2007) (*'Prince v South Africa'*).

Human Rights Council, Resolution 6/37: *Elimination of All Forms of Intolerance and of Discrimination Based on Religion or Belief* (14 December 2007).

Interim Report of the Special Rapporteur on the Elimination of All Forms of Religious Intolerance, UN Doc A/52/477 (16 October 1997).

Interim Report of the Special Rapporteur on Freedom of Religion or Belief, UN Doc A/65/207 (29 July 2010).

International Convention for the Elimination of All Forms of Racial Discrimination, adopted 21 December 1965, 660 UNTS 195, reprinted in 5 ILM 352 (1966) (entered into force 4 January 1969).

International Covenant on Civil and Political Rights, opened for signature 16 December 1966, 999 UNTS 171 (entered into force 23 March 1976).

International Covenant on Economic, Social and Cultural Rights, opened for signature 16 December 1966, 999 UNTS 3 (entered into force 3 January 1976).

Optional Protocol to the ICCPR, opened for signature 16 December 1966, 999 UNTS 302 (entered into force 23 March 1976).

Protocol Additional to the Geneva Conventions of 12 August 1949, and Relating to the Protection of Victims of International Armed Conflicts (*Protocol I*), 8 June 1977 (entered into force 7 December 1978), 1125 UNTS 3.

Protocol Additional to the Geneva Conventions of 12 August 1949, and Relating to the Protection of Victims of Non-International Armed Conflicts (*Protocol II*), 8 June 1977 (entered into force 7 December 1978), 1125 UNTS 609.

Protocol No. 1 to the European Convention for the Protection of Human Rights and Fundamental Freedoms, adopted 20 March 1952, 213 UNTS 262, ETS 9 (entered into force 18 May 1954).

Report of the Special Rapporteur on Contemporary Forms of Racism, Racial Discrimination, Xenophobia and Related Intolerance, UN Doc A/HRC/15/53 (12 July 2010).

Report of the Special Rapporteur on Freedom of Religion or Belief on Angola, UN Doc A/HRC/7/10/Add.4 (6 March 2008).

Report of the Special Rapporteur on Freedom of Religion or Belief on Azerbaijan, UN Doc A/HRC/4/21/Add.2 (18 October 2006).

Report of the Special Rapporteur on Freedom of Religion or Belief on India, UN Doc E/CN.4/1997/91/Add.1 (14 February 1997).

Report of the Special Rapporteur on Freedom of Religion or Belief, 'Summary of cases transmitted to Governments and replies received', UN Doc A/HRC/13/40/Add.1 (16 February 2010).

Report of the Special Rapporteur on Freedom of Religion or Belief, UN Doc E/CN.4/1990/46 (12 January 1990).

Report of the Special Rapporteur on Freedom of Religion or Belief, UN Doc E/CN.4/2004/63 (16 January 2004).

Report of the Special Rapporteur on Freedom of Religion or Belief, UN Doc E/CN.4/2005/61 (20 December 2004).

Report of the Special Rapporteur on Freedom of Religion or Belief on Macedonia, UN Doc A/HRC/13/40/Add.2 (28 December 2009).

Report of the Special Rapporteur on Freedom of Religion or Belief on Romania, UN Doc E/CN.4/2004/63/Add.2 (16 December 2003).

Report of the Special Rapporteur on Freedom of Religion or Belief on Tajikistan, UN Doc A/HRC/7/10/Add.2 (27 November 2007).

Report of the Special Rapporteur on Freedom of Religion or Belief on Turkey, UN Doc A/55/280/Add.1 (10 September 2000).

Report of the Special Rapporteur on Freedom of Religion or Belief on Turkmenistan, UN Doc A/HRC/10/8/Add.4 (12 January 2009).

Setting International Standards in the Field of Human Rights, General Assembly Resolution, 97th plen mtg, UN Doc A/RES/41/120 (4 December 1986).

Study on the Rights of Persons Belonging to Ethnic, Religious and Linguistic Minorities, Francesco Capotorti, UN Special Rapporteur of the Sub-Commission on Prevention of Discrimination and Protection of Minorities, E/CN.4/Sub.2/384/Rev.1 (1979), para 242.

Sub-Commission on Prevention of Discrimination and Protection of Minorities, *Draft Declaration on the Elimination of All Forms of Religious Intolerance*, UN Doc E/CN.4/873 (28 January 1964).

Universal Declaration of Human Rights, GA Res 217A (III), UN GAOR, 3rd sess, 183rd plen mtg, UN Doc A/810 (10 December 1948).

Vienna Convention on the Law of Treaties, opened for signature 23 May 1969, 1155 UNTS 331, art 27 (entered into force 27 January 1980).

Other Materials

Amnesty International, *United Nations Special Procedures: Building on a Cornerstone of Human Rights Protection* (2005).

Australian Heritage Council, *Guidelines for the Assessment of Places for the National Heritage List* (Department of the Environment, Water, Heritage and the Arts, 2009).

Black's Law Dictionary (West Publishing Co, 6th edition, 1990).

Branson, Catherine, former President of the Australian Human Rights Commission, 'Using Human Rights to Inform Administrative Decision-Making', *Speech to the Council of Australasian Tribunals*, 25 August 2009.

Bugg, Laura Beth, 'Religious Freedom and the Right to the City: Local Government Planning and the Rejection of Islamic Schools in Sydney, Australia' (Workshop Paper, Twelfth Berlin Roundtables: Religious Pluralism, Irmgard Coninx Stiftung, 7–11 April 2010).

Burnside, Julian, 'It's Time. A Bill of Rights for Australia' (Speech delivered at the 2008 International Human Rights Day Address, Bob Hawke Prime Ministerial Centre, University of South Australia).

Davidson, Naomi, 'Race Rally Fear Over Elermore Vale Mosque', *The Herald*, 3 December 2010.

Durham, W. Cole Jr, 'Places of Worship: Enhancing Implementation of a Core Right' (Introductory Remarks for Session III of the Supplementary Human Dimension Meeting on Freedom of Religion or Belief, Vienna, Austria, 9–10 July 2009).

Evatt, Elizabeth, 'National Implementation: The Cutting Edge of International Human Rights Law', *Centre for International and Public Law, Law and Policy Paper* 12 (Federation Press, 1999).

Ferrari, Silvio and Sabrina Pastorelli, 'The Public Space: The Formal and Substantive Neutrality of the Public Sphere' (Working Paper No. 4, Religious Diversity and Secular Models in Europe: Innovative Approaches to Law and Policy, September 2010).

French, Robert, Chief Justice, *Oil and Water? – International Law and Domestic Law in Australia* (Bond University Brennan Lecture, 2009).

French, Robert, Chief Justice, *Property, Planning and Human Rights* (Planning Institute of Australia, National Congress, Canberra, 25 March 2013).

Gerber, Paula, *From Convention to Classroom: The Long Road to Human Rights Education* (PhD Thesis, University of Melbourne, 2008).

Human Rights Watch, *Hostile to Democracy: The Movement System and Political Repression in Uganda* (Human Rights Watch, 1999).

International Council on Human Rights Policy, *Human Rights Standards: Learning from Experience* (ICHRP, 2006).

Kirby, Michael, *Australian Interfaith and Its Problems* (Speech delivered at the First National Congress of the Interfaith Association of Australia, Macquarie University, 19 November 1996).

Metlikovec, Jane, 'Muslims Quitting Regional Victoria Due to Lack of Mosques', *The Herald Sun*, 2 June 2008.

Mourad, Hassan, *The Development and Land Use Impacts of Local Mosques* (Undergraduate Thesis, Faculty of the Built Environment, Planning and Urban Development Program, University of New South Wales, 2006).

Parkinson, Patrick, 'Enforcing Tolerance: Vilification Laws and Religious Freedom in Australia' (Paper presented at the Eleventh Annual International Law and Religion Symposium: 'Religion in the Public Sphere: Challenges and Opportunities', Provo, Utah, 3–6 October 2004).

Perpitch, Nicolas, 'Bias denied as Swan Valley Mosque Rejected', *The Australian*, 18 December 2009.

Pocket Oxford Hachette French Dictionary (Oxford University Press, 4th edition, 2010).

Skennar, John, 'Sydney, A City Growing Within: The Establishment of Buddhist Centres in Western Sydney' (Paper presented at Centre for Cultural Research, University of Western Sydney: Post-Suburban Sydney Conference, 2005).

Steinbock, Daniel, *Making Silence Together: Collaboration in the Silent Gatherings of Quakers* (PhD Thesis, Stanford University, August 2012).

Thompson, Claire, 'Temple of Division', *Hills Shire Times*, 12 May 2009.

Victorian Local Government Association, 'Human Rights Matter Locally: Preparing your local government to understand and implement the Charter', *Manual* 1 (2011).

Index